Restoration

Restoration Comedies

EDITED WITH AN INTRODUCTION BY
DENNIS DAVISON

OXFORD UNIVERSITY PRESS
LONDON   OXFORD   NEW YORK
1970

Oxford University Press

LONDON OXFORD NEW YORK
GLASGOW TORONTO MELBOURNE WELLINGTON
CAPE TOWN SALISBURY IBADAN NAIROBI LUSAKA DAR ES SALAAM ADDIS ABABA
BOMBAY CALCUTTA MADRAS KARACHI LAHORE DACCA
KUALA LUMPUR SINGAPORE HONG KONG TOKYO

First published as an Oxford University Press
paperback by Oxford University Press, London, 1970

PRINTED IN GREAT BRITAIN
BY RICHARD CLAY (THE CHAUCER PRESS), LTD.,
BUNGAY SUFFOLK

Contents

Introduction

Eleven regicides had been executed and their heads fixed to London Bridge as a grim reminder. The Great Plague of 1665 was hailed by many as God's punishment on a wicked nation, while not a few regarded the devastating Fire of London in the following year as a Catholic plot. National pride was humiliated by the Dutch fleet which sailed up the Thames in June 1667 and destroyed English ships. Dissenters were persecuted, Oxford and Cambridge remained educational backwaters, M.P.s accepted bribes, books were rigidly censored, and only official Government newspapers appeared between 1660 and 1679. Already in 1675 the London coffee-houses had been suppressed, and in 1683 the University of Oxford condemned and burnt treatises on political theory by Hobbes, Milton, and Baxter. Add to this the wars with the Dutch, financial crises, the panic of the Popish Plot years, and the threat of civil war, as Charles II's illegitimate son, Monmouth, was groomed by Shaftesbury to succeed to the throne, and we must, I think, remain surprised at the growth of Restoration comedy in such a climate.

A handful of playwrights, sheltering from these bleak winds at the two theatres patronized by the King and the Duke of York respectively, might be explicable, but between 1660 and 1700 some two hundred dramatists were at work and about a hundred plays of unknown authorship were written. Nobody would claim that Restoration comedy was more than a minor episode in the history of drama, but its special character, its fertility, its impact on English theatre, and its survival on the modern stage justify its study. A few dates and titles must suffice to indicate that the most celebrated successes spanned only some forty years: Etherege's *She Would If She Could* (1668), Buckingham's *The Rehearsal* (1671), Dryden's *The Conquest of Granada* (1670–71), Wycherley's *The Country Wife* (1675) and *The Plain-Dealer* (1676), Etherege's *The Man of Mode* (1676), Dryden's *All For Love* (1677), Otway's *Venice Preserved* (1682), Congreve's *The Double-Dealer* (1693), Vanbrugh's *The Relapse* (1696) and *The Provoked Wife* (1697), Congreve's *The Way of the World* (1700), and Farquhar's *The Beaux Stratagem* (1707).

The theatrical history of the period has proved fascinating, whether one reads the diary-jottings of Samuel Pepys and the pungent, revealing prologues of John Dryden, or modern studies on theatre management, new-style acting, movable scenery, or the private lives of 'all the King's ladies', as the famous actresses of the time have been termed. Perhaps too much has been made of the supposedly scandalous atmosphere at the theatres—the coxcombs and fops seated on the stage, exchanging claret-soaked witticisms, or the masked prostitutes and their noisy escorts, not to mention Nell Gwynn and her companions who did not restrict themselves to selling oranges. Recent studies remind us that this is a satirical picture, provided by hostile critics or ironical playwrights themselves, and many scholars now believe that Restoration audiences were composed of solid middle-class citizens as well as ladies, gentlemen, wits, fops, country visitors, beaux, and 'vizard-masks'. On the other hand, those who consider the two royally sponsored theatres to be essentially sources of a minority aristocratic culture can point to the occasions when the playhouses were so poorly attended that patrons were allowed to see the first act free in an attempt to lure them in. In fact the King's Theatre in 1682 had to merge with the Duke of York's, and here Thomas Betterton reigned supreme for many years, dictating to all the dramatists the kind of juicy acting roles they had to provide for himself, his wife, and certain actresses. So discussion continues about the nature of the Restoration theatre, its 'popular' or 'élite' character, the composition of its audiences, and the freedom of its writers. (When his patron's current mistress is starring as a virginal heroine can the dramatist, one wonders, retain complete control over his dialogue?) But it is generally agreed that the novel employment of women to play female roles and a more naturalistic style of acting, together with more elaborate changeable scenery, made it possible for Restoration comedy—as distinct from the tragedy—to aim at a vivid portrayal of contemporary life.

Although we may marvel that a boy-actor could successfully present Juliet, Cordelia, or Cleopatra—yet a visit to a contemporary Japanese *kabuki* theatre would show us that female impersonation can be utterly convincing—it is obvious that Shakespeare took great care to minimize sensual scenes, embraces, or bodily display. Lady Macbeth is not exactly a sex-kitten, and most of his witty, energetic heroines spend a good deal of their time disguised as boys. On the Restoration stage it was stipulated by royal patent that only women could play women's parts. This theatrical revolution, influenced, like many other features of English theatre, by French practice, provoked an unprecedented stress on sensual realism, sexual candour, and the exploitation of the personal glamour of the actress. Protracted scenes of flirtations, passionate kissing, and even attempted rape, enabled the playwright to enthral the audience with provocatively clad women (some only fourteen years old) exchanging innuendoes or frank bawdy with equally dazzling gallants. Writers deliberately created 'breeches parts' to enable actresses to disguise themselves as boys and thus reveal their outlines to an audience accustomed to the modestly long gowns of the period. (Sometimes women took all the roles in a play or were cast in men's parts.) Those who charge the Restoration stage with catering for peeping-toms forget that, before it became the custom to provide organized strip shows for respectable night-club patrons, the theatre—especially in ballet, comic opera, or musical comedy—frequently welcomed an element of voyeurism. In any case Restoration sexual manners were boldly unpuritanical and where this led to grossness or cynicism their presentation on the stage could also be corrective. No doubt the gallants eventually got used to seeing a woman's clothed legs and thighs, and courtship antics soon became the subject of ironical attention by dramatists, as we may see in *The Man of Mode* when Young Bellair instructs Harriet in the art of flirtation:

> *Y.B.* At one motion play your fan, roll your eyes, and then settle a kind look upon me.
> *H.* So?
> *Y.B.* Now spread your fan, look down upon it, and tell the sticks with a finger.
> *H.* Very modish.
> *Y.B.* Clap your hands up to your bosom, hold down your gown, shrug a little, draw up your breasts and let 'em fall again, gently, with a sigh or two, etc. . . . Clap your fan then, in both your hands, snatch it to your mouth, smile, and with a lively motion fling your body a little forwards. So—now spread it; fall back on the sudden, cover your face with it, and break out into a loud laughter. . . .

Against the portraits of sensual young heroines (who, one notes, never lose their virginities) we must place those satirical sketches of lustful old widows, weary rakes, foppish would-be gallants, aged cuckolds, 'fumbling keepers', and drunken lechers. This whole gallery of sexual types is surely a valid achievement in social realism rather than an indulgence in pornography. The slimy pimp, Coupler, in Vanbrugh's *The Relapse*, is pictured as repugnant:

> *Coupler.* Ah, you young hot lusty thief, let me muzzle you—(*kissing*)—sirrah, let me muzzle you.
> *Young Fashion.* 'Pshaw, the old lecher!

Similarly, Otway's Sir Jolly Jumble in *The Soldier's Fortune* (1680) is absolutely nauseating, though at the same time a gloriously satirical creation and a serious attempt at depicting sexual depravity. Dryden's *The Kind Keeper* (1678) is a ruthless exposure of the exploitation of women, as we see from this scene in which Mrs Overdone brings her daughter Prue to Aldo's house:

> *Mrs. O.* Ask blessing, Prue: he is the best father you ever had.
> *Aldo.* Bless thee, and make thee a substantial, thriving whore. Have your mother in your eye, Prue; it is good to follow good example. How old are you, Prue? Hold up your head, child.

Prue. Going o' my sixteen, father Aldo.

Aldo. And you have been initiated but these two years—loss of time, loss of precious time! Mrs. Overdone, how much have you made off Prue, since she has been man's meat?

Mrs. O. A very small matter, by my troth. . . . I despair of a coach for her. Her first maidenhead brought me in but little, the weather-beaten old knight, that bought her of me, beat down the price so low. . . .

Aldo. Say your prayers, Prue, and go duly to church o' Sundays, you'll thrive the better all the week. Come, have a good heart, child; I will keep thee myself; thou shalt do my little business; and I'll find thee an able young fellow to do thine.

The old charge that Restoration comedy advocates sexual licence and reproduces bawdy conversation is quite often true. Clearly many dramatists shared the outlook and manners of the characters they created for the stage. Traditionally critics have demanded that a playwright should adopt a moral position and ridicule vice and folly from the vantage point of Good Sense or the Golden Mean, as Molière did overtly and Shakespeare obliquely. The Restoration dramatist tended to identify himself with Witty Hedonism, and so his targets were dullness and prudery as he found them among would-be wits, flirtatious old women, city puritans, or mock-modest ladies-of-the-town. In modern times, after the impact of such writers as de Sade, Wedekind, and Genet, it has perhaps become easier to accept plays in which the author's moral values are defiantly opposed to those of most of his audience.

A much more damaging criticism, heard more recently, is that Restoration comedy is trivial and boring. Critics have shown by textual analysis that much of the dialogue is third-rate, the structure of plot and scenes slipshod, and the characterization shallow and stereotyped. I think this is perfectly true of a great deal of the voluminous output of the period—indeed, these are exactly the criticisms which Restoration dramatists hurled noisily at each other's heads. In the best plays, especially those of Congreve and Etherege, there are passages of fine writing which have been rightly admired, but to my mind the notion that one can find page after page of scintillating wit is a delusion. The satirical set-pieces, such as the faded beauty at her formidable *toilette* tasks, ludicrously daydreaming about a new lover, or the comic description of the banality of country life, are usually well written, and pretentious society chatter, countrified naïvety, or hypocritical prurience are often amusingly parodied. But the staple dialogue is fairly barren of imagery, more longwinded than we would expect, and limited in both matter and mood. But do the textual critics, who have rightly made us realize these deficiencies, ever venture into a theatre? The fact that Restoration comedy is constantly revived and enjoyed by audiences indicates that certain theatrical effects are lost or partly concealed when we simply consult a printed text. The comedy of character and the comedy of situation, hardly visible in the dialogue or the brief stage directions, suddenly appear before our eyes when the play is performed. Lord Foppington and Sir Tunbelly Clumsy, and the farcical situations they are involved in, are not to be appreciated merely from the text. Any play gains immensely when staged, but certain types of plays lose much of their vitality when they are reduced to print. I have never heard of anybody *reading* the script of *Charley's Aunt* (1892), but does anyone doubt its success on the stage? How different is a performance of Beckett's *Krapp's Last Tape* from a reading of the 'trivial' text. Neither ancient Greek tragedy and comedy nor the medieval Mystery plays retain more than a small part of their compelling power when the dialogue alone is read silently in the study: one has only to attend performances of these plays to be convinced of this.

Sir George Etherege has often been considered the pioneer of Restoration comedy, and his first play, *The Comical Revenge, or, Love in a Tub*, produced in 1664, was a tremendous success, earning a thousand pounds in a month. His third and last play, *The Man of Mode, or, Sir Fopling Flutter* (1676), has frequently been reprinted and highly admired. His second play, *She Would If She Could*, was also a great success when it was staged in 1668. It is a comedy of frustration and hypocrisy mirrored by the frequency with which characters have to hide in closets, in wood cupboards, or under tables in order to avoid detection by suspicious spouses or lovers who are in turn hiding from somebody else. Life is a game of surface moral feigning and hectic rendezvous with mistresses or drinking companions, and the usual result is exposure to ridicule. Lady Cockwood would be a whore if she could without anyone knowing: Sir Oliver Cockwood would like to be thought a rake if he could only manage it. The noisy reveller, Sir Joslin Jolly, is a parody of the spirit of revelry, but with all his equipment of songs, dances, and music he only succeeds in being an elderly pretender. The characters are grotesque, the situations are farcical, the satirical effect is boisterously critical of middle-aged debauchery and hypocritical married respectability. With the young lovers, whose escapades are equally complicated and frustrating, Etherege succumbs finally to a sentimental happy ending for true love, but *en route* his outspoken heroines puncture the poses of their rakish gallants with their counter-tactics and spirited comments:

> *Gatty.* Truly you seem to be men of great employment, that are every moment rattling from the eating-houses to the playhouses, from the playhouses to the Mulberry Garden, that live in a perpetual hurry. . . .

The moral of the play is that debauchery and drinking are best left to the younger generation and that when young men are tired of sowing their wild oats they should marry charming, witty, sexy, but virginal, young ladies. (It is still a popular philosophy today, with perhaps less insistence on the final qualification.) Etherege himself married 'a rich old widow' and served as the British envoy to the Diet of the Empire at Ratisbon.

The Mulberry Garden by Sir Charles Sedley, produced in 1668, is chiefly interesting for the detailed picture of the two gallants, Henry Modish and Ned Estridge, and the satirical comedy revolving around Sir John Everyoung and Sir Samuel Forecast. More important topics than fashionable dress and pleasures are treated: the education of women and the goal of a good marriage is the underlying concern of the satire. Sir John Everyoung's liberal viewpoint is:

Well, for all this heat, let's everyone govern his own family as he has a mind to't. I never vex myself that your daughters live shut up as if they were in Spain or Italy. Nor pray don't you trouble yourself that mine see plays, balls, and take their innocent diversion as the custom of the country and their age requires.

Sir Samuel's reply is meant to be stuffily old-fashioned but its realism cannot be discounted:

Well, go then, and carry your daughters abroad, and break their bellies with sillabub, 'tis the greatest kindness you can do 'em now. As you have bred 'em you may e'en keep 'em to yourself and save their portions. I believe nobody will be very fond of a Hyde Park filly for a wife, nor an old boy that looks like a pedlar's pack for a father-in-law! But now I think on't you are such·a spark they'd lose their reputations with you—if they had any!

These exchanges and many of the remarks of the young ladies (e.g., 'Nothing venture, nothing win, and for my part I am resolved to allow all innocent liberty. This matrimony is a pill will scarce go down with a young man without gilding') are evidence of Sedley's purpose of exposing on the stage current problems concerning marriage. The 'heroic' love-plot, presented in verse couplets, now seems oddly matched with the comic scenes in prose, but it indicates the ideal values which lay hidden on the obverse side of Restoration cynicism. How far those heroic values were an elaborate pose, a fantasy world for bored idlers, is another question.

Dryden's professional pen has left us some thirty plays of various kinds, and among the comedies *Limberham, or, The Kind Keeper*, is his most devastating social document, a grim and grimy revelation of 'keeping' as a popular alternative to marriage. But his prose-and-verse *Marriage à la Mode* (1672) is a familiar mixture of satirical and romantic plots and characters. Taking the basic recipe of two men and two women, with interchangeable affections and the standard conviction that marriage must be a bore, Dryden spins his erotic merry-go-round until mutual jealousies cause the couples to

revert to their original partners. Surprisingly enough the final moral is in
favour of married love, though on the way Dryden has been able to conduct
us through all the forbidden pleasures of secret assignations, near-discoveries,
jealous passions, and threatened adultery. The funniest comic creation is the
pretentious, snobbish, Frenchified coquette, Melantha, and only by an incredible bit of theatrical jiggery-pokery is she rehabilitated as a possible wife
for Rhodophil. It is curious to realize that the audience which was enjoying
the ironic comedy of affectations and flirtations could also respond to the
high romance of the main plot, expressed in this kind of verse:

> I know too well when my first love began,
> When at our wake you for the chaplet ran:
> Then I was made the lady of the May,
> And, with the garland, at the goal did stay:
> Still, as you ran, I kept you full in view;
> I hoped, and wished, and ran, methought, for you.
> As you came near, I hastily did rise,
> And stretched my arm outright, that held the prize.
> The custom was to kiss when I should crown;
> You kneeled, and in my lap your head laid down:
> I blushed, and blushed, and did the kiss delay;
> At last my subjects forced me to obey:
> But, when I gave the crown, and then the kiss,
> I scarce had breath to say, Take that, —and this.

Perhaps the Restoration comedy best known today is the frequently revived *The Country Wife* by Wycherley, performed at Drury Lane in 1675.
Here again we have the division between the true lovers, Alithea and
Harcourt, with their witty but romantic standpoints, and the cynically
humorous vision of a society peopled by the egotistic would-be wit, Sparkish,
the bevy of sex-seeking ladies-of-honour led by Lady Fidget, the ridiculous
husband, Mr. Pinchwife, the naïve hedonist, Margery Pinchwife, and the
central exploiter of human vices, Horner. Hilarious though the satirical
character-portraits are, the revelation of ugly human motives takes us into
the most sombre moods that comedy can reach. Horner's ruse to enable him
to expose and enjoy all the available society ladies is the logical final strategy
of the libertine code, ensuring total licence and total secrecy, but the end
result of all his busy machinations is passionless copulation with a queue of
brainless women. As he says himself: '. . . for ceremony in love and eating is
as ridiculous as in fighting; falling on briskly is all should be done in those
occasions.' The sophisticated Horner achieves less delight from love than
the joyously, naïvely amoral Margery Pinchwife.

Charles II died in 1685 and so the four plays already discussed fall strictly within the lifetime of the restored monarch. But the impact of the 'new-comedy' of the sixties is still felt at the end of the century, especially in the work of the younger men, Vanbrugh and Congreve. But whereas *The Way of the World* gives the impression of men and manners observed with precision and presented with all the formal discipline—in plot, dialogue, and character—of ballet choreography, Vanbrugh's comedies have a knockabout zest appropriate to their rough-and-ready scene-plotting and hearty characterization. *The Provoked Wife* is particularly farcical and *The Relapse* (1696) owes a good deal of its stage appeal to scenes of satirical farce which the printed text inevitably cannot capture. The fopperies of the town, exemplified by Lord Foppington, come into literal collision with the earthy vulgarities of the country as incarnated in Sir Tunbelly Clumsy, and there is a similar contrast made between the sophisticated Berinthia and the aptly named Miss Hoyden. The hilarious low comedy and slapstick satire have a welcome vitality, and by means of gross farce rather than witty dialogue the sordid motives behind heiress-hunting in rustic Loamshire are pungently revealed.

The five plays reprinted in this volume reveal that Restoration comedy has more variety of treatment than one might have expected from works which deal with a limited segment of society—though, one might add in defence, no more limited than the social scene of Jane Austen's novels. Apart from the strong vein of heroic romance there is comedy at all levels—boisterous farce, 'humours' characters, the cruel ridicule of fops, coquettes, snobs, pimps, would-be wits, poetasters, lecherous gallants (young and old), sensual ladies-of-honour, and the more sympathetic satire against fashionable young men and women who have to learn the graces and tactics of high society. The intention is not didactic, as it was to become in the eighteenth century: wit and pleasure provide the moral guidelines, such as they are, and so prudes, parsons, and poetasters are fair game. But, despite themselves, the playwrights were concerned with morality and the central problem of all their comedies was marriage. The shams of 'arranged marriages'—holy matrimony degraded to the level of the auction room—and the cynical acceptance of adultery or idle pastimes as an escape from the boredom of marriage, constitute the significant theme of these plays. This, together with a cleansing spray of satire directed forcefully at pretenders to virtue and wit, surely encouraged a critical scrutiny of a ruling class which was less and less capable of ruling. The drunken, rakish gentry and their hypocritically sensual wives are always subjected to ridicule. Upper-class fops and would-be wits are laughed off the stage. The marriage-brokers—grasping fathers, rich old lechers, and assorted go-betweens—are exposed and defeated by witty young lovers. Admittedly the heroes cannot always draw the line between crude

debauchery and frank sensuality, and the bold-speaking, sexually emanci-
pated heroines slip easily from clear-sighted realism to old-fashioned co-
quettish tactics (using their virtue, like Richardson's Pamela, as the crucial
bargaining asset). But then the playwrights were no moral revolutionaries,
nor was society ready to give women the same sexual freedom as men. Inside
every bawdy Restoration comedy there is a muddled, romantic, sensual,
rational plea for 'wedded love' struggling to escape. But I doubt whether
John Milton, penning his own celebration of wedded love in his Restoration
epic, would have recognized it.

DENNIS DAVISON

Monash University
Melbourne
Australia
1969

A Note on the Text

The plays reprinted in this volume have been edited from photocopies of first editions held by the Harvard University Library, to which grateful acknowledgement is made. The title-pages are reproduced from copies held by the British Museum. The punctuation and spelling have been modernized and stage directions occasionally moved to a more appropriate place on the page. Prose mistakenly printed as verse has been printed as prose. Any editorial matter has been enclosed within square brackets.

Invaluable assistance in the preparation of the typescript was afforded by Norma Bolton, aided by Barbara Calton, Christine Sutton, Celia Elber, Sadie Stephens, and Sujatha Pannell.

D. D.

SHE WOULD IF SHE COULD

BY

SIR GEORGE ETHEREGE

SIR GEORGE ETHEREGE (*c.* 1635–1691)

She Would If She Could, first performed at Lincoln's Inn Fields, February 1668; first published 1668.

[*The Works of Sir George Etherege*, ed. H. F. B. Brett-Smith, 3 vols., 1927.]

She wou'd if she cou'd,

A

COMEDY.

Acted at His

HIGHNESSE the DUKE of YORK'S
THEATRE.

Written by
GEORGE ETHEREGE Esq;

LONDON,

Printed for *H. Herringman*, at the Sign of the *Blew Anchor* in the
Lower walk of the *New Exchange*. 1668.

DRAMATIS PERSONAE

SIR OLIVER COCKWOOD SIR JOSLIN JOLLY	} Two country knights
MR. COURTALL MR. FREEMAN	} Two honest gentlemen of the town
MY LADY COCKWOOD	
ARIANA GATTY	} Two young ladies, kinswomen of Sir Joslin Jolly's
MRS. SENTRY	My Lady Cockwood's gentlewoman
MRS. GAZETTE MRS. TRINKET	} Two Exchange women
MR. RAKEHELL	A knight of the industry
THOMAS	Sir Oliver Cockwood's man
A SERVANT BELONGING TO MR. COURTALL	
WAITERS, FIDDLERS, AND OTHER ATTENDANTS	

the industry] whoremongering

She Would If She Could

ACT I   SCENE I

A Dining Room.

Enter Courtall *and* Freeman, *and a* Servant *brushing* Courtall.

Court. So, so, 'tis well: let the coach be made ready.
Serv. It shall, sir.   [*Exit* Servant.
Court. Well, Frank, what is to be done today?
Free. Faith, I think we must e'en follow the old trade; eat well, and prepare ourselves with a bottle or two of good burgundy, that our old acquaintance may look lovely in our eyes; for, for ought as I see, there is no hopes of
new.
Court. Well, this is grown a wicked town! It was otherwise in my memory
—a gentleman should not have gone out of his chamber but some civil
officer or other of the game would have been with him, and have given him
notice where he might have had a course or two in the afternoon.   11
Free. Truly, a good motherly woman of my acquaintance t'other day,
talking of the sins of the times, told me, with tears in her eyes, that there are
a company of higgling rascals, who partly for themselves, but more especially
for some secret friends, daily forestall the markets. Nay, and that many
gentlemen who formerly had been persons of great worth and honour are of
late, for some private reasons, become their own purveyors, to the utter
decay and disencouragement of trade and industry.
Court. I know there are some wary merchants who never trust their
business to a factor. But for my part, I hate the fatigue, and had rather be
bound to back my own colts, and man my own hawks, than endure the
impertinencies of bringing a young wench to the lure.   22

Enter Servant.

Serv. Sir, there is a gentlewoman below desires to speak with you.
Court. Ha, Freeman, this may be some lucky adventure.
Serv. She asked me if you were alone.
Court. And did not you say Ay?

10 game] whoremongering   14 higgling] haggling   20 factor] agent   22 lure]
falconer's bait for recalling hawk

Serv. I told her I would go see.

Court. Go, go down quickly, and tell her I am. Frank, prithee let me put thee into this closet a while.

Free. Why, may not I see her?   30

Court. On my life thou shalt have fair play, and go halves, if it be a purchase that may with honour be divided. You may over-hear all: but for decency's sake, in, in man.

Free. Well, good fortune attend thee.

Enter Mrs. Sentry.

Court. Mrs. Sentry, this is a happiness beyond my expectation.

Sent. Your humble servant, sir.

Court. I hope your lady's come to town?

Sent. Sir Oliver, my lady, and the whole family. Well! We have had a sad time in the country. My lady's so glad she's come to enjoy the freedom of this place again, and I daresay longs to have the happiness of your company.

Court. Did she send you hither?   41

Sent. Oh no, if she should but know that I did such a confident trick, she would think me a good one i'faith. The zeal I have to serve you made me venture to call in my way to the Exchange, to tell you the good news, and to let you know our lodgings are in James Street at the Black-Posts, where we lay the last summer.

Court. Indeed it is very obligingly done.

Sent. But I must needs desire you to tell my lady that you came to the knowledge of this by some lucky chance or other, for I would not be discovered for a world.   50

Court. Let me alone, I warrant thee.

Enter Servant.

Serv. Sir Oliver Cockwood, sir, is come to wait on you.

Sent. O heaven, my master! My lady and myself are both undone, undone. . . .

Court. 'Sdeath, why did you not tell him I was busied?

Sent. For heaven's sake, Mr. Courtall, what shall I do?

Court. Leave, leave trembling, and creep into the wood-hole here.

[*She goes into the wood-hole.*

Enter Sir Oliver.

Court. (*Embraces him.*) Sir Oliver Cockwood!

Sir Ol. Honest Ned Courtall, by my troth I think thou tak'st me for a pretty wench, thou hug'st me so very close and heartily.   60

57 wood-hole] firewood storage recess

Court. Only my joy to see you, sir Oliver, and to welcome you to town.

Sir Ol. Methinks, indeed, I have been an age absent, but I intend to redeem the time. And how, and how stand affairs, prithee now? Is the wine good? Are the women kind? Well, faith, a man had better be a vagabond in this town, than a justice of peace in the country. I was e'en grown a sot for want of gentleman-like recreations. If a man do but rap out an oath the people start as if a gun went off; and if one chance but to couple himself with his neighbour's daughter, without the help of the parson of the parish, and leave a little testimony of his kindness behind him, there is presently such an uproar that a poor man is fain to fly his country. As for drunkenness, 'tis true it may be used without scandal, but the drink is so abominable that a man would forbear it for fear of being made out of love with the vice.   72

Court. I see, sir Oliver, you continue still your old humour and are resolved to break your sweet lady's heart.

Sir Ol. You do not think me sure so barbarously unkind, to let her know all this! No, no, these are secrets fit only to be trusted to such honest fellows as thou art.

Court. Well may I, poor sinner, be excused, since a woman of such rare beauty, such incomparable parts, and of such an unblemished reputation, is not able to reclaim you from these wild courses, sir Oliver.   80

Sir Ol. To say the truth, she is a wife that no man need be ashamed of, Ned.

Court. I vow, sir Oliver, I must needs blame you, considering how tenderly she loves you.

Sir Ol. Ay, ay, the more is her misfortune, and mine too Ned. I would willingly give thee a pair of the best coach-horses in my stable, so thou could'st but persuade her to love me less.

Court. Her virtue and my friendship sufficiently secure you against that, sir Oliver.

Sir Ol. I know thou wert never married, but has it never been thy misfortune to have a mistress love thee thus entirely?   91

Court. It never has been my good fortune, sir Oliver. But why do you ask this question?

Sir Ol. Because then, perchance, thou might'st have been a little sensible what a damned trouble it is.

Court. As how, sir Oliver?

Sir Ol. Why look thee, thus: for a man cannot be altogether ungrateful, sometimes one is obliged to kiss, and fawn, and toy, and lie fooling an hour or two, when a man had rather, if it were not for the disgrace sake, stand all that while in the pillory pelted with rotten eggs and oranges.   100

Court. This is a very hard case indeed, sir Oliver.

Sir Ol. And then the inconvenience of keeping regular hours! But above all, that damned fiend jealousy does so possess these passionate lovers, that I protest, Ned, under the rose be it spoken, if I chance to be a little prodigal in my expence on a private friend or so, I am called to so strict an account at night, that for quietness' sake I am often forced to take a dose of cantharides to make up the sum.

Court. Indeed, sir Oliver, everything considered, you are not so much to be envied as one may rashly imagine.   109

Sir Ol. Well, a pox of this tying man and woman together, for better, for worse! Upon my conscience, it was but a trick that the clergy might have a feeling in the cause.

Court. I do not conceive it to be much for their profit, sir Oliver, for I dare lay a good wager, let 'em but allow Christian liberty, and they shall get ten times more by christenings than they are likely to lose by marriages.

Sir Ol. Faith, thou hast hit it right, Ned! And now thou talk'st of Christian liberty, prithee let us dine together today, and be swingingly merry—but with all secrecy.

Court. I shall be glad of your good company, sir Oliver.   119

Sir Ol. I am to call on a very honest fellow, whom I left here hard by making a visit, sir Joslin Jolly, a kinsman of my wife's, and my neighbour in the country. We call brothers—he came up to town with me and lodgeth in the same house. He has brought up a couple of the prettiest kinswomen, heiresses of a very good fortune. Would thou hadst the instructing of 'em a little; faith, if I am not very much mistaken, they are very prone to the study of the mathematics.

Court. I shall be beholding to you for so good an acquaintance.

Sir Ol. This sir Joslin is in great favour with my lady, one that she has an admirable good opinion of, and will trust me with him anywhere. But to say truth, he is as arrant a sinner as the best of us, and will boggle at nothing that becomes a man of honour. We will go and get leave of my lady, for it is not fit I should break out so soon without her approbation, Ned.   132

Court. By no means, sir Oliver.

Sir Ol. Where shall we meet about an hour hence?

Court. At the French House or the Bear.

Sir Ol. At the French House by all means.

Court. Agreed, agreed.

Sir Ol. Would thou could'st bring a fourth man.

Court. What think you of Frank Freeman?

Sir Ol. There cannot be a better. Well—servant, Ned, servant, Ned!

                                                     [*Exit* Sir Oliver.

104 under the rose] *sub rosa*, in confidence   106 cantharides] dried Spanish Fly, an aphrodisiac   135 the French House] probably Chatelain's French tavern in Covent Garden   135 the Bear] a tavern in Drury Lane

Court. Your servant, sir Oliver.—Mrs. Sentry!   141
Sent. (*In the hole.*) Is he gone?
Court. Ay, ay! You may venture to bolt now.
Sent. (*Crawling out.*) Oh heavens! I would not endure such another
fright.
Court. Come, come, prithee be composed.
Sent. I shall not be myself again this fortnight; I never was in such a
taking days of my life. To have been found false, and to one who, to say
truth, has been always very kind and civil to me; but above all, I was con-
cerned for my lady's honour. . . .   150
Court. Come, come—there's no harm done.
Sent. Ah! Mr. Courtall, you do not know sir Oliver so well as I do. He has
strange humours sometimes, and has it enough in's nature to play the tyrant,
but that my lady and myself awe him by our policy.
Court. Well, well, all's well; did you not hear what a tearing blade sir
Oliver is?
Sent. Ah! 'tis a vile dissembling man; how fairly he carries it to my lady's
face! But I dare not discover him for fear of betraying myself.
Court. Well, Mrs. Sentry, I must dine with 'em, and after I have entered
them with a beer glass or two, if I can I will slip away and pay my respects to
your lady.   161
Sent. You need not question your welcome, I assure you, sir. . . . Your
servant, sir.
Court. Your servant, Mrs. Sentry. I am very sensible of this favour, I
assure you.
Sent. I am proud it was in my power to oblige you, sir.   [*Exit* Sentry.
Court. Freeman! Come, come out of thy hole. How hast thou been able to
contain?
Free. Faith much ado, the scene was very pleasant! But above all, I admire
thy impudence—I could never have had the face to have wheedled the poor
knight so.   171
Court. Pish, pish, 'twas both necessary and honest. We ought to do all we
can to confirm a husband in the good opinion of his wife.
Free. Pray how long, if without offence a man may ask you, have you been
in good grace with this person of honour? I never knew you had that commendable quality of secrecy before.
Court. You are mistaken, Freeman. Things go not as you wickedly
imagine.
Free. Why, hast thou lost all sense of modesty? Dost thou think to pass
these gross wheedles on me too? Come, come, this good news should make
thee a little merrier: faith, though she be an old acquaintance, she has the

148 taking days] state of agitation   159 entered] initiated

advantage of four or five months' absence. 'Slid, I know not how proud you are, but I have thought myself very spruce ere now in an old suit that has been brushed and laid up a while.

Court. Freeman, I know in cases of this nature thou art an infidel; but yet methinks the knowledge thou hast of my sincere dealing with my friends should make thee a little more confiding.

Free. What devilish oath could she invent to fright thee from a discovery?

Court. Wilt thou believe me if I swear the preservation of her honour has been my fault, and not hers?   190

Free. This is something.

Court. Why then, know that I have still been as careful to prevent all opportunities, as she has been to contrive 'em; and still have carried it so like a gentleman, that there has not had the least suspicion of unkindness. She is the very spirit of impertinence, so foolishly fond and troublesome, that no man above sixteen is able to endure her.

Free. Why did you engage thus far then?

Court. Some conveniences which I had by my acquaintance with the sot her husband made me extraordinary civil to her, which presently by her ladyship was interpreted after the manner of the most obliging women. This wench came hither by her commission today.   201

Free. With what confidence she denied it!

Court. Nay, that's never wanting, I assure you. Now is it expected I should lay by all other occasions, and watch every opportunity to wait upon her. She would by her good will give her lover no more rest than a young squire, that has newly set up a coach, does his only pair of horses.

Free. Faith, if it be as thou say'st, I cannot much blame the hardness of thy heart. But did not the oaf talk of two young ladies?

Court. Well remembered, Frank, and now I think on't, 'twill be very necessary to carry on my business with the old one, that we may better have an opportunity of being acquainted with them. Come, let us go and bespeak dinner, and by the way consider of these weighty affairs.   212

Free. Well, since there is but little ready money stirring, rather than want entertainment I shall be contented to play a while upon tick.

Court. And I—provided they promise fair and we find there's hopes of payment hereafter.

Free. Come along, come along.   [*Exeunt.*

182 'Slid] abbreviation of God's eyelid, a mild oath

SCENE II

Sir Oliver Cockwood's Lodging.

Enter Lady Cockwood.

Lady Cock. 'Tis too late to repent. I sent her, but yet I cannot but be troubled to think she stays so long. Sure if she has so little gratitude to let him, he has more honour than to attempt anything to the prejudice of my affection . . . Oh! Sentry, are you come?

Enter Sentry.

Sent. Oh madam, there has been such an accident!

Lady Cock. Prithee do not fright me, wench. . . .

Sent. As I was discoursing with Mr. Courtall, in came sir Oliver.

Lady Cock. Oh! . . . I'm ruined . . . undone for ever!

Sent. You'll still be sending me on these desperate errands.

Lady Cock. I am betrayed, betrayed . . . by this false . . . what shall I call thee?   11

Sent. Nay, but madam . . . have a little patience. . . .

Lady Cock. I have lost all patience, and will never more have any. . . .

Sent. Do but hear me, all is well. . . .

Lady Cock. Nothing can be well, unfortunate woman.

Sent. Mr. Courtall thrust me into the wood-hole.

Lady Cock. And did not sir Oliver see thee?

Sent. He had not the least glimpse of me. . . .

Lady Cock. Dear Sentry . . . and what good news?

Sent. He intends to wait upon you in the afternoon, madam. . . .   20

Lady Cock. I hope you did not let him know I sent you.

Sent. No, no, madam . . . I'll warrant you I did everything much to the advantage of your honour.

Lady Cock. Ah Sentry! If we could but think of some lucky plot now to get sir Oliver out of the way.

Sent. You need not trouble yourself about that, madam, he has engaged to dine with Mr. Courtall at the French House, and is bringing sir Joslin Jolly to get your good will. When Mr. Courtall has fixed 'em with a beer-glass or two, he intends to steal away and pay his devotion to your ladyship.

Lady Cock. Truly he is a person of much worth and honour.   30

Sent. Had you but been there, madam, to have overheard sir Oliver's discourse, he would have made you bless yourself. There is not such another wild man in the town. All his talk was of wenching, and swearing, and drinking, and tearing.

Lady Cock. Ay, ay, Sentry, I know he'll talk of strange matters behind my back. But if he be not an abominable hypocrite at home, and I am not a woman easily to be deceived, he is not able to play the spark abroad thus, I assure you.

Enter Sir Oliver, *and* Sir Joslin (Sir Joslin *singing*).

My dearest dear, this is kindly done of thee to come home again thus quickly.

Sir Ol. Nay, my dear, thou shalt never have any just cause to accuse me of unkindness.   41

Lady Cock. Sir Joslin, now you are a good man, and I shall trust you with sir Oliver again.

Sir Jos. Nay, if I ever break my word with a lady, I will be delivered bound to Mrs. Sentry here, and she shall have leave to carve me for a capon.

Sent. Do you think I have a heart cruel enough for such a bloody execution?

Sir Jos. Kindly spoke i'faith, girl, I'll give thee a buss for that.

                                                                [Kisses her.

Lady Cock. Fy, fy, sir Joslin, this is not seemly in my presence.

Sir Jos. We have all our failings, lady, and this is mine. A right bred greyhound can as well forbear running after a hare when he sees her, as I can mumbling a pretty wench when she comes in my way.   52

Lady Cock. I have heard indeed you are a parlous man, sir Joslin.

Sir Jos. I seldom brag, lady, but for a true cock of the game, little Joslin dares match with the best of 'em.

Sir Ol. Sir Joslin's merry, my dear.

Lady Cock. Ay, ay, if he should be wicked, I know thou art too much a gentleman to offer an injury to thine own dear lady.

Sir Jos. Faith, madam, you must give my brother Cockwood leave to dine abroad today.   60

Lady Cock. I protest, sir Joslin, you begin to make me hate you too. Well, you are e'en grown as bad as the worst of 'em, you are still robbing me of the sweet society of sir Oliver.

Sir Jos. Come, come, your discipline is too severe, i'faith lady.

Lady Cock. Sir Oliver may do what he pleases, sir, he knows I have ever been his obedient lady.

Sir Ol. Prithee, my dear, be not angry. Sir Joseph was so earnest in his invitation that none but a clown could have refused him.

Sir Jos. Ay, ay, we dine at my uncle sir Joseph Jolly's, lady.

48 buss] kiss   53 parlous] perilous

Lady Cock. Will you be sure now to be a good dear, and not drink, nor stay
out late? 71

Sir Jos. I'll engage for all, and if there be no harm in a merry catch or a
waggish story. . . .

Enter Ariana *and* Mistress Gatty.

Ha, ha! Sly-girl and Mad-cap, are you got up? I know what you have been
meditating on; but never trouble your heads, let me alone to bring you
consolation.

Gatty. We have often been beholding to you, sir; for every time he's drunk
he brings us home a couple of fresh servants.

Sir Ol. Well, farewell my dear, prithee do not sigh thus, but make thee
ready, visit, and be merry. 80

Lady Cock. I shall receive most satisfaction in my chamber.

Sir Jos. Come, come along, brother. Farewell one and all, Lady and Sly-
girl, Sly-girl and Mad-cap, your servant, your servant. . . .

[*Exeunt* Sir Oliver *and* Sir Joslin *singing.*

Lady Cock. (*To* Sentry *aside.*) Sentry, is the new point I bought come home,
and is everything in a readiness?

Sent. Everything, madam.

Lady Cock. Come, come up quickly then, girl, and dress me.

[*Exeunt* Lady Cockwood *and* Sentry.

Ariana. Dost not thou wonder, Gatty, she should be so strangely fond of
this coxcomb?

Gatty. Well, if she does not dissemble, may I still be discovered when I do.
Didst thou not see how her countenance changed, as soon as ever their backs
were turned, and how earnestly she whispered with her woman? There is
some weighty affair in hand, I warrant thee. My dear Ariana, how glad am I
we are in this town again. 94

Ariana. But we have left the benefit of the fresh air, and the delight of
wandering in the pleasant groves.

Gatty. Very pretty things for a young gentlewoman to bemoan the loss of
indeed, that's newly come to a relish of the good things of this world.

Ariana. Very good, sister!

Gatty. Why, hast not thou promised me a thousand times to leave off this
demureness?

Ariana. But you are so quick. 102

Gatty. Why, would it not make anyone mad to hear thee bewail the loss of
the country? Speak but one grave word more, and it shall be my daily prayers
thou may'st have a jealous husband, and then you'll have enough of it I
warrant you!

78 servants] gallants   84 point] lace

Ariana. It may be, if your tongue be not altogether so nimble, I may be conformable. But I hope you do not intend we shall play such mad reaks as we did last summer?

Gatty. 'Slife, dost thou think we come here to be mewed up, and take only the liberty of going from our chamber to the dining room, and from the dining room to our chamber again? And like a bird in a cage, with two perches only, to hop up and down, up and down?   113

Ariana. Well, thou art a mad wench.

Gatty. Would'st thou never have us go to a play but with our grave relations, never take the air but with our grave relations—to feed their pride and make the world believe it is in their power to afford some gallant or other a good bargain?

Ariana. But I am afraid we shall be known again.

Gatty. Pish! The men were only acquainted with our vizards and our petticoats, and they are wore out long since. How I envy that sex! Well, we cannot plague 'em enough when we have it in our power for those privileges which custom has allowed 'em above us!   123

Ariana. The truth is they can run and ramble here, and there, and everywhere, and we poor fools rather think the better of 'em.

Gatty. From one playhouse to the other playhouse, and if they like neither the play nor the women, they seldom stay any longer than the combing of their periwigs, or a whisper or two with a friend—and then they cock their caps and out they strut again!

Ariana. But whatsoever we do, prithee now let us resolve to be mighty honest.   131

Gatty. There I agree with thee.

Ariana. And if we find the gallants like lawless subjects, who the more their princes grant, the more they impudently crave. . . .

Gatty. We'll become absolute tyrants, and deprive 'em of all the privileges we gave 'em. . . .

Ariana. Upon these conditions I am contented to trail a pike under thee.
. . . March along girl!   [*Exeunt.*

---

108 reaks] pranks   110 mewed up] caged   120 vizards] small masks

ACT II SCENE I

The Mulberry Garden.

Enter Courtall *and* Freeman.

Court. Was there ever a couple of fops better matched than these two knights are?

Free. They are harp and violin—nature has so tuned 'em as if she intended they should always play the fool in consort.

Court. Now is sir Oliver secure, for he dares not go home till he's quite drunk, and then he grows valiant, insults, and defies his sweet lady—for which with prayers and tears he's forced to feign a bitter repentance the next morning.

Free. What do we here idling in the Mulberry Garden? Why do not we make this visit then?   10

Court. Now art thou as mad upon this trail as if we were upon a hot scent.

Free. Since we know the bush, why do we not start the game?

Court. Gently, good Frank! First know that the laws of honour prescribed in such nice cases will not allow me to carry thee along with me. And next, hast thou so little wit to think that a discreet lady, that has had the experience of so much human frailty, can have so good an opinion of the constancy of her servant as to lead him into temptation?

Free. Then we must not hope her ladyship should make us acquainted with these gentlewomen.

Court. Thou may'st as reasonably expect that an old rook should bring a young snap acquainted with his bubble; but advantages may be hereafter made by my admission into the family.   22

Free. What is to be done then?

Court. Why, look you, thus I have contrived it. Sir Oliver, when I began to grow resty, that he might incline me a little more to drunkenness, in my ear discovered to me the humour of his dear friend sir Joslin. He assured me that when he was in that good natured condition, to requite their courtesy he always carried the good company home with him, and recommended them to his kinswomen.

Free. Very good!   30

Court. Now after the fresh air has breathed on us a while, and expelled the vapours of the wine we have drunk, thou shalt return to these two sots,

s.d. *Mulberry Garden*] pleasure-ground, planted with mulberry trees, on the site of the present Buckingham Palace   20 rook] swindler   21 snap] fellow   21 bubble] dupe
25 resty] restive, or, sluggish

whom we left at the French House, according to our promise, and tell 'em I am a little stayed by some unlucky business, and will be with 'em presently. Thou wilt find 'em tired with long fight, weak and unable to observe their order. Charge 'em briskly and in a moment thou shalt rout 'em, and with little or no damage to thyself gain an absolute victory.

Free. Very well!

Court. In the meantime I will make my visit to the longing lady, and order my business so handsomely, that I will be with thee again immediately to make an experiment of the good humour of sir Joslin.   41

Free. Let's about it.

Court. 'Tis yet too early—we must drill away a little time here, that my excuses may be more probable and my persecution more tolerable.

    Enter Ariana *and* Gatty *with vizards, and pass nimbly over the stage.*

Free. Ha, ha—how wantonly they trip it! There is temptation enough in their very gait to stir up the courage of an old alderman. Prithee let us follow 'em.

Court. I have been so often baulked with these vizard-masks that I have at least a dozen times forsworn 'em. They are a most certain sign of an ill face, or what is worse, an old acquaintance.   50

Free. The truth is nothing but some such weighty reason is able to make women deny themselves the pride they have to be seen.

Court. The evening's fresh and pleasant, and yet there is but little company.

Free. Our course will be the better, these deer cannot herd. Come, come man, let's follow.

Court. I find it is a mere folly to forswear anything—it does but make the devil the more earnest in his temptation.   [*They go after the* Women.

        Enter Women *again, and cross the stage.*

Ariana. Now if these should prove two men-of-war that are cruising here to watch for prizes!

Gatty. Would they had courage enough to set upon us—I long to be engaged!   61

Ariana. Look, look yonder! I protest they chase us.

Gatty. Let us bear away then. If they be truly valiant they'll quickly make more sail and board us.

    The Women *go out, and go about behind the scenes to the other door.*

         Enter Courtall *and* Freeman.

Free. 'Sdeath, how fleet they are! Whatsoever faults they have, they cannot be broken-winded.

---

   48 baulked] thwarted, or, disappointed

Court. Sure, by that little mincing step they should be country fillies that have been breathed at course a park, and barley-break! We shall never reach 'em.

Free. I'll follow directly. Do thou turn down the cross-walk and meet 'em.

Enter the Women, *and after 'em* Courtall *at the lower door,*
and Freeman *at the upper on the contrary side.*

Court. By your leave, ladies. . . .   71

Gatty. I perceive you can make bold enough without it.

Free. Your servant, ladies. . . .

Ariana. Or any other ladies' that will give themselves the trouble to entertain you.

Free. 'Slife, their tongues are as nimble as their heels.

Court. Can you have so little good nature to dash a couple of bashful young men out of countenance, who came out of pure love to tender you their service?

Gatty. 'Twere pity to baulk 'em, sister.   80

Ariana. Indeed methinks they look as if they never had been flipped before.

Free. Yes faith, we have had many a fair course in this paddock, have been very well fleshed, and dare boldly fasten.

                              [*They kiss their hands with a little force.*

Ariana. Well, I am not the first unfortunate woman that has been forced to give her hand, where she never intends to bestow her heart.

Gatty. Now, do you think 'tis a bargain already?

Court. Faith, would there were some lusty earnest given, for fear we should unluckily break off again.

Free. Are you so wild that you must be hooded thus?

Court. Fy, fy, put off these scandals to all good faces.   90

Gatty. For your reputations' sake we shall keep 'em on. 'Slife we should be taken for your relations if we durst shew our faces with you thus publicly.

Ariana. And what a shame that would be to a couple of young gallants! Methinks you should blush to think on't.

Court. These were pretty toys, invented first merely for the good of us poor lovers to deceive the jealous, and to blind the malicious; but the proper use is so wickedly perverted that it makes all honest men hate the fashion mortally.

Free. A good face is as seldom covered with a vizard-mask as a good hat with an oiled case—and yet on my conscience you are both handsome.

Court. Do but remove 'em a little to satisfy a foolish scruple.   101

68 breathed] exercised to improve breathing   68 course a park] a country game in which a girl called out a man to chase her   68 barley-break] a country game requiring hard running   81 flipped] whipped   83 fleshed] incited

Ariana. This is a just punishment you have brought upon yourselves by that unpardonable sin of talking.

Gatty. You can only brag now of your acquaintance with a farendon gown and a piece of black velvet.

Court. The truth is there are some vain fellows whose loose behaviour of late has given great discouragement to the honourable proceedings of all virtuous ladies.   110

Free. But I hope you have more charity than to believe us of the number of the wicked.

Ariana. There's not a man of you to be trusted.

Gatty. What a shame is it to your whole sex that a woman is more fit to be a privy-counsellor, than a young gallant a lover?

Court. This is a pretty kind of fooling, ladies, for men that are idle, but you must bid a little fairer if you intend to keep us from our serious business.

Gatty. Truly you seem to be men of great employment, that are every moment rattling from the eating-houses to the play-houses, from the play-houses to the Mulberry Garden, that live in a perpetual hurry, and have little leisure for such an idle entertainment.

Court. Now would not I see thy face for the world; if it should but be half so good as thy humour thou would'st dangerously tempt me to dote upon thee, and forgetting all shame, become constant.   122

Free. I perceive, by your fooling here, that wit and good humour may make a man in love with a blackamore. That the devil should contrive it so, that we should have earnest business now.

Court. Would they would but be so kind to meet us here again tomorrow.

Gatty. You are full of business, and 'twould but take you off of your employments.

Ariana. And we are very unwilling to have the sin to answer for—of ruining a couple of such hopeful young men.   130

Free. Must we then despair?

Ariana. The ladies you are going to will not be so hard-hearted.

Court. (*To* Freeman.) On my conscience, they love us—begin to grow jealous already.

Free. Who knows but this may prove the luckier adventure of the two?

Court. Come, come, we know you have a mind to meet us. We cannot see you blush; speak it out boldly.

Gatty. Will you swear then not to visit any other women before that time?

Ariana. Not that we are jealous, but because we would not have you tired with the impertinent conversation of our sex, and come to us dull and out of humour.   142

104 farendon] cloth of silk with wool or hair

Court. Invent an oath, and let it be so horrid 'twould make an atheist start to hear it.

Free. And I will swear it readily, that I will not so much as speak to a woman till I speak to you again.

Gatty. But are you troubled with that foolish scruple of keeping an oath?

Free. O most religiously!

Court. And may we not enlarge our hopes upon a little better acquaintance?   150

Ariana. You see all the freedom we allow.

Gatty. It may be we may be entreated to hear a fiddle, or mingle in a country dance, or so.

Court. Well! we are in too desperate a condition to stand upon articles, and are resolved to yield on any terms.

Free. Be sure you be punctual now!

Ariana. Will you be sure?

Court. Or else may we become a couple of credulous coxcombs, and be jilted ever after.—Your servants, ladies.   [*Exeunt* Men.

Ariana. I wonder what they think of us!   160

Gatty. You may easily imagine, for they are not of a humour so little in fashion to believe the best. I assure you the most favourable opinion they can have is that we are still a little wild, and stand in need of better manning.

Ariana. Prithee, dear girl, what dost think of 'em?

Gatty. Faith, so well that I'm ashamed to tell thee.

Ariana. Would I had never seen 'em!

Gatty. Ha! Is it come to that already?

Ariana. Prithee, let's walk a turn or two more and talk of 'em.

Gatty. Let us take care then we are not too particular in their commendations, lest we should discover we intrench upon one another's inclinations, and so grow quarrelsome.   [*Exeunt.*

SCENE II

Sir Oliver's *Lodgings.*

Enter Lady Cockwood *and* Sentry.

Sent. Dear madam, do not afflict yourself thus unreasonably. I dare lay my life it is not want of devotion but opportunity that stays him.

Lady Cock. Ingrateful man! To be so insensible of a lady's passion!

Sent. If I thought he were so wicked I should hate him strangely. But, madam . . .

Lady Cock. Do not speak one word in his behalf—I am resolved to forget him. Perfidious mortal, to abuse so sweet an opportunity!

Sent. Hark, here is somebody coming upstairs.

Lady Cock. Peace, he may yet redeem his honour.

Enter Courtall.

Court. Your humble servant, madam.   10

Lady Cock. (*Starting.*) Mr. Courtall, for heaven sake how came you hither?

Court. Guided by my good fortune, madam. . . . Your servant, Mrs. Sentry.

Sent. Your humble servant, sir. I protest you made me start too, to see you come in thus unexpectedly.

Lady Cock. I did not imagine it could be known I was in town yet.

Court. Sir Oliver did me the favour to make me a visit and dine with me today, which brought me to the knowledge of this happiness, madam; and as soon as I could possibly, I got the freedom to come hither and enjoy it.

Lady Cock. You have ever been extreme obliging, sir.   20

Sent. (*Aside.*) 'Tis a worthy gentleman, how punctual he is to my directions!

Lady Cock. Will you be pleased to repose, sir? Sentry, set some chairs.

[*Exit* Sentry.

Court. With much difficulty, madam, I broke out of my company, and was forced by the importunity of one sir Joslin Jolly, I think they call him, to engage my honour I would return again immediately.

Lady Cock. You must not so soon rob me of so sweet a satisfaction.

Court. No consideration, madam, could take me from you, but that I know my stay at this time must needs endanger your honour; and how often I have denied myself the greatest satisfaction in the world to keep that unblemished, you yourself can witness.   31

Lady Cock. Indeed I have often had great trials of your generosity in those many misfortunes that have attended our innocent affections.

Court. Sir Oliver, madam, before I did perceive it, was got near that pitch of drunkenness which makes him come reeling home and unmanfully insult over your ladyship. And how subject he is then to injure you with an unjust suspicion, you have often told me—which makes me careful not to be surprised here.

Lady Cock. Repose yourself a little, but a little, dear sir. These virtuous principles make you worthy to be trusted with a lady's honour. Indeed sir Oliver has his failings, yet I protest, Mr. Courtall, I love him dearly—but cannot be altogether unsensible of your generous passion.   42

Court. (*Aside.*) Ay, ay, I am a very passionate lover!—Indeed this escape has only given me leisure to look upon my happiness.

Lady Cock. Is my woman retired?

Court. Most dutifully, madam.

Lady Cock. Then let me tell you, sir . . . yet we may make very good use of it.

Court. (*Aside.*) Now am I going to be drawn in again.

Lady Cock. If sir Oliver be in that indecent condition you speak of, to-morrow he will be very submissive, as it is meet for so great a misdemeanour. Then can I, feigning a desperate discontent, take my own freedom without the least suspicion.   53

Court. This is very luckily and obligingly thought on, madam.

Lady Cock. Now if you will be pleased to make an assignation, sir.

Court. Tomorrow about ten o'clock in the lower walk of the New Exchange, out of which we can quickly pop into my coach.

Lady Cock. But I am still so pestered with my woman, I dare not go without her. On my conscience she's very sincere, but it is not good to trust our reputations too much to the frailty of a servant.   60

Court. I will bring my chariot, madam, that will hold but two.

Lady Cock. O most ingeniously imagined, dear sir. For by that means I shall have a just excuse to give her leave to see a relation and bid her stay there till I call her.

Court. It grieves me much to leave you so soon, madam, but I shall comfort myself with the thoughts of the happiness you have made me hope for.

Lady Cock. I wish it were in my power eternally to oblige you, dear sir.

Court. Your humble servant, madam.

Lady Cock. Your humble servant, sweet sir.   [*Exit* Courtall.
Sentry . . . why Sentry . . . where are you?   70

Enter Sentry.

Sent. Here, madam.

Lady Cock. What a strange thing is this! Will you never take warning, but still be leaving me alone in these suspicious occasions?

Sent. I was but in the next room, madam.

Lady Cock. What may Mr. Courtall think of my innocent intentions? I protest if you serve me so again I shall be strangely angry. You should have more regard to your lady's honour.

Sent. (*Aside.*) If I stay in the room she will not speak kindly to me in a week after. And if I go out she always chides me thus! This is a strange infirmity she has, but I must bear with it—for on my conscience, custom has made it so natural she cannot help it.   81

Lady Cock. Are my cousins come home yet?

Sent. Not yet, madam.

Lady Cock. Dost thou know whither they went this evening?

Sent. I heard them say they would go take the air, madam.

Lady Cock. Well, I see it is impossible with virtuous counsel to reclaim them. Truly they are so careless of their own, I could wish sir Joslin would remove 'em, for fear they should bring an unjust imputation on my honour.

Sent. Heavens forbid, madam!

Enter Ariana *and* Gatty.

Lady Cock. Your servant, cousins.   90

Ambo. Your servant, madam.

Lady Cock. How have you spent the cool of the evening?

Gatty. As the custom is, madam, breathing the fresh air in the Park and Mulberry Garden.

Lady Cock. Without the company of a relation, or some discreet body to justify your reputations to the world! You are young, and may be yet insensible of it, but this is a strange censorious age, I assure you.

Noise of music without.

Ariana. Hark! What music's this?

Gatty. I'll lay my life my uncle's drunk, and hath picked us up a couple of worthy servants and brought them home with him in triumph.   100

Enter the Music *playing*, Sir Oliver *strutting and swaggering*, Sir Joslin *singing and dancing with* Mr. Courtall *and* Mr. Freeman *in each hand:* Gatty *and* Ariana *seeing* Courtall *and* Freeman *shriek and exeunt.*

Sir Jos. Hey-day! I told you they were a couple of skittish fillies, but I never knew 'em boggle at a man before! I'll fetch 'em again, I warrant you boys.   [*Exit after them.*

Free. (*To* Courtall.) These are the very self-same gowns and petticoats.

Court. Their surprise confirms us it must be them.

Free. 'Slife, we have betrayed ourselves very pleasantly.

Court. Now am I undone to all intents and purposes, for they will innocently discover all to my lady, and she will have no mercy.

Sir Ol. (*Strutting.*) Dan, dan, da ra, dan, &c. Avoid my presence. The very sight of that face makes me more impotent than a eunuch.   110

Lady Cock. (*Offering to embrace him.*) Dear sir Oliver!

Sir Ol. Forbear your conjugal clippings! I will have a wench! Thou shalt fetch me a wench, Sentry.

91 *Ambo.*] Ariana and Gatty both speak together.

Sent. Can you be so inhuman to my dear lady?

Sir Ol. Peace, Envy, or I will have thee executed for petty treason—thy skin flayed off, stuffed and hung up in my hall in the country, as a terror to my whole family.

Court. What crime can deserve this horrid punishment?

Sir Ol. I'll tell thee, Ned. 'Twas my fortune t'other day to have an intrigue with a tinker's wife in the country, and this malicious slut betrayed the very ditch, where we used to make our assignations, to my lady.   122

Free. She deserves your anger indeed, sir Oliver. But be not so unkind to your virtuous lady.

Sir Ol. Thou dost not know her, Frank. I have had a design to break her heart ever since the first month that I had her, and 'tis so tough that I have not yet cracked one string on't.

Court. You are too unmerciful, sir Oliver.

Sir Ol. Hang her, Ned, by wicked policy she would usurp my empire, and in her heart is a very Pharaoh—for every night she's a-putting me upon making brick without straw!   131

Court. I cannot see a virtuous lady so afflicted without offering her some consolation. (*Aside to her.*) Dear madam, is it not as I told you?

Lady Cock. (*To* Courtall *aside.*) The fates could not have been more propitious, and I shall not be wanting to the furthering of our mutual happiness.

Enter Sir Joslin, *with* Ariana *and* Gatty *in each hand, dancing and singing.*

CATCH

> *This is fly and pretty,*
> *And this is wild and witty;*
> *If either stayed*
> *Till she died a maid,*   140
> *I'faith 'twould be great pity.*

Sir Jos. Here they are, boys i'faith, and now little Joslin's a man of his word. Heuk! Sly-girl and Mad-cap, to 'em to 'em, boys halloo! (*Flings them to* Courtall *and* Freeman, *who kiss their hands.*) What's yonder, your lady in tears, brother Cockwood? Come, come I'll make up all breaches. (*He sings.*) *And we'll all be merry and frolic.* Fy, fy, though man and wife are seldom in good humour alone, there are few want the discretion to dissemble it in company.

Sir Joslin, Sir Oliver *and* Lady Cockwood *stand talking together.*

143 Heuk!] exclamation of surprise

Free. I knew we should surprise you, ladies.

Court. Faith, I thought this conjuring to be but a mere jest till now, and could not believe the astrological rascal had been so skilful.   151

Free. How exactly he described 'em, and how punctual he was in his directions to apprehend 'em!

Gatty. Then you have been with a conjurer, gentlemen.

Court. You cannot blame us, ladies. The loss of our hearts was so considerable that it may well excuse the indirect means we took to find out the pretty thieves that stole 'em.

Ariana. Did not I tell you what men of business these were, sister?

Gatty. I vow I innocently believed they had some pre-engagement to a scrivener or a surgeon, and wished 'em so perfidious.   160

Free. Why, we have kept our oaths, ladies.

Ariana. You are much beholding to providence.

Gatty. But we are more, sister! For had we once been deluded into an opinion they had been faithful, who knows into what inconveniences that error might have drawn us?

Court. Why should you be so unreasonable, ladies, to expect that from us we should scarce have hoped for from you? Fy, fy, the keeping of one's word is a thing below the honour of a gentleman.

Free. A poor shift! Fit only to uphold the reputation of a paltry citizen.

Sir Jos. Come, come, all will be well again, I warrant you, lady.   171

Lady Cock. These are insupportable injuries, but I will bear 'em with an invincible patience, and tomorrow make him dearly sensible how unworthy he has been.

Sir Jos. Tomorrow my brother Cockwood will be another man. . . . So, boys, and how do you like the flesh and blood of the Jollies? . . . Heuk, Sly-girl . . . and Mad-cap, Hey . . . come, come, you have heard them exercise their tongues a while. Now you shall see them play their feet a little. This is a clean-limbed wench, and has neither spavin, splinter, nor wind-gall. Tune her a jig, and play't roundly, you shall see her bounce it away like a nimble frigate before a fresh gale. . . . Hey, methinks I see her under sail already.

Gatty dances a jig.

Hey my little Mad-cap. . . . Here's a girl of the true breed of the Jollies, i'faith. . . . But hark you, hark you, a consultation, gentlemen. . . . Bear up, brother Cockwood, a little. What think you if we pack these idle housewives to bed now, and retire into a room by ourselves and have a merry catch, and

---

151 astrological] magical   154 conjurer] magician   179 spavin] disease of horse's hock-joint   179 splinter] disease in horse's foreleg   179 wind-gall] soft tumour on horse's fetlock-joint

a bottle or two of the best, and perfect the good work we have so unanimously carried on today?

Sir Ol. A most admirable intrigue ... tan, dan, da, ra, dan ... come, come, march to your several quarters! Go, we have sent for a civil person or two and are resolved to fornicate in private.   190

Lady Cock. This is a barbarous return of all my kindness.

Free. and Court. Your humble servant, madam.

[*Exit* Lady Cockwood *and* Sentry.

Court. Hark you! Hark you! Ladies, do not harbour too ill an opinion of us, for faith, when you have had a little more experience of the world, you'll find we are no such abominable rascals.

Gatty. We shall be so charitable to think no worse of you than we do of all mankind, for your sakes,—only that you are perjured, perfidious, inconstant, ingrateful!

Free. Nay, nay, that's enough in all conscience, ladies! And now you are sensible what a shameful thing it is to break one's word, I hope you'll be more careful to keep yours tomorrow.   201

Gatty. 'Invent an oath, and let it be so horrid. . . .'

Court. Nay, nay it is too late for raillery, i'faith, ladies.

Gatty and Ariana. Well, your servant then.

Free. and Court. Your servant, ladies.

Sir Ol. Now the enemy's marched out. . . .

Sir Jos. Then the castle's our own, boys . . . Hey!

> *And here and there I had her,*
> *And everywhere I had her,*
> *Her toy was such, that every touch*
> *Would make a lover madder.*

Free. and Court. Hey brave sir Joslin!

Sir Ol. Ah my dear little witty Joslin, let me hug thee.

Sir Jos. Strike up, you obstreperous rascals, and march along before us.

[*Exeunt singing and dancing.*

The end of the Second Act.

ACT III   SCENE I

The New Exchange.

Mrs. Trinket *sitting in a shop, people passing by as in the Exchange.*

Trink. What d'ye buy? What d'ye lack, gentlemen? Gloves, ribbons, and essences? Ribbons, gloves, and essences?

Enter Mr. Courtall.

Mr. Courtall! I thought you had a quarrel to the Change, and were resolved we should never see you here again.

Court. Your unkindness, indeed, Mrs. Trinket, had been enough to make a man banish himself for ever.

Enter Mrs. Gazette.

Trink. Look you, yonder comes fine Mrs. Gazette. Thither you intended your visit, I am sure.

Gaz. Mr. Courtall! Your servant.

Court. Your servant, Mrs. Gazette.   10

Gaz. This happiness was only meant to Mrs. Trinket. Had it not been my good fortune to pass by, by chance, I should have lost my share on't.

Court. This is too cruel Mrs. Gazette, when all the unkindness is on your side, to rally your servant thus.

Gaz. I vow this tedious absence of yours made me believe you intended to try an experiment on my poor heart, to discover that hidden secret—how long a despairing lover may languish without the sight of the party.

Court. You are always very pleasant on this subject, Mrs. Gazette.

Gaz. And have not you reason to be so too?

Court. Not that I know of.   20

Gaz. Yes, you hear the good news.

Court. What good news?

Gaz. How well this dissembling becomes you! But now I think better on't, it cannot concern you. You are more a gentleman than to have an amour last longer than an Easter term with a country lady. And yet there are some I see as well in the country as in the city, that have a pretty way of huswifing a lover, and can spin an intrigue out a great deal farther than others are willing to do.

Court. What pretty art have they, good Mrs. Gazette?

Gaz. When tradesmen see themselves in an ill condition, and are afraid of

s.d. *The New Exchange*] arcade of shops in the Strand

breaking, can they do better than to take in a good substantial partner to help
to carry on their trading?   32

Court. Sure you have been at 'riddle me, riddle me,' lately, you are so
wondrous witty.

Gaz. And yet I believe my lady Cockwood is so haughty she had rather give
over the vanity of an intrigue than take in a couple of young handsome
kinswomen to help to maintain it.

Court. I knew it would out at last. Indeed it is the principle of most good
women that love gaming, when they begin to grow a little out of play themselves, to make an interest in some young gamester or other in hopes to rook
a favour now and then. But you are quite out in your policy, my lady Cockwood is none of these, I assure you. . . . Hark you, Mrs. Gazette, you must
needs bestir yourself a little for me this morning, or else heaven have mercy
on a poor sinner.   44

Gaz. I hope this wicked woman has no design upon your body already.
Alas! I pity your tender conscience.

Court. I have always made thee my confidant, and now I come to thee as to
a faithful counsellor.

Gaz. State your case.

Court. Why, this ravenous kite is upon wing already—is fetching a little
compass, and will be here within this half hour to swoop me away.   51

Gaz. And you would have me your scarecrow?

Court. Something of that there is in't. She is still your customer?

Gaz. I have furnished her and the young ladies with a few fashionable toys
since they came to town to keep 'em in countenance at a play or in the
Park.

Court. I would have thee go immediately to the young ladies, and by some
device or other entice 'em hither.

Gaz. I came just now from taking measure of 'em for a couple of handker-
chiefs.   60

Court. How unlucky's this!

Gaz. They were calling for their hoods and scarfs, and are coming hither to
lay out a little money in ribbons and essences. I have recommended them to
Mrs. Trinket's shop here.

Court. This falls out more luckily than what I had contrived myself, or
could have done, for here will they be busy just before the door where we
have made our appointment. But if this long-winged devil should chance to
truss me before they come!

Gaz. I will only step up and give some directions to my maid about a little
business that is in haste, and come down again and watch her. If you are
snapped I'll be with you presently, and rescue you, I warrant you, or at least

50-51 fetching a little compass] going a roundabout way   71 presently] at once

stay you till more company come. She dares not force you away in my sight. She knows I am great with sir Oliver, and as malicious a devil as the best of 'em. . . . Your servant, sir.   [*Exit.*

Enter Freeman.

Court. Freeman! 'Tis well you are come.   75
Free. Well! what counter-plot? What hopes of disappointing the old, and of seeing the young ladies? I am ready to receive your orders.
Court. Faith, things are not so well contrived as I could have wished 'em, and yet I hope by the help of Mrs. Gazette to keep my word, Frank.
Free. Nay, now I know what tool thou hast made choice of, I make no question but the business will go well forward. But I am afraid this last unlucky business has so distasted these young trouts they will not be so easily tickled as they might have been.   83
Court. Never fear it. Whatsoever women say, I am sure they seldom think the worse of a man for running at all—'tis a sign of youth and high mettle, and makes them rather *piqué* who shall tame him. That which troubles me most is we lost the hopes of variety, and a single intrigue in love is as dull as a single plot in a play, and will tire a lover worse than t'other does an audience.
Free. We cannot be long without some under-plots in this town; let this be our main design, and if we are anything fortunate in our contrivance we shall make it a pleasant comedy.   91
Court. Leave all things to me, and hope the best. Be gone, for I expect their coming immediately. Walk a turn or two above, or fool a while with pretty Mrs. Anvil, and scent your eye-brows and periwig with a little essence of oranges, or jessamine. And when you see us altogether at Mrs. Gazette's shop, put in as it were by chance. I protest yonder comes the old haggard. To your post quickly! 'Sdeath, where's Gazette and these young ladies now?
                    [*Exit* Freeman.

Enter Lady Cockwood, *and* Sentry.

O madam, I have waited here at least an hour, and time seems very tedious when it delays so great a happiness as you bring with you.
Lady Cock. I vow, sir, I did but stay to give sir Oliver his due correction for those unseemly injuries he did me last night. Is your coach ready?
Court. Yes, madam, but how will you dispose of your maid?   102
Lady Cock. My maid! For heaven's sake, what do you mean, sir? Do I ever use to go abroad without her?
Court. 'Tis upon no design, madam, I speak it, I assure you. But my

---

     86 *piqué*] plume themselves on   95 jessamine] jasmin, a shrub with fragrant flowers
96 haggard] untamed adult hawk

glass coach broke last night and I was forced to bring my chariot, which can hold but two.

Lady Cock. O heaven! You must excuse me, dear sir, for I shall deny myself the sweetest recreations in the world, rather than yield to anything that may bring a blemish upon my spotless honour. 110

Enter Gazette.

Gaz. Your humble servant, madam. Your servant, Mr. Courtall.

Lady Cock. & Court. Your servant, Mrs. Gazette.

Gaz. I am extremely glad to see your ladyship here. I intended to send my maid to your lodgings this afternoon, madam, to tell you I have a parcel of new lace come in, the prettiest patterns that ever were seen; for I am very desirous so good a customer as your ladyship should see 'em first, and have your choice.

Lady Cock. I am much beholding to you, Mrs. Gazette. I was newly come into the Exchange and intended to call at your shop before I went home.

Enter Ariana *and* Gatty; Gazette *goes to 'em.*

Court. 'Sdeath, here are your cousins too! Now there is no hopes left for a poor unfortunate lover to comfort himself withall. 121

Lady Cock. Will fate never be more propitious?

Ariana and Gatty. Your servant, madam.

Lady Cock. I am newly come into the Exchange, and by chance met with Mr. Courtall here, who will needs give himself the trouble to play the gallant and wait upon me.

Gatty. Does your ladyship come to buy?

Lady Cock. A few trifles. Mrs. Gazette says she has a parcel of very fine new laces. Shall we go look upon 'em?

Ariana. We will only fancy a suit of knots or two at this shop, and buy a little essence, and wait upon your ladyship immediately. 131

Gatty. Mrs. Gazette, you are skilled in the fashion—pray let our choice have your approbation.

All go to the shop to look upon ware, but Courtall *and* Lady Cockwood.

Gaz. Most gladly, madam.

Court. 'Sdeath, madam, if you had made no ceremony, but stepped into the coach presently, we had escaped this mischief.

Lady Cock. My over-tenderness of my honour has blasted all my hopes of happiness.

Court. To be thus unluckily surprised in the height of all our expectation leaves me no patience. 140

Lady Cock. Moderate your passion a little, sir. I may yet find out a way.

Court. Oh 'tis impossible, madam, never think on't now you have been seen with me. To leave 'em upon any pretence will be so suspicious, that my concern for your honour will make me so feverish and disordered, that I shall lose the taste of all the happiness you give me.

Lady Cock. Methinks you are too scrupulous, heroic sir.

Court. Besides the concerns I have for you, madam, you know the obligations I have to sir Oliver, and what professions of friendship there are on both sides; and to be thought perfidious and ingrateful, what an affliction would that be to a generous spirit!   150

Lady Cock. Must we then unfortunately part thus?

Court. Now I have better thought on't, that is not absolutely necessary neither.

Lady Cock. These words revive my dying joys. Dear sir, go on.

Court. I will by and by, when I see it most convenient, beg the favour of your ladyship, and your young kinswomen, to accept of a treat and a fiddle. You make some little difficulty at first, but upon earnest persuasion comply, and use your interest to make the young ladies do so too. Your company will secure their reputations, and their company take off from you all suspicion.

Lady Cock. The natural inclination they have to be jigging will make them very ready to comply. But what advantage can this be to our happiness, dear sir?   162

Court. Why, first, madam, if the young ladies, or Mrs. Gazette, have any doubts upon their surprising us together, our joining company will clear 'em all. Next, we shall have some satisfaction in being an afternoon together, though we enjoy not that full freedom we so passionately desire.

Lady Cock. Very good, sir.

Court. But then lastly, madam, we gain an opportunity to contrive another appointment tomorrow, which may restore us unto all those joys we have been so unfortunately disappointed of today.   170

Lady Cock. This is a very prevailing argument indeed. But since sir Oliver believes I have conceived so desperate a sorrow, 'tis fit we should keep this from his knowledge.

Court. Are the young ladies secret?

Lady Cock. They have the good principles not to betray themselves, I assure you.

Court. Then 'tis but going to a house that is not haunted by the company, and we are secure. And now I think on't, the Bear in Drury Lane is the fittest place for our purpose.

Lady Cock. I know your honour, dear sir, and submit to your discretion. ... Have you gratified your fancies, cousins?   181

To them Ariana, Gatty, *and* Gazette *from the shop.*

Ariana. We are ready to wait upon you, madam.

Gatty. I never saw colours better mingled.

Gaz. How lively they set off one another, and how they add to the complexion!

Lady Cock. Mr. Courtall, your most humble servant.

Court. Pray, madam, let me have the honour to wait upon you and these young ladies, till I see you in your coach.

Lady Cock. Your friendship to sir Oliver would engage you in an unnecessary trouble. 190

Ariana. Let not an idle ceremony take you from your serious business, good sir.

Gatty. I should rather have expected to have seen you, sir, walking in Westminster Hall, watching to make a match at tennis, or waiting to dine with a Parliament man, than to meet you in such an idle place as the Exchange is.

Court. Methinks, ladies, you are well acquainted with me upon the first visit.

Ariana. We received your character before, you know sir, in the Mulberry Garden upon oath. 200

Court. (*Aside.*) 'Sdeath, what shall I do? Now out comes all my roguery.

Gatty. Yet I am apt to believe, sister, that was some malicious fellow that wilfully perjured himself on purpose to make us have an ill opinion of this worthy gentleman.

Court. Some rash men would be apt enough to enquire him out and cut his throat, ladies, but I heartily forgive him whosoever he was—for on my conscience 'twas not so much out of malice to me, as out of love to you he did it.

Gaz. He might imagine Mr. Courtall was his rival.

Court. Very likely, Mrs. Gazette. 210

Lady Cock. Whosoever he was, he was an unworthy fellow I warrant him. Mr. Courtall is known to be a person of worth and honour.

Ariana. We took him for an idle fellow, madam, and gave but very little credit to what he said.

Court. 'Twas very obliging, lady, to believe nothing to the disadvantage of a stranger. . . . (What a couple of young devils are these?)

Lady Cock. Since you are willing to give yourself this trouble. . . .

Court. I ought to do my duty, madam. [*Exeunt all but* Ariana *and* Gatty.

Ariana. How he blushed and hung down his head!

Gatty. A little more had put him as much out of countenance as a country clown is when he ventures to compliment his attorney's daughter. 221

[*They follow.*

SCENE [II]

Sir Oliver's Dining Room.

Enter Sir Joslin *and* Servant *severally.*

Sir Jos. How now old boy! Where's my brother Cockwood today?
Serv. He desires to be in private, sir.
Sir Jos. Why, what's the matter, man?
Serv. This is a day of humiliation, sir, with him for last night's transgression.
Sir Jos. I have business of consequence to impart to him, and must and will speak with him. . . . So, ho! Brother Cockwood!
Sir Ol. (Without.) Who's that? My brother Jolly?
Sir Jos. The same, the same, come away, boy.
Sir Ol. (Without.) For some secret reasons I desire to be in private, brother.
Sir Jos. I have such a design on foot as would draw Diogenes out of the tub to follow it! Therefore I say, come away, come away.   12
Sir Ol. (Entering in a night-gown and slippers.) There is such a strange temptation in thy voice—never stir.
Sir Jos. What, in thy gown and slippers yet! Why, brother, I have bespoke dinner, and engaged Mr. Rakehell, the little smart gentleman I have often promised thee to make thee acquainted withal, to bring a whole bevy of damsels in sky, and pink, and flame-coloured taffetas. Come, come, dress thee quickly! There's to be madam Rampant, a girl that shines and will drink at such a rate she's a mistress for Alexander were he alive again.   20
Sir Ol. How unluckily this falls out! Thomas, what clothes have I to put on?
Serv. None but your penitential suit, sir, all the rest are secured.
Sir Ol. Oh unspeakable misfortune! that I should be in disgrace with my lady now!
Sir Jos. Come, come, never talk of clothes. Put on anything—thou hast a person and a mien will bear it out bravely.
Sir Ol. Nay, I know my behaviour will show I am a gentleman, but yet the ladies will look scurvily upon me, brother.
Sir Jos. That's a jest i'faith! He that has *terra firma* in the country may appear in anything before 'em.   30

> *For he that would have a wench kind,*
> *Ne'er smugs up himself like a ninny;*
> *But plainly tells her his mind,*
> *And tickles her first with a guinea.*

Hey boy—

Sir Ol. I vow thou hast such a bewitching way with thee!

Sir Jos. How lovely will the ladies look when they have a beer-glass in their hands!

Sir Ol. I now have a huge mind to venture. But if this should come to my lady's knowledge?   40

Sir Jos. I have bespoke dinner at the Bear, the privat'st place in town. There will be no spies to betray us, if Thomas be but secret, I dare warrant thee, brother Cockwood.

Sir Ol. I have always found Thomas very faithful—but faith 'tis too unkind, considering how tenderly my lady loves me.

Sir Jos. Fy, fy, a man, and kept so much under correction by a busk and a fan!

Sir Ol. Nay, I am in my nature as valiant as any man, when once I set out; but i'faith I cannot but think how my dear lady will be concerned when she comes home and misses me.   50

Sir Jos. A pox upon these qualms.

Sir Ol. Well, thou hast reduced me. But I shall look so untowardly.

Sir Jos. Again art thou at it? In, in, and make all the haste that may be. Rakehell and the ladies will be there before us else.

Sir Ol. Well, thou art an arrant devil—hey—for the ladies, brother Jolly.

Sir Jos. Hey for the ladies, brother Cockwood.

[*Exit singing 'For he that would,' etc.*

SCENE III

The Bear.

Without. Ho! Francis, Humphrey, show a room there!

Enter Courtall, Freeman, Lady Cockwood, Ariana, Gatty, *and* Sentry.

Court. Pray, madam, be not so full of apprehension. There is no fear that this should come to sir Oliver's knowledge.

Lady Cock. I were ruined if it should, sir! Dear, how I tremble! I never was in one of these houses before.

Sent. (*Aside.*) This is a bait for the young ladies to swallow! She has been in most of the eating-houses about town, to my knowledge.

46 busk] corset   54 Rakehell] profligate, rake

Court. Oh Francis!

Enter Waiter.

Wait. Your worship's welcome, sir; but I must needs desire you to walk into the next room, for this is bespoke.   10

Lady Cock. Mr. Courtall, did not you say this place was private?

Court. I warrant you, madam. What company dines here, Francis?

Wait. A couple of country knights, sir Joslin Jolly and sir Oliver Cockwood, very honest gentlemen.

Lady Cock. Combination to undo me!

Court. Peace, madam, or you'll betray yourself to the waiter.

Lady Cock. I am distracted! Sentry, did not I command thee to secure all sir Oliver's clothes, and leave nothing for him to put on but his penitential suit, that I might be sure he could not stir abroad today?

Sent. I obeyed you in everything, madam, but I have often told you sir Joslin is a wicked seducer.   21

Ariana. If my uncle sees us, sister, what will he think of us?

Gatty. We come but to wait upon her ladyship.

Free. You need not fear. You chickens are secure under the wings of that old hen.

Court. Is there to be nobody, Francis, but sir Oliver and sir Joslin?

Wait. Faith, sir, I was enjoined secrecy—but you have an absolute power over me. Coming lately out of the country, where there is but little variety, they have a design to solace themselves with a fresh girl or two, as I understand the business.   [*Exit* Waiter.

Lady Cock. Oh Sentry! Sir Oliver disloyal! My misfortunes come too thick upon me.   32

Court. (*Aside.*) Now is she afraid of being disappointed on all hands.

Lady Cock. I know what to do, Mr. Courtall. I would not be surprised here myself, and yet I would prevent sir Oliver from prosecuting his wicked and perfidious intentions.

Ariana. Now shall we have admirable sport, what with her fear and jealousy.

Gatty. I lay my life she routs the wenches.

Enter Waiter.

Wait. I must needs desire you to step into the next room. Sir Joslin and sir Oliver are below already.   41

Lady Cock. I have not power to move a foot.

Free. We will consider what is to be done within, madam.

Court. Pray, madam, come. I have a design in my head which shall secure you, surprise sir Oliver, and free you from all your fears.

Lady Cock. It cannot be, sir.

Court. Never fear it. Francis, you may own Mr. Freeman and I are in the
house, if they ask for us. But not a word of these ladies, as you tender the
wearing of your ears.   [*Exeunt.*

Enter Sir Joslin, Sir Oliver, *and* Waiter.

Sir Jos. Come, brother Cockwood, prithee be brisk.   50
Sir Ol. I shall disgrace myself for ever, brother.
Sir Jos. Pox upon care, never droop like a cock in moulting time. Thou art
spark enough in all conscience.
Sir Ol. But my heart begins to fail me when I think of my lady.
Sir Jos. What, more qualms yet?
Sir Ol. Well, I will be courageous. But it is not necessary these strangers
should know this is my penitential suit, brother.
Sir Jos. They shall not, they shall not. Hark you, old boy, is the meat
provided? Is the wine and ice come? And are the melodious rascals at hand I
spoke for?   60
Wait. Everything will be in a readiness, sir.
Sir Jos. If Mr. Rakehell, with a coach full or two of vizard-masks and silk
petticoats, call at the door, usher 'em up to the place of execution.
Wait. You shall be obeyed, sir.   [*Exit* Waiter.

Enter Rakehell.

Sir Jos. Ho, here's my little Rakehell come! Brother Cockwood, let me
commend this ingenious gentleman to your acquaintance. He is a knight of
the industry—has many admirable qualities, I assure you.
Sir Ol. I am very glad, sir, of this opportunity to know you.
Rake. I am happy, sir, if you esteem me your servant. Hark you, sir Joslin,
is this sir Oliver Cockwood in earnest?
Sir Jos. In very good earnest I assure you. He is a little fantastical now and
then, and dresses himself up in an odd fashion—but that's all one among
friends, my little Rakehell.   72
Sir Ol. Where are the damsels you talked of, brother Jolly? I hope Mr.
Rakehell has not forgot 'em.
Rake. They are arming for the rancounter.
Sir Jos. What, tricking and trimming?
Rake. Even so, and will be here immediately.
Sir Ol. They need not make themselves so full of temptation—my brother
Jolly and I can be wicked enough without it.
Sir Jos. The truth is, my little Rakehell, we are both mighty men at arms,
and thou shalt see us charge anon to the terror of the ladies.   81

75 rancounter] contest

Rake. Methinks that dress, sir Oliver, is a little too rustical for a man of your capacity.

Sir Ol. I have an odd humour, sir, now and then, but I have wherewithal at home to be as spruce as any man.

Rake. Your periwig is too scandalous, sir Oliver—your black cap and border is never wore but by a fiddler or a waiter.

Sir Jos. Prithee, my little Rakehell, do not put my brother Cockwood out of conceit of himself. Methinks your calotte is a pretty ornament, and makes a man look both polite and politic.   90

Rake. I will allow you, 'tis a grave ware and fit for men of business that are every moment bending of their brows and scratching of their heads, every project would claw out another periwig. But a lover had better appear before his mistress with a bald pate. 'Twill make the ladies apprehend a favour, stop their noses, and avoid you. 'Slife, love in a cap is more ridiculous than love in a tub, or love in a pipkin.

Sir Ol. I must confess your whole head is now in fashion, but there was a time when your calotte was not so despicable.

Rake. Here's a peruke, sir.

Sir Ol. A very good one.   100

Rake. A very good one? 'Tis the best in England! Pray, sir Joslin, take him in your hand, and draw a comb through him, there is not such another frizz in Europe.

Sir Jos. 'Tis a very fine one indeed.

Rake. Pray, sir Oliver, do me the favour to grace it on your head a little.

Sir Ol. To oblige you, sir.

Rake. You never wore anything became you half so well in all your life before.

Sir Jos. Why, you never saw him in your life before!

Rake. That's all one, sir, I know 'tis impossible. Here's a beaver, sir Oliver —feel him! For fineness, substance, and for fashion, the court of France never saw a better. I have bred him but a fortnight and have him at command already. Clap him on boldly! Never hat took the forecock and the hind-cock at one motion so naturally.   114

Sir Ol. I think you have a mind to make a spark of me before I see the ladies.

Rake. Now you have the mien of a true cavalier, and with one look may make a lady kind, and a hector humble. And since I named a hector, here's a sword, sir. Sa, fa, fa, try him, sir Joslin—put him to't, cut through the staple, run him through the door, beat him to the hilts! If he breaks you shall have liberty to break my pate and pay me never a groat of the ten for't.   120

---

89 calotte] skull-cap   96 pipkin] small earthenware pot   102 frizz] mass of small curls   113 forecock and . . . hind-cock] brim upturned at front and back   117 hector] bully   118 staple] column; hasp; snout-ring

Sir Jos. 'Tis a very pretty weapon indeed, sir.

Rake. The hilt is true French-wrought, and *dorée* by the best workman in France. This sword and this castor, with an embroidered button and loop, which I have to vary him upon occasion, were sent me out of France for a token by my elder brother, that went over with a handsome equipage to take the pleasure of this champaign.

Sir Ol. Have you a mind to sell these things, sir?

Rake. That is below a gentleman . . . yet if a person of honour or a particular friend, such as I esteem you, sir Oliver, take at any time a fancy to a band, a cravat, a velvet coat, a vest, a ring, a flageolet, or any other little toy I have about me, I am good-natured and may be easily persuaded to play the fool upon good terms.   132

Enter Freeman.

Sir Jos. Worthy Mr. Freeman!

Sir Ol. Honest Frank, how cam'st thou to find us out, man?

Free. By mere chance, sir. Ned Courtall is without, writing a letter, and I came in to know whether you had any particular engagements, gentlemen.

Sir Ol. We resolved to be in private . . . but you are men without exception.

Free. Methinks you intended to be in private indeed, sir Oliver. 'Sdeath, what disguise have you got on? Are you grown grave since last night, and come to sin *incognito*?   140

Sir Ol. Hark you in your ear, Frank, this is my habit of humiliation, which I always put on the next day after I have transgressed, the better to make my pacification with my incensed lady. . . .

Free. Ha! ha! ha!

Rake. Mr. Freeman, your most humble servant, sir.

Free. Oh my little dapper officer! Are you here?

Sir Jos. Ha, Mr. Freeman, we have bespoke all the jovial entertainment that a merry wag can wish for—good meat, good wine, and a wholesome wench or two. For the digestion we shall have Madam Rampant, the glory of the town, the brightest she that shines, or else my little Rakehell is not a man of his word, sir.   151

Rake. I warrant you she comes, sir Joslin.

Sir Joslin *sings.*

> *And if she comes, she shall not scape,*
> *If twenty pounds will win her;*
> *Her very eye commits a rape,*
> *'Tis such a tempting sinner.*

Enter Courtall.

122 *dorée*] gilded   123 castor] beaver fur hat   126 champaign] open country
130 flageolet] small flute

Court. Well said, sir Joslin, I see you hold up still, and bate not an ace of your good humour.

Sir Jos. Noble Mr. Courtall!

Court. Bless me, sir Oliver, what—are you going to act a droll? How the people would throng about you if you were but mounted on a few deal boards in Covent Garden now!　　　　　　　　　　　　　162

Sir Ol. Hark you, Ned, this is the badge of my lady's indignation for my last night's offence. Do not insult over a poor sober man in affliction.

Court. Come, come, send home for your clothes. I hear you are to have ladies, and you are not to learn at these years how absolutely necessary a rich vest and a peruke are to a man that aims at their favours.

Sir Ol. A pox on't, Ned, my lady's gone abroad in a damned jealous melancholy humour, and has commanded her woman to secure 'em.

Court. Under lock and key?　　　　　　　　　　　　　　　170

Sir Ol. Ay, ay, man, 'tis usual in these cases, out of pure love in hopes to reclaim me, and to keep me from doing myself an injury by drinking two days together.

Court. What a loving lady 'tis!

Sir Ol. There are sots that would think themselves happy in such a lady, Ned. But to a true bred gentleman all lawful solace is abomination.

Rake. Mr. Courtall, your most humble servant, sir.

Court. Oh! my little knight of the industry. I am glad to see you in such good company.

Free. Courtall, hark you, are the masking-habits which you sent to borrow at the playhouse come yet?　　　　　　　　　　　　　181

Court. Yes, and the ladies are almost dressed. This design will add much to our mirth and give us the benefit of their meat, wine, and music for our entertainment.

Free. 'Twas luckily thought of.

Sir Ol. Hark, the music comes.　　　　　　　　　　　　[*Music.*

Sir Jos. Hey, boys—let 'em enter, let 'em enter.

Enter Waiter.

Wait. An't please your worships, there is a mask of ladies without, that desire to have the freedom to come in and dance.

Sir Jos. Hey! boys. . . .　　　　　　　　　　　　　　　190

Sir Ol. Did you bid 'em come *en masquerade*, Mr. Rakehell?

Rake. No, but Rampant is a mad wench. She was half a dozen times a-mumming in private company last Shrovetide, and I lay my life she has put 'em all upon this frolic.

160 droll . . . Covent Garden] an allusion to the puppet shows in the fashionable pleasure-grounds of Covent Garden

Court. They are mettled girls, I warrant them, sir Joslin, let 'em be what they will.

Sir Jos. Let 'em enter, let 'em enter, ha boys. . . .

Enter Music *and the* Ladies *in an antic, and then they take out,* my Lady Cockwood, Sir Oliver, *the young* Ladies, Courtall *and* Freeman, *and* Sentry, Sir Joslin, *and dance a set dance.*

Sir Ol. Oh my little rogue! Have I got thee? How I will turn and wind, and feague thy body!

Sir Jos. Mettle on all sides, mettle on all sides, i'faith! How swimmingly would this pretty little ambling filly carry a man of my body!   201

(Sings.)

> *She's so bonny and brisk,*
> *How she'd curvet and frisk,*
> *If a man were once mounted upon her!*
> *Let me have but a leap*
> *Where 'tis wholesome and cheap,*
> *And a fig for your person of honour!*

Sir Ol. 'Tis true, little Joslin, i'faith.

Court. They have warmed us, sir Oliver.

Sir Ol. Now am I as rampant as a lion, Ned, and could love as vigorously as a seaman that is newly landed after an East India voyage.   211

Court. Take my advice, sir Oliver, do not in your rage deprive yourself of your only hope of an accommodation with your lady.

Sir Ol. I had rather have a perpetual civil war, than purchase peace at such a dishonourable rate. A poor fiddler, after he has been three days persecuted at a country wedding, takes more delight in scraping upon his old squeaking fiddle, than I do in fumbling on that domestic instrument of mine.

Court. Be not so bitter, sir Oliver, on your own dear lady.

Sir Ol. I was married to her when I was young, Ned, with a design to be baulked, as they tie whelps to the bell-wether; where I have been so butted, 'twere enough to fright me, were I not pure mettle, from ever running at sheep again.   222

Court. That's no sure rule, sir Oliver, for a wife's a dish of which, if a man once surfeit, he shall have a better stomach to all others ever after.

Sir Ol. What a shape is here, Ned! So exact and tempting, 'twould persuade a man to be an implicit sinner, and take her face upon credit.

---

s.d. *antic*] fancy dress   199 feague] whip (as a top)   220 bell-wether] leading sheep of a flock, with bell on neck

Sir Jos. Come, brother Cockwood, let us get 'em to lay aside these masking fopperies, and then we'll feague 'em in earnest. Give us a bottle, waiter.

Free. Not before dinner, good sir Joslin. . . .

Sir Ol. Lady, though I have out of drollery put myself into this contemptible dress at present, I am a gentleman, and a man of courage, as you shall find anon by my brisk behaviour.   232

Rake. Sir Joslin! Sir Oliver! These are none of our ladies! They are just come to the door in a coach, and have sent for me down to wait upon 'em up to you.

Sir Jos. Hey boys! more game, more game! Fetch 'em up, fetch 'em up.

Sir Ol. Why, what a day of sport will here be, Ned!   [*Exit* Rakehell.

Sir Jos. They shall all have fair play, boys.

Sir Ol. And we will match ourselves, and make a prize on't. Ned Courtall and I, against Frank Freeman and you brother Jolly, and Rakehell shall be judge for gloves and silk stockings, to be bestowed as the conqueror shall fancy.   242

Sir Jos. Agreed, agreed, agreed.

Court. & Free. A match, a match.

Sir Ol. Hey, boys!

Lady Cockwood counterfeits a fit.

Sent. (*Pulling off her mask.*) Oh heavens! my dear lady! Help, help!

Sir Ol. What's here? Sentry and my lady! 'Sdeath, what a condition am I in now, brother Jolly! You have brought me into this *premunire.* For heaven's sake run down quickly, and send the rogue and whores away. Help, help! oh help! dear madam, sweet lady!   250

[Exit Sir Joslin. Sir Oliver kneels down by her.

Sent. Oh she's gone, she's gone!

Free. Give her more air.

Court. Fetch a glass of cold water, Freeman.

Sir Ol. Dear madam speak, sweet madam speak.

Sent. Out upon thee for a vile hypocrite! Thou art the wicked author of all this. Who but such a reprobate, such an obdurate sinner as thou art, could go about to abuse so sweet a lady?

Sir Ol. Dear Sentry, do not stab me with thy words, but stab me with thy bodkin rather, that I may here die a sacrifice at her feet for all my disloyal actions.   260

Sent. No! Live, live, to be a reproach and a shame to all rebellious husbands! Ah, that she had but my heart! But thou hast bewitched her affections. Thou shouldst then dearly smart for this abominable treason.

---

248 *premunire*] predicament

Gatty. So, now she begins to come to herself.

Ariana. Set her more upright, and bend her a little forward.

Lady Cock. Unfortunate woman! Let me go. Why do you hold me? Would I had a dagger at my heart, to punish it for loving that ungrateful man.

Sir Ol. Dear madam, were I but worthy of your pity and belief.

Lady Cock. Peace, peace, perfidious man, I am too tame and foolish! Were I every day at the plays, the Park, and Mulberry Garden, with a kind look secretly to indulge the unlawful passion of some young gallant; or did I associate myself with the gaming madams, and were every afternoon at my lady Brief's and my lady Meanwell's at ombre and quebas, pretending ill luck to borrow money of a friend, and then pretending good luck to excuse the plenty to a husband, my suspicious demeanour had deserved this. But I who out of a scrupulous tenderness to my honour, and to comply with thy base jealousy, have denied myself all those blameless recreations, which a virtuous lady might enjoy—to be thus inhumanely reviled in my own person, and thus unreasonably robbed and abused in thine too!

Court. Sure she will take up anon, or crack her mind, or else the devil's in't. 281

Lady Cock. Do not stay and torment me with thy sight! Go, graceless wretch, follow thy treacherous resolutions, do, and waste that poor stock of comfort which I should have at home, upon those your ravenous cormorants below. I feel my passion begin to swell again. [*She has a little fit again.*

Court. Now will she get an absolute dominion over him, and all this will be my plague in the end.

Sir Ol. (*Running up and down.*) Ned Courtall, Frank Freeman, cousin Ariana, and dear cousin Gatty, for heaven's sake join all, and moderate her passion. . . . Ah Sentry! forbear thy unjust reproaches, take pity on thy master! Thou hast a great influence over her, and I have always been mindful of thy favours. 292

Sent. You do not deserve the least compassion, nor would I speak a good word for you, but that I know for all this 'twill be acceptable to my poor lady.—Dear madam, do but look up a little, sir Oliver lies at your feet, an humble penitent.

Ariana. How bitterly he weeps! How gladly he sighs!

Gatty. I daresay he counterfeited his sin and is real in his repentance.

Court. Compose yourself a little, pray, madam. All this was mere raillery, a way of talk, which sir Oliver being well-bred has learned among the gay people of the town. 301

Free. If you did but know, madam, what an odious thing it is to be thought to love a wife in good company, you would easily forgive him.

Lady Cock. No, no, 'twas the mild correction which I gave him for his

273 ombre] card game   273 quebas] card game

insolent behaviour last night, that has encouraged him again thus to insult over my affections.

Court. Come, come sir Oliver, out with your bosom-secret, and clear all things to your lady. Is it not as we have said?

Sir Ol. Or may I never have the happiness to be in her good grace again. And as for the harlots, dear madam, here is Ned Courtall and Frank Freeman, that have often seen me in company of the wicked. Let 'em speak if they ever knew me tempted to a disloyal action in their lives.   312

Court. On my conscience, madam, I may more safely swear that sir Oliver has been constant to your ladyship, than that a girl of twelve-years old has her maiden-head this warm and ripening age.

Enter Sir Joslin.

Sir Ol. Here's my brother Jolly too can witness the loyalty of my heart, and that I did not intend any treasonable practice against your ladyship in the least.

Sir Jos. Unless feaguing 'em with a beer-glass be included in the statute. Come, Mr. Courtall, to satisfy my lady, and put her in a little good humour, let us sing the catch I taught you yesterday, that was made by a country vicar on my brother Cockwood and me.   322

(They sing.)

> *Love and wenching are toys,*
> *Fit to please beardless boys,*
> *Th'are sports we hate worse than a leaguer;*
> *When we visit a miss,*
> *We still brag how we kiss,*
> *But 'tis with a bottle we feague her.*

Sir Jos. Come, come, madam, let all things be forgot. Dinner is ready, the cloth is laid in the next room, let us in and be merry. There was no harm meant as I am true little Joslin.   331

Lady Cock. Sir Oliver knows I can't be angry with him, though he plays the naughty man thus. But why, my dear, would y'expose yourself in this ridiculous habit to the censure of both our honours?

Sir Ol. Indeed I was to blame to be over-persuaded. I intended dutifully to retire into the pantry and there civilly to divert myself at back-gammon with the butler.

Sir Jos. Faith, I must ev'n own the fault was mine. I enticed him hither, lady.

Sir Ol. How the devil, Ned, came they to find us out here!   340

Court. No blood-hound draws so sure as a jealous woman.

328 *feague*] do for

Sir Ol. I am afraid Thomas has been unfaithful. Prithee, Ned, speak to my lady, that there may be a perfect understanding between us, and that Sentry may be sent home for my clothes that I may no longer wear the marks of her displeasure.

Court. Let me alone, sir Oliver.

[*He goes to my* Lady Cockwood.

How do you find yourself, madam, after this violent passion?

Lady Cock. This has been a lucky adventure, Mr. Courtall. Now am I absolute mistress of my own conduct for a time.

Court. Then shall I be a happy man, madam. I knew this would be the consequence of all and yet could not I forbear the project.   351

Sir Ol. (*To* Sir Joslin.) How didst thou shuffle away Rakehell and the ladies, brother?

Sir Jos. I have appointed 'em to meet us at six o'clock at the new Spring Garden.

Sir Ol. Then will we yet, in spite of the stars that have crossed us, be in conjunction with madam Rampant, brother.

Court. Come, gentlemen, dinner is on the table.

Sir Jos. Ha! Sly-girl and Mad-cap, I'll enter you, i'faith; since you have found the way to the Bear, I'll feague you.

(*Sings.*)

When we visit a miss,
We still brag how we kiss;
But 'tis with a bottle we feague her.

[*Exeunt singing.*

ACT IV   SCENE I

A Dining Room.

Enter Lady Cockwood.

Lady Cock. A lady cannot be too jealous of her servant's love this faithless and inconstant age. His amorous carriage to that prating girl today, though he pretends it was to blind sir Oliver, I fear will prove a certain sign of his revolted heart. The letters I have counterfeited in these girls' name will clear all. If he accept of that appointment, and refuses mine, I need not any longer doubt.

Enter Sentry.

Sentry, have the letters and message been delivered, as I directed?

Sent. Punctually, madam. I knew they were to be found at the latter end of a play—I sent a porter first with the letter to Mr. Courtall, who was at the King's House. He sent for him out by the door-keeper and delivered it into his own hands.   11

Lady Cock. Did you keep on your vizard, that the fellow might not know how to describe you?

Sent. I did, madam.

Lady Cock. And how did he receive it?

Sent. Like a traitor to all goodness, with all the signs of joy imaginable.

Lady Cock. Be not angry, Sentry, 'tis as my heart wished it. What did you do with the letter to Mr. Freeman? For I thought fit to deceive 'em both, to make my policy less suspicious to Courtall.

Sent. The porter found him at the Duke's House, madam, and delivered it with like care.   21

Lady Cock. Very well.

Sent. After the letters were delivered, madam, I went myself to the playhouse, and sent in for Mr. Courtall, who came out to me immediately. I told him your ladyship presented your humble service to him, and that sir Oliver was going into the city with sir Joslin to visit his brother Cockwood, and that it would add much more to your ladyship's happiness if he would be pleased to meet you in Gray's Inn walks this lovely evening.

Lady Cock. And how did he entertain the motion?

Sent. Bless me! I tremble still to think upon it! I could not have imagined he had been so wicked. He counterfeited the greatest passion, railed at his fate, and swore a thousand horrid oaths, that since he came into the playhouse he had notice of a business that concerned both his honour and fortune . . . and that he was an undone man if he did not go about it presently . . . prayed me to desire your ladyship to excuse him this evening, and that tomorrow he would be wholly at your devotion.   36

Lady Cock. Ha, ha, ha! he little thinks how much he has obliged me.

Sent. I had much ado to forbear upbraiding him with his ingratitude to your ladyship.

Lady Cock. Poor Sentry! Be not concerned for me. I have conquered my affection and thou shalt find it is not jealousy has been my counsellor in this. Go, let our hoods and masks be ready, that I may surprise Courtall and make the best advantage of this lucky opportunity.

Sent. I obey you, madam.   [*Exit* Sentry.

28 Gray's Inn walks] tree-planted lawns north of South Square, Gray's Inn

Lady Cock. How am I filled with indignation! To find my person and my passion both despised, and what is more, so much precious time fooled away in fruitless expectation. I would poison my face, so I might be revenged on this ingrateful villain.

Enter Sir Oliver.

Sir Ol. My dearest!

Lady Cock. My dearest dear! Prithee do not go into the city tonight.

Sir Ol. My brother Jolly is gone before, and I am to call him at councillor Trott's chamber in the Temple.   52

Lady Cock. Well, if you did but know the fear I have upon me when you are absent, you would not seek occasions to be from me thus.

Sir Ol. Let me comfort thee with a kiss. What should'st thou be afraid of ?

Lady Cock. I cannot but believe that every woman that sees thee must be in love with thee, as I am. Do not blame my jealousy.

Sir Ol. I protest I would refuse a countess rather than abuse thee, poor heart.

Lady Cock. And then you are so desperate upon the least occasion, I should have acquainted you else with something that concerns your honour.   61

Sir Ol. My honour! You ought in duty to do it.

Lady Cock. Nay, I knew how passionate you would be presently—therefore you shall never know it.

Sir Ol. Do not leave me in doubt! I shall suspect everyone I look upon. I will kill a Common Council man or two before I come back, if you do not tell me!

Lady Cock. Dear, how I tremble! Will you promise me you will not quarrel then? If you tender my life and happiness, I am sure you will not.

Sir Ol. I will bear anything rather than be an enemy to thy quiet, my dear.

Lady Cock. I could wish Mr. Courtall a man of better principles, because I know you love him, my dear.   72

Sir Ol. Why, what has he done?

Lady Cock. I always treated him with great respects out of my regard to your friendship, but he, like an impudent man as he is, today misconstruing my civility, in most unseemly language made a foul attempt upon my honour.

Sir Ol. Death and hell and furies, I will have my pumps and long sword!

Lady Cock. Oh, I shall faint! Did not you promise me you would not be so rash?

Sir Ol. Well, I will not kill him, for fear of murdering thee, my dear.

Lady Cock. You may decline your friendship and by your coldness give him no encouragement to visit our family.   82

Sir Ol. I think thy advice the best for this once indeed, for it is not fit to

77 pumps] light duelling shoes

publish such a business. But if he should be ever tempting or attempting, let me know it, prithee, my dear.

Lady Cock. If you moderate yourself according to my directions now, I shall never conceal anything from you that may increase your just opinion of my conjugal fidelity.

Sir Ol. Was ever man blessed with such a virtuous lady! (*Aside.*) Yet cannot I forbear going a-ranging again.—Now must I to the Spring Garden to meet my brother Jolly and madam Rampant.   91

Lady Cock. Prithee, be so good to think how melancholy I spend my time here; for I have joy in no company but thine, and let that bring thee home a little sooner.

Sir Ol. Thou hast been so kind in this discovery that I am loth to leave thee.

Lady Cock. I wish you had not been engaged so far.

Sir Ol. Ay, that's it: farewell, my virtuous dear.   [*Exit* Sir Oliver.

Lady Cock. Farewell, my dearest dear. . . . I know he has not courage enough to question Courtall; but this will make him hate him, increase his confidence of me, and justify my banishing that false fellow our house. It is not fit a man that has abused my love should come hither and pry into my actions. Besides, this will make his access more difficult to that wanton baggage!   103

Enter Ariana *and* Gatty *with their hoods and masks.*

Whither are you going, cousins?

Gatty. To take the air upon the water, madam.

Ariana. And for variety, to walk a turn or two in the new Spring Garden.

Lady Cock. I heard you were gone abroad with Mr. Courtall and Mr. Freeman.

Gatty. For heaven's sake, why should your ladyship have such an ill opinion of us?

Lady Cock. The truth is, before I saw you I believed it merely the vanity of that prating man. Mr. Courtall told Mrs. Gazette this morning that you were so well acquainted already that you would meet him and Mr. Freeman anywhere, and that you had promised 'em to receive and make appointment by letters.   115

Gatty. Oh impudent man!

Ariana. Now you see the consequence, sister, of our rambling. They have raised this false story from our innocent fooling with 'em in the Mulberry Garden last night.

Gatty. I could almost foreswear ever speaking to a man again.

Lady Cock. Was Mr. Courtall in the Mulberry Garden last night?

90 Spring Garden] the new pleasure-grounds in Lambeth, named after the demolished Spring Garden at Charing Cross, which had an artificial jet of water to sprinkle the unwary

Ariana. Yes, madam.

Lady Cock. And did he speak to you?

Gatty. There passed a little harmless raillery betwixt us; but you amaze me, madam.

Ariana. I could not imagine any man could be thus unworthy.

Lady Cock. He has quite lost my good opinion too. In duty to sir Oliver I have hitherto showed him some countenance, but I shall hate him hereafter for your sakes. But I detain you from your recreations, cousins.

Gatty. We are very much obliged to your ladyship for this timely notice.

Ariana and Gatty. Your servant, madam.   [*Exeunt* Ariana *and* Gatty.

Lady Cock. Your servant, cousins.—In the Mulberry Garden last night! When I sat languishing and vainly expecting him at home! This has incensed me so, that I could kill him. I am glad these girls are gone to the Spring Garden. It helps my design. The letters I have counterfeited have appointed Courtall and Freeman to meet them there. They will produce 'em, and confirm all I have said. I will daily poison these girls with such lies as shall make their quarrel to Courtall irreconcileable, and render Freeman only suspected —for I would not have him thought equally guilty. He secretly began to make an address to me at the Bear, and this breach shall give him an opportunity to pursue it.   141

Enter Sentry.

Sent. Here are your things, madam.

Lady Cock. That's well. Oh Sentry, I shall once more be happy! For now Mr. Courtall has given me an occasion, that I may without ingratitude check his unlawful passion, and free myself from the trouble of an intrigue that gives me every day such fearful apprehensions of my honour.

[*Exeunt* Lady Cockwood *and* Sentry.

SCENE II

New Spring Garden.

Enter Sir Joslin, Rakehell, *and* Waiter.

Wait. Will you be pleased to walk into an arbour, gentlemen?

Sir Jos. By and by, good sir.

Rake. I wonder sir Oliver is not come yet.

Sir Jos. Nay, he will not fail, I warrant thee, boy. But what's the matter with thy nose, my little Rakehell?

Rake. A foolish accident. Jesting at the Fleece this afternoon I mistook my

man a little, a dull rogue that could not understand raillery—make a sudden
repartee with a quart-pot, sir Joslin.

Sir Jos. Why didst not thou stick him to the wall, my little Rakehell?

Rake. The truth is, sir Joslin, he deserved it; but look you, in case of a
doubtful wound, I am unwilling to give my friends too often the trouble to
bail me. And if it should be mortal, you know a younger brother has not
wherewithal to rebate the edge of a witness, and mollify the hearts of a jury.

Sir Jos. This is very prudently considered indeed.   14

Rake. 'Tis time to be wise, sir. My courage has almost run me out of a
considerable annuity. When I lived first about this town I agreed with a
surgeon for twenty pounds a quarter to cure me of all the knocks, bruises and
green wounds I should receive, and in one half year the poor fellow begged me
to be released of his bargain, and swore I would undo him else in lint and balsom.

Enter Sir Oliver.

Sir Jos. Ho! here's my brother Cockwood come. . . .   20

Sir Ol. Ay, brother Jolly, I have kept my word, you see. But it is a barbarous thing to abuse my lady: I have had such a proof of her virtue—I will tell
thee all anon. But where's madam Rampant and the rest of the ladies, Mr.
Rakehell?

Rake. Faith, sir, being disappointed at noon they were unwilling any more
to set a certainty at hazard. 'Tis term-time and they have severally betook
themselves, some to their chamber-practice, and others to the places of public
pleading.

Sir Ol. Faith, brother Jolly, let us ev'n go into an arbour, and then feague
Mr. Rakehell.   30

Sir Jos. With all my heart—would we had madam Rampant!

(*Sings.*)

> *She's as frolic and free,*
> *As her lovers dare be,*
> *Never awed by a foolish punctilio;*
> *She'll not start from her place,*
> *Though thou nam'st a black ace,*
> *And will drink a beer-glass to Spudilio.*

Hey, boys! Come, come, come! Let's in, and delay our sport no longer.

> [*Exit singing, 'She'll not start from her,' etc.*

Enter Courtall *and* Freeman *severally.*

Court. Freeman!

Free. Courtall, what the devil's the matter with thee? I have observed thee

18 green] fresh   29 feague] do for or beat   36 *black ace*] card term   37 *Spudilio*]
ace of spades

prying up and down the walks like a citizen's wife that has dropped her holy-day pocket-handkercher. 42

Court. What unlucky devil has brought thee hither?

Free. I believe a better natured devil than yours, Courtall, if a leveret be better meat than an old puss that has been coursed by most of the young fellows of her country. I am not working my brain for a counter-plot—a disappointment is not my business.

Court. You are mistaken, Freeman. Prithee begone, and leave me the garden to myself, or I shall grow as testy as an old fowler that is put by his shoot after he has crept half a mile upon his belly. 50

Free. Prithee be thou gone, or I shall take it as unkindly as a chymist would if thou shouldst kick down his limbec in the very minute that he looked for projection.

Court. Come, come, you must yield, Freeman—your business cannot be of such consequence as mine.

Free. If ever thou hadst a business of such consequence in thy life as mine is, I will condescend to be made incapable of affairs presently.

Court. Why, I have an appointment made me, man, without my seeking, by a woman for whom I would have mortgaged my whole estate to have had her abroad but to break a cheese-cake. 60

Free. And I have an appointment made me without my seeking too, by such as she that I will break the whole ten commandments rather than disappoint her of her breaking one.

Court. Come, you do but jest, Freeman. A forsaken mistress could not be more malicious than thou art. Prithee begone!

Free. Prithee do thou begone!

Court. 'Sdeath! The sight of thee will scare my woman for ever.

Free. 'Sdeath! The sight of thee will make my woman believe me the falsest villain breathing.

Court. We shall stand fooling till we are both undone, and I know not how to help it. 71

Free. Let us proceed honestly like friends, discover the truth of things to one another, and if we cannot reconcile our business we will draw cuts and part fairly.

Court. I do not like that way, for talk is only allowable at the latter end of an intrigue and should never be used at the beginning of an amour, for fear of frighting a young lady from her good intentions—yet I care not, though I read the letter, but I will conceal the name.

---

44 leveret] young hare   51 chymist] alchemist   52 limbec] alembic, distilling flask
53 projection] transmutation of metals   73 draw cuts] draw lots (with sticks of different lengths)

Free. I have a letter too, and am content to do the same.

Court. (*Reads.*) 'Sir, in sending you this letter, I proceed against the
modesty of our sex. . . .'   82

Free. 'Sdeath, this begins just like my letter.

Court. Do you read on then. . . .

Free. (*Reads.*) 'But let not the good opinion I have conceived of you make
you too severe in your censuring of me. . . .'

Court. Word for word!

Free. Now do you read again.

Court. (*Reads.*) 'If you give yourself the trouble to be walking in the new
Spring Garden this evening, I will meet you there and tell you a secret, which
I have reason to fear, because it comes to your knowledge by my means, will
make you hate your humble servant.'   92

Free. Verbatim my letter, hey-day!

Court. Prithee let's compare the hands.   [*They compare 'em.*

Free. 'Sdeath, the hand's the same.

Court. I hope the name is not the same too. . . .

Free. If it be, we are finely jilted, faith.

Court. I long to be undeceived. Prithee do thou show first, Freeman.

Free. No—but both together, if you will.

Court. Agreed.   100

Free. Ariana.

Court. Gatty . . . Ha! ha! ha!

Free. The little rogues are masculine in their proceedings and have made
one another confidants in their love.

Court. But I do not like this altogether so well, Frank. I wish they had
appointed us several places, for though 'tis evidence they have trusted one
another with the bargain, no woman ever seals before witness.

Free. Prithee how didst thou escape the snares of the old devil this afternoon?

Court. With much ado! Sentry had set me; if her ladyship had got me into
her clutches there had been no getting off without a rescue, or paying down
the money, for she always arrests upon execution!   112

Free. You made a handsome lie to her woman.

Court. For all this, I know she's angry—for she thinks nothing a just excuse
in these cases, though it were to save the forfeit of a man's estate or reprieve
the life of her own natural brother.

Free. Faith, thou hast not done altogether like a gentleman with her. Thou
should'st fast thyself up to a stomach now and then, to oblige her. If there
were nothing in it but the hearty welcome, methinks 'twere enough to make
thee bear sometimes with the homeliness of the fare.   120

Court. I know not what I might do in a camp where there were no other woman, but I shall hardly in this town, (where there is such plenty,) forbear good meat to get myself an appetite to horseflesh!

Free. This is rather an aversion in thee, than any real fault in the woman. If this lucky business had not fallen out, I intended with your good leave to have outbid you for her ladyship's favour.

Court. I should never had consented to that, Frank. Though I am a little resty at present, I am not such a jade but I should strain if another rid against me. I have ere now liked nothing in a woman that I have loved at last in spite only, because another had a mind to her.   130

Free. Yonder are a couple of vizards tripping towards us.

Court. 'Tis they, i'faith.

Free. We need not divide, since they come together.

Court. I was a little afraid when we compared letters, they had put a trick upon us; but now I am confirmed they are mighty honest.

Enter Ariana *and* Gatty.

Ariana. We cannot avoid 'em.

Gatty. Let us dissemble our knowledge of their business a little and then take 'em down in the height of their assurance.

Court. & Free. Your servant, ladies.

Ariana. I perceive it is as impossible, gentlemen, to walk without you as without our shadows. Never were poor women so haunted by the ghosts of their self-murdered lovers.   142

Gatty. If it should be our good fortunes to have you in love with us, we will take care you shall not grow desperate and leave the world in an ill humour.

Ariana. If you should, certainly your ghosts would be very malicious.

Court. 'Twere pity you should have your curtains drawn in the dead of the night, and your pleasing slumbers interrupted by anything but flesh and blood, ladies.

Free. Shall we walk a turn?

Ariana. By yourselves, if you please.   150

Gatty. Our company may put a constraint upon you, for I find you daily hover about these gardens as a kite does about a back-side, watching an opportunity to catch up the poultry.

Ariana. Woe be to the daughter or wife of some merchant-taylor or poor felt-maker now—for you seldom row to Fox Hall without some such plot against the city.

Free. You wrong us, ladies. Our business has happily succeeded, since we have the honour to wait upon you.

Gatty. You could not expect to see us here.

---

128 resty] sluggish   152 back-side] back premises   155 Fox Hall] The New Spring Garden was at Fox Hall, spelt Vauxhall from about 1700.

Court. Your true lover, madam, when he misses his mistress, is as restless as a spaniel that has lost his master. He ranges up and down the plays, the park and all the gardens, and never stays long but where he has the happiness to see her.   163

Gatty. I suppose your mistress, Mr. Courtall, is always the last woman you are acquainted with.

Court. Do not think, madam, I have that false measure of my acquaintance, which poets have of their verses, always to think the last best—though I esteem you so in justice to your merit.

Gatty. Or if you do not love her best you always love to talk of her most— as a barren coxcomb, that wants discourse, is ever entertaining company out of the last book he read in.   171

Court. Now you accuse me most unjustly, madam! Who the devil that has common sense will go a-birding with a clack in his cap?

Ariana. Nay, we do not blame you, gentlemen. Every one in their way—a huntsman talks of his dogs, a falconer of his hawks, a jockey of his horse, and a gallant of his mistress!

Gatty. Without the allowance of this vanity an amour would soon grow as dull as matrimony.

Court. Whatsoever you say, ladies, I cannot believe you think us men of such abominable principles.   180

Free. For my part, I have ever held it as ingrateful to boast of the favours of a mistress as to deny the courtesies of a friend.

Court. A friend that bravely ventures his life in the field to serve me deserves but equally with a mistress that kindly exposes her honour to oblige me—especially when she does it as generously too and with as little ceremony.

Free. And I would no more betray the honour of such a woman than I would the life of a man that should rob on purpose to supply me.

Gatty. We believe you men of honour, and know it is below you to talk of any woman that deserves it.

Ariana. You are so generous you seldom insult after a victory!   190

Gatty. And so vain that you always triumph before it!

Court. 'Sdeath! What's the meaning of all this?

Gatty. Though you find us so kind, Mr. Courtall, pray do not tell Mrs. Gazette tomorrow that we came hither on purpose this evening to meet you.

Court. I would as soon print it and see a fellow to post it up with the play-bills.

Gatty. You have reposed a great deal of confidence in her, for all you pretend this ill opinion of her secrecy now.

Court. I never trusted her with the name of a mistress, that I should be jealous of if I saw her receive fruit and go out of the playhouse with a stranger.

173 clack] rattle, worked by wind, to scare birds

Gatty. For ought as I see, we are infinitely obliged to you, sir.   201
Court. 'Tis impossible to be insensible of so much goodness, madam.
Gatty. What goodness, pray, sir?
Court. Come, come, give over this raillery.
Gatty. You are so ridiculously unworthy that 'twere a folly to reprove you
with a serious look.
Court. On my conscience, your heart begins to fail you now we are coming
to the point, as a young fellow's that was never in the field before.
Gatty. You begin to amaze me.
Court. Since you yourself sent the challenge, you must not in honour fly off
now.   211
Gatty. Challenge! Oh heavens! This confirms all. Were I a man I would
kill thee for the injuries thou hast already done me.
Free. (*To* Ariana.) Let not your suspicion of my unkindness make you thus
scrupulous. Was ever city ill-treated that surrendered without assault or
summons?
Ariana. Dear sister, what ill spirit brought us hither? I never met with so
much impudence in my life.
Court. (*Aside.*) Hey jilts! They are as good at it already as the old one
i'faith.   220
Free. Come, ladies, you have exercised your wit enough; you would not
venture letters of such consequence for a jest only.
Gatty. Letters! Bless me, what will this come to?
Court. To that none of us shall have cause to repent I hope, madam.
Ariana. Let us fly 'em, sister, they are devils and not men—they could
never be so malicious else.

Enter Lady Cockwood *and* Sentry.

Lady Cock. Your servant, cousins.
Court. (*Starting.*) Ho, my lady Cockwood! My ears are grown an inch
already.
Ariana. My lady! She'll think this an appointment, sister.   230
Free. This is madam Machiavel, I suspect, Courtall.
Court. Nay, 'tis her plot doubtless. Now am I as much out of countenance
as I should be if sir Oliver should take me making bold with her lady-
ship.
Lady Cock. Do not let me discompose you—I can walk alone,
cousins.
Gatty. Are you so uncharitable, madam, to think we have any business with
'em?

231 Machiavel] schemer (after Machiavelli, Florentine author of *del Principe*)

Ariana. It has been our ill fortune to meet 'em here, and nothing could be so lucky as your coming, madam, to free us from 'em.   240

Gatty. They have abused us in the grossest manner.

Ariana. Counterfeited letters under our hands.

Lady Cock. Never trouble yourselves, cousins, I have heard this is a common practice with such unworthy men. Did they not threaten to divulge them and defame you to the world?

Gatty. We cannot believe they intend anything less, madam.

Lady Cock. Doubtless they had such a mean opinion of your wit and honour that they thought to fright you to a base compliance with their wicked purposes.

Ariana. I hate the very sight of 'em.   250

Gatty. I could almost wish myself a disease, to breathe infection upon 'em.

Court. Very pretty! We have carried on our designs very luckily against these young ladies!

Free. We have lost their good opinion for ever.

Lady Cock. I know not whether their folly or their impudence be greater. They are not worth your anger—they are only fit to be laughed at and despised.

Court. A very fine old devil this!

Lady Cock. Mr. Freeman, this is not like a gentleman, to affront a couple of young ladies thus. But I cannot blame you so much—you are in a manner a stranger to our family. But I wonder how that base man can look me in the face, considering how civilly he has been treated at our house.   263

Court. The truth is, madam, I am a rascal—but I fear you have contributed to the making me so. Be not as unmerciful as the devil is to a poor sinner.

Sent. Did you ever see the like? Never trust me if he has not the confidence to make my virtuous lady accessary to his wickedness!

Lady Cock. Ay Sentry! 'Tis a miracle if my honour escapes, considering the access which his greatness with sir Oliver has given him daily to me.   271

Free. Faith, ladies, we did not counterfeit these letters. We are abused as well as you!

Court. I received mine from a porter at the King's Playhouse, and I will show it you that you may see if you know the hand.

Lady Cock. Sentry, are you sure they never saw any of your writing?

Court. 'Sdeath! I am so discomposed, I know not where I have put it.

Sent. Oh madam! Now I remember myself, Mrs. Gatty helped me once to indite a letter to my sweetheart.

Lady Cock. Forgetful wench! Then I am undone.   280

Court. Oh here it is.—Hey, who's here?

> *As he has the letter in his hand, enter* Sir Joslin, Sir Oliver,
> *and* Rakehell, *all drunk, with music.*
>
> (*They sing.*)
>
> *She's no mistress of mine*
> *That drinks not her wine,*
> *Or frowns at my friends' drinking motions;*
> *If my heart thou would'st gain,*
> *Drink thy bottle of champagne.*
> *'Twill serve thee for paint and love-potions.*

Sir Ol. Who's here? Courtall, in my lady's company! I'll dispatch him presently. Help me, brother Jolly.   [*He draws.*

Lady Cock. For heaven's sake, sir Oliver!   290

Court. (*Drawing.*) What do you mean, sir?

Sir Ol. I'll teach you more manners than to make your attempts on my lady, sir.

Lady Cock. & Sent. Oh! Murder! Murder!   [*They shriek.*

Lady Cock. Save my dear sir Oliver! Oh my dear sir Oliver!

> *The young* Ladies *shriek and run out; they all draw to part 'em;*
> *they fight off the stage; she shrieks and runs out.*

ACT V   SCENE I

Sir Oliver's *Dining Room.*

(*Table, and carpet.*)

Enter Lady Cockwood.

Lady Cock. I did not think he had been so desperate in his drink. If they had killed one another I had then been revenged and freed from all my fears.

Enter Sentry.

Sentry, your carelessness and forgetfulness some time or other will undo me. Had not sir Oliver and sir Joslin come so luckily into the garden, the letters had been discovered and my honour left to the mercy of a false man and two young fleering girls. Did you speak to Mr. Freeman unperceived in the hurry?

6 fleering] jeering

Sent. I did, madam, and he promised me to disengage himself as soon as possibly he could, and wait upon your ladyship with all secrecy.

Lady Cock. I have some reason to believe him a man of honour.   10

Sent. Methinks indeed his very look, madam, speaks him to be much more a gentleman than Mr. Courtall. But I was unwilling before now to let your ladyship know my opinion for fear of offending your inclinations.

Lady Cock. I hope by his means to get these letters into my own hands and so prevent the inconveniencies they may bring upon my honour.

Sent. I wonder, madam, what should be sir Oliver's quarrel to Mr. Courtall.

Lady Cock. You know how apt he is to be suspicious in his drink. 'Tis very likely he thought Mr. Courtall betrayed him at the Bear today.

Sent. Pray heaven he be not jealous of your ladyship, finding you abroad so unexpectedly! If he be we shall have a sad hand of him when he comes home, madam.   22

Lady Cock. I should have apprehended it much myself, Sentry, if his drunkenness had not unadvisedly engaged him in his quarrel. As soon as he grows a little sober I am sure his fear will bring him home and make him apply himself to me with all humility and kindness—for he is ever underhand fain to use my interest and discretion to make friends to compound these businesses, or to get an order for the securing his person and his honour.

Sent. I believe verily Mr. Courtall would have been so rude to have killed him, if Mr. Freeman and the rest had not civilly interposed their weapons.

Lady Cock. Heavens forbid! Though he be a wicked man I am obliged in duty to love him. Whither did my cousins go after we came home, Sentry?

Sent. They are at the next door, madam, laughing and playing at lantreloo with my old lady Love-youth and her daughters.   34

Lady Cock. I hope they will not come home then to interrupt my affairs with Mr. Freeman. (*Knocking without.*) Hark! Somebody knocks. It may be him! Run down quickly.

Sent. I fly, madam.   [*Exit* Sentry.

Lady Cock. Now if he has a real inclination for my person I'll give him a handsome opportunity to reveal it.

                              Enter Sentry *and* Freeman.

Free. Your servant, madam.

Lady Cock. Oh Mr. Freeman! This unlucky accident has robbed me of all my quiet. I am almost distracted with thinking of the danger sir Oliver's dear life is in.   44

Free. You need not fear, madam. All things will be reconciled again tomorrow.

33-4 lantre-loo] card game

Sent. You would not blame my lady's apprehensions, did you but know the tenderness of her affections.

Lady Cock. Mr. Courtall is a false and merciless man.

Free. He has always owned a great respect for your ladyship, and I never heard him mention you with the least dishonour.   51

Lady Cock. He cannot—without injuring the truth. Heaven knows my innocence. I hope you did not let him know, sir, of your coming hither.

Free. I should never merit the happiness to wait upon you again, had I so abused this extraordinary favour, madam.

Lady Cock. If I have done any thing unbeseeming my honour, I hope you will be just, sir, and impute it to my fear. I know no man so proper to compose this unfortunate difference as yourself, and if a lady's tears and prayers have power to move you to compassion, I know you will employ your utmost endeavour to preserve me my dear sir Oliver.   60

Free. Do not, madam, afflict yourself so much. I dare engage my life, his life and honour shall be both secure.

Lady Cock. You are truly noble, sir. I was so distracted with my fears that I cannot well remember how we parted at the Spring Garden.

Free. We all divided, madam. After your ladyship and the young ladies were gone together, sir Oliver, sir Joslin, and the company with them took one boat, and Mr. Courtall and I another.

Lady Cock. Then I need not apprehend their meeting again tonight.

Free. You need not, madam. I left Mr. Courtall in his chamber, wondering what should make sir Oliver draw upon him, and fretting and fuming about the trick that was put upon us with the letters today.   71

Lady Cock. Oh! I had almost forgot myself. I assure you, sir, those letters were sent by one that has no inclination to be an enemy of yours.

                                   [*Knocking below. Exit* Sentry.
Somebody knocks. If it be sir Oliver, I am undone! He will hate me mortally if he does but suspect I use any secret means to hinder him from justifying his reputation honourably to the world.

                         Enter Sentry.

Sent. Oh madam! Here is Mr. Courtall below in the entry, discharging a coach-man. I told him your ladyship was busy, but he would not hear me, and I find, do what I can, he will come up.

Lady Cock. I would not willingly suspect you, sir.   80

Free. I have deceived him, madam, in my coming hither, and am as unwilling he should find me here as you can be.

Lady Cock. He will not believe my innocent business with you, but will raise a new scandal on my honour and publish it to the whole town.

Sent. Let him step into the closet, madam.

Lady Cock. Quick, sir, quick, I beseech you—I will send him away again immediately.

Enter Courtall.

Lady Cock. Mr. Courtall! Have you no sense of honour nor modesty left? After so many injuries to come into our house, and without my approbation rudely press upon my retirement thus?   90
Court. Pray, madam, hear my business.
Lady Cock. Thy business is maliciously to pursue my ruin. Thou comest with a base design to have sir Oliver catch thee here, and destroy the only happiness I have.
Court. I come, madam, to beg your pardon for the fault I did unwillingly commit, and to know of you the reason of sir Oliver's quarrel to me.
Lady Cock. Thy guilty conscience is able to tell thee that, vain and ungrateful man!
Court. I am innocent, madam, of all things that may offend him, and I am sure, if you would but hear me, I should remove the justice of your quarrel too.   101
Lady Cock. You are mistaken, sir, if you think I am concerned for your going to the Spring Garden this evening. My quarrel is the same with sir Oliver, and is so just that thou deserv'st to be poisoned for what thou hast done.
Court. Pray, madam, let me know my fault.
Lady Cock. I blush to think upon't. Sir Oliver, since we came from the Bear, has heard something thou hast said concerning me, but what it is I could not get him to discover. He told me 'twas enough for me to know he was satisfied of my innocence.   110
Court. This is mere passion, madam.
Lady Cock. This is the usual revenge of such base men as thou art, when they cannot compass their ends, with their venomous tongues to blast the honour of a lady.
Court. This is a sudden alteration, madam. Within these few hours you had a kinder opinion of me.
Lady Cock. 'Tis no wonder you brag of favours behind my back, that have the impudence to upbraid me with kindness to my face! Dost thou think I could ever have a good thought of thee, whom I have always found so treacherous in thy friendship to sir Oliver?   120
[*Knock at the door. Enter* Sentry.
Sent. Oh madam! Here is sir Oliver come home.
Lady Cock. O heavens! I shall be believed guilty now, and he will kill us both.
Court. (*He draws.*) I warrant you, madam, I'll defend your life.

Lady Cock. Oh! There will be murder, murder! For heaven's sake, sir, hide yourself in some corner or other.

Court. I'll step into that closet, madam.

Sent. Hold, hold, sir, by no means—his pipes and his tobacco-box lie there, and he always goes in to fetch 'em.

Lady Cock. Your malice will soon be at an end. Heaven knows what will be the fatal consequence of your being found here.   131

Sent. Madam, let him creep under the table. The carpet is long enough to hide him.

Lady Cock. Have you good nature enough to save the life and reputation of a lady?

Court. Anything to oblige you, madam.   [*He goes under the table.*

Lady Cock. (*Running to the closet.*) Be sure you do not stir, sir, whatsoever happens!

Court. Not unless he pulls me out by the ears.

Sent. Good! He thinks my lady speaks to *him*!   140

Enter Sir Oliver.

Lady Cock. My dear sir Oliver. . . .

Sir Ol. I am unworthy of this kindness, madam.

Lady Cock. Nay, I intend to chide you for your naughtiness anon, but I cannot choose but hug thee and kiss thee a little first. I was afraid I should never have had thee alive within these arms again.

Sir Ol. Your goodness does so increase my shame, I know not what to say, madam.

Lady Cock. Well, I am glad I have thee safe at home. I will lock thee up above in my chamber and will not so much as trust thee downstairs till there be an end of this quarrel.   150

Sir Ol. I was so little myself I knew not what I did, else I had not exposed my person to so much danger before thy face.

Sent. 'Twas cruelly done, sir, knowing the killing concerns my lady has for you.

Lady Cock. If Mr. Courtall had killed thee I was resolved not to survive thee, but before I had died I would have dearly revenged thy murder.

Sir Ol. As soon as I had recollected myself a little I could not rest till I came home to give thee this satisfaction, that I will do nothing without thy advice and approbation, my dear. I know thy love makes thy life depend upon mine and it is unreasonable I should upon my own rash head hazard that, though it be for the justification of thy honour. Uds me, I have let fall a china-orange that was recommended to me for one of the best that came over this year. 'Slife, light the candle, Sentry, 'tis run under the table. 163

161 Uds] God save   162 china-orange] sweet orange, originally from China

Lady Cock. Oh, I am not well!

Sentry *takes up the candle; there is a great knocking at the door;
she runs away with the candle.*

Sent. Oh Heaven! Who's that that knocks so hastily?

Sir Ol. Why, Sentry, bring back the candle! Are you mad to leave us in the
dark and your lady not well? How is it, my dear?

Lady Cock. For heaven's sake run after her, sir Oliver. Snatch the candle
out of her hand and teach her more manners.

Sir Ol. I will, my dear.   170

Lady Cock. What shall I do? Was ever woman so unfortunate in the
management of affairs!

Court. What will become of me now?

Lady Cock. It must be so. I had better trust my honour to the mercy of
them two, than be betrayed to my husband. Mr. Courtall, give me your hand
quickly, I beseech you.

Court. Here, here, madam, what's to be done now?

Lady Cock. I will put you into the closet, sir.

Court. He'll be coming in for his tobacco-box and pipes.

Lady Cock. Never fear that, sir.   180

Free. (Out of the closet door.) Now shall I be discovered! Pox on your
honourable intrigue—would I were safe at Gifford's.

Lady Cock. Here, here, sir, this is the door. Whatsoever you feel, be not
frighted—for should you make the least disturbance, you will destroy the life,
and what is more, the honour of an unfortunate lady.

Court. So, so, if you have occasion to remove again, make no ceremony,
madam.

                    Enter Sir Oliver, Sentry, Ariana, Gatty.

Sir Ol. Here is the candle. How dost thou, my dear?

Lady Cock. I could not imagine, Sentry, you had been so ill-bred to run
away and leave your master and me in the dark.   190

Sent. I thought there had been another candle upon the table, madam.

Lady Cock. Good! You thought! You are always excusing of your carelessness. Such another misdemeanour. . . .

Sir Ol. Prithee, my dear, forgive her.

Lady Cock. The truth is, I ought not to be very angry with her at present—
'tis a good-natured creature. She was so frighted for fear of thy being mis-
chiefed in the Spring Garden that I verily believe she scarce knows what she
does yet.

Sir Ol. Light the candle, Sentry, that I may look for my orange.

Lady Cock. You have been at my lady Love-youth's, cousins, I hear.

Ariana. We have, madam.   201

Gatty. She charged us to remember her service to you.

Sir Ol. So, here it is, my dear, I brought it home on purpose for thee.

Lady Cock. 'Tis a lovely orange indeed! Thank you, my dear. I am so discomposed with the fright I have had that I would fain be at rest.

Sir Ol. Get a candle, Sentry. Will you go to bed, my dear?

Lady Cock. With all my heart, sir Oliver. 'Tis late, cousins, you had best retire to your chamber too.

Gatty. We shall not stay long here, madam.

Sir Ol. Come, my dear.   210

Lady Cock. Good night, cousins.

Gatty and Ariana. Your servant, madam.

             [*Exeunt* Sir Oliver, Lady Cockwood, *and* Sentry.

Ariana. I cannot but think of those letters, sister.

Gatty. That is, you cannot but think of Mr. Freeman, sister. I perceive he runs in thy head as much as a new gown uses to do in the country, the night before 'tis expected from London.

Ariana. You need not talk, for I am sure the losses of an unlucky gamester are not more his meditation than Mr. Courtall is yours.

Gatty. He has made some slight impression on my memory, I confess, but I hope a night will wear him out again, as it does the noise of a fiddle after dancing.   221

Ariana. Love, like some stains, will wear out of itself I know, but not in such a little time as you talk of, sister.

Gatty. It cannot last longer than the stain of a mulberry at most. The next season out that goes and my heart cannot be long unfruitful, sure.

Ariana. Well, I cannot believe they forged these letters. What should be their end?

Gatty. That you may easily guess at, but methinks they took a very improper way to compass it.

Ariana. It looks more like the malice or jealousy of a woman than the design of two witty men.   231

Gatty. If this should prove a fetch of her ladyship's now, that is a-playing the loving hypocrite above with her dear sir Oliver.

Ariana. How unluckily we were interrupted when they were going to show us the hand!

Gatty. That might have discovered all. I have a small suspicion that there has been a little familiarity between her ladyship and Mr. Courtall.

Ariana. Our finding of 'em together in the Exchange and several passages I observed at the Bear have almost made me of the same opinion.

Gatty. Yet I would fain believe the continuance of it is more her desire than his inclination. That which makes me mistrust him most is her knowing we made 'em an appointment.   242

Ariana. If she were jealous of Mr. Courtall she would not be jealous of Mr. Freeman too. They both pretend to have received letters.

Gatty. There is something in it more than we are able to imagine. Time will make it out, I hope, to the advantage of the gentlemen.

Ariana. I would gladly have it so, for I believe should they give us a just cause, we should find it a hard task to hate them.

Gatty. How I love the song I learnt t'other day, since I saw them in the Mulberry Garden!   250

(She sings.)

> *To little or no purpose I spent many days,*
> *In ranging the park, th'Exchange, and th'plays;*
> *For ne'er in my rambles till now did I prove*
> *So lucky to meet with the man I could love.*
> *Oh! how I am pleased when I think on this man,*
> *That I find I must love, let me do what I can!*
>
> *How long I shall love him, I can no more tell,*
> *Than had I a fever, when I should be well.*
> *My passion shall kill me before I will show it,*
> *And yet I would give all the world he did know it.*   260
> *But oh how I sigh, when I think should he woo me,*
> *I cannot deny what I know would undo me!*

Ariana. Fie, sister, thou art so wanton.

Gatty. I hate to dissemble when I need not. 'Twould look as affected in us to be reserved now w'are alone, as for a player to maintain the character she acts in the tiring-room.

Ariana. Prithee sing a good song.

Gatty. Now art thou for a melancholy madrigal composed by some amorous coxcomb who swears in all companies he loves his mistress so well, that he would not do her the injury were she willing to grant him the favour, and it may be is sot enough to believe he would oblige her in keeping his oath too!

Ariana. Well, I will reach thee thy guitar out of the closet, to take thee off of this subject.   273

Gatty. I'd rather be a nun than a lover at thy rate. Devotion is not able to make me half so serious as love has made thee already.

Ariana opens the closet, Courtall and Freeman come out.

Court. Ha, Freeman! Is this your business with a lawyer? Here's a new discovery, i'faith!

[They shriek and run out.

Free. Peace, man, I will satisfy your jealousy hereafter. Since we have made this lucky discovery let us mind the present business.

Courtall and Freeman catch the Ladies, and bring them back.

Court. Nay, ladies, now we have caught you there is no escaping till w'are to a right understanding.   281

Enter Lady Cockwood *and* Sir Oliver *and* Sentry.

Free. Come, never blush, we are as loving as you can be for your hearts, I assure you.

Court. Had it not been our good fortunes to have been concealed here, you would have had ill nature enough to dissemble with us at least a fortnight longer.

Lady Cock. What's the matter with you here? Are you mad, cousins? Bless me, Mr. Courtall and Mr. Freeman in our house at these unseasonable hours!

Sir Ol. Fetch me down my long sword, Sentry! I lay my life Courtall has been tempting the honour of the young ladies.   290

Lady Cock. Oh my dear!   [*She holds him.*

Gatty. We are almost scared out of our wits. My sister went to reach my guitar out of the closet, and found 'em both shut up there.

Lady Cock. Come, come, this will not serve your turn. I am afraid you had a design secretly to convey 'em into your chamber! Well, I will have no more of these doings in my family, my dear. Sir Joslin shall remove these girls tomorrow.

Free. You injure the young ladies, madam. Their surprise shows their innocence.

Court. If anybody be to blame, it is Mrs. Sentry.   300

Sent. What mean you, sir? Heaven knows I know no more of their being here. . . .

Court. Nay, nay, Mrs. Sentry, you need not be ashamed to own the doing of a couple of young gentlemen such a good office.

Sent. Do not think to put your tricks upon me, sir.

Court. Understanding by Mrs. Sentry, madam, that these young ladies would very likely sit and talk in the dining room an hour before they went to bed of the accidents of the day, and being impatient to know whether that unlucky business which happened in the Spring Garden, about the letters, had quite destroyed our hopes of gaining their esteem, for a small sum of money Mr. Freeman and I obtained the favour of her to shut us up where we might over-hear 'em.   312

Lady Cock. Is this the truth, Sentry?

Sent. I humbly beg your pardon, madam.

Lady Cock. (*Aside.*) A lady's honour is not safe, that keeps a servant so subject to corruption; I will turn her out of my service for this.

Sir Ol. Good! I was suspicious their businesses had been with my lady at first.

Lady Cock. Now will I be in charity with him again for putting this off so handsomely.

Sir Ol. Hark you my dear, shall I forbid Mr. Courtall my house? 320

Lady Cock. Oh! By no means, my dear! I had forgot to tell thee, since I acquainted thee with that business, I have been discoursing with my lady Love-youth, and she blamed me infinitely for letting thee know it, and laughed exceedingly at me, believing Mr. Courtall intended thee no injury, and told me 'twas only a harmless gallantry which his French breeding has used him to.

Sir Ol. Faith, I am apt enough to believe it, for on my conscience he is a very honest fellow. Ned Courtall! How the devil came it about that thee and I fell to Sa, Sa, in the Spring Garden?

Court. You are best able to resolve yourself that, sir Oliver. 330

Sir Ol. Well, the devil take me, if I had the least unkindness for thee . . . prithee let us embrace and kiss, and be as good friends as ever we were, dear rogue.

Court. I am so reasonable, sir Oliver, that I will ask no other satisfaction for the injury you have done me.

Free. Here's the letter, madam.

Ariana. Sister, look here, do you know this hand?

Gatty. 'Tis Sentry's.

Lady Cock. Oh heavens! I shall be ruined yet.

Gatty. She has been the contriver of all this mischief. 340

Court. Nay, now you lay too much to her charge in this. She was but my lady's secretary, I assure you, she has discovered the whole plot to us.

Sent. What does he mean?

Lady Cock. Will he betray me at last?

Court. My lady being in her nature severely virtuous is, it seems, offended at the innocent freedom you take in rambling up and down by yourselves— which made her, out of a tenderness to your reputations, counterfeit these letters in hopes to fright you to that reservedness which she approves of.

Lady Cock. (*Aside.*) This has almost redeemed my opinion of his honour.— Cousins, the little regard you had to the good counsel I gave you puts me upon this business. 351

Gatty. Pray, madam, what was it Mrs. Gazette told you concerning us?

Lady Cock. Nothing, nothing, cousins! What I told you of Mr. Courtall was mere invention, the better to carry on my design for your good.

Court. Freeman, pray what brought you hither?

Free. A kind summons from her ladyship.

Court. Why did you conceal it from me?

Free. I was afraid thy peevish jealousy might have destroyed the design I had of getting an opportunity to clear ourselves to the young ladies.

329 Sa, Sa] a challenge cry in duelling

Court. Fortune has been our friend in that beyond expectation. (*To the* Ladies.) I hope, ladies, you are satisfied of our innocence now.   361

Gatty. Well, had you been found guilty of the letters, we were resolved to have counterfeited two contracts under your hands, and have suborned witnesses to swear 'em.

Ariana. That had been a full revenge, for I know you would think it as great a scandal to be thought to have an inclination for marriage, as we should to be believed willing to take our freedom without it.

Court. The more probable thing, ladies, had been only to pretend a promise; we have now and then courage enough to venture so far for a valuable consideration.   370

Gatty. The truth is such experienced gentlemen as you are seldom mortgage your persons without it be to redeem your estates.

Court. 'Tis a mercy we have 'scaped the mischief so long, and are like to do penance only for our own sins. Most families are a wedding behind-hand in the world, which makes so many young men fooled into wives to pay their father's debts. All the happiness a gentleman can desire is to live at liberty till he be forced that way to pay his own.

Free. Ladies, you know we are not ignorant of the good intentions you have towards us. Pray let us treat a little.

Gatty. I hope you are not in so desperate a condition as to have a good opinion of marriage, are you?   381

Ariana. 'Tis to as little purpose to treat with us of anything under that, as it is for those kind ladies, that have obliged you with a valuable consideration, to challenge the performance of your promise.

Sir Ol. Well, and how, and how, my dear Ned, goes the business between you and these ladies? Are you like to drive a bargain?

Court. Faith, sir Oliver, we are about it.

Sir Ol. And cannot agree, I warrant you. They are for having you take a lease for life, and you are for being tenants at will, Ned, is it not so?

Gatty. These gentlemen have found it so convenient lying in lodgings, they'll hardly venture on the trouble of taking a house of their own.   391

Court. A pretty country seat, madam, with a handsome parcel of land, and other necessaries belonging to't, may tempt us; but for a town-tenement that has but one poor conveniency we are resolved we'll never deal.

A noise of music without.

Sir Ol. Hark! My brother Jolly's come home.

Ariana. Now, gentlemen, you had best look to yourselves, and come to an agreement with us quickly, for I'll lay my life my uncle has brought home a couple of fresh chapmen that will outbid you.

Enter Sir Joslin *with* Music.

Sir Jos. Hey boys!   *[Dance.*

(Sings.)

A catch and a glass,   400
A fiddle and a lass,
What more would an honest man have?
Hang your temperate sot,
Who would seem what he's not;
'Tis I am wise, he's but grave.

Sir Jos. What's here? Mr. Courtall and Mr. Freeman?

Sir Ol. Oh man, here has been the prettiest, the luckiest discovery on all sides! We are all good friends again.

Sir Jos. Hark you brother Cockwood, I have got madam Rampant; Rakehell and she are without.   410

Sir Ol. Oh heavens! Dear brother Jolly, send her away immediately—my lady has such an aversion to a naughty woman that she will swound if she does but see her.

Sir Jos. Faith, I was hard put to't, I wanted a lover, and rather than I would break my old wont, I dressed up Rampant in a suit I bought of Rakehell; but since this good company's here, I'll send her away.

Enter Rakehell.

My little Rakehell, come hither. You see here are two powerful rivals; therefore for fear of kicking, or a worse disaster, take Rampant with you and be going quickly.

Rake. Your humble servant, sir.   *[Exit* Rakehell *and* Rampant.

Court. You may hereafter spare yourself this labour, sir Joslin. Mr. Freeman and I have vowed ourselves humble servants to these ladies.   422

Free. I hope we shall have your approbation, sir.

Sir Jos. Nay, if you have a mind to commit matrimony, I'll send for a canonical sir shall dispatch you presently.

Free. You cannot do better.

Court. What think you of taking us in the humour? Consideration may be your foe, ladies.

Ariana. Come, gentlemen, I'll make you a fair proposition. Since you have made a discovery of our inclinations, my sister and I will be content to admit you in the quality of servants.   431

Gatty. And if after a month's experience of your good behaviour, upon serious thoughts you have courage enough to engage further, we will accept of the challenge, and believe you men of honour.

Sir Jos. Well spoke i'faith, girls! And is it a match, boys?

Court. If the heart of man be not very deceitful, 'tis very likely it may be so.

Free. A month is a tedious time, and will be a dangerous trial of our resolutions, but I hope we shall not repent before marriage, whate'er we do after.

Sir Jos. How stand matters between you and your lady, brother Cockwood? Is there peace on all sides?   441

Sir Ol. Perfect concord, man. I will tell thee all that happened since I parted from thee, when we are alone, 'twill make thee laugh heartily. Never man was so happy in a virtuous and a loving lady!

Sir Jos. Though I have led sir Oliver astray this day or two, I hope you will not exclude me the act of oblivion, madam.

Lady Cock. The nigh relation I have to you and the respect I know sir Oliver has for you, makes me forget all that has passed, sir. But pray be not the occasion of any new transgressions.

Sent. I hope, Mr. Courtall, since my endeavours to serve you have ruined me in the opinion of my lady you will intercede for a reconciliation.   451

Court. Most willingly, Mrs. Sentry … faith, madam, since things have fallen out so luckily, you must needs receive your woman into favour again.

Lady Cock. Her crime is unpardonable, sir.

Sent. Upon solemn protestations, madam, that the gentlemen's intentions were honourable, and having reason to believe the young ladies had no aversion to their inclinations, I was of opinion I should have been ill-natured if I had not assisted 'em in the removing those difficulties that delayed their happiness.

Sir Ol. Come, come, girl, confess how many guineas prevailed upon your easy nature.   461

Sent. Ten, an't please you, sir.

Sir Ol. 'Slife, a sum able to corrupt an honest man in office! Faith you must forgive her, my dear.

Lady Cock. If it be your pleasure, sir Oliver, I cannot but be obedient.

Sent. If sir Oliver, madam, should ask me to see this gold, all may be discovered yet.

Lady Cock. If he does, I will give thee ten guineas out of my cabinet.

Sent. I shall take care to put him upon't! 'Tis fit that I who have bore all the blame, should have some reasonable reward for't.   470

Court. I hope, madam, you will not envy me the happiness I am to enjoy with your fair relation.

Lady Cock. Your ingenuity and goodness, sir, have made a perfect atonement for you.

Court. Pray, madam, what was your business with Mr. Freeman?

Lady Cock. Only to oblige him to endeavour a reconciliation between you

446 act of oblivion] amnesty

and sir Oliver; for though I was resolved never to see your face again, it was
death to me to think your life was in danger.

Sent. What a miraculous come off is this, madam!

Lady Cock. It has made me so truly sensible of those dangers to which an
aspiring lady must daily expose her honour, that I am resolved to give over
the great business of this town, and hereafter modestly confine myself to the
humble affairs of my own family.   483

Court. 'Tis a very pious resolution, madam, and the better to confirm you
in it, pray entertain an able chaplain.

Lady Cock. Certainly fortune was never before so unkind to the ambition
of a lady.

Sir Jos. Come, boys, faith we will have a dance before we go to bed! Sly-
girl and Mad-cap, give me your hands, that I may give 'em to these gentlemen. A parson shall join you ere long, and then you will have authority to
dance to some purpose! Brother Cockwood, take out your lady, I am for Mrs.
Sentry.

> *We'll foot it and side it, my pretty little miss,*
> *And when we are aweary, we'll lie down and kiss.*   494

Play away, boys.   [*They dance.*

Court. (*To* Gatty.) Now shall I sleep as little without you, as I should do
with you! Madam, expectation makes me almost as restless as jealousy.

Free. Faith, let us dispatch this business. Yet I never could find the pleasure of waiting for a dish of meat, when a man was heartily hungry.

Gatty. Marrying in this heat would look as ill as fighting in your drink.

Ariana. And be no more a proof of love than t'other is of valour.

Sir Jos. Never trouble your heads further. Since I perceive you are all
agreed on the matter let me alone to hasten the ceremony. Come, gentlemen,
lead 'em to their chambers. Brother Cockwood do you show the way with
your lady . . . Ha, Mrs. Sentry!

(*Sings.*)

> *I gave my love a green-gown*
> *I'th merry month of May,*
> *And down she fell as wantonly,*
> *As a tumbler does at play.*

Hey boys, lead away boys!   510

Sir Ol.   Give me thy hand, my virtuous, my dear.
           Henceforwards may our mutual loves increase,
           And when we are a-bed, we'll sign the peace.

                                                    [*Exeunt omnes.*

                        FINIS

THE MULBERRY GARDEN

BY

SIR CHARLES SEDLEY

SIR CHARLES SEDLEY (1638–1701)

The Mulberry Garden, first performed at Drury Lane, 18 May 1668; first published 1668.

[*The Poetical and Dramatic Works of Sir Charles Sedley*, ed. V. de S. Pinto, 2 vols., 1928.]

THE
Mulberry-Garden,

A

COMEDY.

As it is Acted by
His MAJESTIE'S SERVANTS
AT THE
THEATRE-ROYAL.

Written by the Honourable
Sir *CHARLES SIDLEY.*

LONDON,
Printed for *H. Herringman,* at the Sign of the *Blew Anchor* in the
Lower walk of the *New Exchange.* 1668.

TO
HER GRACE
THE DUCHESS OF
RICHMOND AND LENOX

Madam,

'Tis an unquestioned privilege we authors have of troubling whomsoever we please with an epistle dedicatory, as we call it, when we print a play; kings and princes have never been able to exempt either themselves or their favourites from our persecution. I think your grace (for a person of so great eminence, beauty, indulgence to wit, and other advantages that mark you out to suffer under addresses of this nature) has 'scaped very well hitherto. For I do not remember your name yet made a sanctuary to any of these criminals. But, madam, your time is come, and you must bear it patiently. All the favour I can show you, is that of a good executioner, which is not to prolong your pain. You see, madam, here the unhappiness of being born in our time, in which to that virtue and perfection the Greeks and Romans would have given temples and altars, the highest thing we dare dedicate is a play or some such trifle. This, that I now offer to your grace, you were so kind to when it was in loose sheets, that by degrees you have trained it up to the confidence of appearing in print before you. And I hope you will find it no hard matter to pardon a presumption you have yourself been accessory to, especially in one that is entirely,

Madam,
Your grace's devoted and
obedient servant,
CHARLES SEDLEY

PROLOGUE

New poets (like fresh beauties come to town)
Have all that are decayed to cry 'em down,
All that are envious, or that have writ ill:
For wits and heroes fain would, dying, kill.
Like statesmen in disgrace, they ill endure
A better conduct should our good procure:
As an old sinner, who in's youth has known
Most women bad, dares venture upon none.
Our author, seeing here the fate of plays,
The dangerous rocks upon the coast of praise,   10
The cruel critic and malicious wit,
Who think themselves undone if a play hit:
And like those wretches who on shipwrecks thrive,
Rage if the vessel do the storm out-live,
By others' loss he stood a while forewarned,
But against tempting hope no man is armed:
Amongst great gamesters, when deep play is seen,
Few that have money but at last come in:
He has known many with a trifling sum,
Into vast fortunes by your favours run: 20
This gives him confidence to try his fate,
And makes him hope he is not come too late;
If you'll undo him quite, like rooks begin,
And for this once in cunning let him win.
He hopes the ladies at small faults will wink,
And a new poet, a new servant think.

23 rooks] cardsharpers

DRAMATIS PERSONAE

Sir John Everyoung
Sir Samuel Forecast
Harry Modish
Ned Estridge
Jack Wildish
Snappum
Eugenio
Philander
Horatio
Officer and Assistants
Servant to Sir Samuel Forecast
Musicians and Dancers
Prentices, and Sedan-men
Diana
Althea
Widow Brightstone
Victoria
Olivia

The Mulberry Garden

ACT I SCENE I

Sir John Everyoung's *house stands.*

Enter Sir John Everyoung, *and* Sir Samuel Forecast.

Ever. Well, for all this heat, let's everyone govern his own family as he has a mind to't. I never vex myself that your daughters live shut up as if they were in Spain or Italy. Nor pray don't you trouble yourself that mine see plays, balls, and take their innocent diversion as the custom of the country and their age requires.

Fore. They are my nieces, as they are your daughters, and I'll tell you, you spoil 'em with your own examples. Youth may well be allowed to be stark mad when they see age so extravagant. Is that a dress for my elder brother, and a reverend justice?

Ever. Yes, and a properer than your little cuffs, black cap, and boots there, for a gentleman.   11

Fore. Of eighteen I confess, but not of fifty.

Ever. Yes, though he were as old as any before the Flood, and for my part I'll not bate a riband for all the whole tribe of you can say. You know yourself every fool would fain be thought wise, and why an old man should not desire to be thought young I see no reason. As long as I am whole at heart I'm resolved my clothes shall ne'er betray me.

Fore. There's no need on't, your face does it sufficiently! Come, I'm ashamed to see you every day set out thus powdered and trimmed like an old player to act a young prince. Your periwig I like very well, it serves to keep your bald pate warm, but that flirting hat there looks as it were made rather for your wit than your head. Pray which is most *à-la-mode*, right reverend spark? Points or laces? Girdle or shoulder-belts? What say your letters out of France?   24

Ever. Lord, what pains you take to quarrel at my dress and mirth, as if age were not tedious enough already but we must add neglect of ourselves and moroseness toward others. Children nowadays are not so fond of their parents that we need use any art to make 'em hate us.

Fore. Well, go then, and carry your daughters abroad, and break their

14 riband] ribbon   21 flirting] waving   23 points] tagged laces

bellies with syllabub, 'tis the greatest kindness you can do 'em now. As you have bred 'em you may e'en keep 'em to yourself and save their portions. I believe nobody will be very fond of a Hyde Park filly for a wife, nor an old boy that looks like a pedlar's pack for a father-in-law! But now I think on't you are such a spark they'd lose their reputations with you—if they had any!

Ever. For ought I see, good brother, they stand as fair in the opinion of the world as yours, and have done nothing but what I like very well.   36

Fore. What, do you count it nothing to be all day abroad, to live more in their coach than at home, and if they chance to keep the house an afternoon, to have the yard full of sedans, the hall full of footmen and pages, and their chambers covered all over with feathers and ribands, dancing and playing at cards with 'em till morning?

Ever. Why, where's the hurt of all this?

Fore. Oh no hurt at all! But if they were my daughters I should be looking for cradles and nurses. I should be sorry to hear Diana or Althea went abroad without some discreet body to look after them, or were at home indeed without employing their time in some piece of huswifry, or at least some good book.   47

Ever. You and I shall never hit it, for now I think those women, who have been least used to liberty, most apt to abuse it when they come to't.

Fore. Oh this fine believing gentleman—I should laugh heartily to see him a grandfather without a son-in-law!

Enter to them Victoria *and* Olivia.

Vict. Sir, if you don't use the coach yourself, my sister and I would go abroad this afternoon.

Ever. Take it children, but don't keep the horses out too late.   54

Fore. What! Never ask 'em whither they're going? By your favour I'll put that question to 'em. Come hither Victoria. What visits do you intend this afternoon?

Vict. None, sir, we were only going a-rambling.

Fore. A-rambling! Methinks that word sounds very prettily i'the mouth of a young maid! Next time I ask 'em whither they're going I believe they'll answer me: 'To drink a bottle or two.' But whither, pray?

Oliv. For that, sir, we shall take counsel of the weather. Either up into the city or towards the park.

Fore. What, none but you two?   64

Oliv. We intended to call on my cousins Althea and Diana.

Fore. They took physic this morning and are not well. You'll but lose your labour.

30 syllabub] soft curd of wine and cream   32 Hyde Park filly] courtesan   39 sedans] covered portable chairs   40 feathers and ribands] fops and beaux

Vict. Sir, they sent for us but an hour ago.

Fore. You had better go without 'em, they are all undressed. To stay for 'em would but make you lose the sweet of the evening.   70

Ever. Brother, what! are you jealous of them too? I assure you they are no men in women's clothes.

Fore. I am not jealous of 'em, but since you'd have it so, I'd as lief they'd keep away.

Ever. And I'd as lief you'd keep away, till you understand yourself better. What! you think your daughters, like your money, never safe but under lock and key? Who would you have 'em converse with if not with their relations?

Fore. With those that are akin to 'em in manners and behaviour, such as they may learn some goodness of. I see nothing they can learn here but vanity.   80

Vict. Sister, they begin to be angry. Come, let's leave 'em till the storm be over.   [*Exeunt.*

Fore. What! are they gone? I warrant if we had been reading a play or romance, we should not have been rid of 'em so soon. But I'll spoil their sport at my house!

Ever. A precious design and worthy of your gravity! But if you do, brother, I'll tell you one thing—you'll go near to spoil a match at cross purposes. Farewell.   [*Exeunt.*

SCENE II

Modish's *chamber.*

Enter Henry Modish *and* Ned Estridge.

Mod. Good morrow, Ned, I thought I had left you too deep engaged last night to have been here thus early.

Est. Why, you sneaked away just as the sport began, like a half-bred cock that strikes a stroke or two briskly and then runs.

Mod. Faith, I had so many irons in the fire for today, I durst not run the hazard of a disorder last night. But you know my heart was with you.

Est. You would not have repented it if your whole body and soul had been with us. Jack Wildish sent for a dozen more of champagne and a brace of such girls as we should have made honourable love to in any other place. And sir John Everyoung was in the pleasantest humour—I'd give a piece I could repeat the satire he made of the country.   11

---

87 cross purposes] parlour game of cross-questions   10 piece] coin

Mod. It would be good news to his daughters for they say now and then in a morning he is of another mind.

Est. That's only while his head aches! They need not fear him—he swears he'll ne'er stir beyond Hyde Park or Coleby's at farthest; as long as he has an acre left, they shall all come to him. 'Tis a pleasant old fellow—he has given me a hundred pounds for my gray beard, and is to ride himself this day month twice round the park, against a bay stone-horse of Wildish's, for two hundred more.

Mod. Methought Wildish and you were very intimate—pray how long have you been acquainted?   21

Est. Faith, about a week or so. Time's a thing only necessary for the friendship of vulgar spirits. Oh here comes the gentleman we were speaking of.

Enter Wildish.

Now Jack, what small petticoat do you come from?

Wild. E'en such another as you are going to now with all this bravery. Those cravats that design *the right honourable*, I'll lay a piece will be rumpled by a worse woman than they were washed, yet afore night.

Mod. Would all the world were of his mind, we young men should pass our time well.

Wild. Oh never the better for that. Such *monsieurs* as you by your feathers are known to be birds of prey, and though you catch nothing, you scare all. Besides, every good man is not acquainted with this principle among you, that you can be in love with nothing but yourselves—and may be jealous of his wife when indeed you come innocently to take a view of your persons from head to feet in the great glass . . . comb out your periwig . . . shake your garnitures . . . and be gone.   36

Est. What, dost think we have no other way of entertainment? No discourse, Jack?

Wild. Yes, a little now and then about their dress—whether their patches be too many or too few, too great or too small—whether her handkerchief be *point de Venise* or *Rome*; and having left behind you some proof of your ability in the mode, return to show yourselves at the last act of a play.

Mod. I dare swear, Jack, thy acquaintance puts thee to none of these criticisms—a plain gorget and a black scarf are all their varieties. And 'Are you well mistress?' and 'What company have you kept lately?' thy most familiar questions. But raillery apart—say it were a man's fortune to prevail upon one of these thou believest so impregnable forts, and to be received

---

15 Coleby's] tavern in the Mulberry Garden   18 stone-horse] stallion   36 garnitures] trimmings to costume   41 *point de Venise*] Venetian lace   44 gorget] article of dress covering throat and bosom

where never any but yourself came so near as to be denied—were not that a conquest?

Wild. As great as that of a place not tenable can be. The present plunder indeed is somewhat, but upon the first siege you must look to be driven out. A lady's heart is a kind of fortification that is easier surprised by being well manned, and makes ever the strongest resistance of itself.   53

Est. 'Tis true, Modish, for I have still observed that when one of these persons of honour does a little forget herself, though at first through a secret sympathy and invincible inclination (as they call it) for one particular man, she ever after loves the whole sex the better for it.

Wild. Right. For these good creatures, women, are like cats—if once made tame anyone may play with 'em; if not, there's no coming near 'em.

Mod. Thou think'st thou hast mauled 'em now! Why I tell thee, Jack, a hector is not readier to pick a quarrel with a saucy creditor, and swear he will never pay the rascal, than a man is to have one with his mistress towards the latter end of an amour. Especially if it amount to a handsome occasion of leaving her, 'tis the kindest thing she can do then. What think you, Estridge?   65

Est. Faith, I'm of your mind, yet I have known some unconscionable ladies make their servants wait as long for a just exception, and almost as impatiently, as they did for the first favour.

Wild. Favour and exception, gentlemen, are words I don't meet with in seven years, where I go. My piece makes my compliment when I come in, and my excuse when I go away, and 'tis ever well taken too. I have all the day to bestow upon my business, the night upon my friends, whilst you are kissing the cards at ombre, or presenting oranges at a playhouse.   73

Est. Thou never knew'st, it seems, what 'twas to be in love then?

Wild. No, faith, I never let the disease run on so far. I always took it in time, and then a bottle of wine or two and a she-friend is an approved remedy. There are men in the world though, who in that distemper prescribe some serious employment, continual exercise, spare diet, and the like. But they are philosophers, and in my opinion make the remedy worse than the disease.   80

Est. I do confess yours is the pleasantest cure—if it be one. But I doubt it only gives a little ease for the present, and like small beer in the morning after a merry bout overnight, doth but make us the worse afterwards.

Mod. Ay now, you talk to him of what he understands. What you do tell him of love for—who by his own confession never knew what it was?

Wild. No, but I guess this same love you speak of, gentlemen, to be much like longing in women—a fantastical appetite to some one thing above all others, which if they cannot get, the lover miscarries of his passion, and the

61 hector] bully   73 ombre] Card game; it was Restoration custom to kiss the cards.

lady of her little one. Or if they do, are both quickly satisfied, and it becomes
for ever after very indifferent, if not loathsome.   90

Est. Well, Modish, I perceive we shall do no good on him. Let's take him
to the Mulberry Garden, and see what the ladies can do.

Wild. You shall excuse me, I have a small ramble of my own for an hour or
two this afternoon . . . and so, your servant.   [*Exit.*

Mod. 'Tis time we were going. I warrant they have walked every foot of the
Garden twice over by this time. They are mad to know whether their friends
in town have dealt faithfully with 'em of late, concerning the mode.

Est. These country ladies for the first month take up their places in the
Mulberry Garden as early as a citizen's wife at a new play.

Mod. And for the most part are as easily discovered; they have always
somewhat on that is just left off by the better sort.

Est. They are the antipodes of the court, for when a fashion sets there, it
rises among them.   [*Exeunt.*

SCENE III

[*The Mulberry Garden.*]

Enter Victoria *and* Olivia.

Vict. Sister, whatever the matter is, methinks we don't see half the
company that used to meet here anights when we were last in town.

Oliv. 'Tis true, but methinks 'tis much better than the long walk at home.
For in my opinion half a score young men and fine ladies well dressed, are a
greater ornament to a garden than a wilderness of sycamores, orange and
lemon trees; and the rustling of rich vests and silk petticoats better music
than the purling of streams, chirping of birds, or any of our country entertainments. And *that* I hope the place will afford us yet, as soon as the plays are
done.

Vict. Sister, what would you give to see Estridge come in now?   10

Oliv. 'Tis impossible, he would not miss his devotion to the park (for all I
could give) such an evening as this. Besides the two garnitures he brought out
of France are soiled, his feather broke, and he has been so out of humour
these two days there's no enduring him. He lost his money too last night I
hear, and losing gamesters are but ill company.

Vict. Fie sister, you make him a saver with a look, and fine in but thinking

92 Mulberry Garden] tree-planted pleasure-ground on site of Buckingham Palace
16 saver] gaming term—one who escapes loss without gain

he is so. You deserve not so complete a servant, but I hope you'll be as obliging to his face as you are severe to him behind his back.

Oliv. The only way to oblige most men is to use 'em thus a little now and then. Even to their faces it gives 'em an opinion of our wit, and is consequently a spur to theirs. The great pleasure of gaming were lost if we saw one another's hands; and of love if we knew one another's hearts. There would be no room for good play in the one, nor for address in the other—which are the refined parts of both. But what would you give to see Horatio?

Vict. To see Horatio, as I knew him once,
  I would all other happiness renounce;
  But he is now another's, and my aim
  Is not to nourish, but to starve my flame:
  I dare not hope my captive to regain,   30
  So many charms contribute to his chain.
  Althea's slave, let false Horatio live,
  Whilst I for freedom, not for empire strive.

Oliv. Fie sister, leave this rhyming at least!

Enter to them Estridge *and* Modish.

Est. Ladies, it is our wonder to find anybody here at this time of day, and no less our happiness to meet with you. All the world is at the park, where we had been ourselves but that we saw your livery at the gate.

Vict. I pray let us not keep you here gentlemen. Your mistresses will curse us and yourselves too, by and by, if the garden should not fill.

Est. If we wish any company, ladies, 'tis for your sakes, not our own.   41

Mod. For my part I would ne'er desire a garden fuller than this is now. We are two to two, and may be hand to hand when you please.

Oliv. I don't know what you think, but in my mind the more the merrier, especially in these places.

Est. Ay, for show, madam, but it happens in great companies, as at feasts, we see a great deal and fall to heartily of nothing and for the most part rise hungry. And 'tis with lovers, madam, as with great-bellied women—if they find what they long for they care not whether there be anything else or no.   50

Vict. What, in love already? Sure the air of this place is a great softner of men's hearts.

Mod. How can it choose, having so many lovers' sighs daily mixed with it? But 'twere a much better quality in't, madam, if it could incline ladies to believe and look with pity on those flames they raise.

37 livery] costumed servant   48 great-bellied] pregnant

Oliv. 'Tis too early to make love this two hours. 'Flames' and 'pity' would sound much better in the evening.

Mod. 'Tis not with love, madam, as with meaner arguments. I might entertain you with my passion for an age and yet have as much left for anon as if I had not spoke one word. The sea is easier emptied than a lover's breast!

Oliv. What say you, sir, is this your opinion too?   61

Est. Yes, faith, madam, and I think a lover can no more say at once what he hath to say to his mistress, than a man can eat at once for his whole lifetime.

Oliv. Nay, if it be so endless, I should beg of my servant, whenever I have one, e'en to keep it to himself for altogether.

Est. There you betray your ignorance—with your pardon, madam. To see the fair Olivia and not love her, is not more impossible than to love her and not tell her on't. Silent lovers you may read of, and in romances too, but heavens forbid you should e'er meet with any.   70

Oliv. If they knew how little they were like to get by being otherwise I'm confident I should meet with none else.

Est. Well, madam, I perceive love like wine makes our discourse seem extravagant to those that are not wound up to the same height. But had you any spark of what I feel I should have had another answer.

Oliv. Why, what answer?

Est. Nay, I know not, but some pretty one that love would have devised for you; no more to be imagined by you now than what you shall talk of next in your sleep. In the meantime, ladies, will you do us the honour to eat syllabubs?   80

Oliv. Sister, let's go, so they'll promise to say nothing but what they think to us when we are there.

Mod. You may do what you please, Ned, but 'tis a liberty I dare not use myself to, for fear of an ill habit.

Est. You are very confident of our good opinion, ladies. I believe there are few women in town would accept of our company on these terms.

Vict. Faith, sister, let's bate 'em that circumstance. Truth is a thing merely necessary for witnesses and historians, and in these places doth but curb invention and spoil good company. We will only confine 'em to what's probable.

Mod. Content, and I dare swear 'twill be better for all parties.   [*Exeunt.*

87 bate] deduct

SCENE IV

Sir Samuel Forecast's *House.*

Enter Althea *and* Diana.

Diana. We two, or none, may of our stars complain,
   Who afford us nothing to share but pain;
   Each bears her own, and th'other's portion too;
   This cruel wonder can high friendship do.
Alth. To us how cheap might they have joy allowed,
   Since both had had what they on each bestowed!
   But yet thy loss I rate above my own,
   Fate on thy love till now did never frown:
   Philander thee above the world did prize,
   Thy parents saw him almost with thy eyes: 10
   All things so prosperous were, thou couldst not guess,
   An accident to wound thy happiness.
   I wretched maid, have but a passion lost,
   Which if none else, my parents would have crossed:
   My lowly hopes do but a step descend,
   Whilst thine, from their full height, do headlong bend:
   This hour that promised all, can nothing pay,
   And Hymen steals his lighted torch away.
Diana. Ah, dear Althea, let not thou and I
   Contend who most exceeds in misery;   20
   It is a dismal strife, since were my own
   Less, I'd share thine till they were equal grown.
   Curse on ambition, why should honour take
   A present back again, that love did make?
   On thee Eugenio did his life bestow,
   To me Philander did his service vow;
   Yet both for honour have those ties despised,
   And now are fled, or must be sacrificed.
   Unkind Philander, had love filled thy breast
   With half those flames thou hast so oft expressed, 30
   They had consumèd in their purer fires
   All other thoughts, and thou wou'dst never mind,
   Who were for kings, and who for slaves designed.

18 Hymen] god of marriage

Alth. The noble sense they show of the sad fate
 Of their dear country, sets a higher rate
 Upon their love; for who that had a grain
 Of honour in him, could endure the reign
 Of proud usurpers, whose relentless will,
 Is all the law by which men spare or kill;
 And his true prince in banishment behold,   40
 Worthy of more than fortune can withhold;
 These monstrous with the crimes of prosperous fate,
 The other shining in his adverse state,
 So that each stroke of fortune does but seem
 A step for his heroic mind to climb,
 Till he has got above her reach, and then
 The virtue she has tried she'll love again?
 Though I must truly mourn their ill success,
 I could not wish Eugenio had done less.
Diana. Had their high virtue the least doubt endured, 50
 Even with their death it had been cheaply cured:
 But this brave act is but to me and you,
 A dangerous proof of what before we knew.
Alth. Though their true worth to us before were clear
 This act has made it to the world appear;
 None ever with that obstinacy loved,
 But they were pleased to see their choice approved:
 No joy complete to worthy minds can seem,
 Which is not height'ned by the world's esteem.
Diana. My heart, Althea, does less grieve it has   60
 Ventured its treasure in so loved a cause,
 Than that Philander did not let me know
 The danger he was like to undergo.
Alth. Sister, though laws of decency refuse,
 We shining swords and glittering armour use;
 Yet a decision of what's right or wrong,
 As well as men's, does to our minds belong;
 And we best show it when we most approve
 Those men that fight in quarrels which we love:
 Though they of courage have the ruder part,   70
 The virtue may become a woman's heart,
 Though not her hand; and she that bravely dares
 Expose her love, sure for her life not cares.
 I knew Eugenio must that hazard run,
 Nor could consent he should the danger shun;

And had Philander the like thoughts of you,
He without doubt had dealt as freely too.
Diana. I must confess my love could never yield,
That he again should win it in the field:
Let me the greatness of your mind admire,   80
Whilst I deplore the greatness of my fire,
A fire which lends no light, but that which serves
To show how much what I exposed deserves,
How much he hazards, and how far I am
From vent'ring him for the whole voice of fame,
Whose danger had I known, my eyes, alas!
Had wept a sea, he would have feared to pass;
But we so long of what is past complain,
As if no further mischief did remain,
As if fate here had her whole malice spent,   90
And all the arrows from her quiver sent.
Alth. When fate would harm where virtue does protect,
She does her guilt and impotence detect;
She can but rob the virtuous of that rest,
She must restore again with interest,
And all the danger of these heroes past,
Must needs consider their high worth at last.
Diana. What we desire, how fain we would believe,
And with that fortune knew not to deceive?
But she profusely to some presents makes,   100
And as unjustly from some others takes.
I fear she's so much to their worth in debt,
She'll nothing pay because the whole's too great:
Like tyrants' wealth her bounties still appear,
Who give to few what they from many tear.
Alth. In the meantime I fear our cruel friends
Will not consult our liking but their ends:
I know they'll press I should Horatio wed,
And promise thee unto some stranger's bed.
Diana. They may such matches as they please provide,   110
But here I vow, I'll never be a bride
To any but Philander; in that heart
He taught to love, none else shall have a part.
Alth. I the like vow to my Eugenio make,
Which fate's worst malice shan't have power to break;
As trees exposed to storms take deeper root,
Than those that do in peaceful valleys sprout:

So in all noble minds, a virtuous love
By opposition does the firmer prove.
Diana. 'Tis fit, Althea, I now take my leave,
Whilst you prepare Horatio to receive.
Alth. Farewell, Diana, and be sure you do
Nothing unworthy of your love and vow.

                              [*Exeunt* Diana *and* Althea *severally.*

ACT II   SCENE I

[Sir Samuel Forecast'*s House.*]

Enter Sir Samuel Forecast, Althea, Jack Wildish, *and* Olivia.

Fore. Daughter, we are much beholding to Horatio. The portion I can give
with you does not deserve a man of past half his fortune—six thousand
pounds a year, an estate well wooded, and I am told very improveable. It
makes me young again to think on't. Eugenio I never liked, and as things
stand now, am right glad we had no more to do with him. But that I am one
whose affection and good will to the state has sufficiently manifested itself, I
might be thought to have a hand in their design, and so have been put in the
tower and had my fortune seized on. Eugenio shall never call a child of mine
wife as long as I live!

Wild. But, sir, your zeal to the cause has put you above those apprehensions.

Fore. You say right, Mr. Wildish, but we cannot be in this case too secure,
and I am resolved Althea, to take off all suspicion, shall out of hand marry
with Horatio.   13

Alth. Sir, I hope you will allow me some time to dismiss Eugenio from my
thoughts.

Wild. And pray sir, what prejudice, what exception have you to Eugenio?

Fore. Originally this only—his father made a purchase of some land that
lay next hedge to mine and gave a thousand pounds more than it was worth,
only to buy it over my head. Think no more on him, upon my blessing; he
is not the man he was. He had an estate; 'tis now sequestered; he dare not
show his head. And besides, I would not have a son-in-law of his principles
for six times his fortune. I should be sorry to see any child of mine soliciting
her husband's composition at a committee.   23

Alth. Had I once had the relation of a wife to Eugenio I should have

6 state] The Republic—Sir Samuel is a Roundhead.   10 cause] the Good Old Cause,
i.e., puritan republicanism   20 sequestered] confiscated   23 composition] Royalists
could compound for their loyalty by surrendering part of estate.

thought nothing a trouble that had become my duty, and could as cheerfully have shared an honourable suffering as the most flourishing condition.

Fore. I charge you never receive visit or message from him more, and tell your sister Diana 'tis my pleasure she quit all correspondence with Philander. They are both dangerous persons. (*Turns to* Wildish.) These young wenches, Mr. Wildish, have less forecast than pigeons; so they be billing, they look no farther; ne'er think of building their nests, nor what shall become of their little ones.   32

Wild. Sir, I think they're i' the right, let 'em increase and multiply, and for the rest, trust him that set 'em a' work.

Fore. Mr. Wildish, you are a merry gentleman! But I'll tell you, Mistress Althea, as I have given you life, I'll take care you shan't make it miserable.

Alth. Sir, the happiness of life lies not in wealth, in title, or in show, but in the mind, which is not to be forced. And we are not the less slaves for being bound in chains of gold. A marriage with Horatio may make me appear happy to the envious world, but like those destructive arts which, while they seem to aid, consume our native beauties, indeed must prey upon my inward peace.

Fore. I'll warrant you peace within, and without too! Horatio is a well-natured, proper gentleman, and one that loves you.   43

Wild. Now there, sir Samuel, I'm on your side, for so the fan be played with, the hand kissed—in fine, the passion handsomely discharged—'tis no great matter who does it! As children cry after their old nurses but 'till they are acquainted with their new, so young ladies regret the loss of one servant but till they have got the same familiarity with another; which, by the way, is seldom long first.

Enter a Servant.

Serv. Sir, there's a man out of Pater Noster Row with stuffs.

Fore. Bid him carry 'em into the next room. Come Althea, let's in and look upon 'em.   [*Exeunt* Althea *and* Sir Samuel.

Manent Wildish *and* Olivia.

Oliv. We women are ever sure of your good word, Mr. Wildish. When you have a mistress I hope she'll deserve it from you in particular, and have in perfection all those good qualities you so liberally bestow upon the whole sex in your discourse.   56

Wild. Why, madam, I thought you had understood raillery! Faith, I have so good an opinion of the sex I am ashamed to own it but to one of them in private. This is only the way of talking I have got among my companions where, when we meet over a bottle of wine, 'tis held as great a part of wit to rally women handsomely behind their back as to flatter 'em to their faces.

---

30 forecast] foresight   40 destructive arts] cosmetics   50 Pater Noster Row] famous for mercers   50 stuffs] clothing material   s.d. *Manent*] remain on stage

Oliv. But why do you make us poor women the subject of your mirth?

Wild. You are grown of late so uncharitable and villainous hard-hearted, are incompassed with so many difficulties as decency, honour, and reputation —that we men that love our pleasure begin to hate you worse than beggars do a coach with the glasses drawn up ... despair of relief, and fall a-railing.

Oliv. And if some kind-hearted wretch do chance to relieve one of you, like beggars you tell it presently and send more! I warrant y'are fine fellows! A woman is well helped up that has one of you to her servant.

Wild. Nay, don't put me in among 'em. I am a mere apostate, though not resolute enough to endure the martyrdoms of being continually laughed at by half a score of 'em. All that I have done, of late, has been mere compliance— as papists go to church for fear of the penalty.   73

Oliv. Pray, sir, to what fair saint do we owe your conversion?

Wild. Faith, there are many in the world now would make you guess this half hour, telling you first the colour of her hair, her age, her country, and perhaps the first letter of her name. But I hate that way of fooling ... 'tis yourself ... whom I love.

Oliv. Impudent fellow! Don't you expect I should forbid you the house, or at least, for punishment of such rudeness, condemn your guilty passion to eternal silence and despair? What! men have lived years in deserts for their mistresses' sake, and yet have trembled when they spoke of love; which you venture at with as little ceremony as you'd ask me how I slept last night.   84

Wild. I know not what romances order in this case; I ne'er thought it would be mine, and so ha'n't much studied it. But prithee don't baulk a young beginner. 'Tis my first fault, and so ben't too severe. I shall relapse else beyond redemption.

Oliv. Well, I'm content for once your ignorance should plead your pardon.

Wild. Nay, Mistress Olivia, consider me a little further. I have lost the pleasures of mirth, of wine, and company. All things that were before delightful to me are no longer so. My life is grown but one continued thought of your fair self. And is a pardon all that I must hope for?   93

Oliv. Come, leave your fooling! Your old humour does better with you a thousand times than this whining love. As there are some perfumes so strong that they lose that name with most, so compliments may be so gross that they become injurious.

Wild. Why, here's it now; there are so many cheats in this trade of love too, that like beggars the true go unrelieved because we meet with now and then a counterfeit. On my life, Mistress Olivia, the plenty I have ever lived in puts me as much out of countenance to ask a charity of this kind, as I

66 glasses] windows   69 helped up] assisted   73 penalty] fine for not attending Anglican service

could be should fortune constrain me to intreat one of the other; and would
not trouble you could my pain admit redress from any but yourself.   103

Oliv. Sure, Mr. Wildish, you would think I had an excellent opinion of
myself, or an implicit faith in whatever you say, should I believe all this now.

Wild. If I told a chirurgeon I had broke my leg, do you think he would not
take my word?

Oliv. Yes, sure.

Wild. Why should not you take it then for a wounded heart? They are
neither of 'em matters to brag on, and I would no more lead the life of a
lover, if I were free, than I would that of a sick man if I were well.   111

Oliv. Methinks the sick men, as you call 'em, live so like the well, as one
can scarce know one from th'other.

Wild. In your chamber, perhaps; but abroad we find a thousand differences.

Oliv. As how, I pray?

Wild. Why, your true lover leaves all company when the sport begins, the
table when the bottles are called for, the gaming house when the cards come
up; is more afraid of an engagement than a lawyer in term-time; would less
miss the last act of a play, the park, or indeed any abominable old ladies,
where he may hope to see the party, than a young wench can Gray's Inn
walks the first Sunday of her new gown.   121

Oliv. What, is this all?

Wild. Not half: ask him to sup, he has business; or if he promise, 'tis ten
to one he fails, and if he sees his mistress, is so transported that he forgets to
send his excuse. If he cannot find her, and so chance to keep his word, sits in
such dismal dumps that he spoils the whole company.

Oliv. And will you be such an animal for my sake?

Wild. Faith, I'm afraid so—but if not well used I shall find the way home
again.

Oliv. Whatever you think, sir, I shall contribute no more to the keeping
you my servant than I did to the making you so.   131

Wild. Well, do but use as proper means to keep me your servant as you
have done to make me so, and I am satisfied.

Oliv. Why, what means?

Wild. As your beauty bred my affection, so let your kindness nourish it.

Oliv. Mr. Wildish, you have been so pleasant upon this new argument, that
I had almost forgot my visit to Diana.

Wild. I'm upon equal terms with you there, for I have made Ned Estridge
and Harry Modish stay this half hour for me at the French House. And so,
your servant.   [*Exeunt.*

106 chirurgeon] surgeon   118 term-time] when court is in session   121-2 Gray's Inn
walks] tree-planted lawns north of South Square, Gray's Inn   139 the French House]
Covent Garden tavern

SCENE II

[Althea's Chamber.]

Enter Althea.

Alth. Under what tyranny are women born!
  Here we are bid to love, and there to scorn;
  As if unfit to be allowed a part
  In choosing him that must have all our heart;
  Or that our liking, like a head-strong beast,
  Were made for nothing, but to be oppressed;
  And below them in this regard we are,
  We may not fly the cruelty we fear.
  The horse may shake the rider from his back,
  The dog his hated master may forsake;   10
  Yet nothing of their native worth impair,
  Nor any conscious sting about them bear.
  But if a virgin an escape contrive,
  She must for ever in dishonour live,
  Condemned within herself, despised of all,
  Into worse mischiefs then she fled from, fall.
  Duty commands I should Horatio wed,
  Love does as strongly for Eugenio plead;
  My mind, distracted thus, a storm abides
  Like seas when winds blow full against their tides.   20

Enter Horatio.

Hora. Madam, methinks you look not pleased; I fear
  My hapless passion did too late appear
  For my content; and only now can prove
  The wretched triumph of some elder love.
  But, fair Althea, you were much to blame
  With your own breath to blow a hopeless flame.
  Ah! had you to its childhood been severe,
  As now to its full growth you cruel are,
  'Thad died with half that pain it now must bear:
  Young plants with ease up by the roots we tear;   30
  But when well grown, the axe must be imployed,
  And they with force and labour are destroyed.

Alth. Generous Horatio, forbear to blame
 Me, as the cruel author of your pain.
 How could I know that you my lover were,
 Until yourself your passion did declare?
 How had it looked in me to have complained
 Of thoughts, perhaps, you never entertained?
 How could I check, alas, those hopes in you,
 Your heart did never harbour, that I knew?   40
Hora. Not know, Althea! why should the same eyes
 So slowly see, so suddenly surprise?
 The very minute I beheld your face,
 You might in mine my growing passion trace.
 Now trembling fear did her pale colour spread,
 Then springing hope brought back the native red:
 Joy may be seen, and grief itself unfold,
 And so may love, though it be never told.
 In every look my passion was confessed,
 And every action my high flame expressed.   50
 As foolish witnesses their cause o'erthrow,
 My arts to hide it, did it clearer show.
Alth. But as fond parents will not seem to know
 A fault they needs must punish when they do;
 So I at first was loth to see a crime
 In one, I otherwise did so esteem:
 For know, Horatio, setting love apart,
 None than yourself is deeper in my heart;
 Your worth and honour I can value, though
 I no requital to your flame allow.   60
Hora. You can give all things else above their due,
 And yet wrong that which most belongs to you:
 Madam, these words, soothe with a cruel art
 Where I less feel, and wound a mortal part;
 With friendship and esteem you strive in vain,
 Kind maid, to ease a lover of his pain:
 For where your beauty once has raised a flame,
 To offer less, and nothing, are the same.
 Love and ambition of their aim denied,
 No other way can e'er be satisfied.   70
Alth. You that could faithless to Victoria prove,
 Methinks should blush even at the name of love.
 Her numerous charms your loud accusers are,
 And call Horatio false, as she is fair.

Hora. You should with pity, not displeasure, see
 The change that your own self creates in me.
 The Roman Senate had their greatness worn
 Perhaps till now, had Caesar ne'er been born.
 Darius 'self could not his Persians blame,
 Because that Alexander overcame.   80
 In love, like war, some victor still there grows,
 Whose spreading empire nothing can oppose.
Alth. Countries are fixed, and cannot fly, although
 They apprehend a certain overthrow.
 Lovers, the force they can't oppose, might shun,
 And may with safety and with honour run.
 Who then would pity him that stays to die,
 When virtue and his duty bid him fly?
Hora. Althea, in love's wars all heroes are,
 Death does less terrible than flight appear;   90
 As gamesters, when they lose, still deeper set,
 Helping ill fortune to increase their debt:
 So lovers, when a nymph gets half their heart,
 Themselves, alas, betray the other part.
Alth. Victoria's wrongs my gratitude deter;
 Your gifts to me are robberies from her.
Hora. I came at first, Althea, 'tis most true
 With love to her, and but respect to you.
 But, ah! how soon within my tortured breast
 You of each other's places are possessed!   100
Alth. Beauty, the wrongs of beauty should revenge,
 And the fair punish, when the faithless change.
Hora. I change Althea, but (as pious men
 Become blessed saints) never to change again.
 If none your matchless beauty must adore,
 But such alone as never loved before,
 You do unjustly, and too high advance
 In love th'already too great power of chance:
 Since that you should their first affection be,
 Let's you their fortune, not their passion see.   110
Alth. It lets me see they falsehood never knew,
 And gives me leave to hope they will be true.
Hora. Sure none can faithless to such beauty prove;
 He that's in heaven, can no higher move.
Alth. A lover's heaven in his fancy lies,
 Which beauty oft neglects, and oft supplies.

Hora. 'Tis not, Althea, that you question mine,
 But 'tis Eugenio's faith does brighter shine;
 'Tis he that makes Victoria's wrong your pain,
 My love a crime, a virtue your disdain.   120
 These tales of falsehood, and of former love,
 Reproaches only, where we like not, prove.
Alth. Horatio, I am glad your disrespect
 Has turned so soon to justice my neglect:
 You that reproach me with a former love,
 Yourself unfit but for my anger prove.   [*Exit* Althea.
Hora. Oh, stay awhile! sure you must joy to see
 The torture you're so pleased to work in me;
 Not that I hope I shall your pity find,
 But that the sight may glut your cruel mind.
 Nature inconstant to her own designs,
 To a fair form a cruel temper joins;
 She makes the heedless lover kneel in vain,
 And in love's temple, to adore Disdain.   [*Exit* Horatio.

[SCENE III]

[*A Street near* Widow Brightstone's *House.*]

Enter Sir Samuel Forecast *and* Jack Wildish.

Fore. When am I to see your fair and wealthy cousin, Mr. Wildish?
Wild. This minute if you please, sir.
Fore. I doubt you are not stirring in the business. You do not lay the necessity of marrying home enough to her. I might have got access ere now else, and our counsel have been drawing the writings.
Wild. It must be done by degrees. If I should have been too forward it might have caused in her a suspicion of my purpose, and so my worthy friend, sir Samuel, have come to her upon some prejudice, which I would not for half her fortune.
Fore. Pray, Mr. Wildish, is she so concerned for her late husband as the world talks?   11
Wild. Ten times more; looks upon his picture all day long, as earnestly as if she were to copy it; since he died, has used no pocket-handkerchers but what was made of his old shirts, and wets two a day of 'em with her tears.

 5 writings] marriage contract

Because he died on a Monday, fasts that day of the week; takes none into her service but Thomases, because 'twas his Christian name, and has now sent into Wales for a Thomas ap Thomas to be her gentleman-usher.

Fore. 'Tis strange she should so affect his name! What think you then, if you called me sir Thomas Forecast?

Wild. Faith, sir, what you please. But I think it will be altogether needless, and if she should come to discover, it might spoil all; s'light, she might mistrust your particular if she should find you put a trick upon her in your name.

Fore. Well, I'll be ruled by you, Mr. Wildish. You know her humour best.

Wild. I can't but think how she'll look upon me when I talk to her of another husband! But I'll venture, sir Samuel, to serve you. Come, let's away, her house is here hard by.   26

[SCENE IV]

They enter the widow's house.

Wild. I show the way, sir.

They find her looking upon her husband's picture, and does not see 'em.

Fore. Excellent woman, she sees us not! Oh the endless treasure of a virtuous wife! It extends even to our memories, and pictures.

Wildish goes up, and speaks to her.

Wild. Madam, here is sir Samuel Forecast come to wait on you.

Widow. Sir, I hope you'll pardon me, if I have let my grief employ any part of that time which was due to my acknowledgment for this favour. You were my husband's friend, and as such will ever be most welcome to me; and though his too scrupulous kindness allowed me not the acquaintance, scarce the sight of any man, yet I did always place a value where he gave his esteem, especially so highly as he did to you.   10

Fore. Madam, I am much bound to you for your good opinion, and come to condole with you. Your husband was an honest, prudent, and a wealthy gentleman, kept good hours, and even reckonings, loved me well, and we have drank many a dish of coffee together.

Widow. Sir, whilst you repeat his virtues, you do but count my loss, and telling me how good he was makes me but more sensibly want him.

Fore. He and I were just of an age, and when we were boys, of a strength.

Widow. And what of that, sir?

17 gentleman-usher] escort   22 your particular] you yourself

Wild. Why, cousin, it makes me think that sir Samuel would make as loving a husband to you, as your last was, and I'll swear it troubles me heartily to see my pretty coz here not yet out of danger of smooth-faced younger brothers, such as marry wives only to keep wenches, and never bring 'em to town but to pass away some part of their estates.   23

Fore. Some such there are—but heaven bless the estate, and widow of my good friend your husband, out of such hands.

Wild. Now I have brought you together, I'll leave you. Cousin, you are not afraid to be left alone with sir Samuel?   [*Exit*.

Widow. I know his virtue, and my own too well.

Fore. Don't you find, madam, business very troublesome?

Widow. I do indeed, and have the misfortune to be involved in it.

Fore. Have you many law-suits?   31

Widow. But one considerable, which being with a man in power, in these corrupt times a woman unfriended and unknown as I am must expect to lose.

Fore. Of what value?

Widow. Five thousand pounds. I shall have enough left however to make me happy with a man that loves me.

Fore. Enough left! Such another word would make me foreswear not only thee but thy whole sex. Five thousand pounds well disposed, why, I tell thee, 'tis able to procure us judgments on half the young prodigals of this age. Thou and I might live comfortably on the forbearance money and let the interest run on.   42

Widow. I did but put the worst—not that I doubt my title if I have common justice.

Fore. No, thou shalt secure thy title. I am a near kinsman to the judge, and a by-way to his favour.

Widow. How do you mean?

Fore. Why I have many times bought a thousand pounds'-worth of other men's lands of him for a hundred.

Widow. I would not corrupt justice for a world.   50

Fore. What, again widow? Nay then, I perceive thou dost it on purpose to lose my heart. But to say truth, it were unreasonable to expect thy tender years should understand the true worth of money so far, that for its sake to trample on those unprofitable and foolish principles the honourable beggars of former times governed their lives by. But thou wilt one day know that age hath its beauties too, as well as youth, and more universally adored.

Widow. Gravity and wisdom, sir, I know men may expect, but our sex has no pretence to them.

21 coz] abbreviation of cousin   41 forbearance money] cash to defer loan repayment
46 by-way] short cut

Fore. No, wealth and power, widow, which awe the grave and wise. Gold and silver are the best red and white; the other, every milkmaid may boast equal with a countess.   61

Enter Sir John Everyoung, Modish, *and* Estridge, *with fiddles playing.*

Widow. What rude fellow's that?

Ever. (*To the Music.*) Hold, let's parley first.—Faith, widow, one that loves you but too well.

Widow. Love me! Upon what acquaintance? I ne'er saw your face before in my days.

Ever. And dost thou like it now?

Widow. Not so well as yourself, you may be confident.

Ever. All this shan't cross my honest purpose. I came in mere charity to prevent thy ruin, and if thou be'st not lost to all sense and reason, nay, even all natural appetite, I'll do't.   71

Widow. I know no ruin near. This is the worst accident has befallen me a good while.

Ever. Hear me but out, and thou shalt bless it. Canst thou be such a traitor to flesh and blood as to count it nothing to be joined to that old trunk there? If he increase or multiply it must be thy bags; interest and brokage are his best instruments.

Widow. You don't consider that all this might be as well applied to your sweet self?

Ever. Yes, most properly! Why, 'tis that makes me hate matrimony and puts me at distance with 'To have and to hold.' I confess my tick is not good and I never desire to game for more than I have about me. Now second me.

Mod. The minute you marry, widow, you are not worth a groat—all is your husband's. And if hereafter you shall come to a sense of your unequal choice, and endeavour to repair it in some young and worthy friend, the old gentleman takes pet, turns you over to a tedious suit for alimony, which your friend furnishes you with money to follow, for a while, and in times grows weary of it himself.

Est. Then, like an old gamester that has lost all he has upon the square, your only way is to turn rook and play upon advantage.   90

Widow. Why, do you know these gentlemen?

Fore. Ay, to my shame. The ringleader of 'em is my brother. There is no remedy but patience.

Widow. Gentlemen, you talk at a strange rate for the first time; but, whomever I marry, my virtue will secure him of my constancy.

Mod. Pray, madam, don't prophane that honourable name; 'tis mere

60 red and white] colours of a woman's face   89 upon the square] honestly   90 rook] sharper   90 play upon advantage] cheat

obstinacy to an old man—a fault methinks you have too ingenious a countenance to be guilty of.

Ever. If thou should'st be so improvident as to neglect the comfort of a gallant, thou'lt never 'scape the scandal, having such a husband.   100

Mod. If you are precise, madam, they'll give you your chaplain. If you love business, your lawyer. If you keep a gentleman-usher, you are undone.

Est. If you take some honest gentleman (which, by my troth, I think is your best course) upon the first hard journey, as the world goes now, 'tis ten to one he falls lame of an old bruise.

Widow. You are very tender of my credit. If you had been as careful, gentlemen, of your own sobriety, I fear I had missed all this good counsel.

Ever. Oh! are you edified? It is good counsel then. And for the warmth that ripened us to this care of thee, be thankful, and enquire no further. But brother, methinks you are over-serious for a man that comes a-suiting.

Widow. He does not find your mirth take so well.

Enter Wildish *apart.*

Wild. 'Slight, here's sir John Everyoung. He'll spoil all if I don't take him off instantly.   113

Wildish *goes out, and brings in three of the widow's maids.*

Fore. Brother, brother, these frolics do you no right in the eye of the world.

Ever. Hang the world, give me the pretty black-eye of the widow.

[*A song.*

Wild. Gentlemen, here's work for you.

Ever. A muss, a muss! You see, Wildish, we found the house, though you would not tell us where it was. 'Tis dangerous to give a hint to men of our parts. Brother, take your widow, show her that you are so far qualified towards a bridegroom as to lead a country dance.

Widow. I'll have no dancing in my house.

Fore. You see they are a little merry. Humour 'em in this; they'll be gone the sooner.   124

Widow. Well, sir Samuel Forecast, anything to serve you.

They dance, and Forecast *steals away.*

Mod. Sir Samuel gone?

Ever. Faith, then the sport's at the best, let's all be gone. Farewell, widow, I have done my part; if thou fallest now, say thou hadst fair warning.

[*Exeunt omnes.*

---

101 precise] scrupulous   110 a-suiting] courting   118 muss] mess, state of confusion

ACT III   SCENE I

[The Lodgings of Eugenio *and* Philander.]

Enter Eugenio, *and* Philander.

Eug. Dear friend, I am in doubt whether I shall
This 'scape, a blessing, or misfortune, call;
Since now I live to hear, Althea must
Be to her duty or to me unjust.
Ye powers that were so kind my life to spare,
Oh why was not my love as much your care?
You saved my life, that I might live to feel
Despair can wound as mortally as steel.
My cause till now my antidote has been,
'Gainst all the mischief it could plunge me in;   10
The strictest prison I have freedom thought,
And been on scaffolds without terror brought.
But these few words: 'Althea is a bride'
More wound my soul than can the world beside.
Phil. Why does Eugenio fancies entertain,
That are Althea's wrongs and his own pain?
Like boys, who in the dark, strange shapes create
In their own brain, themselves to tremble at:
Despair's the portion of the damned below,
And in a generous mind should never grow;   20
Trust to Althea's virtue, trust her love,
And you will safe in either of 'em prove.
Eug. But sure no friend could so my quiet hate,
As this report, of nothing, to create.
Phil. Perhaps her father does no less intend,
And she a while her answer may suspend.
Not that her virtue doubts what it shall do,
But that she may gain time to speak with you:
Every black cloud does not with thunder swell,
Nor every symptom a disease foretell.   30
Some storms blow over; though thy fate appear
Thus gloomy now, anon it may be clear.
Eug. It may, but who can unconcernèd be,
A tempest heard and his whole wealth at sea?
I with more ease all other harms could bear,

Than of Althea's loss but simply hear.
Phil. All that we hear, we are not to believe.
Eug. Our hopes do oft'ner than our fears deceive.
Phil. The advantage man o'er beasts in reason gets
    He pays with interest in fond conceits;   40
    They cannot fear misfortune till it fall,
    And when 'tis gone remember't not at all:
    But man 'gainst his own rest in battle placed,
    Feels mischiefs ere they come, and when they're past.
    The smiles of fortune you so false have found,
    Methinks, you should not mind her when she frowned:
    How would Althea's virtues grieve to find
    Themselves suspected in Eugenio's mind!
    Like princes murdered on the royal throne,
    Where 'till that minute they had brightest shone.   50
Eug. Sure my Althea cannot disapprove
    These fears that spring but from excess of love.
    Of love and courage none too much can share.
Phil. But 'tis their use that does their worth declare:
    Courage, when brutal, ceases to be brave,
    And love, grown jealous, can no merit have.
Eug. A higher mark of love there cannot be,
    We doubt no lover, whom we jealous see.
Phil. So fevers are of life sure proofs we know,
    And yet our lives they often overthrow;   60
    Diseases, though well cured, our bodies mar,
    And fears, although removed, our loves impair:
    True love, like health, should no disorder know.
Eug. But who, alas! such love, or health can show?
    Our passions, like ourselves, are framed to die,
    And have still something they must perish by;
    We none (brave friend) for being hapless blame,
    But all allow, 'tis baseness to be tame;
    He that has raised this tempest in my mind,
    Shall in the billows his own ruin find;   70
    I'll fight him instantly, and make him know,
    I am not more his rival than his foe.
Phil. Thy life, alas, dear friend's no longer thine,
    Thou hast engaged it in a brave design:
    Thy bleeding country, and thy prince's right,
    Are th' only quarrels that thy sword should fight;
    If you into the tyrant's hands should fall,

'Twould pull a sudden ruin on us all.
Which, if you stir, we may have cause to fear,
Since tyrant's eyes and hands are everywhere.   80
Eug. Now thou has touched me in the tend'rest part,
Though love possess, honour must rule my heart;
My nation's fate's too great a sacrifice
For me to make though to Althea's eyes;
No, I am calmed, and happy am to have
A friend so full of temper when I rave,
And hope the gods, whilst I my own neglect,
To fight their quarrel, will my love protect.

                                                        [*Exeunt.*

SCENE II

[*A Room in* Sir John Everyoung's *House.*]

Enter Victoria *and* Olivia.

Vict. Sister, I doubt we are a little too free with our servants, this Modish
and his friend Estridge. Few plays gain audience by being in print, and
fewer women get husbands by being too much known.

Oliv. But ours are most accomplished monsieurs—must be assaulted on all
parts ere they'll yield, must have their ears charmed as well as eyes. 'Twere ill
husbandry in a mercer to be thrifty in his patterns; it often disparages a good
stuff. And too great reserv'dness in one of us, especially at the first, might
give a discouragement to our further acquaintance.

Vict. Now might I have my wish, I would come all new, nay my voice
and name should not be known. Where I would be liked, I would have the
few charms I am mistress of, make their assault at an instant, all at one time.

For sure Horatio did their power subdue,   12
By conquering one, ere he another knew.

Oliv. Fie, sister, think no more of him! But to the matter in hand, whoever
caught anything with a naked hook? Nothing venture, nothing win, and for
my part I am resolved to allow all innocent liberty. This matrimony is a pill
will scarce down with a young man without gilding. Let Estridge believe I am
in love with him, and when he leaves me he'll find I am not.

Enter to them Wildish.

Wild. So he will, when he marries you, or I am deceived, madam.

Vict. What, turned eaves-dropper, Mr. Wildish?   20

Wild. No, ladies, but your heads are so taken up with these heirs apparent, that you can't see a younger brother when he comes into the room.

Oliv. Not when our backs are towards him; but otherwise as an elder, anywhere but before a parson.

Wild. You are in the right. Jointure and allowance for clothes have clearly got the better off. Dear madam, I consider not your portion but your person; give your estate where you please, so you will but settle your affection upon me. My fate depends upon your answer; and the like artillery of unlanded lovers. But I never repine at that, for fine women, like great tables, though they are maintained by men of fortunes, are ever open to men of parts.

Oliv. Why now, Wildish, you talk like yourself again. Ever since I saw you last I have been in most terrible apprehension of a whining copy of verses.

Wild. 'Expectation', you mean, madam! But 'tis not come to that yet. Though I talk a little extravagantly when I see you, I am not so thorough-paced a lover but I can express myself in prose.   35

Vict. But you, being a new convert, can't give too many marks of your devotion. And I should mistrust I were not as I ought to be in my servant's heart, if I did not run sometimes in his head, and then verses follow infallibly.

Wild. Faith, madam, that's much as the head lies. There are some you may search every cranny over, and not find three rhymes—very good lovers too. And to say truth, 'tis unreasonable a man should be put to seek fresh words to express that to his mistress, which has been as well said already by somebody else. I think 'tis very fair if he set his hand to't, and that I am ready to do the most passionate copy of verses you can find!

Oliv. How much love and constancy will you engage for then?   45

Wild. As much as you can find in that paper there.

He gives a paper to Olivia, *she gives it to* Victoria.

Oliv. Sister, here, read 'em. I shall put the accent in the wrong place, stop out of time, or one mischief or other, and so put my poor servant into an agony.

Vict. (*Reads the title.*) 'To a very young lady.'

Oliv. That's I, Wildish. Come, you have been dabbling. Proceed, sister, I fear 'em not; I have no more pity on a rhyming lover than on a beggar that begs in a tone.

Vict. Are not these verses somewhat too weak to allow?

Wild. Faith, madam, I am of your mind. Put a tune to 'em, 'tis an easy stanza.   56

53 in a tone] whining tone

(Sings.)

Vict.   *Ah Cloris! that I now could sit*
As unconcerned, as when
Your infant beauty could beget
No pleasure, nor no pain.   60

2.

When I the dawn used to admire,
And praised the coming day;
I little thought the growing fire
Must take my rest away.

3.

Your charms in harmless childhood lay,
Like metals in the mine,
Age from no face took more away,
Than youth concealed in thine.

4.

But as your charms insensibly
To their perfection pressed,   70
Fond love as unperceived did fly,
And in my bosom rest.

5.

My passion with your beauty grew,
And Cupid at my heart,
Still as his mother favoured you,
Threw a new flaming dart.

6.

Each gloried in their wanton part,
To make a lover he
Employed the utmost of his art,
To make a beauty she.   80

7.

Though now I slowly bend to love
Uncertain of my fate,
If your fair self my chains approve,
I shall my freedom hate.

8.

Lovers, like dying men, may well
At first disordered be,
Since none alive can truly tell
What fortune they must see.

Enter a Servant.

Serv. There's an old gentleman below in a chair enquires for Mr. Wildish. As fine as an emperor—my master sir John is nobody to him! As he peeped through the glass, I thought it was sir Samuel Forecast. 91

Vict. It is impossible it should be he.

Wild. Yes, faith, it is, ladies. I am privy to the plot.

Oliv. Good Mr. Wildish, bring him up. I would give anything to see him.

Wild. Do you step into that closet then, for I must swear the coast is clear. Set the door a little open and you may see him perfectly. His bravery, on my word, is not designed for this place, and he is so politic that he will think your seeing him may be a prejudice to his design.

Wildish *goes out, and brings in* Sir Samuel Forecast.

Wild. Sir Samuel, now you shine indeed. My cousin will be ravished to see you transform yourself thus for her sake. 100

Fore. She is a tender piece, and though her discretion helps her to conceal it, in her heart cannot but love a little bravery. I have two laces in a seam more than my brother Everyoung, and a yard more in my cravat.

Wild. Nay, you are most exact, and in this dress methinks not unlike sir John.

Fore. I came only to show myself to you, and am for my widow presently. Shall I have your company?

Wild. I have a little business here but I'll be with you by that time you are there. I see you came in a chair. 109

Fore. Do you think I had a mind to have the boys follow me in the streets? Pray be secret, Mr. Wildish, for I would have nobody know I am in this dress but yourself and your fair cousin, for a world. And therefore I will make haste from hence. Do you follow me according to your promise.

[*Exit.*

Wild. I shall, sir Samuel.

Oliv. I never saw a city-bridegroom so frizzed, so laced, so perfumed, and so powdered in my life!

Vict. I think verily he was painted too! I vow I should not have known his worship if you had not given us a hint of his bravery before.

Wild. Well, I must recover my old knight. Farewell, ladies.

Oliv. Pray be here anon, and give us an account of this adventure. 120

Vict. Certainly it must be very pleasant.

Wild. I shall obey you, ladies. [*Exit* Wildish.

Enter Everyoung; Victoria *and* Olivia *laughing.*

Ever. Hey-day! what, are the girls mad?

Vict. No, sir, but I think my uncle Forecast's little better.

Ever. Why, what of him?

115 frizzed] with curled hair

Oliv. He is, sir, at this time the greatest spark in London; dressed so like you that if his condition required it I should think, sir, he were going to a scrivener to personate you for a good sum.

Ever. Well, I'll handsel his new clothes and put him as much out of conceit with bravery as ever he was in his life. Boy, call in the three prentices were brought before me for breaking windows last night.   131

Enter three Prentices.

I suppose, young men, you would not scruple at a small piece of service to the man that should procure your liberties.

Omnes. Free us, and command us anything.

Ever. Well then, follow me, and when I show you a certain chair, take the gentleman out of it and cudgel him. I'll be at a little distance, and if you want help, be ready to assist you. Be sure you call him sir John Everyoung and tell him of a lady he affronted.

1 Pren. We shall call him what you please, sir, and beat him as much as you please.   [*Exit* Victoria *and* Olivia.

SCENE *changes.* [*A Street.*]

Forecast *coming by in his chair.*

Ever. That's the chair.

They take out Forecast, *and cudgel him.*

Fore. If you have humanity, if you had women to your mothers, be more merciful, gentlemen! I never injured you nor saw any of you in my life.

[*1*] *Pren.* I perceive, sir John Everyoung, you have forgot the affront you did a lady last night.

Fore. What affront, sir? What lady?

[*1*] *Pren.* The affront, sir, was a great affront, and the lady a great lady that thinks fit to have you beaten for't.

Fore. You mistake, gentlemen, you mistake! For as I am a true servant to the state, I never did kindness or injury to any lady since I was in commission.   11

2 Pren. A true servant to the state, and a man in authority! He shall have three kicks more for that.

Enter Estridge *and* Modish.

128 scrivener] money lender 129 handsel] initiate with ridiculous ceremonies 10-11 in commission] in office

Est. What, three upon one! Whoe'er he be, the cause becomes a gentleman. Let's rescue him at all adventures.

They draw; the Prentices *run away.*

Fore. Estridge and Modish! Nay then, I am utterly undone. I have only 'scaped a little more beating to be laughed at as long as I live.

Est. Sir, we are very happy that our occasions led us this way, since it has given us an opportunity of serving a gentleman especially oppressed by odds.

Fore. I shall take some other time, if you will let me know where to wait on you, to give you thanks for this your seasonable assistance. Now, gentlemen, my hurts require a chirurgion.   [*He offers to go away.*

Mod. Nay, sir, take your hat and sword along with you; there they be.

[*He looks a little for 'em.*

I never heard any man speak so like sir Samuel Forecast in my life.   24

Est. But he is dressed very like Everyoung—a mere medley between the two brothers—but we'll see who he is before we go.

Mod. Have you received any hurt in your face that you cover it with your handkerchief?

Fore. A slight one only.

Est. I have sympathy-powder about me. If you will give me your handkerchief while the blood is warm, will cure it immediately.

Modish *snatches it off, and discovers him.*

Est. Sir Samuel Forecast, why do you hide yourself thus from your friends? We expected nothing for our pains; neither is your hurt so dangerous but it might endure the air.   34

Mod. Methinks you should rather have hid yourself from your enemies. But, sir Samuel, whatever the matter is, I never saw a man so fine in all my life.

Fore. Now the brokers take all fine clothes, and the jail all that love 'em! They have helped me to a fine beating.

Est. Why, do you think the rogues would have had more mercy on your high-crowned hat, black cap, and boots?

Fore. No, but they took me for my brother Everyoung, who, it seems, has lately affronted a lady, and I suffer for it.   43

Mod. The best advice we can give you is to go home and shift, for fear of more mishaps.

Est. Farewell, sir Samuel.   [*Exeunt omnes.*

---

30 sympathy-powder] remedy applied to patient's lost blood and curing 'by sympathy'
44 shift] change clothes

ACT IV   SCENE I

The Mulberry Garden.

Enter Jack Wildish.

Wild. I was to blame no earlier to use myself to these women of honour, as they call 'em; for now, like one that never practised swimming, upon the first occasion I am lost. There are men would have fooled with Olivia, and fooled her too, perhaps, by this time, without ever engaging in one serious thought. Your good fencer always thrusts in guard; he's but a novice that receives hit for hit. This Modish and Estridge—I know not what to make of their continual visits. . . . Methinks love and jealousy come too quick upon a man in one day.

Enter Modish *and* Estridge.

Here come the men! They are open enough to let me know all at large; but I would fain contrive it that the ladies might be witnesses of their servants' most invincible secrecy. I'll steal off ere I am seen, and think on't.   11

Enter Victoria *and* Olivia; *as he goes out he meets 'em.*

Wild. Slip into that arbour, ladies, and trust me for once for a quarter of an hour's diversion.

Oliv. Pray, sister, let us go, he has somewhat in his head, I'm confident.

He puts them into an arbour, and meets Modish *in a walk.*

Wild. Your servant, Modish.

Mod. Oh, your servant!

Est. Your servant, Mr. Wildish.

Wild. What, is there store of game here, gentlemen?

Mod. Troth little, or none; a few citizens that have brought their children out to air 'em and eat cheese-cakes.   20

Wild. I thought this place had been so full of beauties that, like a pack of hounds in a hare-warren, you could not hunt one for another! What think you of an arbour and a bottle of rhenish?

Wildish brings 'em to the next arbour to the ladies.

Est. I like the motion well.

Wild. And how go the ladies? Will they go abroad alone? Are they come to kissing yet?

5 in guard] in a defensive posture   23 rhenish] Rhine wine, hock

Est. What ladies?

Wild. Why, sir John's daughters, the ladies.

Mod. You are merry, Mr. Wildish.

Wild. I should be so indeed, if it were with me as it is with you, gentlemen, that have two such fine women in love with you, and every night sitting up together till morning.   32

Mod. I go only to entertain Victoria in mere friendship to Ned Estridge. 'Tis he that is the happy man.

Est. 'Tis a part of friendship that you discharge very willingly, and very effectually, for sometimes we see neither of you in an hour! And then you return, exclaiming against the heat of the weather and cruelty of your mistress.

Wild. What, that she kept him a little too hard to't, or so?

Mod. Fie, Wildish, they are women of honour.

Wild. Well, here's their health, to make 'em amends! And, faith, they lose none with me, in being civil to an honest gentleman; 'tis the only wealth is left poor women to exercise their good nature with. A friend at court may get you a place, a general of an army give you an employment, a bishop a church-living, and a fair lady a good turn; every one in their way, and I hold him ungrateful that buries an obligation of any sort in silence. Besides, 'twere mere robbery to your friends not to let 'em rejoice in your good fortune.

Mod. But say I have made a vow to the contrary—not that there is, or ever was, any such good fortune; and women's favours, like the gifts of fairies, if once spoke of, vanish.

Wild. Oh, your servant! What say you, Estridge? Are you under a vow too, or are the favours you have received yet only such as the hope of further obliges you to secrecy for a while? But you are so serious, I doubt you intend to commit matrimony!   53

Est. Not as long as I can have simple fornication for love or money! I am not for those ladies that deal by wholesale. A bit off the spit serves my turn as well as the whole joint, and methinks has a prettier relish.

Wild. That is, metaphorically saying, you have sped with your mistress— my service to you, remembering the bit off the spit. (*Drinks to him.*) And how, is she buxom? Does she think happiness consists in motion, or in rest? What sect of philosophers is she of?

Est. A Pythagorean. I, sir, in all these cases say nothing.   61

Wild. Nay, you had as good speak out now, and make me your confidant.

Modish takes Estridge aside.

Mod. Jack Wildish is an honest fellow, 'tis not a pin's matter what we say to him; and they are two of the prettiest women in town. It sounds

---

38 hard to't] unremittingly copulating   59 buxom] pliant; gay; comely; plump
61 Pythagorean] ascetic, like Pythagoras

handsomely to boast some familiarity, you understand me? He knows 'em
not, and will never find us out. I'll begin with him.—I wonder, Wildish, we
could never get you along with us. The ladies have not vowed virginity—
they are no such bugbears as you take 'em for!

Wild. I take 'em for honest women, or, which is e'en as bad, pretenders to
it.   70

Est. There is no harm in pretending to it. That, like a high price, only
serves to keep off ill company.

Wild. Yes, yes, I know what kind of cattle they are, well enough. There's
no having a simple kiss amongst 'em without a journey into the country; nor
getting 'em abroad without a sister, or a cousin at least. And then they must
be at home too by ten o'clock, have the syllabubs and tarts brought into the
coach to 'em; drink more sugar than wine, and so foul all the glasses; put
you to four or five pound charge, and let you see nothing but themselves,
that's man's meat, for't! I have been once or twice plagued with such animals
as these.   80

Mod. Can'st thou imagine, Wildish, we would fool away our time with such
shadows of women as thou describ'st? We have solid and substantial pleasures.

Wild. What? a ribbon, or a lock of hair, I warrant!

Mod. No, two young juicy girls that stick as close to us as the bark to the
tree, and part as unwillingly from us as green fruit does from the stone! And
all this through the reputation of sober and discreet servants to their pleasure.
If such a scandalous fellow as thou come into the house without our introduction, the ladies would cry out, 'Oh my honour!' as far as they could see
thee.   90

Wild. Methinks sir John Everyoung (an old smell-smock as he is) should
take the alarm, and so remove these so juicy girls.

Est. I hope you don't think we mean his daughters all this while? That were
a trick indeed. We speak of two ladies that shall be nameless.

Wild. Faith, gentlemen, I can speak of none such, for all my acquaintance
have two or three names apiece, I assure you.

Mod. Well, Jack, to return your civility in the last health you began,
here's to all those incomparable ladies, that like Roman conquerors have two
or three names apiece! But if thou wouldst leave this rambling, thou wouldst
lose nothing by it. There's as hard drinking in gentlemen's houses now-a-
days as at taverns, and as hot service in many a lady's chamber as at Gifford's.

Wild. But how should a man do to get into reputation? There are your men
of fashion, as well as stuffs, and they go out again nobody knows how.

Mod. 'Tis true. In the first place you must shake hands with your old

91 smell-smock] licentious man   96 names] normally only royalty had more than two
names   101 Gifford's] a notorious brothel   103 stuffs] worthless persons

friends, Hoquemore and Burgundy for a while; leave your Chaste Ling and
La-Frond's, dine with my lord Such-a-one one day, my lady What-d'you-
call'em another. And be sure to talk on't in the next company you come into,
drink wine and water at table, a dish of tea after dinner, like nothing but what
is French before the ladies, lose your money very much like a gentleman to
'em in the afternoon—and the work's done!   110

Wild. This is a hard chapter.

Est. If thou knew'st once the pleasure of such a sprightly girl as Olivia—
the kind quarrels, the fondness, the pretty sullenness after a little absence,
which must be charmed out of it with kisses, and those thousand other
devices that make a lover's happiness—thou wouldst think all this as easy as
lying a-bed in the country in a wet morning.

Mod. Or, if he could but see Victoria's reservedness a little mollified, and
brought to hand with a good supper and the fiddles.

Est. Or Olivia in her morning dress, with her guitar, singing to it most
enticingly, and then as kind in her discourse, her little breasts swelling and
pouting out as if they came half-way to be kissed.   121

Mod. Or the other's haughty look melted into smiles. The pretty combat of
pride and pleasure in her face . . . at some certain times!

Est. My mistress is in the very spring of beauty.

Mod. And mine in the midsummer of perfection.

Est. Mine is. . . .

Wild. Nay, gentlemen, one at once, and no quarrelling I beseech you!
You are happy men both, and have reason to be in love with your sweet lives,
but I thought Victoria had so obstinately doted oŋ her old servant Horatio
that there had been more hope of winning a widow at her husband's funeral
than of any favour for her now.   131

Mod. People will be talking, but on my word she'll ne'er break her heart
for Horatio. I and my fellow-labourer, time, have done his business.

Wild. You are the great masters of your art. These are the two beauties that
the whole town runs mad after.

Est. We know it, we know it! And it is no small part of our felicity to have
that lord send his coach and six to carry 'em to the park; this gentleman
offering to play at angel-beast with 'em, though he scarce know the cards
and has no more visible estate than what he may lose at a sitting: a third
begging to give 'em the four and twenty violins, which his father in the
county hears of and disinherits for, whilst the ladies put 'em off with some
slight excuses and send the whole town over after us.   142

Wild. You have 'em, it seems, in most excellent order!

Mod. Oh there's no true pleasure but in your person of quality. The others

105 Hoquemore] hock   105 Chaste Ling] Chatelain's French tavern   106 La-Frond's]
French tavern   138 angel-beast] card game

love all men so well, they can love none best. They are indeed, like your more
generous creatures, somewhat hard to tame, but I have seen a lion as gentle
as an ox. Time and industry will do anything!

Est. Come, drink a glass round.

Mod. I can't get down a drop of this wine more without a frolic.

Wild. Every man name the woman that has obliged him last, and drink all
their healths in a brimmer!   151

Mod. Content. Begin Estridge.

Est. Olivia! Now, Modish, name yours.

Mod. Victoria, Victoria! We must have your person too, Wildish.

Wild. Mistress Betty.

Mod. Betty what?

Wild. Nay faith, I can go no further, and may very well be mistaken in that
too!

Est. Here's a lock of hair. Shall I dip it for one glass more?

Wild. Whose is it first?   160

Est. Olivia's, whose should it be? Black as jet and shining as her eyes.
Here's her picture too, in little.

Wildish steps a little aside, and looks upon it.

Wild. (*Aside.*) Oh impudence! His sister's picture! He forgot he showed
me a month ago. This lock of hair, produced so confidently, frighted me a
little, till I saw the colour.

Enter to them Snappum.

Snap. Gentlemen, I beg your pardon for pressing thus rudely into your
company, but the business concerns no less than all my fortunes. I have been
long a suitor to a rich widow, and have at last prevailed with her to marry me
suddenly.

Est. What is that to us, sir?   170

Snap. Wildish, you'll, I hope, make my excuse to your friends. Coming
into the garden about half an hour ago, I lost a bracelet of her hair, wrought
with her own hands, so that there is no deceiving her with a counterfeit. A
waiter here tells me he saw one of you take up such a thing.

Wild. Is this it?

Est. That's mine, and composed of hair so dear to me that I would fight
with Hector, the top of your order, for least of 'em.

Snap. And I with Hercules for mine! But pray, Mr. Wildish, let me see it.
If it be that I look for, nobody will quarrel for't, for 'tis full of grey hairs, I
assure you.   180

---

159 dip] drink a toast to   162 in little] a miniature portrait

Wild. Shall he see it?

Est. No.

Wild. I'll make bold for once though.

[*Shows it him.*

Snap. 'Tis my old woman's!

Wild. By the mark I'll swear, for 'tis as grizzled as a silver-haired rabbit. I may venture to let him have it, Estridge, I suppose, mayn't I?

Est. Yes, yes—now I remember me, I sent mine to have a new string put to it.

Snappum *goes off*, Wildish *follows him a little way.*

Wild. Adieu, Snappum.

Snap. Are any of these gentlemen good bubbles, Mr. Wildish?   190

Wild. What do I know? You had best ask 'em!

Snap. No, I thank you, sir, I can be satisfied on easier terms. But you were always a lover of ingenuity; pray tell me.

Wild. Away, away!

[*Exit* Snappum. Wildish *returns.*

I'm sorry your mistress has grey hairs so young; I doubt you are not kind to her, Estridge.

Mod. Nay, Wildish, don't insult upon a mistake.

Estridge *is out of countenance, and looking up and down,*
sees the women in the next arbour.

Est. I think we have neighbours in the next arbour, and fine women they seem to be in their masks.

Mod. Let's entertain 'em.—What, ladies, come a-padding for hearts here in your vizards? A pretty device to make a man in love with he can't tell who!   202

Est. What, rob us of our liberties without one word? Not so much as stand and deliver?

Oliv. If we should rob you of your hearts, gentlemen, 'twere but petty larceny; Victoria and Olivia would never send hue and cry after us.

Mod. You know us, madam.

Oliv. Yes, gentlemen, somewhat better than we did this morning, though I always supposed no less.

Est. Than what?   210

Oliv. Than that you were the vainest coxcombs in the whole town— fellows that would hate a woman that were kind to you because she takes from you the pleasure of belying her.

Est. Olivia?

190 bubbles] dupes   200 a-padding] robbing

Oliv. The very same, sir, whose picture you have in your pocket, and about whose hair you had like to have quarrelled so manfully but now; who sends all the town after you, and puts others off with slight excuses; the obliging lady whose health you drank by that name.

Est. 'Twas another Olivia I meant—one I knew abroad.

Vict. And another Victoria that you meant, Modish?   220

Mod. Right, right! My landlady's daughter ... at the Cheval d'Or ... since gone into a monastery.

Oliv. The daughters of a French Everyoung, I warrant too.

Est. La Jeunesse was their father, which is all one with Everyoung in English.

Mod. On our honours, ladies, we were ever most tender of your dear credits, and are heartily sorry our mistresses light to be of your names.

Oliv. Pray will you do me favour to let me see my picture? I'm confident 'tis very like me.

Est. Your French name-sakes you mean, madam? That maladroit Wildish let it fall and broke the crystal, and I sent it just now away to have a new one put to it, as I hope to be saved, madam.   232

Mod. But, madam, could you think me so senseless as discourse of you at that rate? Here's Jack Wildish has heard us speak of these wenches a hundred times.

Wild. (*Apart.*) 'Slight, these fellows will lie themselves into credit again if I han't a care of 'em instantly.—Gentlemen, I understand no winks; the few lies I'll venture upon I am resolved to keep for my own use.

Est. Prithee, Wildish, help us but this once.

Wild. No, no, go on, methinks you are in a very fair way. I am a stranger; the ladies won't mind what I say.

Oliv. Yes, yes, we'll take your word.   242

Wild. Why then, ladies, I assure you upon the honour of a gentleman, and by my friendship to those worthy persons, I dare answer they are too much servants to discourse so long of any thing but yourselves. And for the French women—you know as much of 'em as I, having never heard tittle of 'em till this minute.

Vict. You have brought a very sufficient witness with you, gentlemen; we do believe him.

Mod. Ours is not the first good cause has been lost by ill witnesses. But I perceive, ladies, you don't know Jack Wildish. He is the verriest droll in the whole town—has a hundred of these fetches.   252

Est. (*To* Wildish *apart.*) Pox on't, thou mayst bring all off yet.

Wild. (*Aloud.*) Faith, my conscience won't give me leave to deceive a lady

227 light] chance

in a friend's behalf.—[*Aside.*] To do it now, and in my own, is all I can obtain of it.

[Estridge *comes up to* Wildish.

Est. 'Sdeath, sir. . . .

Wild. Nay, Estridge, no huffing, you know I mind it not, and 'tis uncivil to fright your mistresses.

Mod. But that we are two to one, and scorn advantages, you should not carry it off thus.   261

Wild. I should be more afraid if you were three to one—but some other time for these matters.

Oliv. Never blame Wildish; we were all the while in the next arbour, so that if he had taken your cue never so readily 't had done you little service.

Vict. Gentlemen, this matter will bear no more raillery. We are sensible of our honours and the injury your extravagant discourse might have done us with any but so worthy a person as Mr. Wildish. But he, we are confident, understands himself too well to have any ill thought of us from your vanity. We can do no less than forbid you our house, and pray forbear it without further ceremony.   271

Wildish takes Victoria; Estridge offers to take Olivia; she refuses.

Oliv. No, sir, you'll say I come to pick you up in the garden one time or other.   [*Exeunt omnes.*

[SCENE II]

[Outside Sir Samuel Forecast's House.]

Enter Eugenio like an Officer, and three more.

Sir Samuel Forecast above.

Enter a Servant.

Serv. Sir, there are some soldiers below say they must search your house for some suspicious person.

Fore. I warrant they mean Eugenio and Philander! I am utterly undone, suspected for a traitor, and all long of those ungracious girls! I am very glad I have got my Christian cloth on again. Go and let 'em in.

Eug. Sir, I hope you will excuse us, we do but follow our orders, and having searched your house for some dangerous persons will leave it you

258 huffing] bullying   4 long of] because of

again in peace. Eugenio and Philander were your sons, and therefore most probably judged to have made your house their sanctuary.

Fore. My house their sanctuary! I had rather it should be their grave. Since they made the state their enemy, I have been so too.   11

Eug. Then you have no thoughts of 'em for your daughters?

Fore. No, sir, I assure you! And to remove all doubt, Althea's shortly to be married to Horatio (one that will bid you welcome, sir, if you please to come to the wedding) and I hope to dispose of Diana ere long to some honest gentleman of our party.

Enter Althea.

Fore. I command you, on my blessing, to answer all things this gentleman questions you about, precisely, as it were myself.

Eug. Sir, you do well, but you must retire a little whilst we examine your daughters. A man, though never so well meaning himself, can't answer for others.   21

[*Exit* Forecast.

Eug. Lady, your father here has showed himself a faithful subject to the commonwealth. It now remains to know what correspondence you entertain with Eugenio and Philander, your former servants.

Alth. Upon my honour, not the least! We are too strictly watched to have a correspondence with any man, and are too careful of ourselves to hold one with persons so obnoxious.

Eug. Are you resolved you never will?

Alth. As things are now they never shall.

Eug. Must you then marry Horatio?   30

Alth. My father tells me so, and I have hitherto been dutiful.

Eug. Horatio's an accomplished gentleman.

Alth. He is, sir, and worthy of more happiness than I can bring him to.

Eug. (*Aside.*) By heaven, she loves him.—You loved Eugenio once, and gave vow for vow.

Alth. I did perhaps.

Eug. A stranger and an enemy as he is, I pity him.

Alth. 'Tis noble in you, sir, but we must all obey our fortunes.

Eugenio *lets fall his disguise.*

Eug. And curse 'em too, if they be all like mine,
That love where beauty, and not virtue, shine.   40
Oh that the tyrants knew that I were here!
Death does more lovely now than life appear.
Since thou art false, 'tis she alone has charms;
Neglected love rests only in your arms:

When I am dead you may your choice avow
Without reproach, which sure you cannot now:
And I shall want the sense of all my wrongs,
My death both to my rest, and thine belongs.
Alth. Can this Eugenio be, and so unkind?
What strange distemper rages in thy mind? 50
Could once my soul of a base thought allow,
He that believes me false should find me so.
Eug. Must you not, madam, with Horatio wed?
'Tis a belief that your own words have bred.
Alth. Forgive my fear, if any word of mine
Unto that hateful sound seemed to incline:
Your rude appearance, of a soldier, made
My tender heart and very love afraid:
I durst not speak what most I did believe,
But used such words as you would best receive. 60
Eug. Alas! Althea, what you told me here,
Did not create, although increase, my fear:
That you must make him happy is not new,
Nor did I learn the killing sounds from you;
The streets are full of it, and everywhere
I can of nothing but this hymen hear.
Alth. 'Tis true, my father does a match design
'Twixt me and this Horatio, and does join
Threats to commands, urges th' uncertain state
Of your affairs, your party, and the fate 70
Of such as do a well-formed power invade;
How they are always conquered or betrayed.
My beauty, fatal to itself the while,
Inflames Horatio, and discourse, like oil,
Foments the fire: of such a love he tells,
As would prevail but where your image dwells;
But still in vain the heart I gave to you,
The one does threaten, and the other woo.
Eug. An absent lover ill maintains the field:
Does not my image to his presence yield? 80
Alth. 'Twere just that faith which you so ill deserve,
For one of nobler thoughts I should reserve.
Eug. We oft are made by a too great concern,
Like too much light, unable to discern.
The leave I gave to your surprise so late,
Now for my own distraction I intreat.

Where there is much of love, there will appear
Mixed with our boldest hope some little fear.
Alth. That fear in a true lover soon would die,
  Which to my virtue is an enemy.   90
Eug. Hope is the passion of a calmer breast,
  But high concernments are with doubt oppressed.
  To few, alas, is such assurance given
  Not to fear hell, although they hope for heaven.
  I not your virtue, but my fate accuse,
  Which still does me with highest rigour use.
Alth. Though fate, Eugenio, for misfortune meant,
  I would refuse to be the instrument.
  That dire necessity it seldom gave
  Of harming them, whom we would only save.   100
Eug. But hark, I think I hear a noise of swords.
Alth. The sound, alas, no room for doubt affords.
  You might perhaps be safe in your disguise.
Spoken within by soldiers. Where are the rest of 'em? Down with the doors
there!
Eug. Their sudden coming all such hope denies;
  'Tis me they seek; I am betrayed. But yet
  Since I can't shun, I'll try to break the net.
  This paper will inform your sister where
  She may of her unhappy servant hear,   110
  Make him remove, help him to shun that fate
  Which does for the unblessed Eugenio wait.
  My rival in their head! By all the gods,
  Horatio, this is an unmanly odds!
  Yet if on thee I can but fall revenged,
  I life for death most happily have changed.
Hora. Eugenio here! I thought of nothing less;
  But my clear meaning this will best express.

                    He fights on Eugenio's *side.*

      Officer. Down with 'em both.

                The soldiers prevail; they are taken.

Eug. Sir, let my life the cruel forfeit pay,   120
  And bear not rashly so much worth away.
  Horatio was too far by virtue led,
  And saved that blood he nobly should have shed:
  He being my rival feared the world might say,

He for my hated life this train did lay.
Honour engaged his sword in my defence,
And honour is a kind of innocence.

Hora. Eugenio, leave to intercede for me.
  I only grieve I could not rescue thee,
  That so thou might'st thy preservation owe 130
  To the same virtue thou so ill didst know:
  And I some fitter time might make thee own
  The injustice of thy mean aspersion,
  To think I came thus rudely to invade
  The place where all that I adore is laid;
  And then to take my rival in a snare,
  Where if I would I knew I could not spare,
  Was an affront thou with that life hadst paid,
  Which I defended: but revenge shows base,
  Which on our honour more dependence has. 140

Eug. Some other time for this dispute we'll take,
  Revenge, by threatening, we the harder make.

Officer. Come, gentlemen, you must away, my orders press; you will have time enough to talk of these things in the Tower.

Enter two Soldiers *bringing in* Sir Samuel.

Officer. Sir, you must along.

Fore. Who, I! For what?

Officer. For harbouring Eugenio here, a known enemy to the state.

Fore. You brought him with you for ought I know—I ne'er saw his face. I answered an officer, and two soldiers that came to search for him even now, and as I thought, gave 'em satisfaction. But when I heard the clashing of swords, because I would not be made accessory to anything that might happen, I confess I retired into a corner of my garret. 152

Officer. Sir, this won't satisfy. The receiver is as bad as the thief. I have found a traitor in your house, and you shall answer it.

Fore. Eugenio, you are an honest gentleman, pray speak. Did I know anything of your being here?

Eug. Not in the least, sir: but my word, I fear, will do you little service.

Enter Wildish.

Wild. What, Sir Samuel, again under persecution? Nay, faith, I can do you no service now; these are a sort of gamesters I dare not meddle withal.

Fore. I am undone! Here's Eugenio found in my house, and they are carrying him to the Tower. 161

144 Tower] Tower of London, used as a prison

Wild. Come, bear up, sir; if there come a turn you'll be a great man.

Fore. I shall be hanged on that side, and to speak my own conscience, I have deserved it.

Wild. No, to lie in prison for concealing cavaliers will be great merit. And let me tell you, as a friend, there's like to be a turn suddenly. 'Tis thought the general will declare like an honest man; I say no more. Therefore carry yourself moderately; this accident may chance to do you good service if you have the grace to make the right use on't. But how came Eugenio and Horatio of a side?   170

Fore. I came but just now among 'em, and know nothing. But 'tis a strange thing a man can't be believed in his own defence. Carry me to prison? I'll see what justice's hand they have for't.

Officer. We shall find hands enough, ne'er fear it.

[*Exeunt omnes.*

ACT V   SCENE I

[Philander'*s Lodgings.*]

Enter Philander *solus.*

Phil. 'Tis strange I nothing of Eugenio hear,
   So long an absence may be worth a fear:
   His friendship was not wont to hide from me
   Of his most secret thoughts the new decree.
   I doubt his love, impatient of delay,
   Has to Althea found some desperate way,
   His passion could not my slow cure attend,
   On which, alas, he did in vain depend.
   I was to blame, no sooner to provide
   Against deluded hope's unruly tide;   10
   Which now I fear has borne him on a shelf,
   Where he'll unkindly perish by himself.

Enter Diana *in man's clothes.*

Ha! a strange face! would I had not been seen;
But 'tis too good for treason to lurk in.

167 general] Monk, instrumental in restoring Charles II   173 hand] warrant

Sure, gentle youth, the place you have mistook,
I cannot be the man for whom you look?
Diana. Philander, in your troubled face I read
Some apprehensions that you are betrayed:
But when you shall my woeful story hear,
A juster sorrow will remove your fear.   20
Phil. Thou hast my name, and yet I know thee not;
Quickly untie, sweet youth, this painful knot.
Diana. Know you this hand?
Phil. Alas, it is my own;
This from Eugenio could be had or none:
Speak, is he dead? Is this his legacy?
And has he sent it, gentle youth, by thee?
Has he Horatio fought? Killing, or slain,
He almost equally would breed my pain.
Diana. He and Horatio fought, but on a side.   30
Phil. What wonder beyond this can fate provide!
I knew, Eugenio, thou wert always brave,
And that thy love was still thy honour's slave.
Diana. On your friend's part you have the virtue brought,
But 'twas Horatio for Eugenio fought.
Phil. Such a prodigious union could not fail.
Diana. A band of soldiers did o'er both prevail.
Phil. Is my unhappy friend a prisoner made?
Diana. He is, and close in the white Tower laid:
He bade me tell you so, that you might shun   40
The desperate hazard that his life must run.
Phil. How came he, gentle youth, thus to expose
My life to one whom he so little knows?
Diana. I am his near relation, and have been
Privy to all design he has been in.
He bids you to remove without delay,
For y'are endangered hourly by your stay:
The soldiers about him a paper took,
Which, though obscurely, of your lodging spoke.
Phil. In vain we to that wretch good counsel give,   50
Resolved to perish, and unfit to live:
When he is gone, what business have I here?
What can again be worth a hope or fear?
The hour he dies, this shall be my relief,
If I could need another wound than grief.

                                        (*Pointing to his sword.*)

Diana. How can you hope to please Eugenio's ghost,
　　In killing him whom he esteems the most?
　　In life our friends we choose, but those we hate
　　We rather wish companions of our fate:
　　If I a present to his shade would send,   60
　　It should be of his foe, and not his friend.
　　But yet I hope Eugenio may escape;
　　Safety has come in an unlooked for shape.
Phil. That hope alone makes me consent to live.
Diana. Can you for life no other reason give?
Phil. None that, alas! is fit for thee to hear.
Diana. Does then Diana's heart so vile appear?
Phil. I hope thou wilt my better genius prove,
　　Since thus thou know'st my business and my love.
Diana. She tells me you have often filled her ears   70
　　With gentle words, and wet her arms with tears;
　　Vowed that your hope and fear, grief and delight,
　　Her frowns or favours only could excite.
Phil. Why so I did, sweet youth, and told her true,
　　But I'm amazed it should be known by you.
Diana. Of late she has worn a face of discontent,
　　That seemed neglected friendship to lament:
　　Eugenio to her sister found a way,
　　Though various hazards in his passage lay.
Phil. Unwisely he the short-lived pleasure sought,   80
　　Too soon 'twas paid for, and too dearly bought;
　　Like Orpheus for one poor untimely look,
　　He has the hope of all he loved forsook.
Diana. That haste expressed a passion, though to blame:
　　Impatience is of love the best extreme.
Phil. That heir's accursed, that for a present sum
　　Resigns the hope of all he has to come.
　　I would Diana to the world prefer,
　　And for her venture anything but her.
　　But, gentle youth, methinks thou speak'st as though   90
　　Thou mad'st a doubt, whether I loved or no.
Diana. Pray heaven Diana mayn't: your fault was great,
　　To think of honour when the day was set
　　For Hymen's rites; when nought else could destroy
　　Your hopes, which then were ripening into joy,
　　You were a traitor to the state declared,
　　And in the glittering toils of fate ensnared.

Phil. Be witness, heaven, and all ye powers above,
    That see our infant passions weakly move,
    E'er they have force into the face to climb,   100
    Or to one action can our wills incline,
    If ever, for one moment, in my breast
    I gave to any, she inspired not, rest.
Diana. Why did you then such daring projects frame,
    And danger court that not concerned your flame?
Phil. 'Tis true, before I knew Diana's charms,
    I courted fame in danger and in arms,
    And thought no cause could lasting glory bring,
    Like the just quarrel of our injured king.
    Eugenio's friendship too that fire improved,   110
    And made me wed that cause I ever loved:
    What since I did was on a former score,
    My fate she can't condemn, but must deplore.
    I was in honour pre-engaged too far,
    E'er to retire, and yet to merit her.
    But whence could'st thou this hated knowledge gain?
    He worse than kills, who makes me live in pain:
    Thy beauty, youth, and words do all persuade,
    Thou happy in her nearest trust art made.

        Diana *here drops a ring, pulling out a handkerchief.*

Ye gods! the ring I to Diana sent!   120
Do not frail man beyond his nature tempt.
The good thou hast done, I thus forget it all,
And let my vengeance on my rival fall.   [*He draws.*
Draw, or I'll leave thee dead upon the ground.

        She pulls off her periwig.

Diana. I dare not draw ... and sure you dare not wound.
Phil. With sudden light I for a while am blind,
    I fought a rival, and a mistress find;
    Where I thought all my rage, my love is due,
    So high a pitch my wishes never flew;
    I am not by degrees to pleasure led,   130
    Nor slowly made the doubtful steps to tread,
    But in an instant, my exalted mind
    Feels all her hopes set free, and fears confined:
    So kings in battles that they gave for gone,
    Redeem their own and win another crown.

Diana. That faith, which nothing should in question bring,
    From a few words you doubt, and from a ring:
    How can I hope a lasting friendship, where
    So light appearance brings so mean a fear?
Phil. Such a surprise a jealous pang might give   140
    To any breast where so much love does live.
    But why, Diana, in this strange disguise?
    Was it to make me happier by surprise?
Diana. Could I my fear, as well as love o'ercome,
    You'd been preserved, and never known by whom;
    Such a concern I would not have betrayed,
    Till I were surer of your passion made.
Phil. What accident, ill understood, could prove
    Of that dire force to make you doubt my love?
    You needs must know how we were all betrayed,   150
    And the hard 'scape I and Eugenio made;
    And since, it had been fatal to be seen,
    So that this chamber my whole world has been.
Diana. What made me doubt, it matters not to know,
    Let it suffice I do no longer so.
    The dreadful sword, which at my breast you held,
    Though with much fear I with more joy beheld:
    For he that truly does his rival hate,
    Declares he loves his mistress at that rate.
Phil. Look on thyself, and measure thence my love,   160
    Think what a flame so bright a form must move:
    That knot be confident will ever last,
    Which passion tied, and reason has made fast.
Diana. Farewell, Philander, think on what I've said,
    And kindly judge the weakness of a maid.
Phil. Thou art too cruel in so short a stay;
    Thus would I gaze my very fight away.
Diana. Though for your safety nothing was too dear,
    Now give me leave for my own self to fear.   [*Exit* Diana.
Phil. She has appeared like lightning to my sight,
    Which, when 'tis vanished, leaves a darker night.

                                      [*Exit* Philander.

[SCENE II]

[Outside the Entrance to the Mulberry Garden.]

Enter Estridge *and* Modish.

Est. 'Twas certainly that rogue Wildish that betrayed us; the arbour and bottle of wine were his motions.

Mod. Without all peradventure, you saw the ladies, when they threw us off, took him home with 'em, nothing could be plainer. . . . What think you if one of us fought him?

Est. Why, faith, I think we had e'en as good let that alone. Hang him, he'll fight; 'twas only a trick he put upon us, and let's rail it off, and serve him in his own kind.

Mod. As how?

Est. Do you remember a certain cousin of his that Everyoung carried us to, the widow of a rich alderman, who died suddenly, and left her all he had? This widow he intends for sir Samuel Forecast, and I make no question but he is to have a round sum for his good word. What think you now, if I order it that one of us marry this widow; then, I hope, we are sufficiently revenged?

Mod. But how is't possible? 15

Est. Nothing so easy. Her maid has promised me to persuade her to take a walk in the Mulberry Garden. This is a time there is little or no company there. 'Tis but waiting at the door with a trusty servant or two, and we may force her whither we please, and then of her own accord she'll marry either of us.

Mod. Why so?

Est. If for no other, for the same reason that men eat horse flesh in a siege— because she can come at nothing else! 23

Mod. If it were a foolish girl we might do somewhat with her indeed. But these widows are like old birds—not to be tamed. She'll fight and scratch, and fly about, there will be no enduring her.

Est. Fear nothing. When she considers she has no other way to save her reputation, she'll hear reason.

Mod. Well. But being equal adventurers, how shall we agree about the prize?

Est. He that marries her shall give the other a statute upon his estate, for two thousand pounds, a pretty good sum, and will serve to stop a gap.

Mod. Content, and I wish thee joy of her with all my heart. 32

Est. You shall find me as good a paymaster as her husband the old alderman would have been. But stand close; here she comes!

Enter the Widow *and her* Maid; *they seize 'em.*

Widow. Thieves, murders, villains! what do you mean?

Est. Nothing, nothing, but I'll make bold to stop that pretty mouth of thine, widow, for once.

They carry 'em off.

Mod. Whither shall we carry 'em?

Est. To a little house I have taken a quarter of a mile off for that purpose, where nobody could hear 'em though they had falconers' or huntsmens' voices.   [*Exeunt.*

[SCENE III]

[Inside the Tower.]

Enter Sir John Everyoung, *and* Sir Samuel Forecast.

Ever. Give you joy, brother, give you joy!

Fore. Of what?

Ever. Why, of your lieutenancy of the Tower. I know you can be here upon no other account, and indeed your fidelity to the public claims no less.

Fore. Sir, give you joy of your new suit and fair periwig there!

Ever. Faith, brother, it sits with no fortune today; whate'er's the matter, I was never worse put together in all my life, and but to congratulate your advancement would not have left the company I dined with.

Fore. I hope to return your kind visit in the Fleet, and see your daughters sell ale and cakes there, and your worship with fewer trappings on—for thither your extravagant courses point.   11

Ever. May my periwig never know a good day, nor be taken for my own hair again, but come off always with my hat if it cost me above twelve pounds.

Fore. Pox on your hat and your periwig! Can you tell how I shall get out?

Ever. No more than how you got in! But you are wise, and know business. Alas, I know nothing but how to sort ribbons, make horse-matches, throw away my money at dice, and keep myself out of the Tower.

Fore. Oh my ungracious girls!

Ever. What of them? Have they broke prison and taken sanctuary in the arms of some sturdy prentice, fencing master, brother of the blade, or any other inferior rascal? You were so strict to 'em I never looked for other.

Fore. Not so fast; but if you can be serious for a minute, do. They are virtuous, but Eugenio, a former servant to Althea, since declared a traitor to

9 Fleet] Fleet Street prison

the state, was taken in my house; I suspected to have been privy to his
being there, and so carried along with him hither. I protested my innocence
to the officers, urged my former service, but all would not do.

Ever. 'Slight! I hope you had more wit: this is the happiest accident that
ever befell mortal, for an old notorious Roundhead to be taken for a Cavalier
at this time! Why, I never thought it had been in you; this was a stratagem
might have become Machiavelli himself.   30

Fore. Why, what's the matter? All's well, I hope.

Ever. Yes, never better, the general has this day to some persons of
quality declared for the king. All Cavaliers are immediately to have their
liberty. Therefore make haste to reconcile with Eugenio and Philander. I
have an order for the delivery of all such prisoners as are here upon the account of loyalty to their prince.

Fore. Philander and Eugenio, on my daughters' account, will do me all the
service they can; and I hope to make some advantage of this imprisonment.

Ever. I'll go and release Eugenio, and bring him to you. Horatio is discharged already. Though we fall out now and then about trifles, we are
brothers, and ought to serve one another in matters of concern.   [*Exeunt.*

[SCENE IV]

[*A Room in* Sir John Everyoung's *House.*]

Enter Victoria, Olivia, *and* Wildish.

Wild. You see now, ladies, what fellows you cast your good opinions on. If
I said anything that was disrespectful to either of you, it ought to go for
nothing; I was merely your decoy in the business.

Oliv. We are very well satisfied on all hands.

Vict. Sure they'll never have the impudence to trouble us again.

Oliv. Now would I were married to Estridge, that I might plague him
soundly.

Wild. How can you make that a plague, madam?

Oliv. A hundred ways: I would never come home till three o'clock in the
morning; tumble my own handkerchief myself, to make him jealous; break
his soundest sleeps in commendation of his bosom-friend, and never leave
till I have made 'em quarrel; fold up all manner of papers, like love letters,
and burn 'em just as he comes into th' room.   13

Wild. I can tell you how to be revenged on him beyond all this.

27 'Slight] God's light—an oath   33 declared] declared his loyalty to

Oliv. Prithee how, Wildish?

Wild. Why, marry me, make a good wife to me, and let him hang himself for rage.

Oliv. I am not so inveterate an enemy; I'll forgive him rather! If I were your wife, I must board half a year with a friend in the country, tumble about the other half in most villainous hackneys, lie two pair of stairs high, and wear black farrendine the whole year about; see you when you had no money to play, and then be kissed out of a ring or a bracelet.   22

Wild. I would not use a city widow of five and fifty so, with seven small children! And am I to suffer nothing all this while?

Oliv. What can you suffer?

Wild. Why, the loss of that which is dearer than life, my liberty; be known for a married man, and so put myself out of all capacity of breaking gold, promising marriage, or any other way of ensuring myself to scrupulous young virgins I shall like hereafter.

Oliv. That is to be taken from the occasion of playing the rascal: is that all?

Wild. Not half; if I make but love to a chambermaid, I shall be answered, 'You have a sweet lady of your own, and why will you wrong her?' If I get acquainted with any young woman, after the fourth or fifth visit be looked upon by her father and mother worse than the tax gatherers in a country village. All this you count nothing?   35

Oliv. Not to a lover, Wildish.

Wild. Well, there is no service so desperate that a gallant man will shrink at if he like his reward. And to give his hand thus to a woman, in him that rightly understands what he does, is as bold an action as Mucius Scaevola's. Yet, that I may use it hereafter where and when I please, upon my dear Olivia I'll venture it.

Oliv. Softly—when you please, and where I please!

Wild. Content, madam. Will you do us the favour to be a witness?

Vict. Well Mr. Wildish, I'll dance bare-foot to serve you.

Wildish leads off Olivia.

Oliv. Hold, hold, Wildish, my heart fails me.   45

Wild. 'Slight, I had a qualm too, there's certainly a more than ordinary providence attends me. I shall 'scape yet, I am now in a twitter—like a gamester upon a great by, that is heartily afraid he shall lose it, and yet his love to the money won't suffer him to draw stakes. I must have her.

Vict. Nay now you are come thus far, e'en go on.

Oliv. Well, Wildish, give me thy hand. The first time thou anger'st me, I'll have a gallant; and the next, make thee a cuckold.   [*Exeunt.*

---

21 farrendine] cheap poplin-like material   39 Scaevola] who thrust his hand into burning coal to show courage   48 by] throw, in dicing

[SCENE V]

[A Room in Sir Samuel Forecast's *House.]*

Enter Horatio *and* Althea.

Hora. Madam, you know your father does command
  That you should shortly give me your fair hand
  Before a priest; but since I find no part
  Goes along with it of your generous heart,
  My mind the charming present can refuse,
  Fearing t'indulge a passion you accuse;
  My joy with your least trouble weighed must still
  Appear, to my own self the greater ill.
Alth. Such words as these, Horatio, but heap more
  Upon a debt that was too great before;   10
  I'm covered with confusion when I weigh
  How much I owe, how little I can pay:
  You may with ease a fairer mistress find,
  And with more ease such worth will make her kind;
  And if I e'er that happy virgin know,
  I'll sue to make her pay you what I owe.
Hora. To change your thoughts, I will no longer try,
  But with the stream I cannot turn, comply:
  I to Victoria will my suit renew,
  And hope to find an advocate in you.   20
Alth. You may command me, and Victoria's mind
  Is of itself to you too well inclined.
Hora. All this methinks should your belief persuade,
  I no contrivance with those villains had,
  To take my rival in so mean a way,
  But only came their sudden rage to stay:
  All that confusion, and surprise could do,
  My passion made me apprehend for you.
Alth. Horatio's honour does too brightly shine,
  To be accused of such a low design;   30
  Had you within the bounds of friendship stayed,
  Yourself and me you had both happy made.
Hora. With ease from friendship we to love are led;
  That slippery path who can securely tread?

Enter Sir Samuel Forecast, Sir John Everyoung, *and* Eugenio.

Alth. I see my father, and Eugenio here,
    And in all faces sudden joys appear.

Forecast, Everyoung, *and* Horatio *seem to discourse.*

Eug. Fortune, I pardon thee thy short-lived spite,
    I for thy constant temper took a fit,
    Th'art kind, and gentle, and 'tis we are blind,
    Who do mistrust the ways thou hast designed   40
    To make us blessed, though better than our own.
Alth. Can you have joy, and yet Althea none?
Eug. May I all misery first undergo,
    E'er joy divided from Althea know.
Alth. What is this wonder hangs upon thy tongue?
    Delay does only to ill news belong.
Eug. Madam, your father licenses my flame,
    And you alone can now oppose my claim;
    That cause which armies did in vain support,
    And noblest spirits did, successless, court,   50
    We shining in a bloodless triumph see,
    Without the dire effects of victory,
    For in the general's breast (the noblest scene)
    The fate of England has transacted been:
    On Albion's throne he will our monarch place,
    Our neighbour's terror, and our nation's grace,
    Whilst at his blessed approach all factious minds
    Vanish, like leaves before autumnal winds.
Alth. Such truth in love and loyalty y'ave shown,
    What less for both could by just heaven be done?   60
Eug. This happiness, though great, yet is not all;
    My dearest friend I soon shall brother call;
    Diana must his deathless flame repay.
Alth. Fate, to be pardoned, had no other way.
Eug. See how your father kindly strives to evade
    His former promise to Horatio made.
Alth. That work's so nobly in his breast begun,
    That a few words will finish what's undone:
    Horatio does all happiness despise,
    From my obedience, which my love denies.   70

Forecast *to* Eugenio.

Fore. Horatio has released me of my promise to him, and seeing your changeless love to one another, was resolved to have moved it to me, if I had not prevented him.

Eug. Such honour, noble youth, I must confess,
Gives wonder equal to my happiness.

Hora. Althea I resign; my guilty flame
Was too unjust to reach so fair an aim:
Victoria's wrongs did my success oppose,
And my lost passion its own penance grows.
So some offenders are their duty taught   80
By th' ill effect and nature of their fault.

Eug. My apprehensions by these words are cleared,
And I dare love that virtue which I feared.
In love alone this mystery we find,
Men best agree when of a different mind.

Hora. There now remains but one thing more to do,
'Tis that Philander may be sent for too.
But see, he comes.

Enter Philander.

Fore. Brother, if your daughter were here, we might have a dance. Sir, you are heartily welcome; I kept my girl safe for you, she has not been so much as blown upon since you saw her. I knew honest men would not be always kept from their own—there would come a time.

Phil. Sir, I was ever most obliged to you. . . .   93
Eugenio here! Then I am doubly blessed,
And only fear to be with joy oppressed.

Eug. The joys of friendship well prepare our mind
For the high raptures we in love shall find:
The name of brothers we shall soon obtain.

Phil. Friendship so perfect by no name can gain.

Enter Diana.

Fate is at length ashamed, or weary grown   100
Upon a flame you smiled so long, to frown;
As vessels tossed upon the raging main,
With greater joy the wished-for port obtain;
Our love this short, fierce tempest having past,
Will joys more high, since less expected, taste.

Diana. But in the storm did you throw nothing out?

Phil. Wrong not my love with so unkind a doubt.

Enter Everyoung, Victoria, Olivia, Wildish.

Ever. Wildish, thou'rt an honest fellow; I'm glad I found thee.

Wild. Sir, the honest fellow desires to be known to you by another name, having newly married your daughter Olivia.   110

Ever. When, pray, Mr. Wildish?

Wild. Just now, sir; the words are scarce out of our mouths.

Ever. Well, this is a day I could not have been angry if thou hadst got her with child upon a contract; but you might have asked my leave, ere you went about to make me a grandfather.

Wild. If I had had a good jointure to offer, so I would, but if I do make you a grandfather, 'tis not done maliciously, I'll swear!

Hora. My guilty cause myself I dare not plead,
     But beg your innocence will intercede:
     Since all my fault your matchless beauty made,   120
     Your goodness now should my excuse persuade.

Alth. I in Victoria will my int'rest try,
     You, and me both, she hardly shall deny.

Hora. Victoria's mind I cannot hope to move,
     Unless a parent's power assist my love;
     Her duty will not your commands withstand,
     She'll take a worthless servant from your hand.

Ever. I'm sure she can have no exception to so deserving a person as Horatio. Lovers, like spaniels, do but show their mettle in a little ranging: though you had a twittering to Althea, you'll make ne'er the worse husband to Victoria. Victoria!   131

Vict. Sir, what's your pleasure?

Ever. That which will prove yours in the end! I charge you upon my blessing, give Horatio your hand, go and be married with your cousins, and make but one work of it.

Vict. Sir, I am all obedience: whoe'er strove
     At once against her duty, and her love?

Wild. But Estridge, what fine lady have you got there?

Est. A certain widow which I have cast myself away upon: a kinswoman of yours, Wildish, that you formerly designed for the right worshipful sir Formal there. Do you know her now?—Sir, we made bold with her without your consent.   142

Wild. Old acquaintance, i'faith, how is't? I have made as bold, and been as welcome too, as e'er you'll be, sir. But why did you steal a marriage thus?

Widow. You know I always loved stolen pleasures, but this marriage stole me. Your old knight was uncertain, came on by inches; this gentleman leaped into the matter, forced me into a coach, and married me in an instant.

130 twittering] hankering

I could have been content to have been a lady, that I might have taken place
of my mistress when she comes to town.   150
    Est. Why, have you a mistress?
    Widow. As sure as you have had a hundred, and now have a wife.
    Mod. I doubt as things go, I shall scarce find you as good a paymaster as
the old alderman.

Estridge pulls his hand from her, and looks angry.

    Wild. Nay, never use her ill now; 'twas none of her fault. She is a very good
creature, and one that I placed to personate my cousin, on purpose to catch
sir Samuel Forecast. You know he took the forfeiture of a mortgage that concerned a very good friend of mine, and I was resolved to be revenged of him?
If you will needs run your head into the noose that's prepared for another,
who can help it? My cousin is married in Ireland, whither she went last
summer to look after some money due to her last husband.   161
    Widow. I am a housekeeper though, and can bid you welcome till she
returns.
    Oliv. A pretty pert thing—I like her humour, she carries it off well! But
Wildish, you shall visit her no more now we are married.
    Wild. Fear not, Estridge will take order for that.

Horatio to Victoria.

Hora. How I do hate myself! that could so long
    At once such beauty and such goodness wrong.
Vict. My kindness has forgot you were to blame,
    You[r] guilt consumed in your reviving flame.   170
Ever. Now you are all paired, let's have a dance.

After the dance, a great shout within.

Eug. I hear the people's voice in joyful cries,
    Like conquering troops o'er flying enemies;
    They seem to teach us in a ruder way
    The honour due to this all-healing day.
Phil. Let's part a while, and vie who shall express
    The highest sense of this great happiness.

EPILOGUE

Poets, of all men, have the hardest game,
Their best endeavours can no favours claim.
The lawyer, if o'erthrown, though by the laws,
He quits himself, and lays it on your cause.
The soldier is esteemed a man of war,
And honour gains, if he but bravely dare.
The grave physician, if his patient die,
He shakes his head, and blames mortality.
Only poor poets their own faults must bear,
Therefore grave judges be not too severe:
Our author humbly hopes to 'scape your rage,
Being no known offender on the stage,
He came by chance, is a mere traveller;
All countries civil unto strangers are:
Yet, faith, he's armed howe'er your censures go,
And can prevent the harm, though not the blow.
No poet can from this one comfort fall,
The best ne'er pleased, nor worst displeased, you all.

FINIS

MARRIAGE À LA MODE

BY

JOHN DRYDEN

JOHN DRYDEN (1631–1700)

Marriage à la Mode, first performed at Lincoln's Inn Fields, 1672; first published 1673.

[*The Dramatic Works of John Dryden*, ed. Montague Summers, 6 vols., 1931–2; *Marriage à la Mode*, ed. J. R. Sutherland, Temple Dramatists, 1934.]

MARRIAGE
A-la-Mode.

A
COMEDY.

As it is Acted at the
THEATRE-ROYAL.

Written by *JOHN DRYDEN* Servant
to His Majesty.

————— ———— *Quicquid sum ego, quamvis*
Infra Lucilli censum ingeniumque, tamen me
Cum magnis vixisse, invita fatebitur usque
Invidia, & fragili quærens illidere dentem
Offendet solido.

Horat. Serm.

LONDON,
Printed by *T. N.* for *Henry Herringman,* and are to be
sold at the *Anchor* in the Lower Walk of
the *New Exchange.* 1673.

TO THE RIGHT HONOURABLE
THE EARL OF
ROCHESTER

My lord,

I humbly dedicate to your lordship that poem of which you were pleased to appear an early patron before it was acted on the stage. I may yet go farther, with your permission, and say that it received amendment from your noble hands ere it was fit to be presented. You may please likewise to remember with how much favour to the author, and indulgence to the play, you commended it to the view of His Majesty, then at Windsor, and by his approbation of it in writing made way for its kind reception on the Theatre. In this dedication therefore I may seem to imitate a custom of the ancients, who offered to their gods the firstlings of the flock, which I think they called *ver sacrum*, because they helped 'em to increase. I am sure, if there be anything in this play wherein I have raised myself beyond the ordinary lowness of my comedies, I ought wholly to acknowledge it to the favour of being admitted into your lordship's conversation. And not only I, who pretend not to this way, but the best comic writers of our age will join with me to acknowledge that they have copied the gallantries of courts, the delicacy of expression, and the decencies of behaviour from your lordship with more success than if they had taken their models from the court of France. But this, my lord, will be no wonder to the world, which knows the excellency of your natural parts and those you have acquired in a noble education. That which with more reason I admire, is, that being so absolute a courtier, you have not forgot either the ties of friendship or the practice of generosity. In my little experience of a court (which I confess I desire not to improve) I have found in it much of interest, and more of detraction. Few men there have that assurance of a friend, as not to be made ridiculous by him when they are absent. There are a middling sort of courtiers who become happy by their want of wit; but they supply that want by an excess of malice to those who have it. And there is no such persecution as that of fools: they can never be considerable enough to be talked of themselves; so that they are safe only in their obscurity, and grow mischievous to witty men, by the great diligence of their envy, and by being always present to represent and aggravate their faults. In the meantime they are forced, when they endeavour to be pleasant, to live on the offals of their wit, whom they decry; and either to quote it, (which they do unwillingly) or to pass it upon others for their own. These are the men who make it their business to chase wit from the knowledge of princes, lest it should disgrace their ignorance. And this kind of malice your lordship has not so much avoided as surmounted. But if by the excellent temper of a royal master, always more ready to hear good than ill, if by his inclination to love you, if by your own merit and address, if by the charms of your conversation, the grace of your behaviour, your knowledge of greatness and habitude in courts, you having been able to preserve yourself with honour in the midst of so dangerous a course; yet at least the remembrance of those hazards has inspired you with pity for other men, who being of an inferior wit and quality to you, are yet persecuted for being that in little, which your lordship is in great. For the quarrel of those people extends itself to anything of sense; and if I may be so vain to own it amongst the rest of the poets, has sometimes reached to the very borders of it, even to me. So that if our general good fortune had not raised up your lordship to defend us, I know not whether anything had been more ridiculous in court than writers. 'Tis to your lordship's favour we generally owe our protection and patronage, and to the nobleness of your nature, which will not suffer the least shadow of your wit to be contemned in other men. You have been often pleased not only to excuse my imperfections, but to vindicate what was tolerable in my writings from their censures. And what I never can forget, you have not only been careful of my reputation, but of my fortune. You have been solicitous to supply my neglect of myself; and to overcome the fatal modesty of poets, which submits them to perpetual wants, rather than to become importunate with those people who have the liberality of kings in their disposing; and who, dishonouring the bounty of their master, suffer such to be in necessity, who endeavour at least to please him: and for whose entertainment he has generously provided, if the fruits of his royal favour were not often stopped in other hands. But your lordship has given me occasion not to complain of courts whilst you are there. I have found the effects of your mediation in all my concernments, and they were so much the more noble in you because they were wholly voluntary. I became your lordship's (if I may venture on the similitude) as the world was made, without knowing him who made it; and brought only a passive obedience to be your creature. This nobleness of yours I think myself the rather obliged to own, because otherwise it must have been lost to all remembrance, for you are endued with that excellent quality of a frank nature, to forget the good which you have done.

But, my lord, I ought to have considered that you are as great a judge as you are a patron; and that in praising you ill I shall incur a higher note of ingratitude than that I thought to have avoided. I stand in need of all your accustomed goodness for the dedication of this play: which though, perhaps it be the best of my comedies, is yet so faulty that I should have feared you, for my critic, if I had not with some policy given you the trouble of being my protector. Wit seems to have lodged itself more nobly in this age than in any of the former: and people of my mean condition are only writers because some of the nobility, and your lordship in the first place, are above the narrow praises which poesy could give you. But let those who love to see themselves exceeded encourage your lordship in so dangerous a quality: for my own part, I must confess, that I have so much of self-interest as to be content with reading some papers of your verses, without desiring you should proceed to a scene or play: with the common prudence of those who are worsted in a duel and declare they are satisfied when they are first wounded. Your lordship has but another step to make, and from the patron of wit you may become its tyrant, and oppress our little reputations with more ease than you now protect them. But these, my lord, are designs which I am sure you harbour not; any more than the French king is contriving the conquest of the Swissers. 'Tis a barren triumph, which is not worth your pains, and would only rank him amongst your slaves, who is already,

My lord,
Your lordship's
Most obedient and most faithful servant,
JOHN DRYDEN

PROLOGUE

Lord, how reformed and quiet we are grown,
Since all our braves and all our wits are gone:
Fop-corner now is free from civil war:
White wig and vizard make no longer jar.
France, and the fleet, have swept the town so clear,
That we can act in peace, and you can hear.
'Twas a sad sight, before they marched from home,
To see our warriors, in red waistcoats, come,
With hair tucked up, into our tiring-room.
But 'twas more sad to hear their last adieu,   10
The women sobbed, and swore they would be true;
And so they were, as long as e'er they could:
But powerful guinea cannot be withstood,
And they were made of playhouse flesh and blood.
Fate did their friends for double use ordain,
In wars abroad they grinning honour gain,
And mistresses, for all that stay, maintain.
Now they are gone 'tis dead vacation here,
For neither friends nor enemies appear.
Poor pensive punk now peeps ere plays begin,   20
Sees the bare bench and dares not venture in:
But manages her last half-crown with care,
And trudges to the Mall, on foot, for air.
Our city friends so far will hardly come,
They can take up with pleasures nearer home;
And see gay shows, and gawdy scenes elsewhere:
For we presume they seldom come to hear.
But they have now ta'n up a glorious trade,
And cutting Moorcraft struts in masquerade.
There's all our hope, for we shall show today,   30
A Masking Ball to recommend our Play:
Nay, to endear 'em more, and let 'em see
We scorn to come behind in courtesy,
We'll follow the new mode which they begin,
And treat 'em with a room and couch within:
For that's one way, howe'er the play fall short,
T'oblige the town, the city, and the court.

3 *Fop-corner*] part of pit frequented by fops   9 *tiring-room*] dressing-room   25 *nearer home*] the rival Dorset Garden theatre   29 *cutting Moorcraft*] swaggering gallant, after the character in Beaumont and Fletcher's *The Scornful Lady*

PERSONS REPRESENTED

Men

POLYDAMAS, usurper of Sicily	*Mr. Wintershall*
LEONIDAS, the rightful prince, unknown	*Mr. Kynaston*
ARGALEON, favourite to Polydamas	*Mr. Lydall*
HERMOGENES, foster-father to Leonidas	*Mr. Cartwright*
EUBULUS, his friend and companion	*Mr. Watson*
RHODOPHIL, captain of the guards	*Mr. Mohun*
PALAMEDE, a courtier	*Mr. Hart*

Women

PALMYRA, daughter to the usurper	*Mrs. Coxe*
AMALTHEA, sister to Argaleon	*Mrs. James*
DORALICE, wife to Rhodophil	*Mrs. Marshall*
MELANTHA, an affected lady	*Mrs. Bowtell*
PHILOTIS, woman to Melantha	*Mrs. Reeve*
BELISA, woman to Doralice	*Mrs. Slade*
ARTEMIS, a court lady	*Mrs. Uphill*

Scene : Sicily

Marriage à la Mode

ACT I   SCENE I

Walks near the Court.

Enter Doralice *and* Beliza.

Dor. Beliza, bring the lute into this arbour, the walks are empty: I would try the song the princess Amalthea bade me learn.

(They go in, and sing.)

1.

Why should a foolish marriage vow
Which long ago was made,
Oblige us to each other now
When passion is decayed?
We loved, and we loved, as long as we could,
Till our love was loved out in us both:
But our marriage is dead, when the pleasure is fled;
'Twas pleasure first made it an oath.   10

2.

If I have pleasures for a friend,
And farther love in store,
What wrong has he whose joys did end,
And who could give no more?
'Tis a madness that he
Should be jealous of me,
Or that I should bar him of another:
For all we can gain,
Is to give ourselves pain,
When neither can hinder the other.   20

Enter Palamede, *in riding habit, and hears the song.*

Re-enter Doralice *and* Beliza.

Bel. Madam, a stranger.

Dor. I did not think to have had witnesses of my bad singing.

Palamede. If I have erred, madam, I hope you'll pardon the curiosity of a stranger; for I may well call myself so, after five years' absence from the court. But you have freed me from one error.

Dor. What's that, I beseech you?

Palamede. I thought good voices and ill faces had been inseparable, and that to be fair and sing well had been only the privilege of angels.

Dor. And how many more of these fine things can you say to me?

Palamede. Very few, madam. For if I should continue to see you some hours longer, you look so killingly that I should be mute with wonder.

Dor. This will not give you the reputation of a wit with me. You travelling *monsieurs* live upon the stock you have got abroad, for the first day or two; to repeat with a good memory, and apply with a good grace, is all your wit. And, commonly, your gullets are sewed up, like cormorants; when you have regorged what you have taken in you are the leanest things in nature.   36

Palamede. Then, madam, I think you had best make that use of me. Let me wait on you for two or three days together, and you shall hear all I have learnt of extraordinary in other countries. And one thing which I never saw till I came home, that is, a lady of a better voice, better face, and better wit than any I have seen abroad. And, after this, if I should not declare myself most passionately in love with you, I should have less wit than yet you think I have.

Dor. A very plain and pithy declaration. I see, sir, you have been travelling in Spain or Italy, or some of the hot countries, where men come to the point immediately. But are you sure these are not words of course? For I would not give my poor heart an occasion of complaint against me, that I engaged it too rashly, and then could not bring it off.   47

Palamede. Your heart may trust itself with me safely. I shall use it very civilly while it stays, and never turn it away—without fair warning to provide for itself.

Dor. First, then, I do receive your passion with as little consideration, on my part, as ever you gave it me, on yours. And now see what a miserable wretch you have made yourself.

Palamede. Who, I miserable? Thank you for that. Give me love enough, and life enough, and I defy Fortune.

Dor. Know then, thou man of vain imagination, know, to thy utter confusion, that I am virtuous.   57

Palamede. Such another word, and I give up the ghost.

Dor. Then, to strike you quite dead, know, that I am married too.

35 cormorants] voracious sea-birds   45 words of course] mere words

Palamede. Art thou married? O thou damnable, virtuous woman!   60

Dor. Yes, married to a gentleman—young, handsome, rich, valiant, and with all the good qualities that will make you despair and hang yourself.

Palamede. Well, in spite of all that, I'll love you! Fortune has cut us out for one another, for I am to be married within these three days. Married past redemption to a young, fair, rich, and virtuous lady. And it shall go hard but I will love my wife as little as I perceive you do your husband.

Dor. Remember I invade no propriety. My servant you are only till you are married.

Palamede. In the meantime you are to forget you have a husband.

Dor. And you, that you are to have a wife.   70

Bel. (*Aside to her lady.*) O madam, my lord's just at the end of the walks, and if you make not haste will discover you.

Dor. Some other time, new servant, we'll talk further of the premises. In the meanwhile break not my first commandment, that is, not to follow me.

Palamede. But where then shall I find you again?

Dor. At court. Yours for two days, sir.

Palamede. And nights, I beseech you, madam. [*Exit* Doralice *and* Beliza.

Palamede. Well, I'll say that for thee, thou art a very dextrous executioner; thou hast done my business at one stroke. Yet I must marry another—and yet I must love this. And if it lead me into some little inconveniences, as jealousies, and duels, and death, and so forth, yet while sweet love is in the case, Fortune do thy worst, and avaunt Mortality.   82

Enter Rhodophil, *who seems speaking to one within.*

Rhod. Leave them with my lieutenant, while I fetch new orders from the king. (*Sees* Palamede.) How? Palamede!

Palamede. Rhodophil!

Rhod. Who thought to have seen you in Sicily?

Palamede. Who thought to have found the court so far from Syracuse?

Rhod. The king best knows the reason of the progress. But answer me, I beseech you. What brought you home from travel?

Palamede. The commands of an old rich father.   90

Rhod. And the hopes of burying him?

Palamede. Both together, as you see, have prevailed on my good nature. In few words, my old man has already married me, for he has agreed with another old man, as rich and as covetous as himself. The articles are drawn and I have given my consent for fear of being disinherited, and yet know not what kind of woman I am to marry.

Rhod. Sure your father intends you some very ugly wife, and has a mind to keep you in ignorance till you have shot the gulf.

82 avaunt] begone   98 shot the gulf] passed through the straits, i.e., married

Palamede. I know not that; but obey I will, and must.

Rhod. Then I cannot choose but grieve for all the good girls and courtesans of France and Italy. They have lost the most kind-hearted, doting, prodigal, humble servant in Europe.   102

Palamede. All I could do in these three years I stayed behind you, was to comfort the poor creatures for the loss of you. But what's the reason that in all this time a friend could never hear from you?

Rhod. Alas, dear Palamede, I have had no joy to write, nor indeed to do anything in the world to please me. The greatest misfortune imaginable is fallen upon me.

Palamede. Prithee, what's the matter?

Rhod. In one word, I am married; wretchedly married; and have been above these two years. Yes, faith, the devil has had power over me in spite of my vows and resolutions to the contrary.   112

Palamede. I find you have sold yourself for filthy lucre; she's old, or ill-conditioned.

Rhod. No, none of these. I'm sure she's young, and, for her humour, she laughs, sings, and dances eternally. And, which is more, we never quarrel about it, for I do the same.

Palamede. You're very unfortunate indeed. Then the case is plain—she is not handsome.

Rhod. A great beauty too, as people say.   120

Palamede. As people say? Why, you should know that best yourself.

Rhod. Ask those, who have smelt to a strong perfume two years together, what's the scent.

Palamede. But here are good qualities enough for one woman.

Rhod. Ay, too many, Palamede. If I could put 'em into three or four women I should be content.

Palamede. O, now I have found it. You dislike her for no other reason but because she's your wife.

Rhod. And is not that enough? All that I know of her perfections now is only by memory. I remember, indeed, that about two years ago I loved her passionately, but those golden days are gone, Palamede. Yet I loved her a whole half-year, double the natural term of any mistress, and think in my conscience I could have held out another quarter. But then the world began to laugh at me, and a certain shame of being out of fashion seized me. At last we arrived at that point that there was nothing left in us to make us new to one another. Yet still I set a good face upon the matter, and am infinite fond of her before company. But when we are alone, we walk like lions in a room, she one way, and I another. And we lie with our backs to each other far distant as if the fashion of great beds was only invented to keep husband and wife sufficiently asunder.   140

Palamede. The truth is, your disease is very desperate; but though you cannot be cured, you may be patched up a little. You must get you a mistress, Rhodophil. That indeed is living on cordials, but as fast as one fails you must supply it with another. You're like a gamester who has lost his estate; yet in doing that you have learned the advantages of play, and can arrive to live upon't.

Rhod. Truth is, I have been thinking on't, and have just resolved to take your counsel. And, faith, considering the damned disadvantages of a married man, I have provided well enough for a humble sinner that is not ambitious of great matters.

Palamede. What is she, for a woman?   150

Rhod. One of the stars of Syracuse, I assure you: young enough, fair enough, and but for one quality just such a woman as I would wish.

Palamede. O friend, this is not an age to be critical in beauty. When we had good store of handsome women, and but few chapmen, you might have been more curious in your choice. But now the price is enhanced upon us, and all mankind set up for mistresses, so that poor little creatures without beauty, birth, or breeding, but only impudence, go off at unreasonable rates. And a man, in these hard times, snaps at them, as he does at broad-gold—never examines the weight but takes light or heavy as he can get it.

Rhod. But my mistress has one fault that's almost unpardonable; for, being a town lady without any relation to the court, yet she thinks herself undone if she be not seen there three or four times a day with the princess Amalthea. And for the king, she haunts and watches him so narrowly in a morning that she prevents even the chymists who beset his chamber to turn their mercury into his gold.   165

Palamede. Yet hitherto, methinks, you are no very unhappy man.

Rhod. With all this she's the greatest gossip in nature, for, besides the court, she's the most eternal visitor of the town: and yet manages her time so well, that she seems ubiquitary. For my part I can compare her to nothing but the sun; for like him she takes no rest, nor ever sets in one place but to rise in another.

Palamede. I confess she had need be handsome with these qualities.

Rhod. No lady can be so curious of a new fashion as she is of a new French word. She's the very mint of the nation, and as fast as any bullion comes out of France, coins it immediately into our language.   175

Palamede. And her name is . . . ?

Rhod. No naming—that's not like a cavalier! Find her if you can by my description, and I am not so ill a painter that I need write the name beneath the picture.

---

154 chapmen] buyers   158 broad-gold] twenty-shilling coin, often clipped round the edges   164 prevents] arrives before   164 chymists] alchemists   169 ubiquitary] to go everywhere

Palamede. Well then, how far have you proceeded in your love?   180
Rhod. 'Tis yet in the bud, and what fruit it may bear I cannot tell. For this insufferable humour of haunting the court is so predominant, that she has hitherto broken all her assignations with me for fear of missing her visits there.

Palamede. That's the hardest part of your adventure. But, for ought I see, Fortune has used us both alike. I have a strange kind of mistress too, in court, besides her I am to marry.

Rhod. You have made haste to be in love then; for, if I am not mistaken, you are but this day arrived.

Palamede. That's all one. I have seen the lady already, who has charmed me, seen her in these walks, courted her, and received, for the first time, an answer that does not put me into despair.   192

To them, Argaleon, Amalthea, Artemis.

I'll tell you at more leisure my adventures. The walks fill apace, I see. Stay, is not that the young lord Argaleon, the king's favourite?

Rhod. Yes, and as proud as ever, as ambitious and as revengeful.

Palamede. How keeps he the king's favour with these qualities?

Rhod. Argaleon's father helped him to the crown. Besides, he gilds over all his vices to the king, and, standing in the dark to him, sees all his inclinations, interests and humours, which he so times and soothes, that in effect he reigns.   200

Palamede. His sister Amalthea, who, I guess, stands by him, seems not to be of his temper.

Rhod. O she's all goodness and generosity.

Arg. Rhodophil, the king expects you earnestly.

Rhod. 'Tis done, my lord, what he commanded. I only waited his return from hunting. Shall I attend your lordship to him?

Arg. No. I go first another way.   [*Exit hastily.*

Palamede. He seems in haste and discomposed.

Amal. (*To* Rhodophil *after a short whisper.*) Your friend? Then he must needs be of much merit.   210

Rhod. When he has kissed the king's hand, I know he'll beg the honour to kiss yours. Come, Palamede.

                [*Exeunt* Rhodophil *and* Palamede *bowing to* Amalthea.

Artem. Madam, you tell me most surprising news.

Amal. The fear of it, you see,
    Has discomposed my brother; but to me
    All that can bring my country good is welcome.

Artem. It seems incredible that this old king,
    Whom all the world thought childless,

Should come to search the farthest parts of Sicily
In hope to find an heir.   220
Amal. To lessen your astonishment I will
Unfold some private passages of state,
Of which you are yet ignorant. Know, first,
That this Polydamas, who reigns, unjustly
Gained the crown.
Artem. Somewhat of this I have confusedly heard.
Amal. I'll tell you all in brief: Theagenes,
Our last great King,
Had, by his queen, one only son, an infant
Of three years old, called, after him, Theagenes;   230
The general, this Polydamas, then married:
The public feasts for which were scarcely past,
When a rebellion in the heart of Sicily
Called out the king to arms.
Artem.   Polydamas
Had then a just excuse to stay behind.
Amal. His temper was too warlike to accept it.
He left his bride and the new joys of marriage,
And followed to the field. In short, they fought;
The rebels were o'ercome; but in the fight
The too bold king received a mortal wound.   240
When he perceived his end approaching near,
He called the general, to whose care he left
His widow queen and orphan son; then died.
Artem. Then false Polydamas betrayed his trust?
Amal. He did; and with my father's help, for which
Heaven pardon him, so gained the soldiers' hearts,
That in few days he was saluted king:
And when his crimes had impudence enough
To bear the eye of day,
He marched his army back to Syracuse.   250
But see how heaven can punish wicked men
In granting their desires: the news was brought him,
That day he was to enter it, that Eubulus,
Whom his dead master had left governor,
Was fled, and with him bore away the queen,
And royal orphan; but, what more amazed him,
His wife, now big with child, and much detesting
Her husband's practices, had willingly
Accompanied their flight.

Artem. How I admire her virtue!
Amal.   What became   260
    Of her and them, since that, was never known.
    Only, some few days since, a famous robber
    Was taken with some jewels of vast price,
    Which, when they were delivered to the king,
    He knew had been his wife's; with these, a letter,
    Much torn, and sullied, but which yet he knew
    To be her writing.
Artem.   Sure from hence he learned
    He had a son.
Amal.   It was not left so plain.
    The paper only said she died in childbed;
    But when it should have mentioned son or daughter,   270
    Just there it was torn off.
Artem.   Madam, the king.

        To them, Polydamas, Argaleon, Guard, *and* Attendants.

Arg. The robber, though thrice racked, confessed no more
    But that he took those jewels near this place.
Poly. But yet the circumstances strongly argue
    That those for whom I search are not far off.
Arg. I cannot easily believe it.
Artem.   (*Aside.*) No,
    You would not have it so.
Poly. Those I employed have, in the neighbouring hamlet,
    Amongst the fishers' cabins made discovery
    Of some young persons whose uncommon beauty   280
    And graceful carriage make it seem suspicious
    They are not what they seem. I therefore sent
    The captain of my guards, this morning early,
    With orders to secure and bring 'em to me.

           Enter Rhodophil *and* Palamede.

    O here he is. Have you performed my will?
Rhod. Sir, those whom you commanded me to bring,
    Are waiting in the walks.
Poly.   Conduct 'em hither.
Rhod. First, give me leave
    To beg your notice of this gentleman.
Poly. He seems to merit it. His name and quality?   290
Rhod. Palamede, son to lord Cleodemus of Palermo,
    And new returned from travel.

Palamede *approaches, and kneels to kiss the* King's *hand.*

Poly. You're welcome.
I knew your father well; he was both brave
And honest. We two once were fellow-soldiers
In the last civil wars.
Palamede. I bring the same unquestioned honesty
And zeal to serve your majesty; the courage
You were pleased to praise in him,
Your royal prudence, and your people's love,
Will never give me leave to try like him   300
In civil wars; I hope it may in foreign.
Poly. Attend the court, and it shall be my care
To find out some employment worthy you.
Go, Rhodophil, and bring in those without.
[*Exeunt* Rhodophil *and* Palamede.

Rhodophil *returns again immediately, and with him enter* Hermogenes,
Leonidas, *and* Palmyra.

Poly. (*Looking earnestly on* Leonidas *and* Palmyra.)
Behold two miracles!
Of different sexes, but of equal form:
So matchless both, that my divided soul
Can scarcely ask the gods a son, or daughter,
For fear of losing one. If from your hands,
You powers, I shall this day receive a daughter,   310
Argaleon, she is yours; but, if a son,
Then Amalthea's love shall make him happy.
Arg. Grant, heaven, this admirable nymph may prove
That issue which he seeks.
Amal. Venus Urania, if thou art a goddess,
Grant that sweet youth may prove the prince of Sicily.
Poly. (*To* Hermogenes.) Tell me, old man, and tell me true, from whence
Had you that youth and maid?
Herm. From whence you had
Your sceptre, sir: I had 'em from the gods.
Poly. The gods then have not such another gift.   320
Say who their parents were.
Herm. My wife and I.
Arg. It is not likely a virgin of so excellent a beauty
Should come from such a stock.
Amal. Much less that such a youth, so sweet, so graceful,
Should be produced from peasants.

Herm. Why, nature is the same in villages,
    And much more fit to form a noble issue
    Where it is least corrupted.
Poly. He talks too like a man that knew the world
    To have been long a peasant. But the rack   330
    Will teach him other language. Hence with him.

    As the Guard *are carrying him away his peruke falls off.*

    Sure I have seen that face before. Hermogenes!
    'Tis he, 'tis he who fled away with Eubulus,
    And with my dear Eudoxia.
Herm. Yes, sir, I am Hermogenes.
    And if to have been loyal be a crime,
    I stand prepared to suffer.
Poly. If thou would'st live, speak quickly.
    What is become of my Eudoxia?
    Where is the queen and young Theagenes?   340
    Where Eubulus? (*Pointing to* Leonidas *and* Palmyra.) And which of
    these is mine?
Herm. Eudoxia is dead; so is the queen,
    The infant king her son, and Eubulus.
Poly. Traitor, 'tis false: produce 'em or . . .
Herm.   Once more
    I tell you, they are dead; but leave to threaten,
    For you shall know no further.
Poly. Then prove indulgent to my hopes, and be
    My friend for ever. Tell me, good Hermogenes,
    Whose son is that brave youth?
Herm.   Sir, he is yours.
Poly. Fool that I am, thou see'st that so I wish it,   350
    And so thou flatter'st me.
Herm.   By all that's holy!
Poly. Again! Thou canst not swear too deeply.
    Yet hold, I will believe thee—yet I doubt.
Herm. You need not, sir.
Arg. Believe him not; he sees you credulous,
    And would impose his own base issue on you,
    And fix it to your crown.
Amal. Behold his goodly shape and feature, sir;
    Methinks he much resembles you.

345 leave] cease

Arg. I say, if you have any issue here,   360
    It must be that fair creature;
    By all my hopes I think so.
Amal. Yes, brother, I believe you by your hopes,
    For they are all for her.
Poly.   Call the youth nearer.
Herm. Leonidas, the king would speak with you.
Poly. Come near, and be not dazzled with the splendour
    And greatness of a court.
Leon. I need not this encouragement.
    I can fear nothing but the gods.
    And for this glory, after I have seen   370
    The canopy of state spread wide above
    In the abyss of heaven, the court of stars,
    The blushing morning, and the rising sun,
    What greater can I see?
Poly. (*Embracing him.*) This speaks thee born a prince; thou art thyself
    That rising sun, and shalt not see on earth
    A brighter than thyself. All of you witness
    That for my son I here receive this youth,
    This brave, this . . . but I must not praise him further,
    Because he now is mine.   380
Leon. (*Kneeling.*) I wonnot, sir, believe
    That I am made your sport;
    For I find nothing in myself but what
    Is much above a scorn; I dare give credit
    To whatsoe'er a king, like you, can tell me.
    Either I am, or will deserve to be your son.
Arg. I yet maintain it is impossible
    This young man should be yours; for, if he were,
    Why should Hermogenes so long conceal him
    When he might gain so much by his discovery?   390
Herm. (*To the* king.) I stayed a while to make him worthy,
    Sir, of you. But in that time I found
    Somewhat within him, which so moved my love,
    I never could resolve to part with him.
Leon. (*To* Argaleon.) You ask too many questions, and are
    Too saucy for a subject.
Arg. You rather over-act your part, and are
    Too soon a prince.
Arg.   Too soon you'll find me one.

381 wonnot] will not

Poly. Enough, Argaleon;
    I have declared him mine: and you, Leonidas,   400
    Live well with him I love.
Arg. Sir, if he be your son, I may have leave
    To think your queen had twins; look on this virgin;
    Hermogenes would enviously deprive you
    Of half your treasure.
Herm.   Sir, she is my daughter.
    I could, perhaps, thus aided by this lord,
    Prefer her to be yours; but truth forbid
    I should procure her greatness by a lie.
Poly. Come hither, beauteous maid: are you not sorry
    Your father will not let you pass for mine?   410
Palmyra. I am content to be what heaven has made me.
Poly. Could you not wish yourself a princess then?
Palmyra. Not to be sister to Leonidas.
Poly. Why, my sweet maid?
Palmyra   Indeed I cannot tell;
    But I could be content to be his handmaid.
Arg. (*Aside.*) I wish I had not seen her.
Palmyra. (*To* Leonidas.) I must weep for your good fortune;
    Pray pardon me, indeed I cannot help it.
    Leonidas, (alas, I had forgot,
    Now I must call you prince) but must I leave you?   420
Leon. (*Aside.*) I dare not speak to her; for if I should,
    I must weep too.
Poly. No, you shall live at court, sweet innocence,
    And see him there. Hermogenes,
    Though you intended not to make me happy,
    Yet you shall be rewarded for th'event.
    Come, my Leonidas, let's thank the gods;
    Thou for a father, I for such a son.
                    [*Exeunt all but* Leonidas *and* Palmyra.
Leon. My dear Palmyra, many eyes observe me,
    And I have thoughts so tender, that I cannot   430
    In public speak 'em to you: some hours hence
    I shall shake off these crowds of fawning courtiers,
    And then . . .   [*Exit* Leonidas.
Palmyra. Fly swift, you hours! You measure time for me in vain,
    Till you bring back Leonidas again.
    Be shorter now; and to redeem that wrong,
    When he and I are met, be twice as long.   [*Exit.*

ACT II SCENE I

Melantha and Philotis.

Phil. Count Rhodophil's a fine gentleman indeed, madam, and I think deserves your affection.

Mel. Let me die but he's a fine man! He sings and dances *en français*, and writes the *billets doux* to a miracle.

Phil. And those are no small talents to a lady that understands and values the French air, as your ladyship does.

Mel. How charming is the French air! And what an *étourdie bête* is one of our untravelled islanders! When he would make his court to me, let me die, but he is just Æsop's Ass, that would imitate the courtly French in his addresses; but, instead of those, comes pawing upon me, and doing all things so *mal à droitly*.   11

Phil. 'Tis great pity Rhodophil's a married man, that you may not have an honourable intrigue with him.

Mel. Intrigue, Philotis! That's an old phrase; I have laid that word by: *amour* sounds better. But thou art heir to all my cast words, as thou art to my old wardrobe. Oh Count Rhodophil! Ah *mon cher!* I could live and die with him.

Enter Palamede *and a* Servant.

Serv. Sir, this is my lady.

Palamede. Then this is she that is to be divine, and nymph, and goddess, and with whom I am to be desperately in love.

[*Bows to her, delivering a letter.*

This letter, madam, which I present you from your father, has given me both the happy opportunity, and the boldness, to kiss the fairest hands in Sicily.

Mel. Came you lately from Palermo, sir?   23

Palamede. But yesterday, madam.

Mel. (*Reading the letter.*) *Daughter, receive the bearer of this letter, as a gentleman whom I have chosen to make you happy;* (O Venus, a new servant sent me! And let me die but he has the air of a *galant homme*) *his father is the rich lord Cleodemus, our neighbour: I suppose you'll find nothing disagreeable in his person or his converse; both which he has improved by travel. The treaty is already concluded, and I shall be in town within these three days; so that you have nothing to do but to obey your careful father.* (*To* Palamede.) Sir, my father, for whom I have a blind obedience, has commanded me to receive

---

7 *étourdie bête*] foolish creature   9 Æsop's Ass] which imitated a fawning dog
15 cast] discarded

your passionate addresses; but you must also give me leave to avow that I cannot merit 'em from so accomplished a cavalier.   34

Palamede. I want many things, madam, to render me accomplished; and the first and greatest of 'em is your favour.

Mel. Let me die, Philotis, but this is extremely French; but yet Count Rhodophil. . . . A gentleman, sir, that understands the *grand monde* so well, who has haunted the best *conversations*, and who (in short) has *voyage*d, may pretend to the good *graces* of any lady.

Palamede. (*Aside.*) Hey-day! *Grand monde*! *conversation*! *voyage*d! and good *graces*! I find my mistress is one of those that run mad in new French words.   43

Mel. I suppose, sir, you have made the *tour* of France; and having seen all that's fine there, will make a considerable reformation in the rudeness of our court: for, let me die, but an unfashioned, untravelled, mere Sicilian, is a *bête*; and has nothing in the world of an *honnête homme*.

Palamede. I must confess, madam, that. . . .

Mel. And what new *menuets* have you brought over with you? Their *menuets* are to a miracle! And our Sicilian jigs are so dull and *fades* to 'em!

Palamede. For *menuets*, madam. . . .   51

Mel. And what new plays are there in vogue? And who danced best in the last *grand ballet*? Come, sweet servant, you shall tell me all.

Palamede. (*Aside.*) Tell her all? Why, she asks all, and will hear nothing.— To answer in order, madam, to your demands. . . .

Mel. I am thinking what a happy couple we shall be! For you shall keep up your correspondence abroad, and everything that's new writ in France, and fine, I mean all that's delicate, and *bien tourné*, we will have first.

Palamede. But, madam, our fortune. . . .

Mel. I understand you, sir; you'll leave that to me: for the *ménage* of a family, I know it better than any lady in Sicily.   61

Palamede. Alas, madam, we. . . .

Mel. Then, we will never make visits together, nor see a play, but always apart; you shall be every day at the king's *levée*, and I at the queen's, and we will never meet, but in the drawing-room.

Phil. Madam, the new prince is just passed by the end of the walk.

Mel. The new prince, say'st thou? Adieu, dear servant; I have not made my court to him these two long hours. O, 'tis the sweetest prince! So *obligeant*, *charmant*, *ravissant*, that. . . . Well, I'll make haste to kiss his hands; and then make half a score visits more, and be with you again in a twinkling.

[*Exit running with* Philotis.

38 *grand monde*] high society   47 *honnête homme*] well-bred man   49 *menuets*] minuets   50 to a miracle] marvellous   50 *fades*] insipid   58 *bien tourné*] stylish 60 *ménage*] housekeeping

Palamede. (*Solus.*) Now heaven, of thy mercy, bless me from this tongue; it may keep the field against a whole army of lawyers, and that in their own language, French gibberish. 'Tis true, in the daytime, 'tis tolerable, when a man has field-room to run from it; but to be shut up in a bed with her, like two cocks in a pit—humanity cannot support it! I must kiss all night in my own defence, and hold her down like a boy at cuffs, nay, and give her the rising blow every time she begins to speak.

Enter Rhodophil.

But here comes Rhodophil. 'Tis pretty odd that my mistress should so much resemble his: the same newsmonger, the same passionate lover of a court, the same. ... But *basta*, since I must marry her, I'll say nothing, because he shall not laugh at my misfortune. 81

Rhod. Well, Palamede, how go the affairs of love? You've seen your mistress?

Palamede. I have so.

Rhod. And how, and how? Has the old Cupid, your father, chosen well for you? Is he a good woodman?

Palamede. She's much handsomer than I could have imagined. In short, I love her, and will marry her.

Rhod. Then you are quite off from your other mistress?

Palamede. You are mistaken. I intend to love 'em both, as a reasonable man ought to do. For, since all women have their faults and imperfections, 'tis fit that one of 'em should help out t'other. 92

Rhod. This were a blessed doctrine, indeed, if our wives would hear it. But they're their own enemies. If they would suffer us but now and then to make excursions, the benefit of our variety would be theirs. Instead of one continued, lazy, tired love, they would in their turns have twenty vigorous, fresh and active loves.

Palamede. And I would ask any of 'em whether a poor narrow brook, half dry the best part of the year, and running ever one way, be to be compared to a lusty stream, that has ebbs and flows? 100

Rhod. Ay, or is half so profitable for navigation?

Enter Doralice, *walking by and reading.*

Palamede. Ods my life, Rhodophil, will you keep my counsel?

Rhod. Yes: where's the secret?

Palamede. (*Showing* Doralice.) There 'tis. I may tell you, as my friend, *sub sigillo*, etc. this is that very numerical lady, with whom I am in love.

73 French gibberish] legal terms in Norman French   74 field-room] open space 76 at cuffs] fighting   77 rising blow] upper-cut (with sexual innuendo)   80 *basta*] enough   86 woodman] marksman   104-5 *sub sigillo*] in secret   105 numerical] identical

Rhod. (*Aside.*) By all that's virtuous, my wife!

Palamede. You look strangely: how do you like her? Is she not very handsome?

Rhod. (*Aside.*) Sure he abuses me. (*To him.*) Why the devil do you ask my judgment? 110

Palamede. You are so dogged now, you think no man's mistress handsome but your own. Come, you shall hear her talk too. She has wit, I assure you.

Rhod. (*Going back.*) This is too much, Palamede.

Palamede. (*Pulling him forward.*) Prithee do not hang back so: of an old tried lover, thou art the most bashful fellow!

Dor. (*Looking up.*) Were you so near, and would not speak, dear husband?

Palamede. (*Aside.*) Husband, quoth a! I have cut out a fine piece of work for myself.

Rhod. Pray, spouse, how long have you been acquainted with this gentleman?

Dor. Who, I acquainted with this stranger? To my best knowledge I never saw him before. 121

Enter Melantha, at the other end.

Palamede. (*Aside.*) Thanks, Fortune, thou hast helped me.

Rhod. Palamede, this must not pass so: I must know your mistress a little better.

Palamede. It shall be your own fault else. Come, I'll introduce you.

Rhod. Introduce me! Where?

Palamede. (*Pointing to* Melantha, *who swiftly passes over the stage.*) There. To my mistress.

Rhod. Who? Melantha! O heavens, I did not see her.

Palamede. But I did. I am an eagle where I love. 130
I have seen her this half hour.

Dor. (*Aside.*) I find he has wit, he has got off so readily. But it would anger me if he should love Melantha.

Rhod. (*Aside.*) Now I could e'en wish it were my wife he loved: I find he's to be married to my mistress.

Palamede. Shall I run after and fetch her back again to present you to her?

Rhod. No, you need not. I have the honour to have some small acquaintance with her.

Palamede. (*Aside.*) O Jupiter! What a blockhead was I not to find it out! My wife that must be, is his mistress. I did a little suspect it before. Well, I must marry her, because she's handsome, and because I hate to be disinherited for a younger brother, which I am sure I shall be if I disobey. And yet I must keep in with Rhodophil, because I love his wife. (*To* Rhodophil.) I must desire you to make my excuse to your lady, if I have been so unfortunate to cause any mistake; and, withal, to beg the honour of being known to her.

Rhod. O, that's but reason. Hark you, spouse, pray look upon this gentle-man as my friend; whom, to my knowledge, you have never seen before this hour.

Dor. I'm so obedient a wife, sir, that my husband's commands shall ever be a law to me.   150

Enter Melantha *again, hastily, and runs to embrace* Doralice.

Mel. O, my dear, I was just going to pay my *devoirs* to you; I had not time this morning, for making my court to the king, and our new prince. Well, never nation was so happy, and all that, in a young prince; and he's the kindest person in the world to me, let me die, if he is not.

Dor. He has been bred up far from court, and therefore. . . .

Mel. That imports not. Though he has not seen the *grand monde*, and all that, let me die but he has the air of the court, most absolutely.

Palamede. But yet, madam, he. . . .

Mel. O, servant, you can testify that I am in his good graces. Well, I can-not stay long with you, because I have promised him this afternoon to. . . . But hark you, my dear, I'll tell you a secret.   161

[*Whispers to* Doralice.

Rhod. (*Aside.*) The devil's in me, that I must love this woman.

Palamede. (*Aside.*) The devil's in me, that I must marry this woman.

Mel. (*Raising her voice.*) So the prince and I. . . . But you must make a secret of this, my dear, for I would not for the world your husband should hear it, or my tyrant, there, that must be.

Palamede. (*Aside.*) Well, fair impertinent, your whisper is not lost, we hear you.

Dor. I understand then, that. . . .

Mel. I'll tell you, my dear, the prince took me by the hand, and pressed it because the king was near, made the *doux yeux* to me, and *en suite*, said a thousand *galanteries*, or let me die, my dear.   172

Dor. Then I am sure you. . . .

Mel. You are mistaken, my dear.

Dor. What, before I speak?

Mel. But I know your meaning; you think, my dear, that I assumed some-thing of *fierté* into my countenance, to *rebute* him; but, quite contrary, I regarded him, I know not how to express it in our dull Sicilian language, *d'un air enjoué*; and said nothing but *à d'autres, à d'autres*, and that it was all *grimace*, and would not pass upon me.   180

Enter Artemis: Melantha *sees her, and runs away from* Doralice.

151 *devoirs*] respects   171 *doux yeux*] ogled   171 *en suite*] afterwards   177 *fierté*] haughtiness   177 *rebute*] rebuff   179 *d'un air enjoué*] with a playful look   179 *à d'autres*] others might believe you!

(*To* Artemis.) My dear, I must beg your pardon, I was just making a loose from Doralice, to pay my respects to you. Let me die, if I ever pass time so agreeably as in your company, and if I would leave it for any lady's in Sicily.

Artem. The princess Amalthea is coming this way.   184

Enter Amalthea: Melantha *runs to her.*

Mel. O dear madam! I have been at your lodgings, in my new *galèche*, so often to tell you of a new *amour* betwixt two persons whom you would little suspect for it, that, let me die, if one of my coach-horses be not dead, and another quite tired and sunk under the *fatigue.*

Amal. O Melantha, I can tell you news. The prince is coming this way.

Mel. The prince! O sweet prince! He and I are to . . . and I forgot it. Your pardon, sweet madam, for my abruptness. *Adieu*, my dears. Servant, Rhodophil; servant, servant, servant all.   192

[Exit running.

Amal. (*Whispers.*) Rhodophil, a word with you.

Dor. (*To* Palamede.) Why do you not follow your mistress, sir?

Palamede. Follow her? Why, at this rate, she'll be at the Indies within this half-hour.

Dor. However, if you can't follow her all day you'll meet her at night I hope?

Palamede. But can you in charity suffer me to be so mortified without affording me some relief? If it be but to punish that sign of a husband there— that lazy matrimony, that dull insipid taste, who leaves such delicious fare at home to dine abroad, on worse meat, and to pay dear for't into the bargain.

Dor. All this is in vain. Assure yourself, I will never admit of any visit from you in private.   204

Palamede. That is to tell me, in other words, my condition is desperate.

Dor. I think you in so ill a condition, that I am resolved to pray for you this very evening in the close walk behind the terrace; for that's a private place and there I am sure nobody will disturb my devotions. And so good-night sir.   [*Exit.*

Palamede. This is the newest way of making an appointment I ever heard of. Let women alone to contrive the means; I find we are but dunces to 'em. Well, I will not be so profane a wretch as to interrupt her devotions; but to make 'em more effectual I'll down upon my knees and endeavour to join my own with 'em.   [*Exit.*

Amal. (*To* Rhodophil.) I know already they do not love each other and that my brother acts but a forced obedience to the king's commands; so that, if a quarrel should arise betwixt the prince and him I were most miserable on both sides.

---

181 making a loose] leaving the company of   185 *galèche*] calash, light carriage

Rhod. There shall be nothing wanting in me, madam, to prevent so sad a
consequence.   220

      Enter the King, Leonidas; *the* King *whispers* [*to*] Amalthea.

(*To himself.*) I begin to hate this Palamede, because he is to marry my
mistress. Yet break with him I dare not, for fear of being quite excluded
from her company. 'Tis a hard case when a man must go by his rival to his
mistress: but 'tis at worst but using him like a pair of heavy boots in a dirty
journey; after I have fouled him all day, I'll throw him off at night. [*Exit.*
  Amal. (*To the* king.) This honour is too great for me to hope.
  Poly. You shall this hour have the assurance of it.
    Leonidas, come hither; you have heard,
    I doubt not, that the father of this princess
    Was my most faithful friend, while I was yet   230
    A private man; and when I did assume
    This crown, he served me in that high attempt.
    You see, then, to what gratitude obliges me;
    Make your addresses to her.
  Leon. Sir, I am yet too young to be a courtier;
    I should too much betray my ignorance,
    And want of breeding, to so fair a lady.
  Amal. Your language speaks you not bred up in deserts,
    But in the softness of some Asian court,
    Where luxury and ease invent kind words,   240
    To cozen tender virgins of their hearts.
  Poly. You need not doubt
    But in what words soe'er a prince can offer
    His crown and person, they will be received.
    You know my pleasure, and you know your duty.
  Leon. Yes, sir, I shall obey, in what I can.
  Poly. In what you can, Leonidas? Consider,
    He's both your king, and father, who commands you.
    Besides, what is there hard in my injunction?
  Leon. 'Tis hard to have my inclination forced.   250
    I would not marry, sir; and, when I do,
    I hope you'll give me freedom in my choice.
  Poly. View well this lady,
    Whose mind as much transcends her beauteous face
    As that excels all others.
  Amal. My beauty, as it ne'er could merit love,
    So neither can it beg: and, sir, you may
    Believe that what the king has offered you,

I should refuse, did I not value more
Your person than your crown.
Leon.   Think it not pride   260
Or my new fortunes swell me to contemn you;
Think less, that I want eyes to see your beauty;
And least of all think duty wanting in me
T'obey a father's will: but . . .
Poly.   But what, Leonidas?
For I must know your reason; and be sure
It be convincing too.
Leon.   Sir, ask the stars,
Which have imposed love on us like a fate,
Why minds are bent to one, and fly another?
Ask why all beauties cannot move all hearts?
For though there may   270
Be made a rule for colour, or for feature,
There can be none for liking.
Poly. Leonidas, you owe me more
Than to oppose your liking to my pleasure.
Leon. I owe you all things, sir; but something too
I owe myself.
Poly. You shall dispute no more; I am a king,
And I will be obeyed.
Leon. You are a king, sir; but you are no god;
Or if you were, you could not force my will.   280
Poly. (*Aside.*) But you are just, you gods! O you are just,
In punishing the crimes of my rebellion
With a rebellious son!
Yet I can punish him, as you do me.
Leonidas, there is no jesting with
My will: I ne'er had done so much to gain
A crown, but to be absolute in all things.
Amal. O, sir, be not so much a king, as to
Forget you are a father: soft indulgence
Becomes that name. Though nature gives you power,   290
To bind his duty, 'tis with silken bonds:
Command him, then, as you command yourself:
He is as much a part of you, as are
Your appetite and will, and those you force not,
But gently bend, and make 'em pliant to your reason.
Poly. It may be I have used too rough a way:
Forgive me, my Leonidas; I know

I lie as open to the gusts of passion,
As the bare shore to every beating surge.
I will not force thee, now; but I intreat thee,   300
Absolve a father's vow to this fair virgin:
A vow, which hopes of having such a son
First caused.
Leon. Show not my disobedience by your prayers,
For I must still deny you, though I now
Appear more guilty to myself than you:
I have some reasons, which I cannot utter,
That force my disobedience; yet I mourn
To death, that the first thing you e'er enjoined me,
Should be that only one command in nature   310
Which I could not obey.
Poly. I did descend too much below myself
When I intreated him. Hence, to thy desert!
Thou'rt not my son, or art not fit to be.
Amal. (*Kneeling.*) Great sir, I humbly beg you, make not me
The cause of your displeasure. I absolve
Your vow: far, far from me, be such designs;
So wretched a desire of being great,
By making him unhappy. You may see
Something so noble in the prince's nature,   320
As grieves him more not to obey, than you
That you are not obeyed.
Poly.   Then, for your sake,
I'll give him one day longer to consider
Not to deny; for my resolves are firm
As fate, that cannot change.   [*Exeunt* King *and* Amalthea.
Leon.   And so are mine.
This beauteous princess, charming as she is,
Could never make me happy: I must first
Be false to my Palmyra, and then wretched.
But, then, a father's anger!
Suppose he should recede from his own vow,   330
He never would permit me to keep mine.

              Enter Palmyra; Argaleon *following her, a little after.*

See, she appears!
I'll think no more of anything but her.
Yet I have one hour good ere I am wretched.
But, oh, Argaleon follows her! So night

Treads on the footsteps of a winter's sun
And stalks all black behind him.
Palmyra.   O Leonidas,
  (For I must call you still by that dear name)
  Free me from this bad man.
Leon. I hope he dares not be injurious to you.   340
Arg. I rather was injurious to myself,
  Than her.
Leon. That must be judged when I hear what you said.
Arg. I think you need not give yourself that trouble.
  It concerned us alone.
Leon. You answer saucily, and indirectly:
  What interest can you pretend in her?
Arg. It may be, sir, I made her some expressions
  Which I would not repeat, because they were
  Below my rank, to one of hers.   350
Leon. What did he say, Palmyra?
Palmyra. I'll tell you all. First, he began to look,
  And then he sighed, and then he looked again;
  At last, he said my eyes wounded his heart:
  And, after that, he talked of flames, and fires;
  And such strange words that I believed he conjured.
Leon. O my heart! Leave me, Argaleon.
Arg. Come, sweet Palmyra,
  I will instruct you better in my meaning:
  You see he would be private.
Leon.   Go yourself,   360
  And leave her here.
Arg.   Alas, she's ignorant,
  And is not fit to entertain a prince.
Leon. First learn what's fit for you; that's to obey.
Arg. I know my duty is to wait on you.
  A great king's son, like you, ought to forget
  Such mean converse.
Leon.   What? A disputing subject?
  Hence; or my sword shall do me justice on thee.
Arg. (*Going.*) Yet I may find a time. . . .
Leon. (*Going after him.*) What's that you mutter—
  To find a time?
Arg.   To wait on you again. . . .   370
  (*Softly.*) In the meantime I'll watch you.
                  [*Exit, and watches during the scene.*

   Leon. How precious are the hours of love in courts!
     In cottages, where love has all the day,
     Full, and at ease, he throws it half away.
     Time gives himself and is not valued there;
     But sells at mighty rates each minute here.
     There, he is lazy, unemployed and slow;
     Here, he's more swift; and yet has more to do.
     So many of his hours in public move
     That few are left for privacy and love.   380
   Palmyra. The sun, methinks, shines faint and dimly here;
     Light is not half so long nor half so clear.
     But, oh, when every day was yours and mine,
     How early up! What haste he made to shine!
   Leon. Such golden days no prince must hope to see;
     Whose ev'ry subject is more blessed than he.
   Palmyra. Do you remember, when their talks were done,
     How all the youth did to our cottage run?
     While winter winds were whistling loud without,
     Our cheerful hearth was circled round about: 390
     With strokes in ashes maids their lovers drew;
     And still you fell to me, and I to you.
   Leon. When love did of my heart possession take,
     I was so young my soul was scarce awake:
     I cannot tell when first I thought you fair;
     But sucked in love, insensibly as air.
   Palmyra. I know too well when first my love began,
     When, at our wake, you for the chaplet ran:
     Then I was made the Lady of the May,
     And with the garland at the goal did stay: 400
     Still as you ran I kept you full in view;
     I hoped and wished, and ran, methought, for you.
     As you came near I hastily did rise,
     And stretched my arm outright, that held the prize.
     The custom was to kiss whom I should crown:
     You kneeled; and, in my lap, your head laid down.
     I blushed, and blushed, and did the kiss delay:
     At last, my subjects forced me to obey;
     But when I gave the crown and then the kiss,
     I scarce had breath to say: Take that—and this.   410

---

391 strokes in ashes] falling ashes forming the lover's initial   398 wake] parish annual festival   398 chaplet] floral wreath

Leon. I felt the while a pleasing kind of smart;
 The kiss went tingling to my very heart.
 When it was gone the sense of it did stay;
 The sweetness clinged upon my lips all day,
 Like drops of honey loth to fall away.
Palmyra. Life, like a prodigal, gave all his store
 To my first youth, and now can give no more.
 You are a prince; and, in that high degree,
 No longer must converse with humble me.
Leon. 'Twas to my loss the gods that title gave;   420
 A tyrant's son is doubly born a slave:
 He gives a crown; but, to prevent my life
 From being happy, loads it with a wife.
Palmyra. Speak quickly; what have you resolved to do?
Leon. To keep my faith inviolate to you.
 He threatens me with exile and with shame,
 To lose my birth-right and a prince's name;
 But there's a blessing which he did not mean,
 To send me back to love and you again.
Palmyra. Why was not I a princess for your sake? 430
 But heaven no more such miracles can make:
 And since that cannot, this must never be;
 You shall not lose a crown for love of me.
 Live happy, and a nobler choice pursue;
 I shall complain of fate, but not of you.
Leon. Can you so easily without me live?
 Or could you take the counsel which you give?
 Were you a princess would you not be true?
Palmyra. I would; but cannot merit it from you.
Leon. Did you not merit, as you do, my heart; 440
 Love gives esteem; and then it gives desert.
 But if I basely could forget my vow,
 Poor helpless innocence, what would you do?
Palmyra. In woods, and plains, where first my love began,
 There would I live, retired from faithless man:
 I'd sit all day within some lonely shade,
 Or that close arbour which your hands have made:
 I'd search the groves, and every tree, to find
 Where you had carved our names upon the rind:
 Your hook, your scrip, all that was yours I'd keep, 450
 And lay 'em by me when I went to sleep.

450 hook] shepherd's crook 450 scrip] satchel

Thus would I live: and maidens, when I die,
Upon my hearse white true-love-knots should tie:
And thus my tomb should be inscribed above:
Here the forsaken virgin rests from love.
Leon. Think not that time or fate shall e'er divide
Those hearts which love and mutual vows have tied:
But we must part; farewell, my love.
Palmyra.   Till when?
Leon. Till the next age of hours we meet again.
Meantime . . . we may,   460
When near each other we in public stand,
Contrive to catch a look, or steal a hand:
Fancy will every touch and glance improve,
And draw the most spirituous parts of love.
Our souls sit close and silently within,
And their own web from their own entrails spin.
And when eyes meet far off, our sense is such,
That, spider-like, we feel the tender'st touch.   *[Exeunt.*

ACT III   SCENE I

Enter Rhodophil, *meeting* Doralice *and* Artemis.
Rhodophil *and* Doralice *embrace.*

Rhod. My own dear heart!
Dor. My own true love! (*She starts back.*) I had forgot myself to be so
kind. Indeed I am very angry with you, dear; you are come home an hour
after you appointed. If you had stayed a minute longer I was just considering
whether I should stab, hang or drown myself.   *[Embracing him.*
Rhod. Nothing but the king's business could have hindered me; and I was
so vexed that I was just laying down my commission rather than have failed
my dear.   *[Kissing her hand.*
Artem. Why, this is love as it should be betwixt man and wife. Such
another couple would bring marriage into fashion again. But is it always thus
betwixt you?   11
Rhod. Always thus! This is nothing. I tell you there is not such a pair of
turtles in all Sicily. There is such an eternal cooing and kissing betwixt us,
that indeed it is scandalous before civil company.
Dor. Well, if I had imagined I should have been this fond fool, I would

never have married the man I loved. I married to be happy; and have made myself miserable by over-loving. Nay, and now my case is desperate, for I have been married above these two years, and find myself every day worse and worse in love. Nothing but madness can be the end on't.

Artem. Dote on, to the extremity, and you are happy.   20

Dor. He deserves so infinitely much, that the truth is there can be no doting in the matter. But to love well, I confess, is a work that pays itself: 'tis telling gold, and after taking it for one's pains.

Rhod. By that I should be a very covetous person; for I am ever pulling out my money, and putting it into my pocket again.

Dor. O dear Rhodophil!

Rhod. O sweet Doralice!   [*Embracing each other.*

Artem. (*Aside.*) Nay, I am resolved, I'll never interrupt lovers. I'll leave 'em as happy as I found 'em.   [*Steals away.*

Rhod. (*Looking up.*) What, is she gone?   30

Dor. Yes; and without taking leave.

Rhod. Then there's enough for this time.   [*Parting from her.*

Dor. Yes sure, the scene's done, I take it.

They walk contrary ways on the stage; he, with his hands in his pocket, whistling: she, singing a dull melancholy tune.

Rhod. Pox o'your dull tune, a man can't think for you.

Dor. Pox o'your damned whistling; you can neither be company to me yourself, nor leave me to the freedom of my own fancy.

Rhod. Well, thou art the most provoking wife!

Dor. Well, thou art the dullest husband, thou art never to be provoked.

Rhod. I was never thought dull till I married thee; and now thou hast made an old knife of me, thou hast whetted me so long till I have no edge left.

Dor. I see you are in the husband's fashion; you reserve all your good humours for your mistresses, and keep your ill for your wives.   42

Rhod. Prithee leave me to my own cogitations; I am thinking over all my sins, to find for which of them it was I married thee.

Dor. Whatever your sin was, mine's the punishment.

Rhod. My comfort is, thou art not immortal; and when that blessed, that divine day comes, of thy departure, I'm resolved I'll make one Holy Day more in the almanac, for thy sake.

Dor. Ay, you had need make a Holy Day for me, for I am sure you have made me a martyr.   50

Rhod. Then, setting my victorious foot upon thy head, in the first hour of thy silence, (that is, the first hour thou art dead, for I despair of it before) I will swear by thy ghost, an oath as terrible to me as Styx is to the gods, never more to be in danger of the banes of matrimony.

Dor. And I am resolved to marry the very same day thou diest, if it be but to show how little I'm concerned for thee.

Rhod. Prithee, Doralice, why do we quarrel thus a-days, ha? This is but a kind of heathenish life and does not answer the ends of marriage. If I have erred, propound what reasonable atonement may be made, before we sleep, and I shall not be refractory: but withal consider, I have been married these three years, and be not too tyrannical.   61

Dor. What, should you talk of a peace abed, when you can give no security for performance of articles?

Rhod. Then, since we must live together, and both of us stand upon our terms, as to matter of dying first, let us make ourselves as merry as we can with our misfortunes. Why there's the devil on't! If thou couldst make my enjoying thee but a little less easy, or a little more unlawful, thou shouldst see what a termagant lover I would prove. I have taken such pains to enjoy thee, Doralice, that I have fancied thee all the fine women in the town, to help me out. But now there's none left for me to think on, my imagination is quite jaded. Thou art a wife, and thou wilt be a wife, and I can make thee another no longer.   [*Exit* Rhodophil.

Dor. Well, since thou art a husband, and wilt be a husband, I'll try if I can find out another! 'Tis a pretty time we women have on't, to be made widows while we are married. Our husbands think it reasonable to complain, that we are the same, and the same to them, when we have more reason to complain, that they are not the same to us. Because they cannot feed on one dish, therefore, we must be starved. 'Tis enough that they have a sufficient ordinary provided, and a table ready spread for 'em: if they cannot fall to and eat heartily, the fault is theirs; and 'tis pity, methinks, that the good creature should be lost, when many a poor sinner would be glad on't.   81

Enter Melantha, *and* Artemis *to her.*

Mel. Dear, my dear, pity me; I am so *chagrine* today; and have had the most signal affront at court! I went this afternoon to do my *devoir* to princess Amalthea, found her, conversed with her, and helped to make her court some half an hour. After which she went to take the air, chose out two ladies to go with her, that came in after me, and left me most barbarously behind her.

Artem. You are the less to be pitied, Melantha, because you subject yourself to these affronts by coming perpetually to court, where you have no business nor employment.   90

Mel. I declare, I had rather of the two be *raillée*'d, nay, *mal traitée* at court,

63 articles] agreements   82 *chagrine*] annoyed   91 *raillée*'d] bantered

than be deified in the town: for, assuredly, nothing can be so *ridicule*, as a mere town-lady.

Dor. Especially at court. How I have seen 'em crowd and sweat in the drawing-room on a holiday night! For that's their time to swarm and invade the presence. O how they catch at a bow, or any little salute from a courtier, to make show of their acquaintance! And rather than be thought to be quite unknown they curtsy to one another. But they take true pains to come near the circle, and press and peep upon the princess, to write letters into the country how she was dressed, while the ladies that stand about make their court to her with abusing them.   101

Artem. These are sad truths, Melantha, and therefore I would e'en advise you to quit the court, and live either wholly in the town, or, if you like not that, in the country.

Dor. In the country! Nay, that's to fall beneath the town; for they live there upon our offals here. Their entertainment of wit is only the re-membrance of what they had when they were last in town. They live this year upon the last year's knowledge, as their cattle do all night by chewing the cud of what they eat in the afternoon.

Mel. And they tell, for news, such unlikely stories. A letter from one of us is such a present to 'em, that the poor souls wait for the carrier's day with such devotion, that they cannot sleep the night before.   112

Artem. No more than I can the night before I am to go a journey.

Dor. Or I, before I am to try on a new gown.

Mel. A song that's stale here will be new there a twelve-month hence; and if a man of the town by chance come amongst 'em, he's reverenced for teach-ing 'em the tune.

Dor. A friend of mine, who makes songs sometimes, came lately out of the west, and vowed he was so put out of countenance with a song of his; for at the first country gentleman's he visited, he saw three tailors cross-legged upon the table in the hall, who were tearing out as loud as ever they could sing: *After the pangs of a desperate lover, etc.* And all that day he heard nothing else but the daughters of the house and the maids humming it over in every corner, and the father whistling it.   124

Artem. Indeed I have observed of myself, that when I am out of town but a fortnight, I am so humble that I would receive a letter from my tailor or mercer for a favour.

Mel. When I have been at grass in the summer, and am new come up again, methinks I'm to be turned into *ridicule* by all that see me. But when I have been once or twice at court I begin to value myself again and to despise my country acquaintance.   131

Artem. There are places where all people may be adored, and we ought to know ourselves so well as to choose 'em.

Dor. That's very true. Your little courtier's wife, who speaks to the King but once a month, need but go to a town-lady, and there she may vapour and cry, *The King and I*, at every word. Your town-lady, who is laughed at in the circle, takes her coach into the city, and there she's called *Your Honour*, and has a banquet from the merchant's wife, whom she laughs at for her kindness. And, as for my finical cit, she removes but to her country house, and there insults over the country gentlewoman that never comes up; who treats her with frumenty and custard, and opens her dear bottle of *mirabilis* beside, for a gill glass of it at parting.   142

Artem. At last, I see, we shall leave Melantha where we found her; for, by your description of the town and country, they are become more dreadful to her than the court, where she was affronted. But you forget we are to wait on the princess Amalthea. Come, Doralice.

Dor. Farewell, Melantha.

Mel. Adieu, my dear.

Artem. You are out of charity with her, and therefore I shall not give your service.   150

Mel. Do not omit it, I beseech you; for I have such a *tendre* for the court, that I love it even from the drawing-room to the lobby, and can never be *rebutée* by any usage. But, hark you, my dears, one thing I had forgot of great concernment.

Dor. Quickly then, we are in haste.

Mel. Do not call it my service, that's too vulgar! But do my *baisemains* to the princess Amalthea. That is *spirituel*!

Dor. To do you service then, we will *prendre* the *carosse* to court, and do your *baisemains* to the princess Amalthea, in your phrase *spirituel*.

[*Exeunt* Artemis *and* Doralice.

Enter Philotis, *with a paper in her hand.*

Mel. O, you are there, minion? And, well, are not you a most precious damsel, to retard all my visits for want of language, when you know you are paid so well for furnishing me with new words for my daily conversation? Let me die, if I have not run the *risque* already, to speak like one of the vulgar; and if I have one phrase left in all my store that is not thread-bare and *usée*, and fit for nothing but to be thrown to peasants.   165

Phil. Indeed, madam, I have been very diligent in my vocation; but you have so drained all the French plays and romances, that they are not able to supply you with words for your daily expenses.

---

135 vapour] boast   139 finical cit] affected citizen   141 frumenty] wheat boiled in milk   141 *mirabilis*] aqua mirabilis, a cordial   151 *tendre*] fondness   153 *rebutée*] discouraged   156 *baisemains*] kissing of hands   157 *spirituel*] witty   158 *prendre* the *carosse*] take the coach   164 *usée*] worn out

Mel. Drained? What a word's there! *Épuisé*, you sot you! Come, produce your morning's work.   170

Phil. (*Shows the paper.*) 'Tis here, madam.

Mel. O, my Venus! Fourteen or fifteen words to serve me a whole day! Let me die, at this rate I cannot last till night. Come, read your works: twenty to one, half of 'em will not pass muster neither.

Phil. (*Reads.*) *Sottises.*

Mel. Sottises: bon. That's an excellent word to begin withal. As for example: He, or she, said a thousand *sottises* to me. Proceed.

Phil. Figure. As: what a *figure* of a man is there! *Naïf,* and *Naiveté.*

Mel. Naïf! As how?

Phil. Speaking of a thing that was naturally said: It was so *naïf.* Or such an innocent piece of simplicity: 'Twas such a *naiveté.*   181

Mel. Truce with your interpretations: make haste.

Phil. Faible, chagrin, grimace, embarrassé, double entendre, équivoque, éclaircissement, suite, bévue, façon, penchant, coup d'étourdi, and *ridicule.*

Mel. Hold, hold; how did they begin?

Phil. They began at *sottises,* and ended *en ridicule.*

Mel. Now give me your paper in my hand, and hold you my glass, while I practise my postures for the day.

                                           [Melantha *laughs in the glass.*
How does that laugh become my face?

Phil. Sovereignly well, madam.   190

Mel. Sovereignly! Let me die, that's not amiss. That word shall not be yours. I'll invent it, and bring it up myself. My new point gorget shall be yours upon't. Not a word of the word, I charge you.

Phil. I am dumb, madam.

Mel. That glance, how suits it with my face?

                                           [*Looking in the glass again.*
Phil. 'Tis so *languissant.*

Mel. Languissant! That word shall be mine too, and my last Indian gown thine for't. (*Looks again.*) That sigh?

Phil. 'Twill make many a man sigh, madam. 'Tis a mere *incendiary.*

Mel. Take my gimp petticoat for that truth. If thou hast more of these phrases, let me die but I could give away all my wardrobe and go naked for 'em.   202

Phil. Go naked? Then you would be a Venus, madam. O Jupiter! What had I forgot? This paper was given me by Rhodophil's page.

Mel. (*Reading the letter.*) . . . Beg the favour from you. . . . Gratify my pas-

---

175 *Sottises*] idiocies   184 *éclaircissement*] explanation   184 *bévue*] blunder   192 point gorget] lace wimple   197 Indian gown] ornate undress   200 gimp] wire-threaded material

sion ... so far ... assignation ... in the grotto ... behind the terrace ...
clock this evening. ... Well, for the *billets doux* there's no man in Sicily must
dispute with Rhodophil; they are so French, so *galant*, and so *tendre*, that I
cannot resist the temptation of the assignation. Now go you away, Philotis;
it imports me to practise what I shall say to my servant when I meet him.

[*Exit* Philotis

'Rhodophil, you'll wonder at my assurance to meet you here; let me die, I
am so out of breath with coming, that I can render you no reason of it.'
Then he will make this *repartie*: 'Madam, I have no reason to accuse you for
that which is so great a favour to me.' Then I reply: 'But why have you drawn
me to this solitary place? Let me die but I am apprehensive of some violence
from you.' Then says he: 'Solitude, madam, is most fit for lovers; but by this
fair hand. ...'—'Nay, now I vow you're rude. Sir! O fie, fie, fie; I hope
you'll be honourable?'—'You'd laugh at me if I should, madam. ...'—
'What, do you mean to throw me down thus? Ah me! ah, ah, ah.'

Enter Polydamas, Leonidas, *and* Guards.

O Venus! The King and court. Let me die but I fear they have found my
faible, and will turn me into *ridicule*. [*Exit running.*

Leon. Sir, I beseech you.
Poly. Do not urge my patience. 222
Leon. I'll not deny
But what your spies informed you of is true:
I love the fair Palmyra; but I loved her
Before I knew your title to my blood.

Enter Palmyra, guarded.

See, here she comes; and looks, amidst her guards,
Like a weak dove under the falcon's gripe.
O heaven, I cannot bear it.
Poly. Maid, come hither.
Have you presumed so far, as to receive 230
My son's affection?
Palmyra. Alas, what shall I answer? To confess it
Will raise a blush upon a virgin's face;
Yet I was ever taught 'twas base to lie.
Poly. You've been too bold, and you must love no more.
Palmyra. Indeed I must; I cannot help my love;
I was so tender when I took the bent,
That now I grow that way.
Poly. He is a prince; and you are meanly born.
Leon. Love either finds equality or makes it: 240

> Like death he knows no difference in degrees,
> But planes and levels all.
Palmyra. Alas, I had not rendered up my heart,
> Had he not loved me first; but he preferred me
> Above the maidens of my age and rank;
> Still shunned their company, and still sought mine;
> I was not won by gifts, yet still he gave;
> And all his gifts, though small, yet spoke his love.
> He picked the earliest strawberries in woods,
> The clustered filberts, and the purple grapes: 250
> He taught a prating stare to speak my name;
> And when he found a nest of nightingales,
> Or callow linnets, he would show 'em me,
> And let me take 'em out.
Poly. This is a little mistress, meanly born,
> Fit only for a prince's vacant hours,
> And then, to laugh at her simplicity,
> Not fix a passion there. Now hear my sentence.
Leon. Remember, ere you give it, 'tis pronounced
> Against us both.   260
Poly. First, in her hand
> There shall be placed a player's painted sceptre,
> And, on her head, a gilded pageant crown;
> Thus shall she go,
> With all the boys attending on her triumph:
> That done, be put alone into a boat,
> With bread and water only for three days,
> And so on the sea she shall be set adrift,
> And who relieves her, dies.
Palmyra. I only beg that you would execute   270
> The last part first: let me be put to sea;
> The bread and water, for my three days' life,
> I give you back, I would not live so long;
> But let me 'scape the shame.
Leon. Look to me, piety; and you, O gods,
> Look to my piety:
> Keep me from saying that which misbecomes a son;
> But let me die before I see this done.
Poly. If you for ever will abjure her sight,
> I can be yet a father; she shall live.   280

251 stare] starling

Leon. Hear, O you powers, is this to be a father?
   I see 'tis all my happiness and quiet
   You aim at, sir; and take 'em:
   I will not save e'en my Palmyra's life
   At that ignoble price; but I'll die with her.
Palmyra. So had I done by you,
   Had fate made me a princess: death, methinks,
   Is not a terror now;
   He is not fierce, or grim, but fawns, and soothes me,
   And slides along, like Cleopatra's aspic,   290
   Offering his service to my troubled breast.
Leon. Begin what you have purposed when you please,
   Lead her to scorn, your triumph shall be doubled.
   As holy priests
   In pity go with dying malefactors,
   So will I share her shame.
Poly. You shall not have your will so much; first part 'em,
   Then execute your office.
Leon.   No; I'll die
   In her defence.   [*Draws his sword.*
Palmyra.   Ah, hold and pull not on
   A curse, to make me worthy of my death: 300
   Do not by lawless force oppose your father,
   Whom you have too much disobeyed for me.
Leon. Here, take it, sir, and with it, pierce my heart:
              [*Presenting his sword to his father upon his knees.*
   You have done more, in taking my Palmyra.
   You are my father, therefore I submit.
Poly. Keep him from any thing he may design
   Against his life, whilst the first fury lasts;
   And now perform what I commanded you.
Leon. In vain; if sword and poison be denied me,
   I'll hold my breath and die.   310
Palmyra. Farewell, my last, Leonidas; yet live,
   I charge you live, till you believe me dead.
   I cannot die in peace, if you die first.
   If life's a blessing, you shall have it last.
Poly. Go on with her, and lead him after me.

Enter Argaleon *hastily, with* Hermogenes.

290 aspic] asp

Arg. I bring you, sir, such news as must amaze you,
  And such as will prevent you from an action
  Which would have rendered all your life unhappy.
Poly. Hermogenes, you bend your knees in vain,

Hermogenes kneels.

My doom's already past.   320
Herm. I kneel not for Palmyra, for I know
  She will not need my prayers; but for myself:
  With a feigned tale I have abused your ears,
  And therefore merit death; but since, unforced,
  I first accuse myself, I hope your mercy.
Poly. Haste to explain your meaning.
Herm. Then, in a few words, Palmyra is your daughter.
Poly. How can I give belief to this impostor?
  He who has once abused me, often may.
  I'll hear no more.
Arg.   For your own sake, you must.   330
Herm. A parent's love (for I confess my crime)
  Moved me to say Leonidas was yours;
  But when I heard Palmyra was to die,
  The fear of guiltless blood so stung my conscience,
  That I resolved, e'en with my shame, to save
  Your daughter's life.
Poly. But how can I be certain, but that interest,
  Which moved you first to say your son was mine,
  Does not now move you too, to save your daughter?
Herm. You had but then my word; I bring you now   340
  Authentic testimonies. Sir, in short,
                    [*Delivers on his knees a jewel, and a letter.*
  If this will not convince you, let me suffer.
Poly. I know this jewel well; 'twas once my mother's,
                              [*Looking at the jewel.*
  Which, marrying, I presented to my wife.
  And this, O this, is my Eudoxia's hand.
  (*Reads.*) 'This was the pledge of love given to Eudoxia,
  Who, dying, to her young Palmyra leaves it:
  And this when you, my dearest lord, receive,
  Own her, and think on me, dying Eudoxia.'
  (*To* Argaleon.) Take it; 'tis well there is no more to read,   350
  My eyes grow full, and swim in their own light.
                              [*He embraces* Palmyra.

Palmyra. I fear, sir, this is your intended pageant.
 You sport yourself at poor Palmyra's cost;
 But if you think to make me proud,
 Indeed I cannot be so: I was born
 With humble thoughts, and lowly like my birth.
 A real fortune could not make me haughty,
 Much less a feigned.
Poly.   This was her mother's temper.
 I have too much deserved thou shouldst suspect
 That I am not thy father; but my love   360
 Shall henceforth show I am. Behold my eyes,
 And see a father there begin to flow:
 This is not feigned, Palmyra.
Palmyra. I doubt no longer, sir; you are a king,
 And cannot lie: falsehood's a vice too base
 To find a room in any royal breast;
 I know, in spite of my unworthiness,
 I am your child; for when you would have killed me,
 Methought I loved you then.
Arg. Sir, we forget the prince Leonidas,   370
 His greatness should not stand neglected thus.
Poly. Guards, you may now retire. Give him his sword,
 And leave him free.
Leon. Then the first use I make of liberty
 Shall be, with your permission, mighty sir,
 To pay that reverence to which nature binds me.
          [*Kneels to* Hermogenes.
Arg. Sure you forget your birth thus to misplace
 This act of your obedience; you should kneel
 To nothing but to heaven, and to a king.
Leon. I never shall forget what nature owes,   380
 Nor be ashamed to pay it; though my father
 Be not a king, I know him brave and honest,
 And well deserving of a worthier son.
Poly. (*To* Hermogenes.) He bears it gallantly.
Leon. Why would you not instruct me, sir, before
 Where I should place my duty?
 From which, if ignorance have made me swerve,
 I beg your pardon for an erring son.
Palmyra. I almost grieve I am a princess, since
 It makes him lose a crown.   390
Leon. And next, to you, my king, thus low I kneel,

T'implore your mercy; if in that small time
I had the honour to be thought your son,
I paid not strict obedience to your will:
I thought, indeed, I should not be compelled,
But thought it as your son; so what I took
In duty from you, I restored in courage;
Because your son should not be forced.

Poly. You have my pardon for it.

Leon. To you, fair princess, I congratulate   400
  Your birth; of which I ever thought you worthy:
  And give me leave to add, that I am proud
  The gods have picked me out to be the man
  By whose dejected fate yours is to rise;
  Because no man could more desire your fortune,
  Or franklier part with his to make you great.

Palmyra. I know the king, though you are not his son,
  Will still regard you as my foster-brother,
  And so conduct you downward from a throne,
  By slow degrees, so unperceived and soft,   410
  That it may seem no fall: or, if it be,
  May fortune lay a bed of down beneath you.

Poly. He shall be ranked with my nobility,
  And kept from scorn by a large pension given him.

Leon. (*Bowing.*) You are all great and royal in your gifts;
  But at the donor's feet I lay 'em down:
  Should I take riches from you, it would seem
  As I did want a soul to bear that poverty
  To which the gods designed my humble birth:
  And should I take your honours without merit,   420
  It would appear, I wanted manly courage
  To hope 'em, in your service, from my sword.

Poly. Still brave, and like yourself.
  The court shall shine this night in its full splendour,
  And celebrate this new discovery.
  Argaleon, lead my daughter: as we go
  I shall have time to give her my commands,
  In which you are concerned.   [*Exeunt all but* Leonidas.

Leon. Methinks I do not want
  That huge long train of fawning followers,   430
  That swept a furlong after me.
  'Tis true, I am alone;
  So was the Godhead ere he made the world,

And better served himself, than served by nature.
And yet I have a soul
Above this humble fate I could command,
Love to do good; give largely to true merit;
All that a king should do. But though these are not
My province, I have scene enough within
To exercise my virtue.   440
All that a heart, so fixed as mine, can move,
Is that my niggard fortune starves my love.   [*Exit*

SCENE II

Palamede *and* Doralice *meet : she, with a book in her hand,*
seems to start at sight of him.

Dor. 'Tis a strange thing that no warning will serve your turn; and that
no retirement will secure me from your impertinent addresses! Did not I
tell you that I was to be private here at my devotions?

Palamede. Yes; and you see I have observed my cue exactly. I am come to
relieve you from them. Come, shut up, shut up your book; the man's come
who is to supply all your necessities.

Dor. Then, it seems, you are so impudent to think it was an assignation?
This, I warrant, was your lewd interpretation of my innocent meaning.

Palamede. Venus forbid that I should harbour so unreasonable a thought of
a fair young lady, that you should lead me hither into temptation. I confess I
might think indeed it was a kind of honourable challenge, to meet privately
without seconds, and decide the difference betwixt the two sexes; but heaven
forgive me if I thought amiss.   13

Dor. You thought too, I'll lay my life on't, that you might as well make
love to me, as my husband does to your mistress.

Palamede. I was so unreasonable to think so too.

Dor. And then you wickedly inferred, that there was some justice in the
revenge of it: or at least but little injury for a man to endeavour to enjoy that,
which he accounts a blessing, and which is not valued as it ought by the dull
possessor. Confess your wickedness, did you not think so?

Palamede. I confess I was thinking so, as fast as I could; but you think so
much before me, that you will let me think nothing.   22

Dor. 'Tis the very thing that I designed. I have forestalled all your

439 scene] stage

arguments, and left you without a word more to plead for mercy. If you have any thing farther to offer, ere sentence pass. . . . Poor animal, I brought you hither only for my diversion.

Palamede. That you may have, if you'll make use of me the right way. But I tell thee, woman, I am now past talking.

Dor. But it may be I came hither to hear what fine things you could say for yourself. 30

Palamede. You would be very angry, to my knowledge, if I should lose so much time to say many of 'em. . . . By this hand you would. . . .

Dor. Fie, Palamede, I am a woman of honour.

Palamede. I see you are; you have kept touch with your assignation. And before we part, you shall find that I am a man of honour. . . . Yet I have one scruple of conscience. . . .

Dor. I warrant you will not want some naughty argument or other to satisfy yourself. . . . I hope you are afraid of betraying your friend?

Palamede. Of betraying my friend! I am more afraid of being betrayed by you to my friend. You women now are got into the way of telling first yourselves. A man who has any care of his reputation will be loth to trust it with you. 42

Dor. O you charge your faults upon our sex. You men are like cocks, you never make love but you clap your wings and crow when you have done.

Palamede. Nay, rather you women are like hens; you never lay, but you cackle an hour after, to discover your nest. . . . But I'll venture it for once.

Dor. To convince you that you are in the wrong, I'll retire into the dark grotto to my devotion, and make so little noise that it shall be impossible for you to find me. . . .

Palamede. But if I find you. . . . 50

Dor. Ay, if you find me. . . . But I'll put you to search in more corners than you imagine. [*She runs in, and he after her.*

Enter Rhodophil *and* Melantha.

Mel. Let me die, but this solitude, and that grotto are scandalous. I'll go no further. Besides, you have a sweet lady of your own.

Rhod. But a sweet mistress, now and then, makes my sweet lady so much more sweet.

Mel. I hope you will not force me?

Rhod. But I will, if you desire it.

Palamede. (*Within.*) Where the devil are you, madam? 'Sdeath, I begin to be weary of this hide-and-seek. If you stay a little longer, till the fit's over, I'll hide in my turn, and put you to the finding me. 61

He enters, and sees Rhodophil *and* Melantha.

How! Rhodophil and my mistress!

Mel. My servant to apprehend me! This is *surprenant au dernier*.

Rhod. I must on! There's nothing but impudence can help me out.

Palamede. Rhodophil, how came you hither in so good company?

Rhod. As you see, Palamede—an effect of pure friendship. I was not able to live without you.

Palamede. But what makes my mistress with you?

Rhod. Why, I heard you were here alone, and could not in civility but bring her to you.   70

Mel. You'll pardon the effects of a passion which I may now avow for you, if it transported me beyond the rules of *bien séance*.

Palamede. But who told you I was here? They that told you that may tell you more, for ought I know.

Rhod. O, for that matter, we had intelligence.

Palamede. But let me tell you, we came hither so very privately that you could not trace us.

Rhod. Us? What us? You are alone.

Palamede. Us! The devil's in me for mistaking. Me, I meant. Or us; that is, you are me, or I you, as we are friends: that's us.   80

Dor. (*Within.*) Palamede, Palamede.

Rhod. I should know that voice? Who's within there, that calls you?

Palamede. Faith I can't imagine; I believe the place is haunted.

Dor. (*Within.*) Palamede, Palamede, all-cocks hidden!

Palamede. Lord, lord, what shall I do? Well, dear friend, to let you see I scorn to be jealous, and that I dare trust my mistress with you, take her back, for I would not willingly have her frighted, and I am resolved to see who's there. I'll not be daunted with a bug-bear, that's certain. Prithee dispute it not, it shall be so. Nay, do not put me to swear, but go quickly. There's an effect of pure friendship for you now!   90

Enter Doralice, *and looks amazed, seeing them.*

Rhod. Doralice! I am thunder-struck to see you here.

Palamede. So am I! Quite thunder-struck. Was it you that called me within? (I must be impudent.)

Rhod. How came you hither, spouse?

Palamede. Ay, how came you hither? And, which is more, how could you be here without my knowledge?

Dor. (*To her husband.*) O, gentleman, have I caught you i'faith! Have I broke forth in ambush upon you! I thought my suspicions would prove true.

Rhod. Suspicions! This is very fine, spouse! Prithee what suspicions?

---

63 *surprenant au dernier*] utterly astounding   72 *bien séance*] good taste   84 all-cocks
hidden!] hide-and-seek call

Dor. O, you feign ignorance: why, of you and Melantha! Here have I stayed these two hours, waiting with all the rage of a passionate, loving wife, but infinitely jealous, to take you two in the manner; for hither I was certain you would come. 103

Rhod. But you are mistaken, spouse, in the occasion; for we came hither on purpose to find Palamede, on intelligence he was gone before.

Palamede. I'll be hanged then if the same party, who gave you intelligence I was here, did not tell your wife you would come hither. Now I smell the malice on't on both sides.

Dor. Was it so, think you? Nay, then, I'll confess my part of the malice too. As soon as ever I spied my husband and Melantha come together, I had a strange temptation to make him jealous in revenge; and that made me call Palamede, Palamede, as though there had been an intrigue between us.

Mel. Nay, I avow, there was an appearance of an intrigue between us too.

Palamede. To see how things will come about! 114

Rhod. (*Embraces.*) And was it only thus, my dear Doralice?

Dor. (*Embracing him.*) And did I wrong none, Rhodophil, with a false suspicion?

Palamede. (*Aside.*) Now am I confident we had all four the same design. 'Tis a pretty odd kind of game this, where each of us plays for double stakes. This is just thrust and parry with the same motion; I am to get his wife, and yet to guard my own mistress. But I am vilely suspicious that while I conquer in the right wing I shall be routed in the left. For both our women will certainly betray their party, because they are each of them for gaining of two, as well as we. And I much fear,

> If their necessities and ours were known,
> They have more need of two, than we of one.

[*Exeunt, embracing one another.*

ACT IV   SCENE I

Enter Leonidas, *musing,* Amalthea *following him.*

Amal. Yonder he is, and I must speak, or die;
And yet 'tis death to speak; yet he must know
I have a passion for him, and may know it
With a less blush; because to offer it
To his low fortunes shows I loved before
His person, not his greatness.

Leon. First scorned, and now commanded from the court!
 The king is good; but he is wrought to this
 By proud Argaleon's malice.
 What more disgrace can love and fortune join   10
 T'inflict upon one man? I cannot now
 Behold my dear Palmyra: she, perhaps, too
 Is grown ashamed of a mean ill-placed love.
Amal. (*Aside.*) Assist me, Venus, for I tremble when
 I am to speak, but I must force myself.
 (*To him.*) Sir, I would crave but one short minute with you,
 And some few words.
Leon.   (*Aside.*) The proud Argaleon's sister!
Amal. (*Aside.*) Alas, it will not out; shame stops my mouth.
 Pardon my error, sir, I was mistaken,
 And took you for another.   20
Leon. (*Aside.*) In spite of all his guards, I'll see Palmyra;
 Though meanly born, I have a kingly soul yet.
Amal. (*Aside.*) I stand upon a precipice, where fain
 I would retire, but love still thrusts me on:
 Now I grow bolder, and will speak to him.
 (*To him.*) Sir, 'tis indeed to you that I would speak,
 And if. . . .
Leon. O, you are sent to scorn my fortunes;
 Your sex and beauty are your privilege;
 But should your brother. . . .   30
Amal. Now he looks angry, and I dare not speak.
 I had some business with you, sir,
 But 'tis not worth your knowledge.
Leon. Then 'twill be charity to let me mourn
 My griefs alone, for I am much disordered.
Amal. 'Twill be more charity to mourn 'em with you:
 Heaven knows I pity you.
Leon.   Your pity, madam,
 Is generous, but 'tis unavailable.
Amal. You know not till 'tis tried.
 Your sorrows are no secret; you have lost   40
 A crown, and mistress.
Leon.   Are not these enough?
 Hang two such weights on any other soul,
 And see if it can bear 'em.
Amal. More; you are banished, by my brother's means,
 And ne'er must hope again to see your princess;

Except as prisoners view fair walks and streets,
And careless passengers going by their grates
To make 'em feel the want of liberty.
But, worse than all,
The king this morning has enjoined his daughter   50
T'accept my brother's love.

Leon.   Is this your pity?
You aggravate my griefs, and print 'em deeper
In new and heavier stamps.

Amal. 'Tis as physicians show the desperate ill
T'endear their art, by mitigating pains
They cannot wholly cure: when you despair
Of all you wish, some part of it, because
Unhoped for, may be grateful; and some other. . . .

Leon. What other?

Amal. Some other may. . . .   60
        (*Aside.*) My shame again has seized me, and I can go
No farther. . . .

Leon. These often failing sighs and interruptions,
Make me imagine you have grief like mine:
Have you ne'er loved?

Amal.   I? Never. (*Aside.*) 'Tis in vain;
I must despair in silence.

Leon. You come as I suspected then, to mock,
At least observe my griefs: take it not ill
That I must leave you.   [*Is going.*
                                                              70
Amal. You must not go with these unjust opinions.
Command my life, and fortunes; you are wise;
Think, and think well, what I can do to serve you.

Leon. I have but one thing in my thoughts and wishes:
If by your means I can obtain the sight
Of my adored Palmyra; or, what's harder,
One minute's time, to tell her, I die hers.
                                              [*She starts back.*

I see I am not to expect it from you;
Nor could, indeed, with reason.

Amal. Name any other thing: is Amalthea
So despicable, she can serve your wishes   80
In this alone?

Leon.   If I should ask of heaven,
I have no other suit.

47 grates] gratings, barred windows

Amal. To show you, then, I can deny you nothing,
   Though 'tis more hard to me than any other,
   Yet I will do't for you.
Leon. Name quickly, name the means.
   Speak, my good angel.
Amal. Be not so much o'erjoyed; for, if you are,
   I'll rather die than do't. This night the court
   Will be in masquerade;   90
   You shall attend on me; in that disguise
   You may both see and speak to her,
   If you dare venture it.
Leon. Yes, were a god her guardian,
   And bore in each hand thunder, I would venture.
Amal. Farewell then; two hours hence I will expect you.
   My heart's so full, that I can stay no longer.   [*Exit.*
Leon. Already it grows dusky; I'll prepare
   With haste for my disguise. But who are these?

         Enter Hermogenes *and* Eubulus.

Herm. 'Tis he; we need not fear to speak to him.   100
Eub. Leonidas.
Leon.   Sure I have known that voice.
Herm. You have some reason, sir; 'tis Eubulus,
   Who bred you with the princess; and, departing,
   Bequeathed you to my care.
Leon. My foster-father! (*Kneeling.*) Let my knees express
   My joys for your return!
Eub. Rise, sir, you must not kneel.
Leon.   E'er since you left me,
   I have been wandering in a maze of fate,
   Led by false fires of a fantastic glory
   And the vain lustre of imagined crowns.   110
   But, ah! why would you leave me? Or how could you
   Absent yourself so long?
Eub. I'll give you a most just account of both:
   And something more I have to tell you, which
   I know must cause your wonder; but this place,
   Though almost hid in darkness, is not safe.

          Torches appear.

Already I discern some coming towards us
With lights, who may discover me. Hermogenes,

Your lodgings are hard by, and much more private.
Herm. There you may freely speak.
Leon.   Let us make haste;   120
For some affairs, and of no small importance,
Call me another way.   [*Exeunt.*

Enter Palamede *and* Rhodophil, *with visor-masks in their hands,*
and torches before them.

Palamede. We shall have noble sport tonight, Rhodophil; this masquerad-
ing is a most glorious invention.
Rhod. I believe it was invented first by some jealous lover to discover the
haunts of his jilting mistress; or perhaps by some distressed servant to gain
an opportunity with a jealous man's wife.
Palamede. No, it must be the invention of a woman, it has so much of
subtlety and love in it.
Rhod. I am sure 'tis extremely pleasant; for to go unknown is the next
degree to going invisible.   131
Palamede. What with our antic habits, and feigned voices, do you know
me? And I know you? Methinks we move and talk just like so many over-
grown puppets.
Rhod. Masquerade is only visor-mask improved; a heightening of the same
fashion.
Palamede. No; masquerade is visor-mask in debauch; and I like it the
better for't. For, with a visor-mask, we fool ourselves into courtship, for the
sake of an eye that glanced, or a hand that stole itself out of the glove sometimes, to give us a sample of the skin. But in masquerade there is nothing to
be known, she's all *terra incognita* and the bold discoverer leaps ashore, and
takes his lot among the wild Indians and savages, without the vile consideration of safety to his person, or of beauty or wholesomeness in his mistress.

Enter Beliza.

Rhod. Beliza, what make you here?   144
Bel. Sir, my lady sent me after you, to let you know she finds herself a little
indisposed, so that she cannot be at court, but is retired to rest in her own
apartment where she shall want the happiness of your dear embraces tonight.
Rhod. A very fine phrase, Beliza, to let me know my wife desires to lie
alone.
Palamede. I doubt, Rhodophil, you take the pains sometimes to instruct
your wife's woman in these elegancies.
Rhod. Tell my dear lady, that since I must be so unhappy as not to wait on
her tonight, I will lament bitterly for her absence. 'Tis true, I shall be at

s.d. *visor-masks*] small face-masks

court, but I will take no *divertissement* there; and when I return to my solitary
bed, if I am so forgetful of my passion as to sleep, I will dream of her; and
betwixt sleep and waking, put out my foot towards her side, for midnight
consolation; and not finding her, I will sigh, and imagine myself a most
desolate widower.   158

 Bel. I shall do your commands, sir.   [*Exit.*

 Rhod. (*Aside.*) She's sick as aptly for my purpose, as if she had contrived
it so. Well, if ever woman was a help-meet for man, my spouse is so; for
within this hour I received a note from Melantha, that she would meet me
this evening in masquerade in boy's habit, to rejoice with me before she
entered into fetters; for I find she loves me better then Palamede, only
because he's to be her husband. There's something of antipathy in the word
marriage to the nature of love; marriage is the mere ladle of affection, that
cools it when 'tis never so fiercely boiling over.

 Palamede. Dear Rhodophil, I must needs beg your pardon. There is an
occasion fallen out which I had forgot: I cannot be at court tonight.   169

 Rhod. Dear Palamede, I am sorry we shall not have one course together at
the herd; but I find your game lies single. Good fortune to you with your
mistress.   [*Exit.*

 Palamede. He has wished me good fortune with his wife: there's no sin in
this then, there's fair leave given. Well, I must go visit the sick; I cannot
resist the temptations of my charity. O what a difference will she find
betwixt a dull resty husband and a quick vigorous lover! He sets out like a
carrier's horse, plodding on, because he knows he must, with the bells of
matrimony chiming so melancholy about his neck, in pain till he's at his
journey's end. And despairing to get thither, he is fain to fortify imagination
with the thoughts of another woman. I take heat after heat, like a well-
breathed courser, and. . . . But hark, what noise is that? Swords! (*Clashing
of swords within.*) Nay, then have with you.   [*Exit* Palamede.

 Re-enter Palamede, *with* Rhodophil*: and* Doralice *in man's habit.*

 Rhod. Friend, your relief was very timely, otherwise I had been oppressed.
 Palamede. What was the quarrel?
 Rhod. What I did was in rescue of this youth.
 Palamede. What cause could he give 'em?
 Dor. The cause was nothing but only the common cause of fighting in
masquerades: they were drunk, and I was sober.
 Rhod. Have they not hurt you?
 Dor. No; but I am exceeding ill, with the fright on't.   190
 Palamede. Let's lead him to some place where he may refresh himself.
 Rhod. Do you conduct him then.

176 resty] sluggish

Palamede. (Aside.) How cross this happens to my design of going to Doralice! For I am confident she was sick on purpose that I should visit her.
Hark you, Rhodophil, could not you take care of the stripling? I am partly
engaged tonight.

Rhod. You know I have business. But come, youth, if it must be so.

Dor. (To Rhodophil.) No, good sir, do not give yourself that trouble. I
shall be safer, and better pleased with your friend here.

Rhod. Farewell then! Once more I wish you good adventure.

Palamede. Damn this kindness! Now must I be troubled with this young
rogue, and miss my opportunity with Doralice.

[*Exit* Rhodophil *alone*, Palamede *with* Doralice.

SCENE II

Enter Polydamas.

Poly. Argaleon counselled well to banish him.
      He has I know not what
      Of greatness in his looks and of high fate,
      That almost awes me; but I fear my daughter,
      Who hourly moves me for him, and I marked
      She sighed when I but named Argaleon to her.
      But see, the maskers: hence my cares, this night;
      At least take truce, and find me on my pillow.

Enter the Princess *in masquerade, with* Ladies : *at the other end,* Argaleon
and Gentlemen *in masquerade : then* Leonidas *leading* Amalthea. *The
King sits. A dance. After the dance,*

Amal. (To Leonidas.) That's the princess;
      I saw the habit ere she put it on.   10
Leon. I know her by a thousand other signs;
      She cannot hide so much divinity.
      Disguised, and silent, yet some graceful motion
      Breaks from her, and shines round her like a glory.

[*Goes to* Palmyra.

Amal. Thus she reveals herself, and knows it not:
      Like love's dark-lantern I direct his steps,
      And yet he sees not that which gives him light.

Palm. (*To* Leonidas.) I know you; but, alas, Leonidas,
   Why should you tempt this danger on yourself?
Leon. Madam, you know me not, if you believe   20
   I would not hazard greater for your sake:
   But you, I fear, are changed.
Palmyra. No, I am still the same;
   But there are many things became Palmyra
   Which ill become the princess.
Leon.   I ask nothing
   Which honour will not give you leave to grant:
   One hour's short audience at my father's house
   You cannot sure refuse me.
Palmyra. Perhaps I should, did I consult strict virtue;
   But something must be given to love and you.   30
   When would you I should come?
Leon. This evening, with the speediest opportunity.
   I have a secret to discover to you,
   Which will surprise, and please you.
Palmyra.   'Tis enough.
   Go now; for we may be observed and known.
   I trust your honour; give me not occasion
   To blame myself, or you.
Leon. You never shall repent your good opinion.
                      [*Kisses her hand and exit.*
Arg. I cannot be deceived; that is the Princess:
   One of her maids betrayed the habit to me;   40
   But who was he with whom she held discourse?
   'Tis one she favours, for he kissed her hand.
   Our shapes are like, are habits near the same:
   She may mistake, and speak to me for him.
   I am resolved, I'll satisfy my doubts,
   Though to be more tormented.   *Exit.*

SONG

I.

Whilst Alexis lay pressed
In her arms he loved best,
With his hands round her neck,
And his head on her breast,   50
He found the fierce pleasure too hasty to stay,
And his soul in the tempest just flying away.

2.

When Celia saw this,
With a sigh, and a kiss,
She cried: 'Oh my dear, I am robbed of my bliss;
'Tis unkind to your love, and unfaithfully done,
To leave me behind you, and die all alone.'

3.

The youth, though in haste,
And breathing his last,
In pity died slowly, while she died more fast;   60
Till at length she cried: 'Now, my dear, now let us go,
Now die, my Alexis, and I will die too.'

4.

Thus entranced they did lie,
Till Alexis did try
To recover new breath, that again he might die:
Then often they died; but the more they did so,
The nymph died more quick, and the shepherd more slow.

Another dance. After it, Argaleon *re-enters, and stands by the* Princess.

Palmyra. (*To* Argaleon.) Leonidas, what means this quick return?
Arg. O heaven! 'Tis what I feared.
Palmyra. Is ought of moment happened since you went?   70
Arg. No, madam, but I understood not fully
   Your last commands.
Palmyra.   And yet you answered to 'em.
   Retire; you are too indiscreet a lover:
   I'll meet you where I promised.   [*Exit.*
Arg. O my cursed fortune! What have I discovered?
   But I will be revenged.   [*Whispers to the* King.
Poly. But are you certain you are not deceived?
Arg. Upon my life.
Poly.   Her honour is concerned.
   Somewhat I'll do; but I am yet distracted,
   And know not where to fix. I wished a child,   80
   And heaven, in anger, granted my request.
   So blind we are, our wishes are so vain,
   That what we most desire proves most our pain.
                                                   [*Exeunt omnes.*

SCENE III

An eating house. Bottles of wine on the table.

Palamede; *and* Doralice *in man's habit.*

Dor. (*Aside.*) Now cannot I find in my heart to discover myself, though I long he should know me.

Palamede. I tell thee, boy, now I have seen thee safe, I must be gone. I have no leisure to throw away on thy raw conversation. I am a person that understands better things, I.

Dor. Were I a woman, oh how you'd admire me! cry up every word I said, and screw your face into a submissive smile. As I have seen a dull gallant act wit, and counterfeit pleasantness, when he whispers to a great person in a playhouse; smile, and look briskly, when the other answers, as if something of extraordinary had past betwixt 'em, when, heaven knows, there was nothing else but: 'What o'clock does your lordship think it is?' and my lord's *repartie* is: ''Tis almost park-time': or, at most: 'Shall we out of the pit, and go behind the scenes for an act or two?' And yet such fine things as these would be wit in a mistress's mouth.   14

Palamede. Ay, boy; there's Dame Nature in the case: he who cannot find wit in a mistress, deserves to find nothing else, boy. But these are riddles to thee, child, and I have not leisure to instruct thee. I have affairs to dispatch, great affairs. I am a man of business.

Dor. Come, you shall not go: you have no affairs but what you may dispatch here, to my knowledge.   20

Palamede. I find now, thou art a boy of more understanding than I thought thee. A very lewd wicked boy! O' my conscience thou wouldst debauch me, and hast some evil designs upon my person.

Dor. You are mistaken, sir, I would only have you show me a more lawful reason why you would leave me, than I can why you should not, and I'll not stay you. For I am not so young but I understand the necessities of flesh and blood, and the pressing occasions of mankind as well as you.

Palamede. A very forward and understanding boy! Thou art in great danger of a page's wit, to be brisk at fourteen, and dull at twenty. But I'll give thee no further account; I must, and will go.   30

Dor. My life on't, your mistress is not at home.

Palamede. This imp will make me very angry. I tell thee, young sir, she is at home; and at home for me; and, which is more, she is abed for me, and sick for me.

12 park-time] time for riding in the park

Dor. For you only?

Palamede. Ay, for me only.

Dor. But how do you know she's sick abed?

Palamede. She sent her husband word so.

Dor. And are you such a novice in love, to believe a wife's message to her husband?

Palamede. Why, what the devil should be her meaning else?   40

Dor. It may be to go in masquerade as well as you; to observe your haunts and keep you company without your knowledge.

Palamede. Nay, I'll trust her for that. She loves me too well to disguise herself from me.

Dor. If I were she, I would disguise on purpose to try your wit; and come to my servant like a riddle: *Read me, and take me.*

Palamede. I could know her in any shape: my good genius would prompt me to find out a handsome woman. There's something in her that would attract me to her without my knowledge.

Dor. Then you make a loadstone of your mistress?   50

Palamede. Yes, and I carry steel about me, which has been so often touched, that it never fails to point to the north pole.

Dor. Yet still my mind gives me that you have met her disguised tonight, and have not known her.

Palamede. This is the most pragmatical conceited little fellow; he will needs understand my business better than myself. I tell thee, once more, thou dost not know my mistress.

Dor. And I tell you, once more, that I know her better than you do.

Palamede. The boy's resolved to have the last word. I find I must go without reply.   [*Exit.*

Dor. Ah mischief, I have lost him with my fooling. Palamede! Palamede!

He returns. She plucks off her peruke, and puts it on again when he knows her.

Palamede. O heavens! Is it you, madam?   62

Dor. Now, where was your good genius that would prompt you to find me out?

Palamede. Why, you see I was not deceived. You yourself were my good genius.

Dor. But where was the steel, that knew the loadstone, ha?

Palamede. The truth is, madam, the steel has lost its virtue; and therefore, if you please, we'll new touch it.

Enter Rhodophil; *and* Melantha *in boy's habit.*
Rhodophil *sees* Palamede *kissing* Doralice's *hand.*

---

50 loadstone] magnetic stone   55 pragmatical] meddlesome

Rhod. Palamede again! Am I fallen into your quarters? What? Engaging with a boy? Is all honourable? 71

Palamede. O, very honourable on my side. I was just chastising this young villain. He was running away without paying his share of the reckoning.

Rhod. Then I find I was deceived in him.

Palamede. Yes, you are deceived in him: 'tis the archest rogue, if you did but know him.

Mel. Good Rhodophil, let us get off *à la dérobée* for fear I should be discovered.

Rhod. There's no retiring now; I warrant you for discovery. Now have I the oddest thought, to entertain you before your servant's face, and he never the wiser; 'twill be the prettiest juggling trick to cheat him when he looks upon us. 83

Mel. This is the strangest *caprice* in you.

Palamede. (*To* Doralice.) This Rhodophil's the unluckiest fellow to me! This is now the second time he has barred the dice when we were just ready to have nicked him; but if ever I get the box again. . . .

Dor. Do you think he will not know me? Am I like myself?

Palamede. No more than a picture in the hangings.

Dor. Nay, then he can never discover me, now the wrong side of the arras is turned towards him. 91

Palamede. At least, 'twill be some pleasure to me to enjoy what freedom I can while he looks on. I will storm the outworks of matrimony even before his face.

Rhod. What wine have you there, Palamede?

Palamede. Old Chios, or the rogue's damned that drew it.

Rhod. Come, to the most constant of mistresses, that I believe is yours, Palamede.

Dor. Pray spare your seconds; for my part I am but a weak brother.

Palamede. Now, to the truest of turtles; that is your wife, Rhodophil, that lies sick at home in the bed of honour. 101

Rhod. Now let's have one common health, and so have done.

Dor. Then, for once, I'll begin it. Here's to him that has the fairest lady of Sicily in masquerade tonight.

Palamede. This is such an obliging health, I'll kiss thee, dear rogue, for thy invention. [*Kisses her.*

Rhod. (*Aside.*) He who has this lady, is a happy man, without dispute.— I'm most concerned in this, I am sure.

Palamede. Was it not well found out, Rhodophil?

---

78 *à la dérobée*] secretly   80 warrant you for] guarantee you against   86 barred the dice] declared throw void   87 nicked] beaten   89 hangings] tapestries

Mel. Ay, this was a *bien trouvé* indeed.   110

Dor. (*To* Melantha.) I suppose I shall do you a kindness to enquire if you
have not been in France, sir?

Mel. To do you service, sir.

Dor. O, monsieur, *votre valet bien humble.*   [*Saluting her.*

Mel. Votre esclave, monsieur, de tout mon cœur.   [*Returning the salute.*

Dor. I suppose, sweet sir, you are the hope and joy of some thriving
citizen, who has pinched himself at home, to breed you abroad, where you
have learnt your exercises, as it appears most awkwardly, and are returned
with the addition of a new-laced bosom and a clap, to your good old father,
who looks at you with his mouth, while you spout French with your *mon
monsieur.*   121

Palamede. Let me kiss thee again for that, dear rogue.

Mel. And you, I imagine, are my young master, whom your mother durst
not trust upon salt water, but left you to be your own tutor at fourteen, to be
very brisk and *entreprenant*, to endeavour to be debauched ere you have
learnt the knack on't, to value yourself upon a clap before you can get it,
and to make it the height of your ambition to get a player for your
mistress.

Rhod. (*Embracing* Melantha.) O dear young bully, thou hast tickled him
with a *repartie* i'faith.   130

Mel. You are one of those that applaud our country plays, where drums,
and trumpets, and blood, and wounds are wit.

Rhod. Again, my boy? Let me kiss thee most abundantly.

Dor. You are an admirer of the dull French poetry, which is so thin, that
it is the very leaf-gold of wit, the very wafers and whipped cream of sense,
for which a man opens his mouth and gapes, to swallow nothing. And to be
an admirer of such profound dulness, one must be endowed with a great
perfection of impudence and ignorance.

Palamede. Let me embrace thee most vehemently.

Mel. I'll sacrifice my life for French poetry.   [*Advancing.*

Dor. I'll die upon the spot for our country wit.   141

Rhod. (*To* Melantha.) Hold, hold, young Mars! Palamede, draw back your
hero.

Palamede. 'Tis time; I shall be drawn in for a second else at the wrong
weapon.

Mel. O that I were a man for thy sake!

Dor. You'll be a man as soon as I shall.

Enter a Messenger *to* Rhodophil.

115 *esclave*] slave   119 clap] venereal disease   125 *entreprenant*] forward

Mess. Sir, the king has instant business with you.
  I saw the guard drawn up by your lieutenant
  Before the palace gate, ready to march.   150
Rhod. 'Tis somewhat sudden; say that I am coming.
                                            [*Exit* Messenger.
Now, Palamede, what think you of this sport? This is some sudden tumult:
will you along?
  Palamede. Yes, yes, I will go; but the devil take me if ever I was less in
humour. Why the pox could they not have stayed their tumult till tomorrow?
Then I had done my business, and had been ready for 'em. Truth is, I had a
little transitory crime to have committed first; and I am the worst man in the
world at repenting, till a sin be thoroughly done. But what shall we do with
the two boys?
  Rhod. Let them take a lodging in the house till the business be over.
  Dor. What, lie with a boy? For my part, I own it, I cannot endure to lie
with a boy.   162
  Palamede. The more's my sorrow I cannot accommodate you with a better
bed-fellow.
  Mel. Let me die, if I enter into a pair of sheets with him that hates the
French.
  Dor. Pish, take no care for us, but leave us in the streets. I warrant you, as
late as it is, I'll find my lodging as well as any drunken bully of 'em all.
  Rhod. (*Aside.*) I'll fight in mere revenge; and wreak my passion
  On all that spoil this hopeful assignation.   170
  Palamede. I'm sure we fight in a good quarrel:
  Rogues may pretend religion, and the laws;
  But a kind mistress is the *Good old Cause*.   [*Exeunt.*

SCENE IV

Enter Palmyra, Eubulus, Hermogenes.

Palmyra. You tell me wonders; that Leonidas
  Is prince Theagenes, the late king's son.
Eub. It seemed as strange to him, as now to you,
  Before I had convinced him. But, besides
  His great resemblance to the king his father,
  The queen his mother lives, secured by me
  In a religious house; to whom each year

173 *Good old Cause*] the Puritan cause

I brought the news of his increasing virtues.
My last long absence from you both was caused
By wounds which in my journey I received   10
When set upon by thieves; I lost those jewels
And letters which your dying mother left.
Herm. The same he means, which, since brought to the king,
Made him first know he had a child alive.
'Twas then my care of prince Leonidas
Caused me to say he was th'usurper's son;
Till, after forced by your apparent danger,
I made the true discovery of your birth,
And once more hid my prince's.

Enter Leonidas.

Leon. Hermogenes, and Eubulus, retire;   20
Those of our party, whom I left without,
Expect your aid and counsel.   [*Exeunt ambo.*
Palmyra. I should, Leonidas, congratulate
This happy change of your exalted fate;
But, as my joy, so you my wonder move;
Your looks have more of business than of love:
And your last words some great design did show.
Leon. I frame not any to be hid from you.
You, in my love, all my designs may see;
But what have love and you designed for me?   30
Fortune once more has set the balance right:
First, equalled us, in lowness; then, in height.
Both of us have so long, like gamesters, thrown,
Till fate comes round and gives to each his own.
As fate is equal so may love appear:
Tell me at least what I must hope or fear.
Palmyra. After so many proofs, how can you call
My love in doubt? Fear nothing; and hope, all.
Think what a prince with honour may receive,
Or I may give without a parent's leave.   40
Leon. You give and then restrain the grace you show;
As ostentatious priests, when souls they woo,
Promise their heaven to all but grant to few.
But do for me, what I have dared for you.
I did no argument from duty bring:
Duty's a name; and love's a real thing.

s.d. *ambo*] together

Palmyra. Man's love may like wild torrents overflow;
    Woman's as deep, but in its banks must go.
    My love is mine; and that I can impart;
    But cannot give my person with my heart.   50
Leon. Your love is then no gift:
    For when the person it does not convey,
    'Tis to give gold, and not to give the key,
Palmyra. Then ask my father.
Leon.   He detains my throne:
    Who holds back mine, will hardly give his own.
Palmyra. What then remains?
Leon.   That I must have recourse
    To arms; and take my love and crown, by force.
    Hermogenes is forming the design;
    And with him, all the brave and loyal join.
Palmyra. And is it thus you court Palmyra's bed?   60
    Can she the murderer of her parent wed?
    Desist from force: so much you well may give
    To love, and me, to let my father live.
Leon. Each act of mine my love to you has shown;
    But you, who tax my want of it, have none.
    You bid me part with you, and let him live;
    But they should nothing ask, who nothing give.
Palmyra. I give what virtue and what duty can,
    In vowing ne'er to wed another man.
Leon. You will be forced to be Argaleon's wife.   70
Palmyra. I'll keep my promise, though I lose my life.
Leon. Then you lose love, for which we both contend;
    For life is but the means, but love's the end.
Palmyra. Our souls shall love hereafter.
Leon.   I much fear,
    That soul which could deny the body here
    To taste of love, would be a niggard there.
Palmyra. Then 'tis past hope: our cruel fate, I see,
    Will make a sad divorce 'twixt you and me.
    For, if you force employ, by heaven I swear,
    And all blessed beings. . . .
Leon.   Your rash oath forbear!   80
Palmyra. I never. . . .
Leon.   Hold once more! But, yet, as he
    Who 'scapes a dangerous leap, looks back to see;
    So I desire, now I am past my fear,

To know what was that oath you meant to swear.
Palmyra. I meant that if you hazarded your life,
Or sought my father's, ne'er to be your wife.
Leon. See now Palmyra how unkind you prove!
Could you with so much ease forswear my love?
Palmyra. You force me with your ruinous design.
Leon. Your father's life is more your care than mine.   90
Palmyra. You wrong me: 'tis not; though it ought to be;
You are my care, heaven knows, as well as he.
Leon. If now the execution I delay,
My honour and my subjects I betray.
All is prepared for the just enterprise;
And the whole city will tomorrow rise.
The leaders of the party are within,
And Eubulus has sworn that he will bring,
To head their arms, the person of their king.
Palmyra. In telling this you make me guilty too;   100
I therefore must discover what I know:
What honour bids you do, nature bids me prevent;
But kill me first, and then pursue your black intent.
Leon. Palmyra, no; you shall not need to die;
Yet I'll not trust too strict a piety.
Within there!

Enter Eubulus.

Eubulus, a guard prepare;
Here, I commit this prisoner to your care.
                    [*Kisses* Palmyra's *hand; then gives it to* Eubulus.
Palmyra. Leonidas, I never thought these bands
Could e'er be given me by a lover's hands.
Leon. (*Kneeling.*) Palmyra, thus your judge himself arraigns;   110
He who imposed these bonds still wears your chains:
When you to love or duty false must be,
Or to your father guilty, or to me,
These chains alone remain to set you free.

Noise of swords clashing.

Poly. (*Within.*) Secure these, first; then search the inner room.
Leon. From whence do these tumultuous clamours come?

Enter Hermogenes, *hastily.*

Herm. We are betrayed; and there remains alone
　　This comfort, that your person is not known.

　　　　Enter the King, Argaleon, Rhodophil, Palamede, Guards;
　　　　　　　some like citizens as prisoners.

Poly. What mean this midnight consultation here,
　　Where I, like an unsummoned guest, appear?   120
Leon. Sir . . .
Arg.　　　　There needs no excuse; 'tis understood;
　　You were all watching, for your prince's good.
Poly. My reverend city friends, you are well met!
　　On what great work were your grave wisdoms set?
　　Which of my actions were you scanning here?
　　What French invasion have you found to fear?
Leon. They are my friends, and come, sir, with intent
　　To take their leaves before my banishment.
Poly. Your exile, in both sexes, friends can find:
　　(*Seeing* Palmyra.) I see the ladies, like the men, are kind.   130
Palmyra. (*Kneeling.*) Alas, I came but . . .
Poly.　　　　　　　　　　Add not to your crime
　　A lie: I'll hear you speak some other time.
　　How? Eubulus! Nor time nor thy disguise
　　Can keep thee undiscovered from my eyes.
　　A guard there; seize 'em all.
Rhod. Yield, sir. What use of valour can be shown?
[*Leon.*] One, and unarmed, against a multitude!
　　O for a sword!

　　　　He reaches at one of the guard's halberds, and is seized behind.

　　　　　　　I will not lose my breath
　　In fruitless prayers; but beg a speedy death.
Palmyra. O spare Leonidas, and punish me.   140
Poly. Mean girl, thou want'st an advocate for thee.
　　Now the mysterious knot will be untied;
　　Whether the young king lives, or where he died:
　　Tomorrow's dawn shall the dark riddle clear,
　　Crown all my joys, and dissipate my fear.   [*Exeunt omnes.*

ACT V   SCENE I

Palamede, Straton. Palamede *with a letter in his hand.*

Palamede. This evening, sayest thou? Will they both be here?

Strat. Yes, sir; both my old master, and your mistress's father. The old gentleman ride hard this journey. They say it shall be the last time they will see the town, and both of 'em are so pleased with this marriage, which they have concluded for you, that I am afraid they will live some years longer to trouble you, with the joy of it.

Palamede. But this is such an unreasonable thing, to impose upon me to be married tomorrow. 'Tis hurrying a man to execution without giving him time to say his prayers!   9

Strat. Yet, if I might advise you, sir, you should not delay it: for your younger brother comes up with 'em, and is got already into their favours. He has gained much upon my old master by finding fault with inn-keepers' bills, and by starving us and our horses to show his frugality. And he is very well with your mistress's father, by giving him receipts for the spleen, gout, and scurvy, and other infirmities of old age.

Palamede. I'll rout him, and his country education. Pox on him, I remember him before I travelled, he had nothing in him but mere jockey; used to talk loud, and make matches, and was all for the crack of the field. Sense and wit were as much banished from his discourse, as they are when the court goes out of town to a horse race. Go now and provide your master's lodgings.   21

Strat. I go, sir.   [*Exit.*

Palamede. It vexes me to the heart to leave all my designs with Doralice unfinished; to have flown her so often to a mark, and still to be bobbed at retrieve. If I had but once enjoyed her, though I could not have satisfied my stomach with the feast, at least I should have relished my mouth a little! But now. . . .

Enter Philotis.

Phil. Oh, sir, you are happily met. I was coming to find you.

Palamede. From your lady, I hope.   29

Phil. Partly from her; but more especially from myself. She has just now received a letter from her father, with an absolute command to dispose herself to marry you tomorrow.

---

17 jockey] i.e., race course interests   18 crack] favourite (racehorse)   24-5 flown . . . retrieve.] made her fly so often to the quarry, and still be cheated at the second flight of the spring bird (a sexual innuendo)

Palamede. And she takes it to the death?

Phil. Quite contrary. The letter could never have come in a more lucky minute, for it found her in an ill humour with a rival of yours, that shall be nameless, about the pronunciation of a French word.

Palamede. Count Rhodophil! Never disguise it, I know the *amour*. But I hope you took the occasion to strike in for me?

Phil. It was my good fortune to do you some small service in it. For your sake I discommended him all over: clothes, person, humour, behaviour, everything. And to sum up all, told her it was impossible to find a married man that was otherwise, for they were all so mortified at home with their wives' ill humours, that they could never recover themselves to be company abroad.

Palamede. Most divinely urged!   45

Phil. Then I took occasion to commend your good qualities: as, the sweetness of your humour, the comeliness of your person, your good mien, your valour; but, above all, your liberality.

Palamede. I vow to God I had like to have forgot that good quality in myself, if thou had'st not remembered me on't. Here are five pieces for thee.

Phil. Lord, you have the softest hand, sir! It would do a woman good to touch it. Count Rhodophil's is not half so soft; for I remember I felt it once, when he gave me ten pieces for my New Year's gift.

Palamede. O, I understand you, madam; you shall find my hand as soft again as Count Rhodophil's. There are twenty pieces for you. The former was but a retaining fee; now I hope you'll plead for me.   56

Phil. Your own merits speak enough. Be sure only to ply her with French words, and I'll warrant you'll do your business. Here are a list of her phrases for this day. Use 'em to her upon all occasions, and foil her at her own weapon; for she's like one of the old Amazons, she'll never marry, except it be the man who has first conquered her.

Palamede. I'll be sure to follow your advice: but you'll forget to further my design.

Phil. What, do you think I'll be ungrateful? ... But, however, if you distrust my memory, put some token on my finger to remember it by. That diamond there would do admirably.   66

Palamede. There 'tis. And I ask your pardon heartily for calling your memory into question. I assure you I'll trust it another time without putting you to the trouble of another token.

Enter Palmyra *and* Artemis.

Artem. Madam, this way the prisoners are to pass. Here you may see Leonidas.

Palmyra. Then here I'll stay and follow him to death.

Enter Melantha *hastily.*

Mel. O, here's her highness!—Now is my time to introduce myself and to make my court to her in my new French phrases. Stay, let me read my catalogue—*suite, figure, chagrin, naiveté,* and let me die for the parenthesis of all.

Palamede. (*Aside.*) Do, persecute her; and I'll persecute thee as fast in thy own dialect.

Mel. Madam, the princess! Let me die, but this is a most horrid spectacle, to see a person who makes so grand a *figure* in the court, without the *suite* of a princess, and entertaining your *chagrin* all alone. (*Naiveté* should have been there, but the disobedient word would not come in.)   82

Palmyra. What is she, Artemis?

Artem. An impertinent lady, madam; very ambitious of being known to your highness.

Palamede. (*To* Melantha.) Let me die, madam, if I have not waited you here these two long hours, without so much as the *suite* of a single servant to attend me; entertaining myself with my own *chagrin,* till I had the honour to see your ladyship, who are a person that makes so considerable a *figure* in the court.   90

Mel. Truce with your *douceurs,* good servant; you see I am addressing to the princess; pray do not *embarrass* me—*embarrass* me! What a delicious French word do you make me lose upon you too! (*To the* princess.) Your highness, madam, will please to pardon the *bévue* which I made in not sooner finding you out to be a princess. But let me die if this *éclaircissement* which is made this day of your quality, does not ravish me; and give me leave to tell you. . . .

Palamede. But first give me leave to tell you, madam, that I have so great a *tendre* for your person, and such a *penchant* to do you service, that. . . .

Mel. What, must I still be troubled with your *sottises?* (There's another word lost that I meant for the princess, with a mischief to you!) But your highness, madam. . . .   102

Palamede. But your ladyship, madam. . . .

Enter Leonidas *guarded, and led over the stage.*

Mel. Out upon him, how he looks, madam! Now he's found no prince, he is the strangest figure of a man; how could I make that *coup d'étourdi* to think him one?

Palmyra. Away, impertinent!—My dear Leonidas!

Leon. My dear Palmyra!

Palmyra. Death shall never part us; my destiny is yours.

[*He is led off; she follows.*

75-6 for the parenthesis of all] if I can't fit them all in   105 *coup d'étourdi*] foolish act

Mel. Impertinent! Oh I am the most unfortunate person this day breathing: that the princess should thus *rompre en visière*, without occasion. Let me die but I'll follow her to death, till I make my peace.   112

Palamede. (*Holding her.*) And let me die, but I'll follow you to the infernals till you pity me.

Mel. (*Turning towards him angrily.*) Ay, 'tis long of you that this *malheur* is fallen upon me. Your impertinence has put me out of the good graces of the princess and all that, which has ruined me, and all that, and therefore let me die but I'll be revenged, and all that.

Palamede. Façon, façon, you must and shall love me, and all that; for my old man is coming up, and all that; and I am *désespéré au dernier*, and will not be disinherited, and all that.   121

Mel. How durst you interrupt me so *mal à propos*, when you knew I was addressing to the princess?

Palamede. But why would you address yourself so much *à contretemps* then?

Mel. Ah mal peste!

Palamede. Ah j'enrage!

Phil. Radoucissez-vous, de grâce, madame; vous êtes bien en colère pour peu de chose. Vous n'entendez pas la raillerie galante.

Mel. À d'autres, à d'autres: he mocks himself of me, he abuses me: ah me unfortunate!   [*Cries.*

Phil. You mistake him, madam, he does but accommodate his phrase to your refined language. *Ah, qu'il est un cavalier accompli!* (*To him.*) Pursue your point, sir. . . .   133

Palamede. (*Singing.*) *Ah qu'il fait beau dans ces bocages;*
　　　　　　　　Ah que le ciel donne un beau jour!
There I was with you, with a *menuet.*

Mel. Let me die now, but this singing is fine, and extremely French in him. (*Laughs.*) But then, that he should use my own words, as it were in contempt of me, I cannot bear it.   [*Crying.*

Palamede. (*Singing.*) *Ces beaux séjours, ces doux ramages.* . . .   140

Mel. (*Singing after him.*)
　　　　Ces beaux séjours, ces doux ramages
　　　　Ces beaux séjours, nous invitent a l'amour!
Let me die but he sings *en cavalier*, and so humours the cadence. (*Laughing.*)

Palamede. (*Singing again.*) *Vois, ma Climène, vois sous ce chêne,*
　　　　　　　　S'entrebaiser ces oiseaux amoureux!

---

111 *rompre en visière*] attack brutally   115 *malheur*] misfortune   119 *Façon*] no theatricals!   120 *désespéré au dernier*] in the depths of despair   124 *à contretemps*] at the wrong moment   127 *Radoucissez-vous*] calm yourself   127 *en colère*] angry   128 *entendez*] understand   134 *bocages*] groves   140 *ramages*] chirping of birds   143 *en cavalier*] in a free and easy manner   144 *chêne*] oak   145 *S'entrebaiser*] kissing each other

Let me die now, but that was fine. Ah, now, for three or four brisk French-
men, to be put into masking habits, and to sing it on a theatre, how witty it
would be! And then to dance helter-skelter to a *chanson à boire: Toute la
terre, toute la terre est à moi!* What's [it] matter though it were made, and
sung, two or three years ago in cabarets, how it would attract the admiration,
especially of every one that's an *éveillé!*   151

Mel. Well; I begin to have a *tendre* for you; but yet, upon condition,
that . . . when we are married, you. . . .

Palamede *sings while she speaks.*

Phil. You must down her voice: if she makes her French conditions, you
are a slave for ever.

Mel. First, will you engage that. . . .

Palamede. (Louder.) Fa, la, la, la, etc.

Mel. Will you hear the conditions?

Palamede. No; I will hear no conditions! I am resolved to win you *en
français*: to be very airy, with abundance of noise, and no sense. Fa, la, la, la,
etc.   161

Mel. Hold, hold! I am vanquished with your *gaieté d'esprit.* I am yours, and
will be yours, *sans nulle réserve, ni condition!* And let me die, if I do not think
myself the happiest nymph in Sicily. . . . My dear French dear, stay but a
minute, till I *raccommode* myself with the princess; and then I am yours,
jusqu'à la mort. . . . *Allons donc.* . . .   [*Exeunt* Melantha, Philotis.

Palamede. (Solus, fanning himself with his hat.) I never thought before that
wooing was so laborious an exercise! If she were worth a million I have
deserved her. And now, methinks too, with taking all this pains for her, I
begin to like her. 'Tis so; I have known many, who never cared for hare nor
partridge, but those they caught themselves would eat heartily: the pains,
and the story a man tells of the taking of 'em, makes the meat go down more
pleasantly. Besides, last night I had a sweet dream of her, and, Gad, she I
have once dreamed of, I am stark mad till I enjoy her, let her be never so
ugly.   175

Enter Doralice.

Dor. Who's that you are so mad to enjoy, Palamede?

Palamede. You may easily imagine that, sweet Doralice.

Dor. More easily than you think I can. I met just now with a certain
man who came to you with letters from a certain old gentleman, yclipped

---

148 *chanson à boire*] drinking song   151 *éveillé*] up-to-date sophisticate   152 *tendre*]
inclination   163 *sans nulle réserve, ni condition*] without any reservation or condition
165 *raccommode* myself] make things up   166 *jusqu'à la mort*] till death   166 *Allons
donc*] let's go   179 yclipped] called (archaic)

your father; whereby I am given to understand that tomorrow you are to take an oath in the church to be grave henceforward, to go ill-dressed and slovenly, to get heirs for your estate, and to dandle 'em for your diversion; and, in short, that love and courtship are to be no more.   183

Palamede. Now have I so much shame to be thus apprehended in the manner, that I can neither speak nor look upon you. I have abundance of grace in me, that I find: but if you have any spark of true friendship in you, retire a little with me to the next room that has a couch or bed in't and bestow your charity upon a poor dying man. A little comfort from a mistress, before a man is going to give himself in marriage, is as good as a lusty dose of strong-water to a dying malefactor; it takes away the sense of hell and hanging from him.   191

Dor. No, good Palamede, I must not be so injurious to your bride. 'Tis ill drawing from the bank today, when all your ready money is payable tomorrow.

Palamede. A wife is only to have the ripe fruit that falls off itself; but a wise man will always preserve a shaking for a mistress.

Dor. But a wife for the first quarter is a mistress.

Palamede. But when the second comes.

Dor. When it does come, you are so given to variety, that you would make a wife of me in another quarter.   200

Palamede. No, never, except I were married to you. Married people can never oblige one another, for all they do is duty and consequently there can be no thanks. But love is more frank and generous than he is honest; he's a liberal giver, but a cursed pay-master.

Dor. I declare I will have no gallant; but, if I would, he should never be a married man. A married man is but a mistress's half-servant, as a clergyman is but the king's half-subject. For a man to come to me that smells o'th' wife—'slife, I would as soon wear her old gown after her, as her husband!

Palamede. Yet 'tis a kind of fashion to wear a princess's cast shoes. You see the country ladies buy 'em to be fine in them.   210

Dor. Yes, a princess's shoes may be worn after her, because they keep their fashion, by being so very little used. But generally a married man is the creature of the world the most out of fashion. His behaviour is dumpish. His discourse—his wife and family. His habit so much neglected, it looks as if that were married too. His hat is married, his peruke is married, his breeches are married, and if we could look within his breeches, we should find him married there too.

Palamede. Am I then to be discarded for ever? Pray do but mark how terrible that word sounds. For ever! It has a very damned sound, Doralice.

Dor. Ay, for ever! It sounds as hellishly to me as it can do to you, but there's no help for't.   221

Palamede. Yet if we had but once enjoyed one another! But then, once only is worse than not at all: it leaves a man with such a lingering after it.

Dor. For ought I know 'tis better that we have not. We might upon trial have liked each other less, as many a man and woman, that have loved as desperately as we, and yet when they came to possession, have sighed, and cried to themselves: *Is this all?*

Palamede. That is only if the servant were not found a man of this world; but if, upon trial, we had not liked each other, we had certainly left loving; and faith, that's the greater happiness of the two.   230

Dor. 'Tis better as 'tis. We have drawn off already as much of our love as would run clear; after possessing, the rest is but jealousies, and disquiets, and quarrelling, and piecing.

Palamede. Nay, after one great quarrel, there's never any sound piecing; the love is apt to break in the same place again.

Dor. I declare I would never renew a love; that's like him who trims an old coach for ten years together—he might buy a new one better cheap.

Palamede. Well, madam, I am convinced that 'tis best for us not to have enjoyed; but Gad, the strongest reason is—because I can't help it!

Dor. The only way to keep us new to one another is never to enjoy, as they keep grapes by hanging 'em upon a line. They must touch nothing if you would preserve 'em fresh.   242

Palamede. But then they wither, and grow dry in the very keeping. However I shall have a warmth for you, and an eagerness, every time I see you. And if I chance to out-live Melantha. . . .

Dor. And if I chance to out-live Rhodophil. . . .

Palamede. Well, I'll cherish my body as much as I can upon that hope. 'Tis true, I would not directly murder the wife of my bosom; but to kill her civilly, by the way of kindness, I'll put as fair as another man. I'll begin tomorrow night, and be very wrathful with her, that's resolved on.

Dor. Well, Palamede, here's my hand. I'll venture to be your second wife, for all your threatenings.   252

Palamede. In the meantime I'll watch you hourly, as I would the ripeness of a melon, and I hope you'll give me leave now and then to look on you, and to see if you are not ready to be cut yet.

Dor. No, no, that must not be, Palamede, for fear the gardener should come and catch you taking up the glass.

Enter Rhodophil.

Rhod. (*Aside.*) Billing so sweetly! Now I am confirmed in my suspicions. I must put an end to this, ere it go further. (*To* Doralice.) Cry you mercy, spouse; I fear I have interrupted your recreations.   260

233 piecing] mending   249 put] endeavour

Dor. What recreations?

Rhod. Nay, no excuses, good spouse. I saw fair hand conveyed to lip, and pressed as though you had been squeezing soft wax together for an indenture. Palamede, you and I must clear this reckoning. Why would you have seduced my wife?

Palamede. Why would you have debauched my mistress?

Rhod. What do you think of that civil couple that played at a game called *hide-and-seek* last evening in the grotto?

Palamede. What do you think of that innocent pair who made it their pretence to seek for others, but came indeed to hide themselves there?

Rhod. All things considered I begin vehemently to suspect that the young gentleman I found in your company last night was a certain youth of my acquaintance.   273

Palamede. And I have an odd imagination that you could never have suspected my small gallant if your little villainous Frenchman had not been a false brother.

Rhod. Farther arguments are needless. Draw off! I shall speak to you now by the way of Bilbo.   [*Claps his hand to his sword.*

Palamede. And I shall answer you by the way of Dangerfield.
                                                     [*Claps his hand on his.*

Dor. Hold, hold! Are not you two a couple of mad fighting fools, to cut one another's throats for nothing?   281

Palamede. How for nothing? He courts the woman I must marry.

Rhod. And he courts you whom I have married.

Dor. But you can neither of you be jealous of what you love not.

Rhod. Faith I am jealous, and that makes me partly suspect that I love you better than I thought.

Dor. Pish! A mere jealousy of honour.

Rhod. Gad, I am afraid there's something else in 't. For Palamede has wit, and if he loves you there's something more in ye than I have found: some rich mine, for ought I know, that I have not yet discovered.   290

Palamede. 'Slife, what's this? Here's an argument for me to love Melantha! For he has loved her, and he has wit too, and for ought I know there may be a mine: but if there be I am resolved I'll dig for 't.

Dor. (*To* Rhodophil.) Then I have found my account in raising your jealousy. O 'tis the most delicate sharp sauce to a cloyed stomach! It will give you a new edge, Rhodophil.

Rhod. And a new point too, Doralice, if I could be sure thou art honest.

Dor. If you are wise, believe me for your own sake. Love and religion have but one thing to trust to—that's a good sound faith. Consider, if I have

---

278 Bilbo] sword (Bilbao in Spain was famed for rapiers)   279 Dangerfield] sword (conventional name for a bullying swordsman)

played false, you can never find it out by any experiment you can make upon me.   301

Rhod. No? Why, suppose I had a delicate screwed gun—if I left her clean and found her foul, I should discover to my cost she had been shot in.

Dor. But if you left her clean, and found her only rusty, you would discover to your shame she was only so for want of shooting.

Palamede. Rhodophil, you know me too well to imagine I speak for fear; and therefore in consideration of our past friendship, I will tell you, and bind it by all things holy, that Doralice is innocent.

Rhod. Friend, I will believe you, and vow the same of your Melantha. But the devil on't is, how shall we keep 'em so.   310

Palamede. What dost think of a blessed community betwixt us four, for the solace of the women and relief of the men? Methinks it would be a pleasant kind of life: wife and husband for the standing dish, and mistress and gallant for the dessert!

Rhod. But suppose the wife and the mistress should both long for the standing dish, how should they be satisfied together?

Palamede. In such a case they must draw lots. And yet that would not do either, for they would both be wishing for the longest cut?

Rhod. Then I think, Palamede, we had as good make a firm league not to invade each other's propriety.   320

Palamede. Content, say I. From henceforth let all acts of hostility cease betwixt us; and that in the usual form of treaties, as well by sea as by land, and in all fresh waters.

Dor. I will add but one proviso,—that whoever breaks the league, either by war abroad or by neglect at home, both the women shall revenge themselves by the help of the other party.

Rhod. That's but reasonable. Come away, Doralice; I have a great temptation to be sealing articles in private.

    Palamede. Hast thou so?   [*Claps him on the shoulder.*
    Fall on, Macduff,   330
    And curst be he that first cries: 'Hold, enough.'

    Enter Polydamas, Palmyra, Artemis, Argaleon: *after them*
        Eubulus, *and* Hermogenes, *guarded.*

Palmyra. Sir, on my knees I beg you.
Poly. Away, I'll hear no more.
Palmyra. For my dead mother's sake; you say you loved her,
    And tell me I resemble her. Thus she
    Had begged.

302 screwed] bored   320 propriety] property

Poly.   And thus had I denied her.
Palmyra. You must be merciful.
Arg.   You must be constant.
Poly. Go, bear 'em to the torture; you have boasted
  You have a king to head you: I would know   340
  To whom I must resign.
Eub.   This is our recompense
  For serving thy dead queen.
Herm.   And education
  Of thy daughter.
Arg. You are too modest, in not naming all
  His obligations to you: why did you
  Omit his son, the prince Leonidas?
Poly. That imposture
  I had forgot; their tortures shall be doubled.
Herm. You please me, I shall die the sooner.
Eub. No; could I live an age, and still be racked,   350
  I still would keep the secret.

      As they are going off, enter Leonidas, *guarded.*

Leon. Oh whither do you hurry innocence!
  If you have any justice, spare their lives;
  Or if I cannot make you just, at least
  I'll teach you to more purpose to be cruel.
Palmyra. Alas, what does he seek!
Leon. Make me the object of your hate and vengeance!
  Are these decrepit bodies worn to ruin,
  Just ready, of themselves, to fall asunder,
  And to let drop the soul,   360
  Are these fit subjects for a rack, and tortures?
  Where would you fasten any hold upon 'em?
  Place pains on me; united fix 'em here;
  I have both youth, and strength, and soul to bear 'em:
  And if they merit death, then I much more;
  Since 'tis for me they suffer.
Herm.   Heaven forbid
  We should redeem our pains, or worthless lives,
  By our exposing yours.
Eub. Away with us! Farewell, sir.
  I only suffer in my fears for you.   370
Arg. (*Aside.*) So much concerned for him? Then my
  Suspicion's true.   [*Whispers to the* king.

Palmyra. Hear yet my last request, for poor Leonidas;
 Or take my life with his.
Arg. (*To the* king.) Rest satisfied; Leonidas is he.
Poly. I am amazed: what must be done?
Arg. Command his execution instantly;
 Give him not leisure to discover it;
 He may corrupt the soldiers.
Poly. Hence with that traitor; bear him to his death: 380
 Haste there, and see my will performed.
Leon. Nay, then I'll die like him the gods have made me.
 Hold, gentlemen; I am . . .   [Argaleon *stops his mouth.*
Arg. Thou art a traitor; 'tis not fit to hear thee.
Leon. (*Getting loose a little.*) I say I am the. . . .
Arg. So; gag him, and lead him off.   [*Again stopping his mouth.*

Leonidas, Hermogenes, Eubulus, *led off.* Polydamas *and* Argaleon *follow.*

Palmyra. Duty and love by turns possess my soul
 And struggle for a fatal victory.
 I will discover he's the king; ah, no:
 That will perhaps save him;   390
 But then I am guilty of a father's ruin.
 What shall I do or not do? Either way
 I must destroy a parent, or a lover.
 Break heart; for that's the least of ills to me,
 And death the only cure. (*Swoons.*)
Artem. Help, help the princess.
Rhod. Bear her gently hence, where she may
 Have more succour.   [*She is borne off,* Artemis *follows her.*

   Shouts within, and clashing of swords.

Palamede. What noise is that?

   Enter Amalthea, *running.*

Amal. Oh, gentlemen, if you have loyalty   400
 Or courage, show it now: Leonidas
 Broke on the sudden from his guards, and snatching
 A sword from one, his back against the scaffold,
 Bravely defends himself; and owns aloud
 He is our long-lost king, found for this moment;
 But, if your valours help not, lost for ever.
 Two of his guards, moved by the sense of virtue,
 Are turned for him, and there they stand at bay
 Against an host of foes.

Rhod.   Madam, no more;
 We lose time: my command, or my example,   410
 May move the soldiers to the better cause.
 (*To* Palamede.) You'll second me?
Palamede. Or die with you: no subject e'er can meet
 A nobler fate than at his sovereign's feet.   [*Exeunt.*

        Clashing of swords within, and shouts.
Enter Leonidas, Rhodophil, Palamede, Eubulus, Hermogenes, *and their
        party*, *victorious.* Polydamas *and* Argaleon, *disarmed.*

Leon. That I survive the dangers of this day,
 Next to the gods, brave friends, be yours the honour.
 And let heaven witness for me that my joy
 Is not more great for this my right restored,
 Than 'tis that I have power to recompense
 Your loyalty and valour. Let mean princes   420
 Of abject souls, fear to reward great actions;
 I mean to show,
 That whatsoe'er subjects, like you, dare merit,
 A king, like me, dares give. . . .
Rhod. You make us blush, we have deserved so little.
Palamede. And yet instruct us how to merit more.
Leon. And as I would be just in my rewards,
 So should I in my punishments; these two,
 This the usurper of my crown, the other
 Of my Palmyra's love, deserve that death   430
 Which both designed for me.
Poly.   And we expect it.
Arg. I have too long been happy to live wretched.
Poly. And I too long have governed, to desire
 A life without an empire.
Leon. You are Palmyra's father; and as such,
 Though not a king, shall have obedience paid
 From him who is one. Father, in that name,
 All injuries forgot, and duty owned.   [*Embraces him.*
Poly. O, had I known you could have been this king,
 Thus god-like, great and good, I should have wished   440
 T'have been dethroned before. 'Tis now I live,
 And more than reign; now all my joys flow pure,
 Unmixed with cares, and undisturbed by conscience.

        Enter Palmyra, Amalthea, Artemis, Doralice *and* Melantha.

Leon. See, my Palmyra comes! The frighted blood
  Scarce yet recalled to her pale cheeks,
  Like the first streaks of light broke loose from darkness,
  And dawning into blushes. (*To* Polydamas.) Sir, you said,
  Your joys were full. Oh, would you make mine so!
  I am but half-restored without this blessing.
Poly. The gods, and my Palmyra, make you happy,   450
  As you make me. (*Gives her hand to* Leonidas.)
Palmyra. Now all my prayers are heard:
  I may be dutiful, and yet may love.
  Virtue and patience have at length unravelled
  The knots which fortune tied.
Mel. Let me die, but I'll congratulate his majesty: how admirably well his
royalty becomes him! Becomes! That is *lui sied*, but our damned language
expresses nothing.
Palamede. How? Does it become him already? 'Twas but just now you
said, he was such a *figure* of a man.   460
Mel. True, my dear, when he was a private man he was a *figure*; but since
he is a king, methinks he has assumed another *figure*: he looks so grand, and
so august.   [*Going to the* king.
Palamede. Stay, stay; I'll present you when it is more convenient. I find I
must get her a place at court; and when she is once there, she can no longer
be ridiculous; for she is young enough, and pretty enough, and fool enough,
and French enough, to bring up a fashion there to be affected.
Leon. (*To* Rhodophil.) Did she then lead you to this brave attempt?
  (*To* Amalthea.) To you, fair Amalthea, what I am,
  And what all these, from me, we jointly owe: 470
  First, therefore, to your great desert, we give
  Your brother's life; but keep him under guard,
  Till our new power be settled. What more grace
  He may receive, shall from his future carriage
  Be given, as he deserves.
Arg. I neither now desire, nor will deserve it;
  My loss is such as cannot be repaired,
  And to the wretched, life can be no mercy.
Leon. Then be a prisoner always: thy ill fate,
  And pride will have it so: but since, in this, I cannot,   480
  Instruct me, generous Amalthea, how
  A king may serve you.
Amal.   I have all I hope,
  And all I now must wish; I see you happy.

457 *lui sied*] sits well on (suits) him

    Those hours I have to live, which heaven in pity
    Will make but few, I vow to spend with vestals:
    The greatest part, in prayers for you; the rest
    In mourning my unworthiness.
    Press me not farther to explain myself;
    'Twill not become me, and may cause your trouble.
Leon. (*Aside.*) Too well I understand her secret grief,   490
    But dare not seem to know it. (*To* Palmyra.) Come my fairest,
    Beyond my crown, I have one joy in store;
    To give that crown to her whom I adore.   [*Exeunt omnes.*

485 vestals] nuns

EPILOGUE

Thus have my spouse and I informed the nation,
And led you all the way to reformation.
Not with dull morals, gravely writ, like those
Which men of easy phlegm, with care compose.
Your poet's of stiff words and limber sense,
Born on the confines of indifference.
But by examples drawn, I dare to say,
From most of you who hear and see the play.
There are more Rhodophils in this theatre,
More Palamedes, and some few wives, I fear.   10
But yet too far our poet would not run,
Though 'twas well offered, there was nothing done.
He would not quite the woman's frailty bare,
But stripped 'em to the waist, and left 'em there.
And the men's faults are less severely shown,
For he considers that himself is one.
Some stabbing wits, to bloody satire bent,
Would treat both sexes with less compliment:
Would lay the scene at home, of husbands tell,
For wenches, taking up their wives i' th' Mell,   20
And a brisk bout which each of them did want,
Made by mistake of mistress and gallant.
Our modest author thought it was enough
To cut you off a sample of the stuff:
He spared my shame, which you, I'm sure, would not,
For you were all for driving on the plot:
You sighed when I came in to break the sport,
And set your teeth when each design fell short.
To wives and servants all good wishes lend,
But the poor cuckold seldom finds a friend.   30
Since therefore court and town will take no pity,
I humbly cast myself upon the city.

FINIS

5 limber] nimble   20 Mell] Mall

THE COUNTRY WIFE

BY

WILLIAM WYCHERLEY

WILLIAM WYCHERLEY (*c.* 1640–1716)

The Country Wife, first performed at Drury Lane, 12 January 1675; first published 1675.

[*The Complete Works of William Wycherley*, ed. Montague Summers, 4 vols., 1924; *The Country Wife*, ed. T. H. Fujimura, Regents Restoration Drama Series, 1965.]

THE

Country-Wife,

A

COMEDY,

Acted at the

THEATRE ROYAL.

Written by Mr. *Wycherley.*

Indignor quicquam reprehendi, non quia crassè
Compositum illepidéve putetur, sed quia nuper:
Nec veniam Antiquis, sed honorem & præmia posci.
Horat.

LONDON,

Printed for *Thomas Dring*, at the *Harrow*, at the
Corner of *Chancery-Lane* in *Fleet-street*. 1675.

PROLOGUE

Spoken by Mr. Hart.

Poets, like cudgelled bullies, never do
At first or second blow submit to you;
But will provoke you still, and ne'er have done
Till you are weary, first, with laying on:
The late so baffled scribbler of this day,
Though he stands trembling, bids me boldly say
What we before most plays are used to do,
For poets out of fear first draw on you;
In a fierce prologue the still pit defie,
And ere you speak, like Castril, give the lie;   10
But though our Bayes's battles oft I've fought,
And with bruised knuckles their dear conquests bought;
Nay, never yet feared odds upon the stage,
In prologue dare not hector with the age,
But would take quarter from your saving hands,
Though Bayes within all yielding countermands,
Says you confed'rate wits no quarter give,
Therefore his play shan't ask your leave to live:
Well, let the vain rash fop, by huffing so,
Think to obtain the better terms of you;   20
But we the actors humbly will submit,
Now, and at any time, to a full pit;
Nay, often we anticipate your rage,
And murder poets for you on our stage:
We set no guards upon our tiring-room,
But when with flying colours there you come,
We patiently, you see, give up to you
Our poets, virgins, nay our matrons too.

5 scribbler] perhaps Wycherley   10 Castril] the angry character in Jonson's *The Alchemist* (1610)   11 Bayes's] poet's. Also name given to Dryden in Buckingham's *The Rehearsal* (1672)   19 huffing] bullying   25 tiring-room] dressing-room

THE PERSONS

MR. HORNER	*Mr. Hart*
MR. HARCOURT	*Mr. Kenaston*
MR. DORILANT	*Mr. Lydal*
MR. PINCHWIFE	*Mr. Mohun*
MR. SPARKISH	*Mr. Haynes*
SIR JASPER FIDGET	*Mr. Cartwright*
MRS. MARGERY PINCHWIFE	*Mrs. Bowtel*
MRS. ALITHEA	*Mrs. James*
MY LADY FIDGET	*Mrs. Knep*
MRS. DAINTY FIDGET	*Mrs. Corbet*
MRS. SQUEAMISH	*Mrs. Wyatt*
OLD LADY SQUEAMISH	*Mrs. Rutter*
WAITERS, SERVANTS, AND ATTENDANTS	
A BOY	
A QUACK	*Mr. Schotterel*
LUCY, ALITHEA'S MAID	*Mrs. Cory*

The Scene : London

The Country Wife

ACT I SCENE I

Enter Horner, *and* Quack *following him at a distance.*

Horn. (*Aside.*) A quack is as fit for a pimp as a midwife for a bawd. They are still but in their way both helpers of nature. Well, my dear doctor, hast thou done what I desired?

Quack. I have undone you for ever with the women, and reported you throughout the whole town as bad as an eunuch, with as much trouble as if I had made you one in earnest.

Horn. But have you told all the midwives you know, the orange wenches at the playhouses, the city husbands, and old fumbling keepers of this end of the town? For they'll be the readiest to report it!

Quack. I have told all the chamber-maids, waiting-women, tire-women and old women of my acquaintance; nay, and whispered it as a secret to 'em, and to the whisperers of Whitehall. So that you need not doubt 'twill spread, and you will be as odious to the handsome young women as ... 13

Horn. As the smallpox. Well ...

Quack. And to the married women of this end of the town as ...

Horn. As the great ones; nay, as their own husbands.

Quack. And to the city dames as Aniseed Robin of filthy and contemptible memory; and they will frighten their children with your name, especially their females.

Horn. And cry, 'Horner's coming to carry you away!' I am only afraid 'twill not be believed. You told 'em 'twas by an English-French disaster, and an English-French chirurgeon, who has given me at once not only a cure but an antidote for the future against that damned malady, and that worse distemper, love, and all other women's evils? 24

Quack. Your late journey into France has made it the more credible, and your being here a fortnight before you appeared in public looks as if you apprehended the shame—which I wonder you do not. Well, I have been hired by young gallants to belie 'em t'other way, but you are the first would be thought a man unfit for women.

8 keepers] men who maintain a mistress 10 tire-women] dressers 17 Aniseed Robin] a well-known hermaphrodite

Horn. Dear Mr. doctor, let vain rogues be contented only to be thought abler men than they are. Generally 'tis all the pleasure they have, but mine lies another way.   32

Quack. You take, methinks, a very preposterous way to it, and as ridiculous as if we operators in physic should put forth bills to disparage our medicaments, with hopes to gain customers.

Horn. Doctor, there are quacks in love, as well as physic, who get but the fewer and worse patients for their boasting. A good name is seldom got by giving it oneself, and women no more than honour are compassed by bragging. Come, come, doctor, the wisest lawyer never discovers the merits of his cause till the trial. The wealthiest man conceals his riches, and the cunning gamester his play. Shy husbands and keepers, like old rooks, are not to be cheated but by a new unpractised trick. False friendship will pass now no more than false dice upon 'em—no, not in the city.   43

Enter Boy.

Boy. There are two ladies and a gentleman coming up.

Horn. A pox! Some unbelieving sisters of my former acquaintance who, I am afraid, expect their sense should be satisfied of the falsity of the report. No—this formal fool and women!

Enter Sir Jasper Fidget, Lady Fidget, *and* Mrs. Dainty Fidget.

Quack. His wife and sister.

Sir Jas. My coach breaking just now before your door, sir, I look upon as an occasional reprimand to me, sir, for not kissing your hands, sir, since your coming out of France, sir; and so my disaster, sir, has been my good fortune, sir; and this is my wife and sister, sir.   52

Horn. What then, sir?

Sir Jas. My lady and sister, sir.—Wife, this is master Horner.

Lady Fidg. Master Horner, husband!

Sir Jas. My lady, my lady Fidget, sir.

Horn. So, sir.

Sir Jas. Won't you be acquainted with her, sir? (*Aside.*) So, the report is true, I find, by his coldness or aversion to the sex; but I'll play the wag with him. Pray salute my wife, my lady, sir.   60

Horn. I will kiss no man's wife, sir, for him, sir; I have taken my eternal leave, sir, of the sex already, sir.

Sir Jas. (*Aside.*) Ha, ha, ha,! I'll plague him yet.—Not know my wife, sir?

Horn. I do know your wife, sir, she's a woman, sir, and consequently a monster, sir, a greater monster than a husband, sir.

Sir Jas. A husband! How, sir?

Horn. (*Makes horns.*) So, sir. But I make no more cuckolds, sir.

39 discovers] reveals   41 rooks] swindlers   60 salute] kiss

Sir Jas. Ha, ha, ha! Mercury, Mercury!

Lady Fidg. Pray, sir Jasper, let us be gone from this rude fellow.

Dain. Who, by his breeding, would think he had ever been in France?

Lady Fidg. Foh! he's but too much a French fellow, such as hate women of quality and virtue for their love to their husbands, sir Jasper. A woman is hated by 'em as much for loving her husband as for loving their money. But pray let's be gone.   74

Horn. You do well, madam, for I have nothing that you came for. I have brought over not so much as a bawdy picture, new postures, nor the second part of the *Ecole des Filles*, nor. . . .

Quack. (*Apart to* Horner.) Hold for shame, sir! What d'ye mean? You'll ruin yourself for ever with the sex. . . .

Sir Jas. Ha, ha, ha! He hates women perfectly, I find.

Dain. What pity 'tis he should.

Lady Fidg. Ay, he's a base rude fellow for't; but affectation makes not a woman more odious to them than virtue.

Horn. Because your virtue is your greatest affectation, madam.   84

Lady Fidg. How, you saucy fellow! Would you wrong my honour?

Horn. If I could.

Lady Fidg. How d'y mean, sir?

Sir Jas. Ha, ha, ha! No, he can't wrong your ladyship's honour; upon my honour! He poor man—hark you in your ear—a mere eunuch.

Lady Fidg. O filthy French beast! foh, foh! Why do we stay? Let's be gone. I can't endure the sight of him.   91

Sir Jas. Stay but till the chairs come. They'll be here presently.

Lady Fidg. No, no.

Sir Jas. Nor can I stay longer. 'Tis—let me see—a quarter and a half quarter of a minute past eleven. The Council will be sat, I must away. Business must be preferred always before love and ceremony with the wise, Mr. Horner.

Horn. And the impotent, sir Jasper.

Sir Jas. Ay, ay, the impotent, Master Horner, ha, ha, ha!

Lady Fidg. What, leave us with a filthy man alone in his lodgings?   100

Sir Jas. He's an innocent man now, you know. Pray stay, I'll hasten the chairs to you.—Mr. Horner, your servant; I should be glad to see you at my house. Pray come and dine with me, and play at cards with my wife after dinner—you are fit for women at that game yet, ha, ha! (*Aside.*) 'Tis as much a husband's prudence to provide innocent diversion for a wife as to hinder her unlawful pleasures, and he had better employ her than let her employ herself.—Farewell.   [*Exit* Sir Jasper.

76 new postures] lewd illustrations to erotic poems   77 *Ecole des Filles*] a pornographic book   92 chairs] sedan chairs   92 presently] at once

Horn. Your servant, sir Jasper.

Lady Fidg. I will not stay with him, foh!

Horn. Nay, madam, I beseech you stay, if it be but to see I can be as civil
to ladies yet as they would desire.   111

Lady Fidg. No, no, foh! You cannot be civil to ladies.

Dain. You as civil as ladies would desire!

Lady Fidg. No, no, no! foh, foh, foh!

> [*Exeunt* Lady Fidget *and* Dainty.

Quack. Now I think, I, or you yourself rather, have done your business
with the women!

Horn. Thou art an ass. Don't you see already, upon the report and my
carriage, this grave man of business leaves his wife in my lodgings, invites me
to his house and wife, who before would not be acquainted with me out of
jealousy?   120

Quack. Nay, by this means you may be the more acquainted with the husbands, but the less with the wives.

Horn. Let me alone; if I can but abuse the husbands, I'll soon disabuse
the wives! Stay—I'll reckon you up the advantages I am like to have by
my stratagem. First, I shall be rid of all my old acquaintances, the most
insatiable sorts of duns, that invade our lodgings in a morning. And next
to the pleasure of making a new mistress is that of being rid of an old
one. And of all old debts, love, when it comes to be so, is paid the most
unwillingly.

Quack. Well, you may be so rid of your old acquaintances, but how will
you get any new ones?   131

Horn. Doctor, thou wilt never make a good chemist, thou art so incredulous
and impatient. Ask but all the young fellows of the town, if they do not lose
more time, like huntsmen, in starting the game, than in running it down.
One knows not where to find 'em, who will, or will not. Women of quality
are so civil you can hardly distinguish love from good breeding, and a man is
often mistaken! But now I can be sure she that shows an aversion to me loves
the sport—as those women that are gone, whom I warrant to be right. And
then the next thing is, your women of honour, as you call 'em, are only
chary of their reputations, not their persons, and 'tis scandal they would
avoid, not men. Now may I have, by the reputation of an eunuch, the privileges of one; and be seen in a lady's chamber in a morning as early as her
husband; kiss virgins before their parents or lovers; and may be, in short,
the *passe partout* of the town. Now, doctor. . . .   144

Quack. Nay, now you shall be the doctor! And your process is so new that
we do not know but it may succeed.

---

132 chemist] alchemist   138 right] sexy   144 *passe partout*] master key

Horn. Not so new neither. *Probatum est*, doctor.

Quack. Well, I wish you luck and many patients whilst I go to mine.

[*Exit* Quack.

Enter Harcourt *and* Dorilant *to* Horner.

Harc. Come, your appearance at the play yesterday has, I hope, hardened you for the future against the women's contempt and the men's raillery, and now you'll abroad as you were wont.   151

Horn. Did I not bear it bravely?

Dor. With a most theatrical impudence! Nay, more than the orange-wenches show there, or a drunken vizard-mask, or a great-bellied actress. Nay, or the most impudent of creatures—an ill poet. Or, what is yet more impudent, a second-hand critic!

Horn. But what say the ladies? Have they no pity?

Harc. What ladies? The vizard-masks, you know, never pity a man when all's gone, though in their service.

Dor. And for the women in the boxes, you'd never pity them when 'twas in your power.   161

Harc. They say, 'tis pity but all that deal with common women should be served so.

Dor. Nay, I dare swear, they won't admit you to play at cards with them, go to plays with 'em, or do the little duties which other shadows of men are wont to do for 'em.

Horn. Who do you call shadows of men?

Dor. Half-men.

Horn. What, boys?

Dor. Ay, your old boys, old *beaux garçons*, who like superannuated stallions are suffered to run, feed, and whinny with the mares as long as they live, though they can do nothing else.   172

Horn. Well, a pox on love and wenching! Women serve but to keep a man from better company. Though I can't enjoy *them*, I shall *you* the more. Good fellowship and friendship are lasting, rational and manly pleasures.

Harc. For all that, give me some of those pleasures you call effeminate too! They help to relish one another.

Horn. They disturb one another.

Harc. No, mistresses are like books—if you pore upon them too much they doze you and make you unfit for company, but if used discreetly you are the fitter for conversation by 'em.   181

Dor. A mistress should be like a little country retreat near the town—not

147 *Probatum est*] it has been proved   154 vizard-mask] whore   154 great-bellied] pregnant

to dwell in constantly, but only for a night and away, to taste the town the
better when a man returns.

Horn. I tell you, 'tis as hard to be a good fellow, a good friend, and a lover
of women, as 'tis to be a good fellow, a good friend, and a lover of money.
You cannot follow both, then choose your side. Wine gives you liberty, love
takes it away.

Dor. Gad, he's in the right on't.

Horn. Wine gives you joy, love grief and tortures, besides the chirurgeon's.
Wine makes us witty, love, only sots. Wine makes us sleep; love breaks it.

Dor. By the world he has reason, Harcourt.   192

Horn. Wine makes. . . .

Dor. Ay, wine makes us . . . makes us princes; love makes us beggars, poor
rogues, i'gad . . . and wine. . . .

Horn. So, there's one converted. No, no, love and wine—oil and vinegar.

Harc. I grant it; love will still be uppermost!

Horn. Come, for my part I will have only those glorious, manly pleasures
of being drunk and very slovenly.

Enter Boy.

Boy. Mr. Sparkish is below, sir.   200

Harc. What, my dear friend! A rogue that is fond of me only, I think, for
abusing him.

Dor. No, he can no more think the men laugh at him than that women jilt
him, his opinion of himself is so good.

Horn. Well, there's another pleasure by drinking I thought not of—I shall
lose *his* acquaintance, because he cannot drink! And you know 'tis a very
hard thing to be rid of him for he's one of those nauseous offerers at wit,
who, like the worst fiddlers, run themselves into all companies.

Harc. One that by being in the company of men of sense would pass for
one.   210

Horn. And may so to the short-sighted world, as a false jewel amongst
true ones is not discerned at a distance. His company is as troublesome to us
as a cuckold's when you have a mind to his wife's.

Harc. No, the rogue will not let us enjoy one another, but ravishes our
conversation, though he signifies no more to't than sir Martin Mar-all's
gaping, and awkward thrumming upon the lute does to his man's voice and
music.

Dor. And to pass for a wit in town shows himself a fool every night to us,
that are guilty of the plot.

Horn. Such wits as he are, to a company of reasonable men, like rooks to

183 taste] relish   215 sir Martin Mar-all] the foolish lover in Dryden's comedy of that
name (1667)

the gamesters, who only fill a room at the table, but are so far from contributing to the play that they only serve to spoil the fancy of those that do.

Dor. Nay, they are used like rooks too, snubbed, checked, and abused; yet the rogues will hang on. 224

Horn. A pox on 'em, and all that force nature, and would be still what she forbids 'em! Affectation is her greatest monster.

Harc. Most men are the contraries to that they would seem. Your bully, you see, is a coward with a long sword; the little, humbly fawning physician with his ebony cane is he that destroys men.

Dor. The usurer, a poor rogue possessed of mouldy bonds and mortgages; and we they call spendthrifts are only wealthy, who lay out his money upon daily new purchases of pleasure. 232

Horn. Ay, your arrantest cheat is your trustee, or executor; your jealous man, the greatest cuckold; your churchman, the greatest atheist; and your noisy, pert rogue of a wit, the greatest fop, dullest ass, and worst company as you shall see—for here he comes!

Enter Sparkish *to them.*

Spark. How is't, sparks, how is't? Well, faith, Harry, I must rally thee a little, ha, ha, ha! upon the report in town of thee, ha, ha, ha! I can't hold i'faith —shall I speak?

Horn. Yes, but you'll be so bitter then. 240

Spark. Honest Dick and Frank here shall answer for me, I will not be extreme bitter, by the universe.

Harc. We will be bound in ten thousand pound bond, he shall not be bitter at all.

Dor. Nor sharp, nor sweet.

Horn. What, not downright insipid?

Spark. Nay then, since you are so brisk and provoke me, take what follows. You must know, I was discoursing and rallying with some ladies yesterday, and they happened to talk of the fine new signs in town.

Horn. Very fine ladies, I believe. 250

Spark. Said I, 'I know where the best new sign is.' 'Where?' says one of the ladies. 'In Covent Garden,' I replied. Said another, 'In what street?' 'In Russell Street,' answered I. 'Lord,' says another, 'I'm sure there was ne'er a fine new sign there yesterday.' 'Yes, but there was,' said I again, 'and it came out of France, and has been there a fortnight.'

Dor. A pox! I can hear no more, prithee.

Horn. No, hear him out; let him tune his crowd a while.

Harc. The worst music, the greatest preparation.

249 signs] traders' signboards or inn signs 252 Covent Garden] fashionable London district   253 Russell Street] fashionable residential area   257 crowd] fiddle

Spark. Nay, faith, I'll make you laugh. 'It cannot be,' says a third lady.
'Yes, yes,' quoth I again. Says a fourth lady. . . .   260

Horn. Look to't, we'll have no more ladies.

Spark. No . . . then mark, mark, now. Said I to the fourth, 'Did you never
see Mr. Horner? He lodges in Russell Street, and he's a *sign of a man*, you
know, since he came out of France!' He, ha, he!

Horn. But the devil take me, if thine be the sign of a jest.

Spark. With that they all fell a-laughing, till they bepissed themselves!
What, but it does not move you, methinks? Well, I see one has as good go
to law without a witness, as break a jest without a laughter on one's side.
Come, come sparks, but where do we dine? I have left at Whitehall an earl to
dine with you.   270

Dor. Why, I thought thou hadst loved a man with a title better than a suit
with a French trimming to't.

Harc. Go to him again.

Spark. No, sir, a wit to me is the greatest title in the world.

Horn. But go dine with your earl, sir; he may be exceptious. We are your
friends, and will not take it ill to be left, I do assure you.

Harc. Nay, faith, he shall go to him.

Spark. Nay, pray, gentlemen.

Dor. We'll thrust you out, if you wo'not. What, disappoint anybody for us?

Spark. Nay, dear gentlemen, hear me.   280

Horn. No, no, sir, by no means; pray go, sir.

Spark. Why, dear rogues.

Dor. No, no.

They all thrust him out of the room.

All. Ha, ha, ha!

Sparkish *returns.*

Spark. But, sparks, pray hear me. What, d'ye think I'll eat then with gay
shallow fops and silent coxcombs? I think wit as necessary at dinner as a
glass of good wine, and that's the reason I never have any stomach when I eat
alone. Come, but where do we dine?

Horn. Even where you will.

Spark. At Chateline's?   290

Dor. Yes, if you will.

Spark. Or at the Cock?

Dor. Yes, if you please.

Spark. Or at the Dog and Partridge?

290 Chateline's] French restaurant in Covent Garden   292 Cock] Bow Street tavern
294 Dog and Partridge] Fleet Street tavern

Horn. Ay, if you have a mind to't, for we shall dine at neither.

Spark. Pshaw! with your fooling we shall lose the new play. And I would no more miss seeing a new play the first day than I would miss sitting in the wits' row. Therefore I'll go fetch my mistress and away.   *Exit* Sparkish.

Manent Horner, Harcourt, Dorilant. *Enter to them* Mr. Pinchwife.

Horn. Who have we here? Pinchwife?

Pinch. Gentlemen, your humble servant.   300

Horn. Well, Jack, by thy long absence from the town, the grumness of thy countenance, and the slovenliness of thy habit, I should give thee joy, should I not, of marriage?

Pinch. (*Aside.*) Death! does he know I'm married too? I thought to have concealed it from him at least—My long stay in the country will excuse my dress, and I have a suit of law, that brings me up to town, that puts me out of humour. Besides, I must give Sparkish tomorrow five thousand pound to lie with my sister.

Horn. Nay, you country gentlemen, rather than not purchase, will buy anything; and he is a cracked title, if we may quibble. Well, but am I to give thee joy? I heard thou wert married.   311

Pinch. What then?

Horn. Why, the next thing that is to be heard is, thou'rt a cuckold.

Pinch. (*Aside.*) Unsupportable name!

Horn. But I did not expect marriage from such a whoremaster as you, one that knew the town so much, and women so well.

Pinch. Why, I have married no London wife.

Horn. Pshaw! that's all one. That grave circumspection in marrying a country wife is like refusing a deceitful, pampered Smithfield jade to go and be cheated by a friend in the country.   320

Pinch. (*Aside.*) A pox on him and his simile!—At least we are a little surer of the breed there, know what her keeping has been, whether foiled or unsound.

Horn. Come, come, I have known a clap gotten in Wales. And there are cousins, justices' clerks, and chaplains in the country—I won't say coachmen! But she's handsome and young?

Pinch. (*Aside.*) I'll answer as I should do.—No, no, she has no beauty but her youth; no attraction but her modesty; wholesome, homely, and housewifely, that's all.

Dor. He talks as like a grazier as he looks.   330

Pinch. She's too awkward, ill-favoured, and silly to bring to town.

Harc. Then methinks you should bring her, to be taught breeding.

---

301 grumness] moroseness   315 whoremaster] fornicator   319 Smithfield jade] Smithfield market nag, i.e., a whore   322 foiled] deflowered   324 clap] venereal disease

Pinch. To be taught! No, sir, I thank you. Good wives and private soldiers should be ignorant. (*Aside.*) I'll keep her from your instructions, I warrant you.

Harc. (*Aside.*) The rogue is as jealous as if his wife were not ignorant.

Horn. Why, if she be ill-favoured, there will be less danger here for you than by leaving her in the country. *We* have such variety of dainties that we are seldom hungry.

Dor. But they have always coarse, constant, swingeing stomachs in the country.   341

Harc. Foul feeders indeed.

Dor. And your hospitality is great there.

Harc. Open house, every man's welcome!

Pinch. So, so, gentlemen.

Horn. But, prithee, why would'st thou marry her? If she be ugly, ill-bred, and silly, she must be rich then?

Pinch. As rich as if she brought me twenty thousand pound out of this town; for she'll be as sure not to spend her moderate portion as a London baggage would be to spend hers, let it be what it would; so 'tis all one. Then, because she's ugly, she's the likelier to be my own; and being ill-bred, she'll hate conversation; and since silly and innocent, will not know the difference betwixt a man of one-and-twenty and one of forty.   353

Horn. Nine—to my knowledge; but if she be silly, she'll expect as much from a man of forty-nine as from him of one-and-twenty. But methinks wit is more necessary than beauty, and I think no young woman ugly that has it, and no handsome woman agreeable without it.

Pinch. 'Tis my maxim he's a fool that marries, but he's a greater that does not marry a fool. What is wit in a wife good for, but to make a man a cuckold?

Horn. Yes, to keep it from his knowledge.

Pinch. A fool cannot contrive to make her husband a cuckold.   361

Horn. No, but she'll club with a man that can; and what is worse, if she cannot make her husband a cuckold, she'll make him jealous, and pass for one, and then 'tis all one.

Pinch. Well, well, I'll take care for one, my wife shall make me no cuckold, though she had your help Mr. Horner; I understand the town, sir.

Dor. (*Aside.*) His help!

Harc. (*Aside.*) He's come newly to town, it seems, and has not heard how things are with him.

Horn. But tell me, has marriage cured thee of whoring, which it seldom does?   371

Harc. 'Tis more than age can do.

Horn. No, the word is, I'll marry and live honest. But a marriage vow is

340 swingeing] huge

like a penitent gamester's oath, and entering into bonds and penalties to stint himself to such a particular small sum at play for the future, which makes him but the more eager, and not being able to hold out, loses his money again, and his forfeit to boot.

Dor. Ay, ay, a gamester will be a gamester whilst his money lasts, and a whoremaster whilst his vigour.

Harc. Nay, I have known 'em, when they are broke and can lose no more, keep a-fumbling with the box in their hands to fool with only, and hinder other gamesters.   382

Dor. That had wherewithal to make lusty stakes.

Pinch. Well, gentlemen, you may laugh at me, but you shall never lie with my wife; I know the town.

Horn. But prithee, was not the way you were in better? Is not keeping better than marriage?

Pinch. A pox on't! The jades would jilt me; I could never keep a whore to myself.

Horn. So, then you only married to keep a whore to yourself? Well, but let me tell you, women, as you say, are like soldiers, made constant and loyal by good pay rather than by oaths and covenants. Therefore I'd advise my friends to keep rather than marry, since too I find, by your example, it does not serve one's turn—for I saw you yesterday in the eighteen-penny place with a pretty country wench!   395

Pinch. (*Aside.*) How the devil! Did he see my wife then? I sat there that she might not be seen. But she shall never go to a play again.

Horn. What, dost thou blush at nine-and-forty for having been seen with a wench?

Dor. No, faith, I warrant 'twas his wife, which he seated there out of sight, for he's a cunning rogue, and understands the town.

Harc. He blushes! Then 'twas his wife—for men are now more ashamed to be seen with them in public than with a wench.

Pinch. (*Aside.*) Hell and damnation! I'm undone, since Horner has seen her, and they know 'twas she.   405

Horn. But prithee, was it thy wife? She was exceedingly pretty; I was in love with her at that distance.

Pinch. You are like never to be nearer to her. Your servant, gentlemen. (*Offers to go.*)

Horn. Nay, prithee stay.

Pinch. I cannot, I will not.

Horn. Come, you shall dine with us.

Pinch. I have dined already.

386 keeping] supporting a mistress   394 eighteen-penny place] part of theatre frequented by whores

Horn. Come, I know thou hast not. I'll treat thee, dear rogue. Thou sha't spend none of thy Hampshire money today.   414
Pinch. (*Aside.*) Treat me! So, he uses me already like his cuckold!
Horn. Nay, you shall not go.
Pinch. I must, I have business at home.   [*Exit* Pinchwife.
Harc. To beat his wife! He's as jealous of her as a Cheapside husband of a Covent Garden wife.
Horn. Why, 'tis as hard to find an old whoremaster without jealousy and the gout, as a young one without fear or the pox.

As gout in age from pox in youth proceeds,
So wenching past, then jealousy succeeds—
The worst disease that love and wenching breeds.

ACT II   SCENE I

Mrs. Margery Pinchwife *and* Alithea: Mr. Pinchwife *peeping behind at the door.*

Mrs. Pinch. Pray, sister, where are the best fields and woods to walk in, in London?
Alith. A pretty question! Why, sister, Mulberry Garden and St. James's Park; and for close walks, the New Exchange.
Mrs. Pinch. Pray, sister, tell me why my husband looks so grum here in town, and keeps me up so close, and will not let me go a-walking, nor let me wear my best gown yesterday?
Alith. Oh, he's jealous, sister.
Mrs. Pinch. Jealous? What's that?
Alith. He's afraid you should love another man.   10
Mrs. Pinch. How should he be afraid of my loving another man, when he will not let me see any but himself.
Alith. Did he not carry you yesterday to a play?
Mrs. Pinch. Ay, but we sat amongst ugly people. He would not let me come near the gentry, who sat under us, so that I could not see 'em. He told me none but naughty women sat there, whom they toused and moused. But I would have ventured for all that.

418 Cheapside husband] city merchant husband   419 Covent Garden wife] fashionable wife or, possibly, high-class mistress   3 Mulberry Garden] fashionable walk   3-4 St. James's Park] noted for its Mall   4 New Exchange] arcade of shops in the Strand   16 toused and moused] rumpled and toyed with

Alith. But how did you like the play?

Mrs. Pinch. Indeed I was a-weary of the play, but I liked hugeously the actors! They are the goodliest, properest men, sister. 20

Alith. Oh, but you must not like the actors, sister.

Mrs. Pinch. Ay, how should I help it, sister? Pray, sister, when my husband comes in, will you ask leave for me to go a-walking?

Alith. (*Aside.*) A-walking! Ha, ha! Lord, a country gentlewoman's leisure is the drudgery of a foot-post; and she requires as much airing as her husband's horses.

Enter Mr. Pinchwife *to them.*

But here comes your husband; I'll ask, though I'm sure he'll not grant it.

Mrs. Pinch. He says he won't let me go abroad for fear of catching the pox.

Alith. Fie, the smallpox you should say.

Mrs. Pinch. Oh my dear, dear bud, welcome home! Why dost thou look so fropish? Who has nangered thee? 31

Pinch. You're a fool!

Mrs. Pinchwife goes aside and cries.

Alith. Faith, so she is, for crying for no fault, poor tender creature!

Pinch. What, you would have her as impudent as yourself, as arrant a jill-flirt, a gadder, a magpie, and to say all—a mere notorious town-woman?

Alith. Brother, you are my only censurer; and the honour of your family shall sooner suffer in your wife there than in me, though I take the innocent liberty of the town.

Pinch. Hark you, mistress, do not talk so before my wife. The innocent liberty of the town! 40

Alith. Why, pray, who boasts of any intrigue with me? What lampoon has made my name notorious? What ill women frequent my lodgings? I keep no company with any women of scandalous reputations.

Pinch. No, you keep the men of scandalous reputations company.

Alith. Where? Would you not have me civil? Answer 'em in a box at the plays, in the drawing room at Whitehall, in St. James's Park, Mulberry Garden, or. . . .

Pinch. Hold, hold! Do not teach my wife where the men are to be found! I believe she's the worse for your town documents already. I bid you keep her in ignorance, as I do. 50

Mrs. Pinch. Indeed, be not angry with her, bud. She will tell me nothing of the town though I ask her a thousand times a day.

Pinch. Then you are very inquisitive to know, I find!

---

25 foot-post] letter-carrier on foot   31 fropish] peevish   31 nangered] angered
34-5 jill-flirt] wanton girl   35 magpie] idle chatterer

Mrs. Pinch. Not I, indeed, dear. I hate London. Our placehouse in the country is worth a thousand of't. Would I were there again!

Pinch. So you shall, I warrant. But were you not talking of plays and players when I came in? (*To* Alithea.) You are her encourager in such discourses.

Mrs. Pinch. No, indeed, dear; she chid me just now for liking the player-men.

Pinch. (*Aside.*) Nay, if she be so innocent as to own to me her liking them, there is no hurt in't.—Come, my poor rogue, but thou lik'st none better than me?   62

Mrs. Pinch. Yes, indeed, but I do; the playermen are finer folks.

Pinch. But you love none better than me?

Mrs. Pinch. You are mine own dear bud, and I know you; I hate a stranger.

Pinch. Ay, my dear, you must love me only, and not be like the naughty town-women, who only hate their husbands and love every man else—love plays, visits, fine coaches, fine clothes, fiddles, balls, treats, and so lead a wicked town-life.

Mrs. Pinch. Nay, if to enjoy all these things be a town-life, London is not so bad a place, dear.   71

Pinch. How! If you love me, you must hate London.

Alith. (*Aside.*) The fool has forbid me discovering to her the pleasures of the town, and he is now setting her agog upon them himself.

Mrs. Pinch. But, husband, do the town-women love the playermen too?

Pinch. Yes, I warrant you.

Mrs. Pinch. Ay, I warrant you.

Pinch. Why, you do not, I hope?

Mrs. Pinch. No, no, bud; but why have we no playermen in the country?

Pinch. Ha!—Mistress Minx, ask me no more to go to a play.   80

Mrs. Pinch. Nay, why, love? I did not care for going, but when you forbid me, you make me, as't were, desire it.

Alith. (*Aside.*) So 'twill be in other things, I warrant.

Mrs. Pinch. Pray, let me go to a play, dear.

Pinch. Hold your peace, I wo'not.

Mrs. Pinch. Why, love?

Pinch. Why, I'll tell you.

Alith. (*Aside.*) Nay, if he tell her, she'll give him more cause to forbid her that place.

Mrs. Pinch. Pray, why, dear?   90

Pinch. First, you like the actors, and the gallants may like you.

Mrs. Pinch. What, a homely country girl? No bud, nobody will like me.

Pinch. I tell you, yes, they may.

Mrs. Pinch. No, no, you jest—I won't believe you, I will go.

54 placehouse] country house

Pinch. I tell you then, that one of the lewdest fellows in town, who saw you there, told me he was in love with you.

Mrs. Pinch. Indeed! Who, who, pray who was't?

Pinch. (Aside.) I've gone too far, and slipped before I was aware. How overjoyed she is!

Mrs. Pinch. Was it any Hampshire gallant, any of our neighbours? I promise you, I am beholding to him.   101

Pinch. I promise you, you lie; for he would but ruin you, as he has done hundreds. He has no other love for women, but that; such as he look upon women, like basilisks, but to destroy 'em.

Mrs. Pinch. Ay, but if he loves me, why should he ruin me? Answer me to that. Methinks he should not; I would do him no harm.

Alith. Ha, ha, ha!

Pinch. 'Tis very well; but I'll keep him from doing you any harm, or me either.

Enter Sparkish *and* Harcourt.

But here comes company; get you in, get you in.   110

Mrs. Pinch. But pray, husband, is he a pretty gentleman that loves me?

Pinch. In, baggage, in!   [*Thrusts her in; shuts the door.*
(Aside.) What, all the lewd libertines of the town brought to my lodgings by this easy coxcomb! S'death, I'll not suffer it.

Spark. Here Harcourt, do you approve my choice? *(To* Alithea.) Dear little rogue, I told you I'd bring you acquainted with all my friends, the wits, and. . . .

Harcourt *salutes her.*

Pinch. (Aside.) Ay, they shall know her, as well as you yourself will, I warrant you.

Spark. This is one of those, my pretty rogue, that are to dance at your wedding tomorrow; and him you must bid welcome ever to what you and I have.   122

Pinch. (Aside.) Monstrous!

Spark. Harcourt, how dost thou like her, faith?—Nay, dear, do not look down; I should hate to have a wife of mine out of countenance at any thing.

Pinch. (Aside.) Wonderful!

Spark. Tell me, I say, Harcourt, how dost thou like her? Thou hast stared upon her enough to resolve me.

Harc. So infinitely well that I could wish I had a mistress too, that might differ from her in nothing but her love and engagement to you.   130

---

104 basilisks] mythical serpents whose glance was fatal

Alith. Sir, master Sparkish has often told me that his acquaintance were all wits and railleurs, and now I find it.

Spark. No, by the universe, madam, he does not rally now; you may believe him. I do assure you, he is the honestest, worthiest true-hearted gentleman—a man of such perfect honour, he would say nothing to a lady he does not mean.

Pinch. (*Aside.*) Praising another man to his mistress!

Harc. Sir, you are so beyond expectation obliging, that. . . .

Spark. Nay, i'gad, I am sure you do admire her extremely; I see't in your eyes.—He does admire you, madam.—By the world, don't you?   140

Harc. Yes, above the world, or the most glorious part of it, her whole sex; and till now I never thought I should have envied you, or any man about to marry, but you have the best excuse for marriage I ever knew.

Alith. Nay, now, sir, I'm satisfied you are of the society of the wits and railleurs since you cannot spare your friend even when he is but too civil to you. But the surest sign is, since you are an enemy to marriage, for that, I hear, you hate as much as business or bad wine.

Harc. Truly, madam, I never was an enemy to marriage till now, because marriage was never an enemy to me before.

Alith. But why, sir, is marriage an enemy to you now? Because it robs you of your friend here? For you look upon a friend married as one gone into a monastery, that is—dead to the world.   152

Harc. 'Tis indeed, because you marry him; I see, madam, you can guess my meaning. I do confess heartily and openly, I wish it were in my power to break the match. By heavens I would!

Spark. Poor Frank.

Alith. Would you be so unkind to me?

Harc. No, no, 'tis not because I would be unkind to you.

Spark. Poor Frank! No, gad, 'tis only his kindness to me.

Pinch. (*Aside.*) Great kindness to you indeed! Insensible fop, let a man make love to his wife to his face!   161

Spark. Come, dear Frank, for all my wife there that shall be, thou shalt enjoy me sometimes, dear rogue. By my honour, we men of wit condole for our deceased brother in marriage as much as for one dead in earnest. I think that was prettily said of me, ha, Harcourt? But come, Frank, be not melancholy for me.

Harc. No, I assure you I am not melancholy for you.

Spark. Prithee, Frank, dost think my wife-that-shall-be, there, a fine person?

Harc. I could gaze upon her till I became as blind as you are.

Spark. How, as I am? How?   171

Harc. Because you are a lover, and true lovers are blind, stock blind.

Spark. True, true; but by the world, she has wit too, as well as beauty. Go, go with her into a corner, and try if she has wit; talk to her anything; she's bashful before me.

Harc. Indeed, if a woman wants wit in a corner, she has it nowhere.

Alith. (*Aside to* Sparkish.) Sir, you dispose of me a little before your time. . . .

Spark. Nay, nay, madam let me have an earnest of your obedience, or. . . . Go, go, madam. . . .   180

Harcourt courts Alithea aside.

Pinch. How, sir! If you are not concerned for the honour of a wife, I am for that of a sister; he shall not debauch her. Be a pander to your own wife, bring men to her, let 'em make love before your face, thrust 'em into a corner together, then leave 'em in private! Is this your town wit and conduct?

Spark. Ha, ha, ha! A silly wise rogue would make one laugh more than a stark fool, ha, ha, ha! I shall burst. Nay, you shall not disturb 'em; I'll vex thee, by the world.

[*Struggles with* Pinchwife *to keep him from* Harcourt *and* Alithea.

Alith. The writings are drawn, sir, settlements made; 'tis too late, sir, and past all revocation.

Harc. Then so is my death.   190

Alith. I would not be unjust to him.

Harc. Then why to me so?

Alith. I have no obligation to you.

Harc. My love.

Alith. I had his before.

Harc. You never had it; he wants, you see, jealousy, the only infallible sign of it.

Alith. Love proceeds from esteem; he cannot distrust my virtue. Besides he loves me, or he would not marry me.

Harc. Marrying you is no more sign of his love, than bribing your woman, that he may marry you, is a sign of his generosity. Marriage is rather a sign of interest than love; and he that marries a fortune, covets a mistress, not loves her. But if you take marriage for a sign of love, take it from me immediately.

Alith. No, now you have put a scruple in my head. But in short, sir, to end our dispute—I must marry him, my reputation would suffer in the world else.

Harc. No, if you do marry him, with your pardon, madam, your reputation suffers in the world, and you would be thought in necessity for a cloak.

Alith. Nay, now you are rude, sir.—Mr. Sparkish, pray come hither, your friend here is very troublesome, and very loving.

Harc. (*Aside to* Alithea.) Hold, hold!   210

197 cloak] i.e. to hide pregnancy

Pinch. D'ye hear that?

Spark. Why, d'ye think I'll seem to be jealous, like a country bumpkin?

Pinch. No, rather be a cuckold, like a credulous cit.

Harc. Madam, you would not have been so little generous as to have told him?

Alith. Yes, since you could be so little generous as to wrong him.

Harc. Wrong him! No man can do't, he's beneath an injury; a bubble, a coward, a senseless idiot, a wretch so contemptible to all the world but you that . . .

Alith. Hold, do not rail at him, for since he is like to be my husband, I am resolved to like him. Nay, I think I am obliged to tell him you are not his friend.—Master Sparkish, Master Sparkish!   222

Spark. What, what? Now, dear rogue, has not she wit?

Harc. (*Speaks surlily.*) Not so much as I thought, and hoped she had.

Alith. Mr. Sparkish, do you bring people to rail at you?

Harc. Madam. . . .

Spark. How! No, but if he does rail at me, 'tis but in jest, I warrant—what we wits do for one another and never take any notice of it.

Alith. He spoke so scurrilously of you, I had no patience to hear him; besides, he has been making love to me.   230

Harc. (*Aside.*) True, damned, telltale woman.

Spark. Pshaw! to show his parts—we wits rail and make love often but to show our parts; as we have no affections, so we have no malice; we. . . .

Alith. He said you were a wretch, below an injury.

Spark. Pshaw!

Harc. (*Aside.*) Damned, senseless, impudent, virtuous jade! Well, since she won't let me have her, she'll do as good, she'll make me hate her.

Alith. A common bubble.

Spark. Pshaw!

Alith. A coward.   240

Spark. Pshaw, pshaw!

Alith. A senseless, drivelling idiot.

Spark. How! Did he disparage my parts? Nay, then my honour's concerned. I can't put up that, sir, by the world. Brother, help me to kill him. (*Aside.*) I may draw now, since we have the odds of him! 'Tis a good occasion, too, before my mistress . . .   [*Offers to draw.*

Alith. Hold, hold!

Spark. What, what?

Alith. (*Aside.*) I must not let 'em kill the gentleman neither, for his kindness to me; I am so far from hating him that I wish my gallant had his person and understanding. Nay, if my honour. . . .   251

213 cit] citizen—a term of contempt   217 bubble] gullible fool

Spark. I'll be thy death.

Alith. Hold, hold! Indeed, to tell the truth, the gentleman said after all that what he spoke was but out of friendship to you.

Spark. How! say, I am—I am a fool, that is, no wit, out of friendship to me?

Alith. Yes, to try whether I was concerned enough for you, and made love to me only to be satisfied of my virtue, for your sake.

Harc. (*Aside.*) Kind however. . . .

Spark. Nay, if it were so, my dear rogue, I ask thee pardon. But why would not you tell me so, faith?   261

Harc. Because I did not think on't, faith.

Spark. Come, Horner does not come. Harcourt let's be gone to the new play.—Come, madam.

Alith. I will not go, if you intend to leave me alone in the box and run into the pit, as you use to do.

Spark. Pshaw! I'll leave Harcourt with you in the box to entertain you, and that's as good. If I sat in the box I should be thought no judge but of trimmings.—Come away, Harcourt, lead her down.

> [*Exeunt* Sparkish, Harcourt, *and* Alithea.

Pinch. Well, go thy ways, for the flower of the true town fops, such as spend their estates before they come to 'em, and are cuckolds before they're married. But let me go look to my own freehold—How!   272

Enter My Lady Fidget, Mistress Dainty Fidget, *and* Mistress Squeamish

Lady Fidg. Your servant, sir. Where is your lady? We are come to wait upon her to the new play.

Pinch. New play!

Lady Fidg. And my husband will wait upon you presently.

Pinch. (*Aside.*) Damn your civility.—Madam, by no means; I will not see sir Jasper here till I have waited upon him at home; nor shall my wife see you till she has waited upon your ladyship at your lodgings.

Lady Fidg. Now we are here, sir. . . .   280

Pinch. No, madam.

Dain. Pray let us see her.

Squeam. We will not stir till we see her.

Pinch. (*Aside.*) A pox on you all!   [*Goes to the door, and returns.* She has locked the door, and is gone abroad.

Lady Fidg. No, you have locked the door, and she's within.

Dain. They told us below, she was here.

Pinch. (*Aside.*) Will nothing do? Well, it must out then.—To tell you the truth, ladies, which I was afraid to let you know before, least it might

269 trimmings] clothes

endanger your lives, my wife has just now the smallpox come out upon her. Do not be frightened; but pray, be gone, ladies; you shall not stay here in danger of your lives; pray get you gone, ladies.   292

Lady Fidg. No, no, we have all had 'em.

Squeam. Alack, alack!

Dain. Come, come, we must see how it goes with her; I understand the disease.

Lady Fidg. Come.

Pinch. (*Aside.*) Well, there is no being too hard for women at their own weapon, lying; therefore I'll quit the field.

                                                    [*Exit* Pinchwife.

Squeam. Here's an example of jealousy!   300

Lady Fidg. Indeed, as the world goes, I wonder there are no more jealous, since wives are so neglected.

Dain. Pshaw! as the world goes, to what end should they be jealous?

Lady Fidg. Foh! 'tis a nasty world.

Squeam. That men of parts, great acquaintance, and quality should take up with and spend themselves and fortunes in keeping little playhouse creatures, foh!

Lady Fidg. Nay, that women of understanding, great acquaintance, and good quality should fall a-keeping too of little creatures, foh!

Squeam. Why, 'tis the men of quality's fault. They never visit women of honour and reputation as they used to do; and have not so much as common civility for ladies of our rank, but use us with the same indifferency and ill-breeding as if we were all married to 'em.   313

Lady Fidg. She says true! 'Tis an arrant shame women of quality should be so slighted. Methinks, birth—birth should go for something. I have known men admired, courted, and followed for their titles only.

Squeam. Ay, one would think men of honour should not love, no more than marry, out of their own rank.

Dain. Fie, fie upon 'em! They are come to think cross-breeding for themselves best, as well as for their dogs and horses.

Lady Fidg. They are dogs, and horses for't!

Squeam. One would think, if not for love, for vanity a little.   322

Dain. Nay, they do satisfy their vanity upon us sometimes, and are kind to us in their report—tell all the world they lie with us.

Lady Fidg. Damned rascals! That we should be only wronged by 'em. To report a man has . . . had a person, when he has not . . . had a person, is the greatest wrong in the whole world that can be . . . done to a person.

Squeam. Well, 'tis an arrant shame noble persons should be so wronged and neglected.

Lady Fidg. But still 'tis an arranter shame for a noble person to neglect

her own honour, and defame her own noble person with little inconsiderable
fellows, foh! 332

Dain. I suppose the crime against our honour is the same with a man of
quality as with another.

Lady Fidg. How! No, sure, the man of quality is likest one's husband, and
therefore the fault should be the less.

Dain. But then the pleasure should be the less!

Lady Fidg. Fie, fie, fie, for shame, sister! Whither shall we ramble? Be
continent in your discourse, or I shall hate you.

Dain. Besides, an intrigue is so much the more notorious for the man's
quality. 341

Squeam. 'Tis true, nobody takes notice of a private man, and therefore
with him 'tis more secret, and the crime's the less when 'tis not known.

Lady Fidg. You say true. I'faith, I think you are in the right on't. 'Tis not
an injury to a husband till it be an injury to our honours; so that a woman of
honour loses no honour with a private person; and to say truth. . . .

Dain. (*Apart to* Squeamish.) So, the *little fellow* is grown a *private person*
. . . with her.

Lady Fidg. But still my dear, dear *honour*.

Enter Sir Jasper, Horner, Dorilant.

Sir Jas. Ay, my dear, dear of honour, thou hast still so much honour in thy
mouth. . . . 351

Horn. (*Aside.*) That she has none elsewhere.

Lady Fidg. Oh, what d'ye mean to bring in these upon us?

Dain. Foh! these are as bad as wits.

Squeam. Foh!

Lady Fidg. Let us leave the room.

Sir Jas. Stay, stay; faith, to tell you the naked truth. . . .

Lady Fidg. Fie, sir Jasper, do not use that word *naked*.

Sir Jas. Well, well, in short, I have business at Whitehall, and cannot go
to the play with you, therefore would have you go. . . . 360

Lady Fidg. With those two to a play?

Sir Jas. No, not with t'other, but with Mr. Horner. There can be no more
scandal to go with him than with Mr. Tattle, or Master Limberham.

Lady Fidg. With that nasty fellow! No!

Sir Jas. Nay, prithee dear, hear me.

[*Whispers to* Lady Fidget.

Horn. Ladies. . . .

Horner, Dorilant *drawing near* Squeamish *and* Dainty.

363 Tattle, Limberham] names for harmless gallants

Dain. Stand off!

Squeam. Do not approach us!

Dain. You herd with the wits, you are obscenity all over.

Squeam. I would as soon look upon a picture of Adam and Eve, without fig leaves, as any of you, if I could help it, therefore keep off, and do not make us sick.   372

Dor. What a devil are these?

Horn. Why, these are pretenders to honour, as critics to wit, only by censuring others; and as every raw, peevish, out-of-humoured affected, dull, tea-drinking, arithmetical fop sets up for a wit, by railing at men of sense, so these for honour by railing at the court and ladies of as great honour as quality.

Sir Jas. Come, Mr. Horner, I must desire you to go with these ladies to the play, sir.

Horn. I, sir?   380

Sir Jas. Ay, ay, come, sir.

Horn. I must beg your pardon, sir, and theirs. I will not be seen in women's company in public again for the world.

Sir Jas. Ha, ha! strange aversion!

Squeam. No, he's for women's company in private.

Sir Jas. He—poor man—he! ha, ha, ha!

Dain. 'Tis a greater shame amongst lewd fellows to be seen in virtuous women's company than for the women to be seen with them.

Horn. Indeed, madam, the time was I only hated virtuous women, but now I hate the other too; I beg your pardon ladies.   390

Lady Fidg. You are very obliging, sir, because we would not be troubled with you.

Sir Jas. In sober sadness, he shall go.

Dor. Nay, if he wo'not, I am ready to wait upon the ladies; and I think I am the fitter man.

Sir Jas. You, sir, no, I thank you for that—Master Horner is a privileged man amongst the virtuous ladies; 'twill be a great while before you are so, he, he, he! He's my wife's gallant, he, he, he! No, pray withdraw, sir, for as I take it, the virtuous ladies have no business with you.

Dor. And I am sure he can have none with them. 'Tis strange a man can't come amongst virtuous women now but upon the same terms as men are admitted into the great Turk's seraglio; but heaven keep me from being an ombre player with 'em! But where is Pinchwife?   403

[*Exit* Dorilant.

Sir Jas. Come, come, man; what, avoid the sweet society of woman-kind? —that sweet, soft, gentle, tame, noble creature, woman, made for man's companion. . . .

376 arithmetical] precise   403 ombre] card game

Horn. So is that soft, gentle, tame, and more noble creature a spaniel, and has all their tricks—can fawn, lie down, suffer beating, and fawn the more; barks at your friends when they come to see you; makes your bed hard; gives you fleas, and the mange sometimes. And all the difference is, the spaniel's the more faithful animal, and fawns but upon one master.   411

Sir Jas. He, he, he!

Squeam. Oh, the rude beast!

Dain. Insolent brute!

Lady Fidg. Brute! Stinking, mortified, rotten French wether, to dare. . . .

Sir Jas. Hold, an't please your ladyship.—For shame, master Horner, your mother was a woman.—(*Aside.*) Now shall I never reconcile 'em.— Hark you, madam, take my advice in your anger. You know you often want one to make up your drolling pack of ombre players; and you may cheat him easily, for he's an ill gamester, and consequently loves play. Besides, you know, you have but two old civil gentlemen (with stinking breaths too) to wait upon you abroad; take in the third into your service. The others are but crazy; and a lady should have a supernumerary gentleman-usher, as a supernumerary coachhorse, lest sometimes you should be forced to stay at home.   425

Lady Fidg. But are you sure he loves play, and has money?

Sir Jas. He loves play as much as you, and has money as much as I.

Lady Fidg. Then I am contented to make him pay for his scurrillity; money makes up in a measure all other wants in men.—(*Aside.*) Those whom we cannot make hold for gallants, we make fine.

Sir Jas. (*Aside.*) So, so; now to mollify, to wheedle him.—Master Horner, will you never keep civil company? Methinks 'tis time now, since you are only fit for them. Come, come, man, you must e'en fall to visiting our wives, eating at our tables, drinking tea with our virtuous relations after dinner, dealing cards to 'em, reading plays and gazettes to 'em, picking fleas out of their shocks for 'em, collecting receipts, new songs, women, pages, and footmen for 'em.   437

Horn. I hope they'll afford me better employment, sir.

Sir Jas. He, he, he! 'Tis fit you know your work before you come into your place; and since you are unprovided of a lady to flatter, and a good house to eat at, pray frequent mine, and call my wife mistress, and she shall call you gallant, according to the custom.

Horn. Who, I?

Sir Jas. Faith, thou shalt for my sake; come, for my sake only.

Horn. For your sake. . . .

Sir Jas. Come, come, here's a gamester for you; let him be a little familiar

---

415 mortified] dead   415 wether] castrated ram   423 gentleman-usher] escort
430 fine] pay   436 shocks] poodles   436 receipts] recipes

sometimes; nay, what if a little rude? Gamesters may be rude with ladies, you know.

Lady Fidg. Yes, losing gamesters have a privilege with women.

Horn. I always thought the contrary, that the winning gamester had most privilege with women; for when you have lost your money to a man, you'll lose anything you have, all you have, they say, and he may use you as he pleases.   453

Sir Jas. He, he, he! Well, win or lose, you shall have your liberty with her.

Lady Fidg. As he behaves himself; and for your sake I'll give him admittance and freedom.

Horn. All sorts of freedom, madam?

Sir Jas. Ay, ay, ay, all sorts of freedom thou can'st take, and so go to her, begin thy new employment; wheedle her, jest with her, and be better acquainted one with another.   460

Horn. (*Aside.*) I think I know her already, therefore may venture with her, my secret for hers.   [*Horner and* Lady Fidget *whisper.*

Sir Jas. Sister, cuz, I have provided an innocent playfellow for you there.

Dain. Who, he!

Squeam. There's a playfellow indeed!

Sir Jas. Yes, sure, what, he is good enough to play at cards, blindman's buff, or the fool with sometimes.

Squeam. Foh! we'll have no such playfellows.

Dain. No, sir, you shan't choose playfellows for us, we thank you.

Sir Jas. Nay, pray hear me.   [*Whispering to them.*

Lady Fidg. But, poor gentleman, could you be so generous, so truly a man of honour, as for the sakes of us women of honour, to cause yourself to be reported no man? No man! And to suffer yourself the greatest shame that could fall upon a man, that none might fall upon us women by your conversation? But indeed, sir, as perfectly, perfectly, the same man as before your going into France, sir? As perfectly, perfectly, sir?   476

Horn. As perfectly, perfectly, madam. Nay, I scorn you should take my word; I desire to be tried only, madam.

Lady Fidg. Well, that's spoken again like a man of honour; all men of honour desire to come to the test. But, indeed, generally you men report such things of yourselves, one does not know how or whom to believe; and it is come to that pass we dare not take your words no more than your tailor's, without some staid servant of yours be bound with you. But I have so strong a faith in your honour, dear, dear, noble sir, that I'd forfeit mine for yours at any time, dear sir.   485

Horn. No, madam, you should not need to forfeit it for me. I have given you security already to save you harmless, my late reputation being so well known in the world, madam.

Lady Fidg. But if upon any future falling out, or upon a suspicion of my
taking the trust out of your hands, to employ some other, you yourself should
betray your trust, dear sir? I mean, if you'll give me leave to speak obscenely,
you might tell, dear sir.   492

Horn. If I did, nobody would believe me! The reputation of impotency is
as hardly recovered again in the world as that of cowardice, dear madam.

Lady Fidg. Nay then, as one may say, you may do your worst, dear, dear,
sir.

Sir Jas. Come, is your ladyship reconciled to him yet? Have you agreed on
matters? For I must be gone to Whitehall.

Lady Fidg. Why, indeed, sir Jasper, master Horner is a thousand, thousand
times a better man than I thought him. Cousin Squeamish, sister Dainty, I
can name him now; truly, not long ago, you know, I thought his very name
obscenity, and I would as soon have lain with him as have named him.

Sir Jas. Very likely, poor madam.   503

Dain. I believe it.

Squeam. No doubt on't.

Sir Jas. Well, well—that your ladyship is as virtuous as any she, I know,
and him all the town knows—he, he, he! Therefore, now you like him, get
you gone to your business together; go, go, to your business, I say, pleasure,
whilst I go to my pleasure, business.

Lady Fidg. Come then, dear gallant.

Horn. Come away, my dearest mistress.

Sir Jas. So, so; why 'tis as I'd have it.   [*Exit* Sir Jasper.

Horn. And as I'd have it!

Lady Fidg. Who for his business from his wife will run,
          Takes the best care to have her business done!
                                                          [*Exeunt omnes.*

ACT III   SCENE I

Alithea *and* Mrs. Pinchwife.

Alith. Sister, what ails you? You are grown melancholy.

Mrs. Pinch. Would it not make anyone melancholy, to see you go every day
fluttering about abroad, whilst I must stay at home like a poor, lonely, sullen
bird in a cage?

Alith. Ay, sister, but you came young and just from the nest to your cage,

491 obscenely] openly

so that I thought you liked it; and could be as cheerful in't as others that took their flight themselves early, and are hopping abroad in the open air.

Mrs. Pinch. Nay, I confess I was quiet enough till my husband told me what pure lives the London ladies live abroad, with their dancing, meetings, and junketings, and dressed every day in their best gowns; and I warrant you, play at ninepins every day of the week, so they do.   11

Enter Mr. Pinchwife.

Pinch. Come, what's here to do? You are putting the town pleasures in her head, and setting her a-longing.

Alith. Yes, after ninepins! You suffer none to give her those longings, you mean, but yourself.

Pinch. I tell her of the vanities of the town like a confessor.

Alith. A confessor! Just such a confessor as he that, by forbidding a silly ostler to grease the horse's teeth, taught him to do't.

Pinch. Come Mistress Flippant, good precepts are lost when poor examples are still before us. The liberty you take abroad makes her hanker after it, and out of humour at home. Poor wretch! she desired not to come to London; I would bring her.   22

Alith. Very well.

Pinch. She has been this week in town, and never desired, till this afternoon, to go abroad.

Alith. Was she not at a play yesterday?

Pinch. Yes, but she ne'er asked me. I was myself the cause of her going.

Alith. Then, if she ask you again, you are the cause of her asking, and not my example.

Pinch. Well, tomorrow night I shall be rid of you; and the next day, before 'tis light, she and I'll be rid of the town, and my dreadful apprehensions. Come, be not melancholy, for thou shalt go into the country after tomorrow, dearest.   33

Alith. Great comfort!

Mrs. Pinch. Pish! what d'ye tell me of the country for?

Pinch. How's this! What, pish at the country?

Mrs. Pinch. Let me alone, I am not well.

Pinch. O if that be all—what ails my dearest?

Mrs. Pinch. Truly I don't know; but I have not been well since you told me there was a gallant at the play in love with me.

Pinch. Ha!

Alith. That's by my example too!   42

Pinch. Nay, if you are not well, but are so concerned because a lewd fellow chanced to lie and say he liked you, you'll make me sick too.

Mrs. Pinch. Of what sickness?

Pinch. Of that which is worse than the plague—jealousy.

Mrs. Pinch. Pish, you jeer! I'm sure there's no such disease in our receipt-book at home.

Pinch. No, thou never met'st with it, poor innocent. (*Aside.*) Well, if thou cuckold me, 'twill be my fault, for cuckolds and bastards are generally makers of their own fortune. ⁵¹

Mrs. Pinch. Well, but pray, bud, let's go to a play tonight.

Pinch. 'Tis just done, she comes from it; but why are you so eager to see a play?

Mrs. Pinch. Faith, dear, not that I care one pin for their talk there, but I like to look upon the playermen, and would see, if I could, the gallant you say loves me; that's all, dear bud.

Pinch. Is that all, dear bud?

Alith. This proceeds from my example!

Mrs. Pinch. But if the play be done, let's go abroad however, dear bud.

Pinch. Come, have a little patience, and thou shalt go into the country on Friday. ⁶²

Mrs. Pinch. Therefore I would see first some sights, to tell my neighbours of. Nay, I will go abroad, that's once.

Alith. I'm the cause of this desire too!

Pinch. But now I think on't, who was the cause of Horner's coming to my lodging today? That was you.

Alith. No, you, because you would not let him see your handsome wife out of your lodging.

Mrs. Pinch. Why, O Lord! did the gentleman come hither to see me indeed? ⁷¹

Pinch. No, no.—You are not cause of that damned question too, Mistress Alithea? (*Aside.*) Well, she's in the right of it. He is in love with my wife . . . and comes after her . . . 'tis so . . . but I'll nip his love in the bud; lest he should follow us into the country, and break his chariot-wheel near our house on purpose for an excuse to come to't. But I think I know the town.

Mrs. Pinch. Come, pray bud, let's go abroad before 'tis late. For I will go, that's flat and plain.

Pinch. (*Aside.*) So! the obstinacy already of a town-wife, and I must, whilst she's here, humour her like one.—Sister, how shall we do, that she may not be seen or known? ⁸²

Alith. Let her put on her mask.

Pinch. Pshaw! A mask makes people but the more inquisitive, and is as ridiculous a disguise as a stage beard; her shape, stature, habit will be known. And if we should meet with Horner he would be sure to take acquaintance with us, must wish her joy, kiss her, talk to her, leer upon her, and the devil

and all. No, I'll not use her to a mask, 'tis dangerous; for masks have made
more cuckolds than the best faces that ever were known.

Alith. How will you do then?   90

Mrs. Pinch. Nay, shall we go? The Exchange will be shut, and I have a
mind to see that.

Pinch. So ... I have it ... I'll dress her up in the suit we are to carry
down to her brother, little sir James; nay, I understand the town tricks.
Come, let's go dress her. A mask! No—a woman masked, like a covered dish,
gives a man curiosity, and appetite, when, it may be, uncovered 'twould turn
his stomach; no, no.

Alith. Indeed your comparison is something a greasy one. But I had a
gentle gallant used to say, 'A beauty masked, like the sun in eclipse, gathers
together more gazers than if it shined out.'

[Exeunt.

SCENE II

The scene changes to the New Exchange.

Enter Horner, Harcourt, Dorilant.

Dor. Engaged to women, and not sup with us?

Horn. Ay, a pox on 'em all.

Harc. You were much a more reasonable man in the morning, and had as
noble resolutions against 'em as a widower of a week's liberty.

Dor. Did I ever think to see you keep company with women in vain?

Horn. In vain! No—'tis, since I can't love 'em, to be revenged on 'em.

Harc. Now your sting is gone, you looked in the box, amongst all those
women, like a drone in the hive, all upon you; shoved and ill-used by 'em all,
and thrust from one side to t'other.

Dor. Yet he must be buzzing amongst 'em still, like other old beetle-
headed, lickerish drones. Avoid 'em, and hate 'em as they hate you.   11

Horn. Because I do hate 'em, and would hate 'em yet more, I'll frequent
'em. You may see by marriage, nothing makes a man hate a woman more,
than her constant conversation. In short, I converse with 'em, as you do with
rich fools, to laugh at 'em, and use 'em ill.

Dor. But I would no more sup with women, unless I could lie with 'em,
than sup with a rich coxcomb, unless I could cheat him.

10-11 beetle-headed] stupid   11 lickerish] lecherous

Horn. Yes, I have known thee sup with a fool for his drinking; if he could set out your hand that way only, you were satisfied, and if he were a wine-swallowing mouth 'twas enough.   20

Harc. Yes, a man drinks often with a fool, as he tosses with a marker, only to keep his hand in ure. But do the ladies drink?

Horn. Yes, sir, and I shall have the pleasure at least of laying 'em flat with a bottle, and bring as much scandal that way upon 'em as formerly t'other.

Harc. Perhaps you may prove as weak a brother amongst 'em that way as t'other.

Dor. Foh! drinking with women is as unnatural as scolding with 'em. But 'tis a pleasure of decayed fornicators, and the basest way of quenching love.

Harc. Nay, 'tis drowning love instead of quenching it. But leave us for civil women too!   30

Dor. Ay, when he can't be the better for 'em. We hardly pardon a man that leaves his friend for a wench, and that's a pretty lawful call.

Horn. Faith, I would not leave you for 'em, if they would not drink.

Dor. Who would disappoint his company at Lewis's for a gossiping?

Harc. Foh! Wine and women, good apart, together as nauseous as sack and sugar. But hark you, sir, before you go, a little of your advice; an old maimed general, when unfit for action, is fittest for counsel. I have other designs upon women than eating and drinking with them. I am in love with Sparkish's mistress, whom he is to marry tomorrow. Now how shall I get her?   40

Enter Sparkish, *looking about.*

Horn. Why, here comes one will help you to her.

Harc. He! He, I tell you, is my rival, and will hinder my love.

Horn. No, a foolish rival and a jealous husband assist their rival's designs; for they are sure to make their women hate them, which is the first step to their love for another man.

Harc. But I cannot come near his mistress but in his company.

Horn. Still the better for you, for fools are most easily cheated when they themselves are accessories; and he is to be bubbled of his mistress, as of his money, the common mistress, by keeping him company.

Spark. Who is that, that is to be bubbled? Faith, let me snack, I han't met with a bubble since Christmas. Gad, I think bubbles are like their brother woodcocks, go out with the cold weather.   52

Harc. (*Apart to* Horner.) A pox! he did not hear all I hope.

Spark. Come, you bubbling rogues you, where do we sup?—Oh, Harcourt,

---

21 marker] scorekeeper at dice   22 ure] practice   34 Lewis's] a London tavern
35 sack] sherry   48 bubbled] hoodwinked   50 snack] share   52 woodcocks] dupes

my mistress tells me you have been making fierce love to her all the play
long, ha, ha!—But I. . . .

Harc. I make love to her?

Spark. Nay, I forgive thee; for I think I know thee, and I know her, but I
am sure I know myself.

Harc. Did she tell you so? I see all women are like these of the exchange,
who, to enhance the price of their commodities, report to their fond customers
offers which were never made 'em.   62

Horn. Ay, women are as apt to tell before the intrigue as men after it, and
so show themselves the vainer sex. But hast thou a mistress, Sparkish?
'Tis as hard for me to believe it as that thou ever hadst a bubble, as you
bragged just now.

Spark. Oh, your servant, sir; are you at your raillery, sir? But we were
some of us beforehand with you today at the play. The wits were something
bold with you, sir; did you not hear us laugh?

Harc. Yes, but I thought you had gone to plays to laugh at the poet's
wit, not at your own.   71

Spark. Your servant, sir; no, I thank you. Gad, I go to a play as to a country
treat. I carry my own wine to one, and my own wit to t'other, or else I'm
sure I should not be merry at either. And the reason why we are so often
louder than the players is because we think we speak more wit, and so
become the poet's rivals in his audience. For to tell you the truth, we hate the
silly rogues; nay, so much that we find fault even with their bawdy upon the
stage, whilst we talk of nothing else in the pit as loud.

Horn. But, why should'st thou hate the silly poets? Thou hast too much
wit to be one, and they, like whores, are only hated by each other. And thou
dost scorn writing, I'm sure.   81

Spark. Yes, I'd have you to know, I scorn writing. But women, women,
that make men do all foolish things, make 'em write songs too. Everybody
does it. 'Tis even as common with lovers as playing with fans; and you can no
more help rhyming to your Phyllis than drinking to your Phyllis.

Harc. Nay, poetry in love is no more to be avoided than jealousy.

Dor. But the poets damned your songs, did they?

Spark. Damn the poets! They turned 'em into burlesque, as they call it.
That burlesque is a hocus-pocus trick they have got, which by the virtue of
hictius doctius, *topsy-turvy*, they make a wise and witty man in the world a
fool upon the stage, you know not how. And 'tis therefore I hate 'em too, for
I know not but it may be my own case; for they'll put a man into a play for
looking asquint. Their predecessors were contented to make serving-men
only their stage-fools, but these rogues must have gentlemen, with a pox to
'em, nay knights. And, indeed, you shall hardly see a fool upon the stage but

90 *hictius doctius*] juggler's jargon

he's a knight. And to tell you the truth, they have kept me these six years
from being a knight in earnest, for fear of being knighted in a play, and
dubbed a fool.

Dor. Blame 'em not, they must follow their copy—the age.

Harc. But why should'st thou be afraid of being in a play, who expose
yourself every day in the playhouses, and as public places?   101

Horn. 'Tis but being on the stage, instead of standing on a bench in the pit.

Dor. Don't you give money to painters to draw you like? And are you
afraid of your pictures at length in a playhouse, where all your mistresses
may see you?

Spark. A pox! Painters don't draw the smallpox or pimples in one's face.
Come, damn all your silly authors whatever, all books and booksellers, by the
world, and all readers, courteous or uncourteous.

Harc. But, who comes here, Sparkish?

Enter Mr. Pinchwife, *and his wife in man's clothes,*
Alithea, Lucy *her maid.*

Spark. Oh hide me! There's my mistress too.   110
                    [Sparkish *hides himself behind* Harcourt.

Harc. She sees you.

Spark. But I will not see her. 'Tis time to go to Whitehall, and I must not
fail the drawing-room.

Harc. Pray, first carry me, and reconcile me to her.

Spark. Another time! Faith, the king will have supped.

Harc. Not with the worse stomach for thy absence! Thou art one of those
fools that think their attendance at the king's meals as necessary as his physicians', when you are more troublesome to him than his doctors, or his dogs.

Spark. Pshaw! I know my interest, sir. Prithee, hide me.

Horn. Your servant, Pinchwife.—What, he knows us not!   120

Pinch. (*To his wife aside.*) Come along.

Mrs. Pinch. Pray, have you any ballads? Give me a sixpenny worth?

Clasp. We have no ballads.

Mrs. Pinch. Then give me *Covent Garden Drollery*, and a play or two. . . .
Oh, here's *Tarugo's Wiles*, and *The Slighted Maiden*—I'll have them.

Pinch. (*Apart to her.*) No, plays are not for your reading. Come along; will
you discover yourself?

Horn. Who is that pretty youth with him, Sparkish?

---

123 *Clasp*] a vendor, unlisted in the dramatis personae   124 *Covent Garden Drollery*]
Brome's compilation of songs from plays (1672)   125 *Tarugo's Wiles*] comedy by Sir
Thomas St. Serfe (1667)   125 *The Slighted Maiden*] comedy by Sir Robert Stapleton
(1663)

Spark. I believe his wife's brother, because he's something like her; but I
never saw her but once.   130

Horn. Extremely handsome. I have seen a face like it too. Let us follow 'em.

[*Exeunt* Pinchwife, Mistress Pinchwife. Alithea, Lucy,
Horner, Dorilant *following them.*

Harc. Come, Sparkish, your mistress saw you, and will be angry you go
not to her. Besides I would fain be reconciled to her, which none but you
can do, dear friend.

Spark. Well, that's a better reason, dear friend. I would not go near her
now, for her's or my own sake, but I can deny you nothing; for though I
have known thee a great while, never go, if I do not love thee as well as a new
acquaintance.

Harc. I am obliged to you indeed, dear friend. I would be well with her,
only to be well with thee still; for these ties to wives usually dissolve all ties to
friends. I would be contented she should enjoy you a-nights, but I would
have you to myself a-days, as I have had, dear friend.   142

Spark. And thou shalt enjoy me a-days, dear, dear friend, never stir; and
I'll be divorced from her, sooner than from thee. Come along. . . .

Harc. (*Aside.*) So we are hard put to't, when we make our rival our pro-
curer; but neither she nor her brother would let me come near her now.
When all's done, a rival is the best cloak to steal to a mistress under, without
suspicion; and when we have once got to her as we desire, we throw him off
like other cloaks.

[*Exit* Sparkish, *and* Harcourt *following him.*

Re-enter Mr. Pinchwife, Mistress Pinchwife *in man's clothes.*

Pinch. (*To* Alithea *off-stage.*) Sister, if you will not go, we must leave you.
(*Aside.*) The fool her gallant and she will muster up all the young saunterers of
this place, and they will leave their dear seamstresses to follow us. What a
swarm of cuckolds and cuckold-makers are here!—Come, let's be gone,
Mistress Margery.   154

Mrs. Pinch. Don't you believe that, I han't half my bellyfull of sights yet.

Pinch. Then walk this way.

Mrs. Pinch. Lord, what a power of brave signs are here! Stay—the Bull's
Head, the Ram's Head, and the Stag's Head! Dear. . . .

Pinch. Nay, if every husband's proper sign here were visible, they would
be all alike.

Mrs. Pinch. What d'ye mean by that, bud?

Pinch. 'Tis no matter . . . no matter, bud.

Mrs. Pinch. Pray tell me; nay, I will know.

Pinch. They would all be bulls', stags' and rams' heads!   164

[*Exeunt* Mr. Pinchwife, Mrs. Pinchwife.

Re-enter Sparkish, Harcourt, Alithea, Lucy, *at t'other door.*

Spark. Come, dear madam, for my sake you shall be reconciled to him.

Alith. For your sake I hate him.

Harc. That's something too cruel, madam, to hate me for his sake.

Spark. Ay indeed, madam, too, too cruel to me, to hate my friend for my sake.

Alith. I hate him because he is your enemy; and you ought to hate him too, for making love to me, if you love me.   171

Spark. That's a good one; I hate a man for loving you! If he did love you, 'tis but what he can't help; and 'tis your fault, not his, if he admires you. I hate a man for being of my opinion! I'll ne'er do't, by the world.

Alith. Is it for your honour or mine, to suffer a man to make love to me, who am to marry you tomorrow?

Spark. Is it for your honour or mine, to have me jealous? That he makes love to you, is a sign you are handsome; and that I am not jealous, is a sign you are virtuous. That, I think, is for your honour.

Alith. But 'tis your honour too I am concerned for.   180

Harc. But why, dearest madam, will you be more concerned for his honour, than he is himself? Let his honour alone, for my sake and his. He, he has no honour. . . .

Spark. How's that?

Harc. But what my dear friend can guard himself.

Spark. O ho—that's right again.

Harc. Your care of his honour argues his neglect of it, which is no honour to my dear friend here; therefore once more, let his honour go which way it will, dear madam.

Spark. Ay, ay, were it for my honour to marry a woman whose virtue I suspected, and could not trust her in a friend's hands?   191

Alith. Are you not afraid to lose me?

Harc. He afraid to lose you, madam! No, no—you may see how the most estimable and most glorious creature in the world is valued by him. Will you not see it?

Spark. Right, honest Frank, I have that noble value for her that I cannot be jealous of her.

Alith. You mistake him. He means you care not for me nor who has me.

Spark. Lord, madam, I see you are jealous! Will you wrest a poor man's meaning from his words?   200

Alith. You astonish me, sir, with your want of jealousy.

Spark. And you make me giddy, madam, with your jealousy and fears, and virtue and honour. Gad, I see virtue makes a woman as troublesome as a little reading or learning.

Alith. Monstrous!

Lucy. (*Behind.*) Well, to see what easy husbands these women of quality
can meet with! A poor chambermaid can never have such lady-like luck.
Besides, he's thrown away upon her; she'll make no use of her fortune, her
blessing; none to a gentleman for a pure cuckold, for it requires good breeding to be a cuckold.   210

Alith. I tell you then plainly, he pursues me to marry me.

Spark. Pshaw!

Harc. Come, madam, you see you strive in vain to make him jealous of me.
My dear friend is the kindest creature in the world to me.

Spark. Poor fellow.

Harc. But his kindness only is not enough for me, without your favour.
Your good opinion, dear madam, 'tis that must perfect my happiness. Good
gentleman, he believes all I say; would you would do so. Jealous of me! I
would not wrong him nor you for the world.

Alithea walks carelessly to and fro.

Spark. Look you there; hear him, hear him, and do not walk away so.

Harc. I love you, madam, so. . . .   221

Spark. How's that! Nay—now you begin to go too far indeed.

Harc. So much, I confess, I say I love you, that I would not have you
miserable, and cast yourself away upon so unworthy and inconsiderable a
thing as what you see here.
                        [*Clapping his hand on his breast, points at* Sparkish.

Spark. No, faith, I believe thou would'st not. Now his meaning is plain.
But I knew before thou would'st not wrong me nor her.

Harc. No, no, heavens forbid the glory of her sex should fall so low as into
the embraces of such a contemptible wretch, the last of mankind—my dear
friend here—I injure him.   [*Embracing* Sparkish.

Alith. Very well.   231

Spark. No, no, dear friend, I knew it. Madam, you see he will rather wrong
himself than me, in giving himself such names.

Alith. Do you not understand him yet?

Spark. Yes, how modestly he speaks of himself, poor fellow.

Alith. Methinks he speaks impudently of yourself, since—before yourself
too; insomuch that I can no longer suffer his scurrilous abusiveness to you,
no more than his love to me.   [*Offers to go.*

Spark. Nay, nay, madam, pray stay. His love to you! Lord, madam, has he
not spoke yet plain enough?   240

Alith. Yes indeed, I should think so.

Spark. Well then, by the world, a man can't speak civilly to a woman now
but presently she says he makes love to her! Nay, madam, you shall stay,

with your pardon, since you have not yet understood him, till he has made an
éclaircissement of his love to you, that is, what kind of love it is. (*To* Harcourt.)
Answer to thy catechism. Friend, do you love my mistress here?

Harc. Yes, I wish she would not doubt it.

Spark. But how do you love her?

Harc. With all my soul.

Alith. I thank him; methinks he speaks plain enough now.   250

Spark. (*To* Alithea.) You are out still.—But with what kind of love,
Harcourt?

Harc. With the best and truest love in the world.

Spark. Look you there then, that is with no matrimonial love, I'm
sure!

Alith. How's that? Do you say matrimonial love is not best?

Spark. (*Aside.*) Gad, I went too far ere I was aware.—But speak for thyself,
Harcourt; you said you would not wrong me nor her.

Harc. No, no, madam, e'en take him for heaven's sake. . . .

Spark. Look you there, madam.   260

Harc. Who should in all justice be yours, he that loves you most.

                              [*Claps his hand on his breast.*

Alith. Look you there, Mr. Sparkish, who's that?

Spark. Who should it be?—Go on, Harcourt.

Harc. Who loves you more than women titles, or fortune fools.

                              [*Points at* Sparkish.

Spark. Look you there, he means me still, for he points at me.

Alith. Ridiculous!

Harc. Who can only match your faith and constancy in love.

Spark. Ay.

Harc. Who knows, if it be possible, how to value so much beauty and
virtue.   270

Spark. Ay.

Harc. Whose love can no more be equalled in the world than that heavenly
form of yours.

Spark. No.

Harc. Who could no more suffer a rival than your absence, and yet could
no more suspect your virtue than his own constancy in his love to you.

Spark. No.

Harc. Who, in fine, loves you better than his eyes, that first made him
love you.

Spark. Ay—nay, madam, faith, you shan't go, till. . . .   280

Alith. Have a care, lest you make me stay too long. . . .

Spark. But till he has saluted you; that I may be assured you are friends,

245 *éclaircissement*] explanation

after his honest advice and declaration. Come, pray, madam, be friends with
him.

Enter Master Pinchwife, Mistress Pinchwife.

Alith. You must pardon me, sir, that I am not yet so obedient to you.

Pinch. What, invite your wife to kiss men? Monstrous! Are you not
ashamed? I will never forgive you.

Spark. Are you not ashamed that I should have more confidence in the
chastity of your family than you have? You must not teach me, I am a man of
honour, sir, though I am frank and free. I am frank, sir. . . .   290

Pinch. Very frank, sir, to share your wife with your friends.

Spark. He is an humble, menial friend, such as reconciles the differences
of the marriage bed. You know man and wife do not always agree; I design
him for that use, therefore would have him well with my wife.

Pinch. A menial friend! You will get a great many menial friends by showing your wife as you do.

Spark. What then? It may be I have a pleasure in't, as I have to show fine
clothes at a playhouse the first day, and count money before poor rogues.

Pinch. He that shows his wife or money will be in danger of having them
borrowed sometimes.   300

Spark. I love to be envied, and would not marry a wife that I alone could
love. Loving alone is as dull as eating alone. Is it not a frank age? And I am a
frank person. And to tell you the truth, it may be I love to have rivals in a
wife; they make her seem to a man still but as a kept mistress. And so good
night, for I must to Whitehall.—Madam, I hope you are now reconciled to
my friend; and so I wish you a good night, madam, and sleep if you can, for
tomorrow you know I must visit you early with a canonical gentleman.
Good night, dear Harcourt.   [*Exit* Sparkish.

Harc. Madam, I hope you will not refuse my visit tomorrow, if it should be
earlier with a canonical gentleman than Mr. Sparkish's.   310

Pinch. (*Coming between* Alithea *and* Harcourt.) This gentlewoman is yet
under my care; therefore you must yet forbear your freedom with her, sir.

Harc. Must, sir!

Pinch. Yes, sir, she is my sister.

Harc. 'Tis well she is, sir—for I must be her servant, sir. Madam. . . .

Pinch. Come away, sister. We had been gone if it had not been for you,
and so avoided these lewd rakehells, who seem to haunt us.

Enter Horner, Dorilant *to them.*

Horn. How now, Pinchwife!

Pinch. Your servant.

317 rakehells] dissipated men of fashion, rakes

Horn. What! I see a little time in the country makes a man turn wild and unsociable, and only fit to converse with his horses, dogs, and his herds.

Pinch. I have business, sir, and must mind it. Your business is pleasure, therefore you and I must go different ways.   323

Horn. Well, you may go on, but this pretty young gentleman . . .

[*Takes hold of* Mrs. Pinchwife.

Harc. The lady. . . .

Dor. And the maid. . . .

Horn. Shall stay with us, for I suppose their business is the same with ours—pleasure.

Pinch. (*Aside.*) 'Sdeath, he knows her, she carries it so sillily! Yet if he does not, I should be more silly to discover it first.   330

Alith. Pray, let us go, sir.

Pinch. Come, come.

Horn. (*To* Mrs. Pinchwife.) Had you not rather stay with us?—Prithee, Pinchwife, who is this pretty young gentleman?

Pinch. One to whom I'm a guardian. (*Aside.*) I wish I could keep her out of your hands.

Horn. Who is he? I never saw anything so pretty in all my life.

Pinch. Pshaw! do not look upon him so much; he's a poor bashful youth, you'll put him out of countenance. Come away, brother.

[*Offers to take her away.*

Horn. Oh, your brother?   340

Pinch. Yes, my wife's brother. Come, come, she'll stay supper for us.

Horn. I thought so, for he is very like her I saw you at the play with, whom I told you I was in love with.

Mrs. Pinch. (*Aside.*) O jeminy! Is this he that was in love with me? I am glad on't, I vow, for he's a curious fine gentleman, and I love him already too. (*To* Mr. Pinchwife.) Is this he, bud?

Pinch. (*To his wife.*) Come away, come away.

Horn. Why, what haste are you in? Why won't you let me talk with him?

Pinch. Because you'll debauch him. He's yet young and innocent, and I would not have him debauched for anything in the world. (*Aside.*) How she gazes on him! the devil!   351

Horn. Harcourt, Dorilant, look you here; this is the likeness of that dowdy he told us of, his wife. Did you ever see a lovelier creature? The rogue has reason to be jealous of his wife, since she is like him, for she would make all that see her in love with her.

Harc. And as I remember now, she is as like him here as can be.

Dor. She is indeed very pretty, if she be like him.

Horn. Very pretty? A very pretty commendation! She is a glorious creature, beautiful beyond all things I ever beheld.

Pinch. So, so.   360

Harc. More beautiful than a poet's first mistress of imagination.

Horn. Or another man's last mistress of flesh and blood.

Mrs. Pinch. Nay, now you jeer, sir; pray don't jeer me.

Pinch. Come, come. (*Aside.*) By heavens, she'll discover herself!

Horn. I speak of your sister, sir.

Pinch. Ay, but saying she was handsome, if like him, made him blush.
(*Aside.*) I am upon a rack!

Horn. Methinks he is so handsome he should not be a man.

Pinch. (*Aside.*) Oh, there 'tis out, he has discovered her! I am not able to
suffer any longer. (*To his wife.*) Come, come away, I say.   370

Horn. Nay, by your leave, sir, he shall not go yet. (*To them.*) Harcourt,
Dorilant, let us torment this jealous rogue a little.

Harc. and Dor. How?

Horn. I'll show you.

Pinch. Come, pray let him go, I cannot stay fooling any longer; I tell you
his sister stays supper for us.

Horn. Does she? Come then, we'll all go sup with her and thee.

Pinch. No, now I think on't, having stayed so long for us, I'll warrant she's
gone to bed. (*Aside.*) I wish she and I were well out of their hands.—Come, I
must rise early tomorrow, come.   380

Horn. Well then, if she be gone to bed, I wish her and you a good night.
But pray, young gentleman, present my humble service to her.

Mrs. Pinch. Thank you heartily, sir.

Pinch. (*Aside.*) S'death! she will discover herself yet in spite of me.—He is
something more civil to you, for your kindness to his sister, than I am, it
seems.

Horn. Tell her, dear sweet little gentleman, for all your brother there, that
you have revived the love I had for her at first sight in the playhouse.

Mrs. Pinch. But did you love her indeed, and indeed?

Pinch. (*Aside.*) So, so.—Away, I say.   390

Horn. Nay, stay. Yes, indeed, and indeed, pray do you tell her so, and give
her this kiss from me.   [*Kisses her.*

Pinch. (*Aside.*) O heavens! What do I suffer! Now 'tis too plain he knows
her, and yet . . .

Horn. And this, and this . . .   [*Kisses her again.*

Mrs. Pinch. What do you kiss me for? I am no woman.

Pinch. (*Aside.*) So—there, 'tis out.—Come, I cannot, nor will stay any
longer.

Horn. Nay, they shall send your lady a kiss too. Here, Harcourt, Dorilant,
will you not?   [*They kiss her.*

Pinch. (*Aside.*) How! do I suffer this? Was I not accusing another just now

for this rascally patience, in permitting his wife to be kissed before his face?
Ten thousand ulcers gnaw away their lips!—Come, come.   403

Horn. Good night, dear little gentleman; madam, goodnight; farewell
Pinchwife. (*Apart to* Harcourt *and* Dorilant.) Did I not tell you I would raise
his jealous gall?

> [*Exeunt* Horner, Harcourt *and* Dorilant.

Pinch. So, they are gone at last! Stay, let me see first if the coach be at this
door.   [*Exit.*

> Horner, Harcourt *and* Dorilant *return.*

Horn. What, not gone yet? Will you be sure to do as I desired you, sweet
sir?   410

Mrs. Pinch. Sweet sir, but what will you give me then?

Horn. Anything. Come away into the next walk.

> [*Exit* Horner, *haling away* Mrs. Pinchwife.

Alith. Hold, hold! What d'ye do?

Lucy. Stay, stay, hold. . . .

Harc. Hold, madam, hold! Let him present him, he'll come presently;
nay, I will never let you go till you answer my question.

Lucy. For god's sake, sir, I must follow 'em.

Dor. No, I have something to present you with too; you shan't follow them.

> Alithea, Lucy, *struggling with* Harcourt *and* Dorilant.
> Pinchwife *returns.*

Pinch. Where?—how?—what's become of?—gone!—whither?

Lucy. He's only gone with the gentleman, who will give him something,
an't please your worship.   421

Pinch. Something!—give him something, with a pox!—Where are they?

Alith. In the next walk only, brother.

Pinch. Only, only! Where, where?

> [*Exit* Pinchwife, *and returns presently, then goes out again.*

Harc. What's the matter with him? Why so much concerned? But
dearest madam. . . .

Alith. Pray, let me go, sir; I have said and suffered enough already.

Harc. Then you will not look upon, nor pity, my sufferings?

Alith. To look upon 'em, when I cannot help 'em, were cruelty, not pity;
therefore I will never see you more.   430

Harc. Let me then, madam, have my privilege of a banished lover, com-
plaining or railing, and giving you but a farewell reason why, if you cannot
condescend to marry me, you should not take that wretch, my rival.

Alith. He only, not you, since my honour is engaged so far to him, can give
me a reason, why I should not marry him. But if he be true, and what I think
him to me, I must be so to him. Your servant, sir.

Harc. Have women only constancy when 'tis a vice, and are, like fortune, only true to fools?

Dor. (*To* Lucy, *who struggles to get from him.*) Thou sha't not stir, thou robust creature! You see I can deal with you, therefore you should stay the rather, and be kind.   441

Enter Pinchwife.

Pinch. Gone, gone, not to be found! quite gone! Ten thousand plagues go with 'em! Which way went they?

Alith. But into t'other walk, brother.

Lucy. Their business will be done presently sure, an't please your worship; it can't be long in doing, I'm sure on't.

Alith. Are they not there?

Pinch. No; you know where they are, you infamous wretch, eternal shame of your family, which you do not dishonour enough yourself, you think, but you must help her to do it too, thou legion of bawds!   450

Alith. Good brother. . . .

Pinch. Damned, damned sister!

Alith. Look you here, she's coming.

Enter Mistress Pinchwife *in man's clothes, running, with her hat under her arm, full of oranges and dried fruit;* Horner *following.*

Mrs. Pinch. O dear bud, look you here what I have got, see.

Pinch. (*Aside, rubbing his forehead.*) And what I have got here too, which you can't see.

Mrs. Pinch. The fine gentleman has given me better things yet.

Pinch. Has he so? (*Aside.*) Out of breath and coloured! I must hold yet.

Horn. I have only given your little brother an orange, sir.

Pinch. (*To* Horner.) Thank you, sir. (*Aside.*) You have only squeezed my orange, I suppose, and given it me again. Yet I must have a city-patience. (*To his wife.*) Come, come away.   462

Mrs. Pinch. Stay, till I have put up my fine things, bud.

Enter Sir Jasper Fidget.

Sir Jas. O master Horner, come, come, the ladies stay for you; your mistress, my wife, wonders you make not more haste to her.

Horn. I have stayed this half hour for you here, and 'tis your fault I am not with your wife.

Sir Jas. But pray, don't let her know so much. The truth on't is, I was advancing a certain project to his majesty about—I'll tell you.

Horn. No, let's go, and hear it at your house.—Good night, sweet little gentleman. One kiss more; you'll remember me now, I hope.   [*Kisses her.*

Dor. What, sir Jasper, will you separate friends? He promised to sup with us, and if you take him to your house, you'll be in danger of our company too.

Sir Jas. Alas, gentlemen, my house is not fit for you; there are none but civil women there, which are not for your turn. He, you know, can bear with the society of civil women now, ha, ha, ha! Besides, he's one of my family ... he's ... he, he, he!   477

Dor. What is he?

Sir Jas. Faith, my eunuch, since you'll have it, he, he, he!

                                        [*Exit* Sir Jasper Fidget *and* Horner.

Dor. I rather wish thou wert his, or my cuckold. Harcourt, what a good cuckold is lost there for want of a man to make him one! Thee and I cannot have Horner's privilege, who can make use of it.

Harc. Ay, to poor Horner 'tis like coming to an estate at threescore, when a man can't be the better for't.

Pinch. Come.

Mrs. Pinch. Presently, bud.

Dor. Come, let us go too. (*To* Alithea.) Madam, your servant. (*To* Lucy.) Good night, strapper.

Harc. Madam, though you will not let me have a good day or night, I wish you one; but dare not name the other half of my wish.   490

Alith. Good night, sir, for ever.

Mrs. Pinch. I don't know where to put this here, dear bud. You shall eat it. Nay, you shall have part of the fine gentleman's good things, or treat as you call it, when we come home.

Pinch. Indeed, I deserve it, since I furnished the best part of it.

                                        [*Strikes away the orange.*

    The gallant treats, presents, and gives the ball;
    But 'tis the absent cuckold, pays for all.

ACT IV   SCENE I

In Pinchwife's *house in the morning.*

Lucy, Alithea *dressed in new clothes.*

Lucy. Well, madam, now have I dressed you, and set you out with so many ornaments, and spent upon you ounces of essence and pulvilio; and all this for no other purpose but as people adorn and perfume a corpse for a stinking secondhand grave—such or as bad I think Master Sparkish's bed.

488 strapper] lusty girl   2 pulvilio] scented powder

Alith. Hold your peace.

Lucy. Nay, madam, I will ask you the reason why you would banish poor Master Harcourt for ever from your sight? How could you be so hard-hearted?

Alith. 'Twas because I was not hard-hearted.

Lucy. No, no; 'twas stark love and kindness, I warrant!   10

Alith. It was so. I would see him no more because I love him.

Lucy. Hey-day, a very pretty reason!

Alith. You do not understand me.

Lucy. I wish you may yourself.

Alith. I was engaged to marry, you see, another man, whom my justice will not suffer me to deceive or injure.

Lucy. Can there be a greater cheat or wrong done to a man than to give him your person without your heart? I should make a conscience of it.

Alith. I'll retrieve it for him after I am married a while.

Lucy. The woman that marries to love better will be as much mistaken as the wencher that marries to live better. No, madam, marrying to increase love is like gaming to become rich—alas, you only lose what little stock you had before.   23

Alith. I find by your rhetoric you have been bribed to betray me.

Lucy. Only by his merit, that has bribed your heart, you see, against your word and rigid honour. But what a devil is this honour? 'Tis sure a disease in the head, like the megrim, or falling sickness, that always hurries people away to do themselves mischief. Men lose their lives by it: women what's dearer to 'em, their love, the life of life.

Alith. Come, pray talk you no more of honour, nor Master Harcourt. I wish the other would come to secure my fidelity to him and his right in me.

Lucy. You will marry him then?   32

Alith. Certainly. I have given him already my word, and will my hand too, to make it good when he comes.

Lucy. Well, I wish I may never stick pin more if he be not an errant natural to t'other fine gentleman.

Alith. I own he wants the wit of Harcourt, which I will dispense withal for another want he has, which is want of jealousy which men of wit seldom want.

Lucy. Lord, madam, what should you do with a fool to your husband? You intend to be honest, don't you? Then that husbandly virtue, credulity, is thrown away upon you.   42

Alith. He only that could suspect my virtue should have cause to do it. 'Tis Sparkish's confidence in my truth that obliges me to be so faithful to him.

27 megrim] migraine   35 natural] simpleton

Lucy. You are not sure his opinion may last.

Alith. I am satisfied 'tis impossible for him to be jealous after the proofs I have had of him. Jealousy in a husband—heaven defend me from it! It begets a thousand plagues to a poor woman, the loss of her honour, her quiet, and her. . . .   50

Lucy. And her pleasure!

Alith. What d'ye mean, impertinent?

Lucy. Liberty is a great pleasure, madam.

Alith. I say, loss of her honour, her quiet, nay, her life sometimes; and what's as bad almost, the loss of this town, that is, she is sent into the country, which is the last ill usage of a husband to a wife, I think.

Lucy. (*Aside.*) Oh, does the wind lie there?—Then of necessity, madam, you think a man must carry his wife into the country, if he be wise. The country is as terrible, I find, to our young English ladies as a monastery to those abroad. And on my virginity, I think they would rather marry a London jailer than a high sheriff of a county, since neither can stir from his employment. Formerly women of wit married fools for a great estate, a fine seat, or the like; but now 'tis for a pretty seat only in Lincoln's Inn Fields, St. James's Fields, or the Pall Mall.   64

Enter to them Sparkish, *and* Harcourt *dressed like a parson.*

Spark. Madam, your humble servant, a happy day to you, and to us all.

Harc. Amen.

Alith. Who have we here?

Spark. My chaplain, faith. O madam, poor Harcourt remembers his humble service to you, and in obedience to your last commands, refrains coming into your sight.   70

Alith. Is not that he?

Spark. No, fie, no; but to show that he ne'er intended to hinder our match, has sent his brother here to join our hands. When I get me a wife, I must get her a chaplain, according to the custom. This is his brother, and my chaplain.

Alith. His brother?

Lucy. (*Aside.*) And your chaplain, to preach in your pulpit then!

Alith. His brother!

Spark. Nay, I knew you would not believe it.—I told you, sir, she would take you for your brother Frank.

Alith. Believe it!   80

Lucy. (*Aside.*) His brother! ha, ha, he! He has a trick left still, it seems.

Spark. Come, my dearest, pray let us go to church before the canonical hour is past.

Alith. For shame, you are abused still.

82-3 canonical hour] period permitted for marriage ceremonies (8 a.m. to noon)

Spark. By the world, 'tis strange now you are so incredulous.

Alith. 'Tis strange you are so credulous.

Spark. Dearest of my life, hear me. I tell you this is Ned Harcourt of Cambridge, by the world—you see he has a sneaking college look. 'Tis true he's something like his brother Frank, and they differ from each other no more than in their age, for they were twins.   90

Lucy. Ha, ha, he!

Alith. Your servant, sir; I cannot be so deceived, though you are. But come, let's hear, how do you know what you affirm so confidently?

Spark. Why, I'll tell you all. Frank Harcourt, coming to me this morning to wish me joy and present his service to you, I asked him if he could help me to a parson. Whereupon he told me he had a brother in town who was in orders, and he went straight away and sent him, you see there, to me.

Alith. Yes, Frank goes and puts on a black coat—then tells you he is Ned. That's all you have for't!

Spark. Pshaw, pshaw! I tell you by the same token, the midwife put her garter about Frank's neck to know 'em asunder, they were so like.   101

Alith. Frank tells you this too?

Spark. Ay, and Ned there too. Nay, they are both in a story.

Alith. So, so; very foolish!

Spark. Lord, if you won't believe one, you had best try him by your chambermaid there; for chambermaids must needs know chaplains from other men, they are so used to 'em.

Lucy. Let's see; nay, I'll be sworn he has the canonical smirk, and the filthy, clammy palm of a chaplain.

Alith. Well, most reverend doctor, pray let us make an end of this fooling.

Harc. With all my soul, divine, heavenly creature, when you please.

Alith. He speaks like a chaplain indeed.   112

Spark. Why, was there not 'soul', 'divine', 'heavenly', in what he said.

Alith. Once more, most impertinent black coat, cease your persecution, and let us have a conclusion of this ridiculous love.

Harc. (*Aside.*) I had forgot—I must suit my style to my coat, or I wear it in vain.

Alith. I have no more patience left. Let us make once an end of this troublesome love, I say.

Harc. So be it, seraphic lady, when your honour shall think it meet and convenient so to do.   121

Spark. Gad, I'm sure none but a chaplain could speak so, I think.

Alith. Let me tell you, sir, this dull trick will not serve your turn. Though you delay our marriage, you shall not hinder it.

Harc. Far be it from me, munificent patroness, to delay your marriage. I desire nothing more than to marry you presently, which I might do, if you yourself would; for my noble, good-natured and thrice generous patron here would not hinder it.

Spark. No, poor man, not I, faith.

Harc. And now, madam, let me tell you plainly, nobody else shall marry you. By heavens, I'll die first, for I'm sure I should die after it.   131

Lucy. (*Aside.*) How his love has made him forget his function, as I have seen it in real parsons!

Alith. That was spoken like a chaplain too! Now you understand him, I hope.

Spark. Poor man, he takes it heinously to be refused. I can't blame him, 'tis putting an indignity upon him not to be suffered. But you'll pardon me, madam, it shan't be, he shall marry us. Come away, pray, madam.

Lucy. Ha, ha, he! More ado! 'Tis late.

Alith. Invincible stupidity! I tell you he would marry me as your rival, not as your chaplain.   141

Spark. (*Pulling her away.*) Come, come, madam.

Lucy. I pray, madam, do not refuse this reverend divine the honour and satisfaction of marrying you—for I dare say he has set his heart upon't, good doctor.

Alith. What can you hope or design by this?

Harc. (*Aside.*) I could answer her—a reprieve, for a day only, often revokes a hasty doom. At worst, if she will not take mercy on me and let me marry her, I have at least the lover's second pleasure, hindering my rival's enjoyment, though but for a time.

Spark. Come, madam, 'tis e'en twelve o'clock, and my mother charged me never to be married out of the canonical hours. Come, come! Lord, here's such a deal of modesty, I warrant, the first day.

Lucy. Yes, an't please your worship, married women show all their modesty the first day, because married men show all their love the first day.

[*Exeunt* Sparkish, Alithea, Harcourt *and* Lucy.

[SCENE II]

The scene changes to a bedchamber, where appear Pinchwife, Mrs. Pinchwife.

Pinch. Come, tell me, I say.

Mrs. Pinch. Lord! han't I told it an hundred times over?

Pinch. (*Aside.*) I would try if, in the repetition of the ungrateful tale, I could find her altering it in the least circumstance; for if her story be false, she is so too.—Come, how was't, baggage?

Mrs. Pinch. Lord, what pleasure you take to hear it, sure!

Pinch. No, you take more in telling it, I find. But speak—how was't?

Mrs. Pinch. He carried me up into the house next to the Exchange.

Pinch. So, and you two were only in the room?

Mrs. Pinch. Yes, for he sent away a youth, that was there, for some dried fruit and China oranges.   11

Pinch. Did he so? Damn him for it . . . and for. . . .

Mrs. Pinch. But presently came up the gentlewoman of the house.

Pinch. Oh, 'twas well she did! But what did he do whilst the fruit came?

Mrs. Pinch. He kissed me an hundred times, and told me he fancied he kissed my fine sister, meaning me you know, whom he said he loved with all his soul, and bid me be sure to tell her so, and to desire her to be at her window by eleven of the clock this morning, and he would walk under it at that time.

Pinch. (*Aside.*) And he was as good as his word, very punctual, a pox reward him for't.   21

Mrs. Pinch. Well, and he said if you were not within, he would come up to her, meaning me, you know, bud, still.

Pinch. (*Aside.*) So—he knew her certainly. But for this confession I am obliged to her simplicity.—But what, you stood very still when he kissed you?

Mrs. Pinch. Yes, I warrant you; would you have had me discovered myself?

Pinch. But you told me he did some beastliness to you—as you called it. What was't?

Mrs. Pinch. Why, he put. . . .

Pinch. What?   30

Mrs. Pinch. Why, he put the tip of his tongue between my lips, and so mousled me . . . and I said, I'd bite it.

Pinch. An eternal canker seize it, for a dog!

Mrs. Pinch. Nay, you need not be so angry with him neither, for to say truth, he has the sweetest breath I ever knew.

Pinch. The devil!—You were satisfied with it then, and would do it again?

Mrs. Pinch. Not unless he should force me.

Pinch. Force you, changeling! I tell you no woman can be forced.

Mrs. Pinch. Yes, but she may be sure by such one as he, for he's a proper, goodly strong man—'tis hard, let me tell you, to resist him.   40

Pinch. (*Aside.*) So, 'tis plain she loves him, yet she has not love enough to make her conceal it from me. But the sight of him will increase her aversion for me, and love for him, and that love instruct her how to deceive me and satisfy him, all idiot as she is. Love! 'Twas he gave women first their craft, their art of deluding. Out of nature's hands they came plain, open, silly, and fit for slaves, as she and heaven intended 'em, but damned love . . . well . . . I

32 mousled] rumpled

must strangle that little monster whilst I can deal with him.—Go, fetch pen, ink, and paper out of the next room.

Mrs. Pinch. Yes, bud.

[*Exit* Mrs. Pinchwife.

Pinch. (*Aside.*) Why should women have more invention in love than men? It can only be because they have more desires, more soliciting passions, more lust, and more of the devil. 52

Mrs. Pinchwife *returns.*

Come, minx, sit down and write.

Mrs. Pinch. Ay, dear bud, but I can't do't very well.

Pinch. I wish you could not at all.

Mrs. Pinch. But what should I write for?

Pinch. I'll have you write a letter to your lover.

Mrs. Pinch. O lord, to the fine gentleman a letter!

Pinch. Yes, to the fine gentleman.

Mrs. Pinch. Lord, you do but jeer; sure you jest? 60

Pinch. I am not so merry, come, write as I bid you.

Mrs. Pinch. What, do you think I am a fool?

Pinch. (*Aside.*) She's afraid I would not dictate any love to him, therefore she's unwilling.—But you had best begin.

Mrs. Pinch. Indeed, and indeed, but I won't, so I won't!

Pinch. Why?

Mrs. Pinch. Because he's in town. You may send for him if you will.

Pinch. Very well, you would have him brought to you—is it come to this? I say, take the pen and write, or you'll provoke me.

Mrs. Pinch. Lord, what d'ye make a fool of me for? Don't I know that letters are never writ but from the country to London, and from London into the country? Now, he's in town, and I am in town too; therefore I can't write to him, you know. 73

Pinch. (*Aside.*) So, I am glad it is no worse; she is innocent enough yet.— Yes, you may, when your husband bids you, write letters to people that are in town.

Mrs. Pinch. Oh, may I so? Then I'm satisfied.

Pinch. Come, begin. (*Dictates.*) 'Sir. . . .'

Mrs. Pinch. Shan't I say, 'Dear Sir'? You know one says always something more than bare 'Sir'.

Pinch. Write as I bid you, or I will write 'whore' with this penknife in your face. 82

Mrs. Pinch. Nay, good bud. (*She writes.*) 'Sir'.

Pinch. 'Though I suffered last night your nauseous, loathed kisses and embraces. . . .'—Write!

Mrs. Pinch. Nay, why should I say so? You know I told you he had a sweet breath.

Pinch. Write!

Mrs. Pinch. Let me but put out 'loathed'.

Pinch. Write, I say!   90

Mrs. Pinch. Well then. (*Writes.*)

Pinch. Let's see what have you writ. (*Takes the paper and reads.*) 'Though I suffered last night your kisses and embraces'—Thou impudent creature! Where is 'nauseous' and 'loathed'?

Mrs. Pinch. I can't abide to write such filthy words.

Pinch. Once more write as I'd have you, and question it not, or I will spoil thy writing with this. (*Holds up the penknife.*) I will stab out those eyes that cause my mischief.

Mrs. Pinch. O lord, I will!

Pinch. So . . . so. . . . Let's see now! (*Reads.*) 'Though I suffered last night your nauseous, loathed kisses, and embraces'—go on—'Yet I would not have you presume that you shall ever repeat them.'—So. . . .   102

Mrs. Pinch. (*She writes.*) I have writ it.

Pinch. On then.—'I then concealed myself from your knowledge, to avoid your insolencies. . . .'

Mrs. Pinch. (*She writes.*) So.

Pinch. 'The same reason, now I am out of your hands. . . .'

Mrs. Pinch. (*She writes.*) So.

Pinch. 'Makes me own to you my unfortunate, though innocent frolic, of being in man's clothes. . . .'   110

Mrs. Pinch. (*She writes.*) So.

Pinch. 'That you may forevermore cease to pursue her, who hates and detests you. . . .'   [*She writes on.*

Mrs. Pinch. (*Sighs.*) So -h. . . .

Pinch. What, do you sigh?—'detests you . . . as much as she loves her husband and her honour'.

Mrs. Pinch. I vow, husband, he'll ne'er believe I should write such a letter.

Pinch. What, he'd expect a kinder from you? Come now, your name only.

Mrs. Pinch. What, shan't I say, 'Your most faithful, humble servant till death'?   121

Pinch. No, tormenting fiend! (*Aside.*) Her style, I find, would be very soft. —Come, wrap it up now, whilst I go fetch wax and a candle, and write on the back side, 'For Mr. Horner'.

[*Exit* Pinchwife.

Mrs. Pinch. 'For Mr. Horner'.—So, I am glad he has told me his name. Dear Mr. Horner! But why should I send thee such a letter that will vex

thee and make thee angry with me? . . . Well I will not send it. . . . Ay, but
then my husband will kill me . . . for I see plainly, he won't let me love Mr.
Horner . . . but what care I for my husband? . . . I won't so, I won't send
poor Mr. Horner such a letter . . . but then my husband. . . . But oh, what if I
writ at bottom, my husband made me write it? . . . Ay, but then my husband
would see't. . . . Can one have no shift? Ah, a London woman would have
had a hundred presently. Stay . . . what if I should write a letter, and wrap it
up like this, and write upon't too? Ay, but then my husband would see't. . . .
I don't know what to do. . . . But yet y'vads I'll try, so I will . . . for I will
not send this letter to poor Mr. Horner, come what will on't.   136

> [*She writes, and repeats what she hath writ.*

'Dear, sweet Mr. Horner'. . . . So. . . . 'My husband would have me send you
a base, rude, unmannerly letter . . . but I won't' . . . so . . . 'and would have
me forbid you loving me . . . but I won't' . . . so . . . 'and would have me say
to you, I hate you poor Mr. Horner . . . but I won't tell a lie for him' . . .
there . . . 'for I'm sure if you and I were in the country at cards together' . . .
so . . . 'I could not help treading on your toe under the table' . . . so . . . 'or
rubbing knees with you, and staring in your face 'till you saw me' . . . very
well . . . 'and then looking down, and blushing for an hour together' . . . so
. . . 'but I must make haste before my husband come; and now he has taught
me to write letters you shall have longer ones from me, who am, dear, dear,
poor dear Mr. Horner, your most humble friend, and servant to command
'till death, Margery Pinchwife.'—Stay, I must give him a hint at bottom . . .
so . . . now wrap it up just like t'other . . . so . . . now write 'For Mr. Horner'.
. . But, oh now, what shall I do with it? For here comes my husband.

Enter Pinchwife.

Pinch. (*Aside.*) I have been detained by a sparkish coxcomb, who pretended
a visit to me; but I fear 'twas to my wife.—What, have you done?   152
Mrs. Pinch. Ay, ay, bud, just now.
Pinch. Let's see't. What d'ye tremble for? What, you would not have it go?
Mrs. Pinch. Here. (*Aside.*) No, I must not give him that, so I had been
served if I had given him this.
Pinch. (*He opens and reads the first letter.*) Come, where's the wax and seal?
Mrs. Pinch. (*Aside.*) Lord, what shall I do now? Nay, then, I have it.—
Pray, let me see 't. Lord, you think me so arrant a fool, I cannot seal a letter?
I will do 't, so I will.

> [*Snatches the letter from him, changes it for the other,*
> *seals it, and delivers it to him.*

Pinch. Nay, I believe you will learn that, and other things too, which I
would not have you.

135 y'vads] in faith

Mrs. Pinch. So. Han't I done it curiously? (*Aside.*) I think I have; there's my letter going to Mr. Horner, since he'll needs have me send letters to folks.

Pinch. 'Tis very well; but I warrant, you would not have it go now?

Mrs. Pinch. Yes, indeed, but I would, bud, now.

Pinch. Well you are a good girl then. Come, let me lock you up in your chamber 'till I come back. And be sure you come not within three strides of the window when I am gone, for I have a spy in the street.   170

[*Exit* Mrs. Pinchwife.

[Pinchwife *locks the door.*

At least, 'tis fit she thinks so. If we do not cheat women, they'll cheat us; and fraud may be justly used with secret enemies, of which a wife is the most dangerous. And he that has a handsome one to keep, and a frontier town, must provide against treachery rather than open force. Now I have secured all within, I'll deal with the foe without with false intelligence. (*Holds up the letter.*)   [*Exit* Pinchwife.

[SCENE III]

The scene changes to Horner's *lodging.*

Quack *and* Horner.

Quack. Well, sir, how fadges the new design? Have you not the luck of all your brother projectors, to deceive only yourself at last?

Horn. No, good Domine doctor, I deceive you, it seems, and others too, for the grave matrons and old rigid husbands think me as unfit for love as they are. But their wives, sisters and daughters know some of 'em better things already!

Quack. Already!

Horn. Already, I say. Last night I was drunk with half a dozen of your civil persons, as you call 'em, and people of honour, and so was made free of their society and dressing rooms for ever hereafter; and am already come to the privileges of sleeping upon their pallats, warming smocks, tying shoes and garters, and the like, doctor, already, already, doctor.   12

Quack. You have made use of your time, sir.

Horn. I tell thee, I am now no more interruption to 'em when they sing or talk bawdy than a little squab French page who speaks no English.

Quack. But do civil persons and women of honour drink and sing bawdy songs?

163 curiously] carefully   1 fadges] succeeds   2 projectors] schemers   3 Domine] sir
11 pallats] mattresses   15 squab] chubby

Horn. Oh, amongst friends, amongst friends. For your bigots in honour are just like those in religion. They fear the eye of the world more than the eye of heaven, and think there is no virtue but railing at vice, and no sin but giving scandal. They rail at a poor, little, kept player, and keep themselves some young, modest pulpit comedian to be privy to their sins in their closets, not to tell 'em of them in their chapels.   22

Quack. Nay, the truth on't is, priests amongst the women now have quite got the better of us lay confessors, physicians.

Horn. And they are rather their patients, but . . .

Enter my Lady Fidget, *looking about her.*

Now we talk of women of honour, here comes one. Step behind the screen there, and but observe if I have not particular privileges with the women of reputation already, doctor, already.

Quack *steps behind screen.*

Lady Fidg. Well, Horner, am not I a woman of honour? You see, I'm as good as my word.   30

Horn. And you shall see, madam, I'll not be behindhand with you in honour. And I'll be as good as my word too, if you please but to withdraw into the next room.

Lady Fidg. But first, my dear sir, you must promise to have a care of my dear honour.

Horn. If you talk a word more of your honour, you'll make me incapable to wrong it. To talk of honour in the mysteries of love is like talking of heaven or the deity in an operation of witchcraft, just when you are employing the devil; it makes the charm impotent.

Lady Fidg. Nay, fie, let us not be smutty. But you talk of mysteries, and bewitching to me—I don't understand you.   41

Horn. I tell you, madam, the word 'money' in a mistress's mouth, at such a nick of time, is not a more disheartening sound to a younger brother than that of honour to an eager lover like myself.

Lady Fidg. But you can't blame a lady of my reputation to be chary.

Horn. Chary! I have been chary of it already, by the report I have caused of myself.

Lady Fidg. Ay, but if you should ever let other women know that dear secret, it would come out. Nay, you must have a great care of your conduct, for my acquaintance are so censorious,—oh 'tis a wicked censorious world, Mr. Horner!—I say, are so censorious and detracting that perhaps they'll talk to the prejudice of my honour, though you should not let them know the dear secret.   53

21 pulpit comedian] priest

Horn. Nay, madam, rather than they shall prejudice your honour, I'll prejudice theirs; and to serve you, I'll lie with 'em all, make the secret their own, and then they'll keep it! I am a Machiavel in love, madam.

Lady Fidg. Oh no, sir, not that way.

Horn. Nay, the devil take me, if censorious women are to be silenced any other way!

Lady Fidg. A secret is better kept, I hope, by a single person than a multitude. Therefore pray do not trust anybody else with it, dear, dear Mr. Horner.   [*Embracing him.*

Enter Sir Jasper Fidget.

Sir Jas. How now!   63

Lady Fidg. (*Aside.*) O my husband! . . . prevented! . . . and what's almost as bad, found with my arms about another man . . . that will appear too much . . . what shall I say?—Sir Jasper, come hither. I am trying if Mr. Horner were ticklish, and he's as ticklish as can be. I love to torment the confounded toad. Let you and I tickle him.

Sir Jas. No, your ladyship will tickle him better without me, I suppose. But is this your buying china? I thought you had been at the china house?

Horn. (*Aside.*) China house! That's my cue, I must take it.—A pox! Can't you keep your impertinent wives at home? Some men are troubled with the husbands, but I with the wives. But I'd have you to know, since I cannot be your journeyman by night, I will not be your drudge by day, to squire your wife about and be your man of straw, or scarecrow, only to pies and jays that would be nibbling at your forbidden fruit. I shall be shortly the hackney gentleman-usher of the town.

Sir Jas. (*Aside.*) He, he, he! Poor fellow, he's in the right on't, faith! To squire women about for other folks is as ungrateful an employment as to tell money for other folks. He, he, he!—Ben't angry, Horner.   80

Lady Fidg. No, 'tis I have more reason to be angry, who am left by you to go abroad indecently alone; or, what is more indecent, to pin myself upon such ill-bred people of your acquaintance as this is.

Sir Jas. Nay, prithee, what has he done?

Lady Fidg. Nay, he has done nothing.

Sir Jas. But what d'ye take ill, if he has done nothing?

Lady Fidg. Ha, ha, ha! Faith, I can't but laugh, however. Why, d'ye think the unmannerly toad would not come down to me to the coach? I was fain to come up to fetch him, or go without him, which I was resolved not to do; for he knows china very well, and has himself very good, but will not let me

---

75 pies and jays] fops   76-7 hackney gentleman-usher] hired escort   79 ungrateful] thankless

see it lest I should beg some. But I will find it out, and have what I came for
yet.   92
    [*Exit* Lady Fidget, *and locks the door, followed by* Horner *to the door.*
    Horn. (*Apart to* Lady Fidget.) Lock the door, madam.—So, she has got
into my chamber, and locked me out. Oh, the impertinency of womankind!
Well, Sir Jasper, plain dealing is a jewel. If ever you suffer your wife to
trouble me again here, she shall carry you home a pair of horns, by my Lord
Mayor she shall! Though I cannot furnish you myself, you are sure, yet I'll
find a way.
    Sir Jas. (*Aside.*) Ha, ha, he! At my first coming in and finding her arms
about him, tickling him it seems, I was half jealous, but now I see my folly.—
He, he, he! Poor Horner.   101
    Horn. Nay, though you laugh now, 'twill be my turn ere long. Oh, women,
more impertinent, more cunning, and more mischievous than their monkeys,
and to me almost as ugly! ... Now is she throwing my things about, and
rifling all I have ... but I'll get into her the back way, and so rifle her for it.
    Sir Jas. Ha, ha, ha! Poor angry Horner.
    Horn. Stay here a little, I'll ferret her out to you presently, I warrant.
                        [*Exit* Horner *at t'other door.*
    Sir Jas. Wife! My lady Fidget! Wife! He is coming into you the back way!
    [Sir Jasper *calls through the door to his wife; she answers from within.*
    Lady Fidg. Let him come, and welcome, which way he will.   110
    Sir Jas. He'll catch you, and use you roughly, and be too strong for you.
    Lady Fidg. Don't you trouble yourself, let him if he can.
    Quack. (*Behind.*) This indeed I could not have believed from him, nor
any but my own eyes.

Enter Mistress Squeamish.

    Squeam. Where's this woman-hater, this toad, this ugly, greasy, dirty
sloven?
    Sir Jas. (*Aside.*) So the women all will have him ugly. Methinks he is a
comely person, but his wants make his form contemptible to 'em; and 'tis e'en
as my wife said yesterday, talking of him, that a proper handsome eunuch
was as ridiculous a thing as a gigantic coward.   120
    Squeam. Sir Jasper, your servant. Where is the odious beast?
    Sir Jas. He's within in his chamber, with my wife; she's playing the wag
with him.
    Squeam. Is she so? And he's a clownish beast, he'll give her no quarter,
he'll play the wag with her again, let me tell you. Come, let's go help her ...
What, the door's locked?
    Sir Jas. Ay, my wife locked it.
    Squeam. Did she so? Let us break it open then.

Sir Jas. No, no, he'll do her no hurt.

Squeam. No. (*Aside.*) But is there no other way to get into 'em? Whither goes this? I will disturb 'em.   131

[*Exit* Squeamish *at another door.*

Enter Old Lady Squeamish.

Old L. Squeam. Where is this harlotry, this impudent baggage, this rambling tomrig? O sir Jasper, I'm glad to see you here. Did you not see my viled grandchild come in hither just now?

Sir Jas. Yes.

Old L. Squeam. Ay, but where is she then? where is she? Lord, sir Jasper, I have e'en rattled myself to pieces in pursuit of her. But can you tell what she makes here? They say below, no woman lodges here.

Sir Jas. No.

Old L. Squeam. No! What does she here then? Say, if it be not a woman's lodging, what makes she here? But are you sure no woman lodges here?

Sir Jas. No, nor no man neither—this is Mr. Horner's lodging.   142

Old L. Squeam. Is it so, are you sure?

Sir Jas. Yes, yes.

Old L. Squeam. So—then there's no hurt in't, I hope. But where is he?

Sir Jas. He's in the next room with my wife.

Old L. Squeam. Nay, if you trust him with your wife, I may with my biddy. They say he's a merry, harmless man now, e'en as harmless a man as ever came out of Italy with a good voice, and as pretty harmless company for a lady as a snake without his teeth.   150

Sir Jas. Ay, ay, poor man.

Enter Mrs. Squeamish.

Squeam. I can't find 'em.—Oh, are you here, grandmother? I followed, you must know, my lady Fidget hither. 'Tis the prettiest lodging, and I have been staring on the prettiest pictures.

Enter Lady Fidget *with a piece of china in her hand, and* Horner *following.*

Lady Fidg. And I have been toiling and moiling for the prettiest piece of china, my dear.

Horn. Nay, she has been too hard for me, do what I could.

Squeam. Oh lord, I'll have some china too. Good Mr. Horner, don't you think to give other people china, and me none. Come in with me too.

Horn. Upon my honour, I have none left now.   160

Squeam. Nay, nay, I have known you deny your china before now, but you shan't put me off so. Come.

Horn. This lady had the last there.

133 tomrig] hoyden   133 viled] vile   149 voice] i.e. castrato of Italian opera

Lady Fidg. Yes indeed, madam, to my certain knowledge he has no more left.

Squeam. Oh, but it may be he may have some you could not find.

Lady Fidg. What, d'y think if he had had any left, I would not have had it too? For we women of quality never think we have china enough.

Horn. Do not take it ill, I cannot make china for you all, but I will have a roll-wagon for you too, another time.   170

Squeam. Thank you, dear toad.

Lady Fidg. (*Apart to* Horner.) What do you mean by that promise?

Horn. (*Aside to* Lady Fidget.) Alas, she has an innocent, literal understanding.

Old L. Squeam. Poor Mr. Horner, he has enough to do to please you all, I see.

Horn. Ay, madam, you see how they use me.

Old L. Squeam. Poor gentleman, I pity you.

Horn. I thank you, madam. I could never find pity but from such reverend ladies as you are. The young ones will never spare a man.

Squeam. Come, come, beast, and go dine with us, for we shall want a man at ombre after dinner.   181

Horn. That's all their use of me, madam, you see.

Squeam. Come, sloven, I'll lead you, to be sure of you.
                                    [*Pulls him by the cravat.*

Old L. Squeam. Alas, poor man, how she tugs him! Kiss, kiss her! That's the way to make such nice women quiet.

Horn. No, madam, that remedy is worse than the torment. They know I dare suffer anything rather than do it.

Old L. Squeam. Prithee kiss her, and I'll give you her picture in little, that you admired so last night. Prithee, do!

Horn. Well, nothing but that could bribe me. I love a woman only in effigy, and good painting, as much as I hate them. I'll do't, for I could adore the devil well painted.   [*Kisses* Mrs. Squeamish.

Squeam. Foh, you filthy toad! Nay, now I've done jesting.   174   193

Old L. Squeam. Ha, ha, ha! I told you so.

Squeam. Foh! a kiss of his. . . .

Sir Jas. Has no more hurt in't than one of my spaniel's.

Squeam. Nor no more good neither.

Quack. (*Behind.*) I will now believe anything he tells me.

Enter Mr. Pinchwife.

Lady Fidg. O lord, here's a man! Sir Jasper, my mask, my mask! I would not be seen here for the world.

Sir Jas. What, not when I am with you?

170 roll-wagon] trolley   188 picture in little] miniature

Lady Fidg. No, no, my honour . . . let's be gone.   202

Squeam. Oh, grandmother, let us be gone. Make haste, make haste, I know not how he may censure us.

Lady Fidg. Be found in the lodging of anything like a man! Away!

[*Exeunt* Sir Jasper, Lady Fidget, Old Lady Squeamish, Mrs. Squeamish.

Quack. (*Behind.*) What's here, another cuckold? He looks like one, and none else sure have any business with him.

Horn. Well, what brings my dear friend hither?

Pinch. Your impertinency.   210

Horn. My impertinency! Why, you gentlemen that have got handsome wives think you have a privilege of saying anything to your friends, and are as brutish as if you were our creditors.

Pinch. No, sir, I'll ne'er trust you any way.

Horn. But why not, dear Jack? Why diffide in me thou knowst so well?

Pinch. Because I do know you so well.

Horn. Han't I been always thy friend, honest Jack, always ready to serve thee, in love or battle, before thou wert married, and am so still?

Pinch. I believe so. You would be my second now indeed.

Horn. Well, then, dear Jack, why so unkind, so grum, so strange to me? Come, prithee kiss me, dear rogue. Gad, I was always, I say, and am still as much thy servant as. . . .   222

Pinch. As I am yours, sir. What, you would send a kiss to my wife, is that it?

Horn. So, there 'tis! A man can't show his friendship to a married man, but presently he talks of his wife to you. Prithee, let thy wife alone, and let thee and I be all one, as we were wont. What, thou art as shy of my kindness as a Lombard Street alderman of a courtier's civility at Locket's.

Pinch. But you are overkind to me—as kind as if I were your cuckold already. Yet I must confess you ought to be kind and civil to me, since I am so kind, so civil to you, as to bring you this. Look you there, sir.

[*Delivers him a letter.*

Horn. What is't?   232

Pinch. Only a love letter, sir.

Horn. From whom? . . . How! this is from your wife! (*Reads.*) Hum . . . and hum. . . .

Pinch. Even from my wife, sir. Am I not wondrous kind and civil to you now too?—(*Aside.*) But you'll not think her so!

Horn. (*Aside.*) Ha! Is this a trick of his or hers?

Pinch. The gentleman's surprised, I find. What, you expected a kinder letter?

---

215 diffide in] distrust   228 Lombard Street] noted for rich goldsmiths   228 Locket's] fashionable eating-house

Horn. No, faith, not I, how could I? 241

Pinch. Yes, yes, I'm sure you did. A man so well made as you are, must needs be disappointed if the women declare not their passion at first sight or opportunity.

Horn. (*Aside.*) But what should this mean? Stay, the postscript. (*Reads aside.*) 'Be sure you love me whatsoever my husband says to the contrary, and let him not see this lest he should come home and pinch me, or kill my squirrel.'—(*Aside.*) It seems he knows not what the letter contains.

Pinch. Come, ne'er wonder at it so much.

Horn. Faith, I can't help it. 250

Pinch. Now, I think I have deserved your infinite friendship and kindness, and have showed myself sufficiently an obliging kind friend and husband! Am I not so, to bring a letter from my wife to her gallant?

Horn. Ay, the devil take me, art thou the most obliging, kind friend and husband in the world, ha, ha!

Pinch. Well, you may be merry, sir, but in short I must tell you, sir, my honour will suffer no jesting.

Horn. What dost thou mean?

Pinch. Does the letter want a comment? Then know, sir, though I have been so civil a husband as to bring you a letter from my wife, to let you kiss and court her to my face, I will not be a cuckold, sir, I will not. 261

Horn. Thou art mad with jealousy. I never saw thy wife in my life, but at the play yesterday, and I know not if it were she or no. I court her, kiss her!

Pinch. I will not be a cuckold, I say. There will be danger in making me a cuckold.

Horn. Why, wert thou not well cured of thy last clap?

Pinch. I wear a sword.

Horn. It should be taken from thee lest thou should'st do thyself a mischief with it. Thou art mad, man.

Pinch. As mad as I am, and as merry as you are, I must have more reason from you ere we part. I say again, though you kissed and courted last night my wife in man's clothes, as she confesses in her letter. . . . 272

Horn. (*Aside.*) Ha!

Pinch. Both she and I say, you must not design it again, for you have mistaken your woman, as you have done your man.

Horn. (*Aside.*) Oh . . . I understand something now.—Was that thy wife? Why would'st thou not tell me 'twas she? Faith, my freedom with her was your fault, not mine.

Pinch. (*Aside.*) Faith, so 'twas.

Horn. Fie! I'd never do't to a woman before her husband's face, sure.

Pinch. But I had rather you should do't to my wife before my face than behind my back, and that you shall never do. 282

Horn. No—you will hinder me.

Pinch. If I would not hinder you, you see by her letter, she would.

Horn. Well, I must e'en acquiesce then, and be contented with what she writes.

Pinch. I'll assure you 'twas voluntarily writ. I had no hand in't, you may believe me.

Horn. I do believe thee, faith.

Pinch. And believe her too, for she's an innocent creature, has no dissembling in her—and so fare you well, sir.   291

Horn. Pray, however, present my humble service to her, and tell her I will obey her letter to a tittle, and fulfill her desires, be what they will, or with what difficulty soever I do't, and you shall be no more jealous of me, I warrant her and you.

Pinch. Well, then, fare you well, and play with any man's honour but mine, kiss any man's wife but mine, and welcome.   [*Exit* Mr. Pinchwife.

Horn. Ha, ha, ha! Doctor.

Quack. It seems he has not heard the report of you, or does not believe it.

Horn. Ha, ha! Now, doctor, what think you?   300

Quack. Pray let's see the letter ... hum ... (*Reads the letter.*) 'for ... dear ... love you ...'

Horn. I wonder how she could contrive it! What say'st thou to't? 'Tis an original.

Quack. So are your cuckolds, too, originals, for they are like no other common cuckolds, and I will henceforth believe it not impossible for you to cuckold the Grand Signior amidst his guards of eunuchs, that I say!

Horn. And I say for the letter, 'tis the first love letter that ever was without flames, darts, fates, destinies, lying and dissembling in't.

Enter Sparkish *pulling in* Mr. Pinchwife.

Spark. Come back, you are a pretty brother-in-law, neither go to church, nor to dinner with your sister bride!   311

Pinch. My sister denies her marriage, and you see is gone away from you dissatisfied.

Spark. Pshaw! upon a foolish scruple that our parson was not in lawful orders, and did not say all the Common Prayer. But 'tis her modesty only, I believe. But let women be never so modest the first day, they'll be sure to come to themselves by night, and I shall have enough of her then. In the meantime, Harry Horner, you must dine with me. I keep my wedding at my aunt's in the Piazza.

Horn. Thy wedding! What stale maid has lived to despair of a husband, or what young one of a gallant?   321

307 Grand Signior] Turkish sultan   319 Piazza] arcade near Covent Garden

Spark. Oh, your servant, sir . . . this gentleman's sister then . . . no stale maid.

Horn. I'm sorry for't.

Pinch. (*Aside.*) How comes he so concerned for her?

Spark. You sorry for't? Why, do you know any ill by her?

Horn. No, I know none but by thee. 'Tis for her sake, not yours, and another man's sake that might have hoped, I thought.

Spark. Another man! Another man! What is his name?

Horn. Nay, since 'tis past he shall be nameless. (*Aside.*) Poor Harcourt! I am sorry thou hast missed her.   331

Pinch. (*Aside.*) He seems to be much troubled at the match.

Spark. Prithee tell me—nay, you shan't go, brother.

Pinch. I must of necessity, but I'll come to you to dinner.

[*Exit* Mr. Pinchwife.

Spark. But Harry, what, have I a rival in my wife already? But with all my heart, for he may be of use to me hereafter! For though my hunger is now my sauce, and I can fall on heartily without, but the time will come when a rival will be as good sauce for a married man to a wife as an orange to veal.

Horn. O thou damned rogue, thou hast set my teeth on edge with thy orange!   340

Spark. Then let's to dinner—there I was with you again. Come.

Horn. But who dines with thee?

Spark. My friends and relations, my brother Pinchwife, you see, of your acquaintance.

Horn. And his wife?

Spark. No, gad, he'll ne'er let her come amongst us good fellows. Your stingy country coxcomb keeps his wife from his friends, as he does his little firkin of ale for his own drinking, and a gentleman can't get a smack on't. But his servants, when his back is turned, broach it at their pleasures, and dust it away, ha, ha, ha! Gad, I am witty, I think, considering I was married today, by the world. But come. . . .   351

Horn. No, I will not dine with you, unless you can fetch her too.

Spark. Pshaw! what pleasure can'st thou have with women now, Harry?

Horn. My eyes are not gone—I love a good prospect yet, and will not dine with you unless she does too. Go fetch her, therefore, but do not tell her husband 'tis for my sake.

Spark. Well, I'll go try what I can do. In the meantime come away to my aunt's lodging, 'tis in the way to Pinchwife's.

Horn. The poor woman has called for aid, and stretched forth her hand, doctor. I cannot but help her over the pale out of the briars!   360

[*Exeunt* Sparkish, Horner, Quack.

348 firkin] cask   348 smack] taste   350 dust it away] drink it up   360 pale] fence

[SCENE IV]

The Scene changes to Pinchwife's *house.*

Mrs. Pinchwife *alone leaning on her elbow. A table, pen, ink, and paper.*

Mrs. Pinch. Well, 'tis e'en so, I have got the London disease they call love.
I am sick *of* my husband, and *for* my gallant. I have heard this distemper
called a fever, but methinks 'tis liker an ague, for when I think of my husband
I tremble and am in a cold sweat, and have inclinations to vomit, but when I
think of my gallant, dear Mr. Horner, my hot fit comes and I am all in a
fever, indeed, and as in other fevers my own chamber is tedious to me, and I
would fain be removed to his, and then methinks I should be well. Ah, poor
Mr. Horner! Well, I cannot, will not stay here. Therefore I'll make an end of
my letter to him, which shall be a finer letter than my last, because I have
studied it like anything. Oh, sick, sick!   [*Takes the pen and writes.*

Enter Mr. Pinchwife, *who seeing her writing steals softly behind her,
and looking over her shoulder, snatches the paper from her.*

Pinch. What, writing more letters?   11
Mrs. Pinch. O lord, bud, why d'ye fright me so?
                          [*She offers to run out: he stops her, and reads.*
Pinch. How's this! Nay, you shall not stir, madam. 'Dear, dear, dear, Mr.
Horner. . . .' Very well. . . . I have taught you to write letters to good purpose . . . but let's see't.—'First, I am to beg your pardon for my boldness in
writing to you, which I'd have you to know I would not have done had not
you said first you loved me so extremely, which if you do, you will never
suffer me to lie in the arms of another man, whom I loath, nauseate, and
detest.'—Now you can write these filthy words! But what follows?—'Therefore I hope you will speedily find some way to free me from this unfortunate
match, which was never, I assure you, of my choice, but I'm afraid 'tis already too far gone. However, if you love me, as I do you, you will try what
you can do, but you must help me away before tomorrow, or else, alas, I
shall be forever out of your reach, for I can defer no longer our. . . .' (*The
letter concludes.*) 'Our?' What is to follow 'our'? Speak, what? Our journey
into the country, I suppose? Oh, woman, damned woman! And love, damned
love, their old tempter! For this is one of his miracles. In a moment he can
make those blind that could see, and those see that were blind, those dumb
that could speak, and those prattle who were dumb before—nay, what is
more than all, make these dough-baked, senseless, indocile animals, women,
too hard for us, their politic lords and rulers, in a moment.—But make an

end of your letter, and then I'll make an end of you thus, and all my plagues
together.   [*Draws his sword.*

Mrs. Pinch. O lord, o lord you are such a passionate man, bud!   34

Enter Sparkish.

Spark. How now, what's here to do?

Pinch. This fool here now!

Spark. What, drawn upon your wife? You should never do that but at
night in the dark, when you can't hurt her! This is my sister-in-law, is it
not? (*Pulls aside her handkerchief.*) Ay, faith, e'en our country Margery;
one may know her. Come, she and you must go dine with me; dinner's
ready, come. But where's my wife? Is she not come home yet? Where is she?

Pinch. Making you a cuckold—'tis that they all do, as soon as they can.

Spark. What, the wedding day? No, a wife that designs to make a cully of
her husband will be sure to let him win the first stake of love, by the world.
But come, they stay dinner for us. Come, I'll lead down our Margery.

Mrs. Pinch. No! . . . Sir, go, we'll follow you.

Spark. I will not wag without you.

Pinch. (*Aside.*) This coxcomb is a sensible torment to me amidst the
greatest in the world.

Spark. Come, come, madam Margery.   50

Pinch. No, I'll lead her my way. What, would you treat your friends with
mine, for want of your own wife? (*Leads her to t'other door, and locks her in
and returns.*)—(*Aside.*) I am contented my rage should take breath.

Spark. (*Aside.*) I told Horner this.

Pinch. Come now.

Spark. Lord, how shy you are of your wife! But let me tell you, brother,
we men of wit have amongst us a saying that cuckolding, like the smallpox,
comes with a fear, and you may keep your wife as much as you will out of
danger of infection, but if her constitution incline her to't, she'll have it
sooner or later, by the world, say they.   60

Pinch. (*Aside.*) What a thing is a cuckold, that every fool can make him
ridiculous!—Well, sir, . . . but let me advise you, now you are come to be
concerned, because you suspect the danger, not to neglect the means to
prevent it, especially when the greatest share of the malady will light upon
your own head, for . . .

> Hows'e'er the kind wife's belly comes to swell,
> The husband breeds for her, and first is ill.

---

43 cully] fool   47 wag] stir   48 sensible] acute   56 shy] distrustful

ACT V   SCENE I

Mr. Pinchwife's House.

Enter Mr. Pinchwife *and* Mrs. Pinchwife.

A table and candle.

Pinch. Come, take the pen and make an end of the letter, just as you intended. If you are false in a tittle, I shall soon perceive it, and punish you with this as you deserve. (*Lays his hand on his sword.*) Write what was to follow ... let's see.... 'You must make haste and help me away before tomorrow, or else I shall be for ever out of your reach, for I can defer no longer our. ...' What follows 'our'?

Mrs. Pinch. Must all out then, bud?

[Mrs. Pinchwife *takes the pen and writes.* Look you there, then.

Pinch. Let's see ... 'For I can defer no longer our wedding. Your slighted Alithea.'—What's the meaning of this? My sister's name to't? Speak, unriddle!   11

Mrs. Pinch. Yes, indeed, bud.

Pinch. But why her name to't? Speak—speak I say!

Mrs. Pinch. Ay, but you'll tell her then again. If you would not tell her again. ...

Pinch. I will not. ... I am stunned ... my head turns round. Speak!

Mrs. Pinch. Won't you tell her indeed, and indeed?

Pinch. No, speak, I say.

Mrs. Pinch. She'll be angry with me, but I had rather she should be angry with me than you bud. And to tell you the truth, 'twas she made me write the letter, and taught me what I should write.   21

Pinch. (*Aside.*) Ha! I thought the style was somewhat better than her own. —But how could she come to you to teach you, since I had locked you up alone?

Mrs. Pinch. Oh, through the keyhole, bud.

Pinch. But why should she make you write a letter for her to him, since she can write herself?

Mrs. Pinch. Why, she said because—for I was unwilling to do it.

Pinch. Because what—because?

Mrs. Pinch. Because, lest Mr. Horner should be cruel and refuse her, or vain afterwards, and show the letter, she might disown it, the hand not being hers.   32

Pinch. (*Aside.*) How's this? Ha!—then I think I shall come to myself again. This changeling could not invent this lie, but if she could, why should she? She might think I should soon discover it . . . stay . . . now I think on't too, Horner said he was sorry she had married Sparkish, and her disowning her marriage to me makes me think she has evaded it for Horner's sake. Yet why should she take this course? But men in love are fools; women may well be so.—But hark you, madam, your sister went out in the morning and I have not seen her within since.   40

Mrs. Pinch. Alackaday, she has been crying all day above, it seems, in a corner.

Pinch. Where is she? Let me speak with her.

Mrs. Pinch. (*Aside.*) O lord, then he'll discover all!—Pray hold, bud. What, d'y mean to discover me? She'll know I have told you then. Pray, bud, let me talk with her first.

Pinch. I must speak with her to know whether Horner ever made her any promise; and whether she be married to Sparkish or no.

Mrs. Pinch. Pray, dear bud, don't, till I have spoken with her and told her that I have told you all, for she'll kill me else.   50

Pinch. Go then, and bid her come out to me.

Mrs. Pinch. Yes, yes, bud.

Pinch. Let me see. . . .

Mrs. Pinch. (*Aside.*) I'll go, but she is not within to come to him. I have just got time to know of Lucy her maid, who first set me on work, what lie I shall tell next, for I am e'en at my wits end!   [*Exit* Mrs. Pinchwife.

Pinch. Well, I resolve it; Horner shall have her. I'd rather give him my sister than lend him my wife, and such an alliance will prevent his pretensions to my wife, sure. I'll make him of kin to her, and then he won't care for her.   60

Mrs. Pinchwife returns.

Mrs. Pinch. O lord, bud, I told you what anger you would make me with my sister!

Pinch. Won't she come hither?

Mrs. Pinch. No, no, alackaday, she's ashamed to look you in the face, and she says if you go in to her, she'll run away downstairs, and shamefully go herself to Mr. Horner, who has promised her marriage, she says, and she will have no other, so she won't.

Pinch. Did he so—promise her marriage? Then she shall have no other. Go tell her so, and if she will come and discourse with me a little concerning the means, I will about it immediately. Go!   [*Exit* Mrs. Pinchwife.

His estate is equal to Sparkish's, and his extraction as much better than his as

34 changeling] simpleton

his parts are. But my chief reason is I'd rather be of kin to him by the name
of brother-in-law than of cuckold.   73

Enter Mrs. Pinchwife.

Well, what says she now?

Mrs. Pinch. Why, she says she would only have you lead her to Horner's
lodging—with whom she first will discourse the matter before she talk with
you, which yet she cannot do. For alack, poor creature, she says she can't so
much as look you in the face, therefore she'll come to you in a mask. And you
must excuse her if she make you no answer to any question of yours till you
have brought her to Mr. Horner. And if you will not chide her nor question
her she'll come out to you immediately.   81

Pinch. Let her come. I will not speak a word to her, nor require a word from
her.

Mrs. Pinch. Oh, I forgot—besides, she says, she cannot look you in the
face, though through a mask, therefore would desire you to put out the candle.

Mr. Pinch. I agree to all; let her make haste. There, 'tis out. (*Puts out the
candle.*)   [*Exit* Mrs. Pinchwife.

My case is something better; I'd rather fight with Horner for not lying with
my sister than for lying with my wife, and of the two I had rather find my
sister too forward than my wife. I expected no other from her free education,
as she calls it, and her passion for the town. Well, wife and sister are names
which make us expect love and duty, pleasure and comfort, but we find 'em
plagues and torments, and are equally, though differently troublesome to
their keeper—for we have as much ado to get people to lie with our sisters as
keep 'em from lying with our wives!   94

Enter Mrs. Pinchwife, *masked, and in hood and scarf, and a nightgown
and petticoat of* Alithea's, *in the dark.*

What, are you come, sister? Let us go then . . . but first let me lock up my
wife. Mrs. Margery, where are you?

Mrs. Pinch. Here, bud.

Pinch. Come hither, that I may lock you up. Get you in. (*Locks the door.*)
Come, sister, where are you now?

Mrs. Pinchwife *gives him her hand, but when he lets her go, she steals softly
on t'other side of him, and is led away by him for his sister* Alithea.

[SCENE II]

The scene changes to Horner's *lodging.*

Quack, Horner.

Quack. What, all alone? Not so much as one of your cuckolds here, nor one of their wives! They use to take their turns with you, as if they were to watch you.

Horn. Yes, it often happens that a cuckold is but his wife's spy, and is more upon family duty when he is with her gallant abroad, hindering his pleasure, than when he is at home with her, playing the gallant. But the hardest duty a married woman imposes upon a lover is keeping her husband company always.

Quack. And his fondness wearies you almost as soon as hers.

Horn. A pox! keeping a cuckold company after you have had his wife is as tiresome as the company of a country squire to a witty fellow of the town, when he has got all his money.   12

Quack. And as at first a man makes a friend of the husband to get the wife, so at last you are fain to fall out with the wife to be rid of the husband.

Horn. Ay, most cuckold-makers are true courtiers. When once a poor man has cracked his credit for 'em, they can't abide to come near him.

Quack. But at first, to draw him in, are so sweet, so kind, so dear, just as you are to Pinchwife. But what becomes of that intrigue with his wife?

Horn. A pox! he's as surly as an alderman that has been bit, and since he's so coy, his wife's kindness is in vain, for she's a silly innocent.   20

Quack. Did she not send you a letter by him?

Horn. Yes, but that's a riddle I have not yet solved. Allow the poor creature to be willing, she is silly too, and he keeps her up so close. . . .

Quack. Yes, so close that he makes her but the more willing, and adds but revenge to her love, which two, when met, seldom fail to satisfy each other one way or other.

Horn. What! here's the man we are talking of, I think.

Enter Mr. Pinchwife *leading in his wife, masked,*
muffled, and in her sister's nightgown.

Horn. Pshaw!

Quack. Bringing his wife to you is the next thing to bringing a love letter from her.   30

Horn. What means this?

Pinch. The last time, you know, sir, I brought you a love letter. Now you see a mistress I think you'll say I am a civil man to you!

Horn. Ay, the devil take me, will I say thou art the civilest man I ever met with, and I have known some. I fancy I understand thee now better than I did the letter. But hark thee, in thy ear. . . .

Pinch. What?

Horn. Nothing but the usual question, man; is she sound, on thy word?

Pinch. What, you take her for a wench, and me for a pimp?

Horn. Pshaw! wench and pimp, paw words. I know thou art an honest fellow, and hast a great acquaintance among the ladies, and perhaps hast made love for me rather than let me make love to thy wife.   42

Pinch. Come, sir, in short; I am for no fooling.

Horn. Nor I neither; therefore prithee let's see her face presently. Make her show, man! Art thou sure I don't know her?

Pinch. I am sure you do know her.

Horn. A pox! why dost thou bring her to me then?

Pinch. Because she's a relation of mine. . . .

Horn. Is she, faith, man? Then thou art still more civil and obliging, dear rogue.   50

Pinch. . . . who desired me to bring her to you.

Horn. Then she is obliging, dear rogue.

Pinch. You'll make her welcome, for my sake, I hope.

Horn. I hope she is handsome enough to make herself welcome. Prithee, let her unmask.

Pinch. Do you speak to her. She would never be ruled by me.

Horn. Madam . . .   [Mrs. Pinchwife *whispers to* Horner.
She says she must speak with me in private. Withdraw, prithee.

Pinch. (*Aside.*) She's unwilling, it seems, I should know all her undecent conduct in this business.—Well, then, I'll leave you together, and hope when I am gone you'll agree. If not, you and I shan't agree, sir.   61

Horn. (*Aside.*) What means the fool?—If she and I agree, 'tis no matter what you and I do.

[*Whispers to* Mrs. Pinchwife, *who makes signs
with her hand for* Mr. Pinchwife *to be gone.*

Pinch. In the meantime I'll fetch a parson, and find out Sparkish and disabuse him. You would have me fetch a parson, would you not? Well then. . . . Now I think I am rid of her, and shall have no more trouble with her. Our sisters and daughters, like usurers' money, are safest when put out, but our wives, like their writings, never safe but in our closets under lock and key.   [*Exit* Mr. Pinchwife.

40 paw] improper   44 presently] at once

Enter Boy.

Boy. Sir Jasper Fidget, sir, is coming up.   70
Horn. Here's the trouble of a cuckold, now, we are talking of. A pox on him! Has he not enough to do to hinder his wife's sport, but he must other women's too?—Step in here, madam.   [*Exit* Mrs. Pinchwife.

Enter Sir Jasper.

Sir Jas. My best and dearest friend.
Horn. (*Aside to* Quack.) The old style, doctor.—Well, be short, for I am busy. What would your impertinent wife have now?
Sir Jas. Well guessed, i'faith, for I do come from her.
Horn. To invite me to supper? Tell her I can't come. Go.
Sir Jas. Nay, now you are out, faith, for my lady and the whole knot of the virtuous gang, as they call themselves, are resolved upon a frolic of coming to you tonight in a masquerade, and are all dressed already.   81
Horn. I shan't be at home.
Sir Jas. (*Aside.*) Lord, how churlish he is to women!—Nay, prithee don't disappoint 'em, they'll think 'tis my fault, prithee don't. I'll send in the banquet and the fiddles. But make no noise on't, for the poor virtuous rogues would not have it known for the world, that they go a-masquerading, and they would come to no man's ball but yours.
Horn. Well, well—get you gone, and tell 'em, if they come, 'twill be at the peril of their honour and yours.
Sir Jas. He, he, he! We'll trust you for that, farewell.
                                                        [*Exit* Sir Jasper.
Horn.   Doctor, anon you too shall be my guest,
                 But now I'm going to a private feast.

[SCENE III]

The Scene changes to the Piazza of Covent Garden.

Sparkish, Pinchwife.

Spark. (*With the letter in his hand.*) But who could have thought a woman could have been false to me? By the world, I could not have thought it.
Pinch. You were for giving and taking liberty; she has taken it only, sir, now you find in that letter. You are a frank person, and so is she, you see there.

Spark. Nay, if this be her hand—for I never saw it.

Pinch. 'Tis no matter whether that be her hand or no. I am sure this hand, at her desire, led her to Mr. Horner, with whom I left her just now, to go fetch a parson to 'em, at their desire too, to deprive you of her forever, for it seems yours was but a mock marriage.   10

Spark. Indeed, she would needs have it that 'twas Harcourt himself in a parson's habit that married us, but I'm sure he told me 'twas his brother Ned.

Pinch. Oh, there 'tis out, and you were deceived, not she, for you are such a frank person—but I must be gone. You'll find her at Mr. Horner's. Go and believe your eyes.   [*Exit* Mr. Pinchwife.

Spark. Nay, I'll to her, and call her as many crocodiles, sirens, harpies, and other heathenish names as a poet would do a mistress who had refused to hear his suit, nay more, his verses on her.—But stay, is not that she following a torch at t'other end of the Piazza? And from Horner's certainly—'tis so.

Enter Alithea *following a torch, and* Lucy *behind.*

You are well met, madam, though you don't think so. What, you have made a short visit to Mr. Horner, but I suppose you'll return to him presently. By that time the parson can be with him.   23

Alith. Mr. Horner, and the parson, sir!

Spark. Come, madam, no more dissembling, no more jilting, for I am no more a frank person.

Alith. How's this?

Lucy. (*Aside.*) So, 'twill work, I see.

Spark. Could you find out no easy country fool to abuse? none but me, a gentleman of wit and pleasure about the town? But it was your pride to be too hard for a man of parts, unworthy false woman! False as a friend that lends a man money to lose! False as dice, who undo those that trust all they have to 'em!   33

Lucy. (*Aside.*) He has been a great bubble by his similes, as they say!

Alith. You have been too merry, sir, at your wedding dinner, sure.

Spark. What, d'y mock me too?

Alith. Or you have been deluded.

Spark. By you!

Alith. Let me understand you.

Spark. Have you the confidence—I should call it something else, since you know your guilt—to stand my just reproaches? You did not write an impudent letter to Mr. Horner! who I find now has clubbed with you in deluding me with his aversion for women, that I might not, forsooth, suspect him for my rival.

20 torch] linkboy with torch

Lucy. (*Aside.*) D'y think the gentleman can be jealous now, madam?

Alith. I write a letter to Mr. Horner!

Spark. Nay, madam, do not deny it. Your brother showed it me just now, and told me likewise he left you at Horner's lodging to fetch a parson to marry you to him. And I wish you joy, madam, joy, joy! and to him, too, much joy! and to myself more joy for not marrying you!   50

Alith. (*Aside.*) So I find my brother would break off the match, and I can consent to't, since I see this gentleman can be made jealous.—O Lucy, by his rude usage and jealousy, he makes me almost afraid I am married to him. Art thou sure 'twas Harcourt himself and no parson that married us?

Spark. No, madam, I thank you. I suppose that was a contrivance too of Mr. Horner's and yours, to make Harcourt play the parson. But I would, as little as you, have him one now, no, not for the world, for shall I tell you another truth? I never had any passion for you 'till now, for now I hate you. 'Tis true I might have married your portion, as other men of parts of the town do sometimes, and so your servant. And to show my unconcernedness, I'll come to your wedding and resign you with as much joy as I would a stale wench to a new cully. Nay, with as much joy as I would after the first night, if I had been married to you. There's for you, and so your servant, servant.

[*Exit* Sparkish.

Alith How was I deceived in a man!

Lucy You'll believe, then, a fool may be made jealous now? For that easiness in him, that suffers him to be led by a wife, will likewise permit him to be persuaded against her by others.

Alith. But marry Mr. Horner! My brother does not intend it, sure. If I thought he did, I would take thy advice, and Mr. Harcourt for my husband. And now I wish that if there be any over-wise woman of the town, who, like me, would marry a fool for fortune, liberty, or title, first, that her husband may love play, and be a cully to all the town, but her, and suffer none but fortune to be mistress of his purse. Then, if for liberty, that he may send her into the country under the conduct of some housewifely mother-in-law. And, if for title, may the world give 'em none but that of cuckold.   75

Lucy. And for her greater curse, madam, may he not deserve it.

Alith. Away, impertinent!—Is not this my old lady Lanterlu's?

Lucy. Yes, madam. (*Aside.*) And here I hope we shall find Mr. Harcourt.

[*Exeunt* Alithea, Lucy.

---

77 lady Lanterlu's] lanterloo, or loo, a card game

[SCENE IV]

The scene changes again to Horner's *lodging.*

Horner, Lady Fidget, Mrs. Dainty Fidget, Mrs. Squeamish.

A table, banquet, and bottles.

Horn. (*Aside.*) A pox! they are come too soon . . . before I have sent back my new mistress. All I have now to do is to lock her in, that they may not see her.

Lady Fidg. That we may be sure of our welcome, we have brought our entertainment with us, and are resolved to treat thee, dear toad.

Dain. And that we may be merry to purpose, have left sir Jasper and my old lady Squeamish quarrelling at home at backgammon.

Squeam. Therefore, let us make use of our time, lest they should chance to interrupt us.

Lady Fidg. Let us sit then.   10

Horn. First, that you may be private, let me lock this door and that, and I'll wait upon you presently.

Lady Fidg. No, sir, shut 'em only and your lips for ever, for we must trust you as much as our women.

Horn. You know all vanity's killed in me.—I have no occasion for talking.

Lady Fidg. Now, ladies, supposing we had drank each of us our two bottles, let us speak the truth of our hearts.

Dain. and Squeam. Agreed.

Lady Fidg. By this brimmer, for truth is nowhere else to be found. (*Aside to* Horner.) Not in thy heart, false man!   20

Horn. (*Aside to* Lady Fidget.) You have found me a true man, I'm sure!

Lady Fidg. (*Aside to* Horner.) Not every way.—But let us sit and be merry.

(Lady Fidget *sings.*)

I.

Why should our damned tyrants oblige us to live
On the pittance of pleasure which they only give?
    We must not rejoice,
    With wine and with noise.
In vain we must wake in a dull bed alone,
Whilst to our warm rival, the bottle, they're gone.
    Then lay aside charms,
    *And take up these arms.**   [* *The glasses.*

2.

'Tis wine only gives 'em their courage and wit,   31
Because we live sober, to men we submit.
  If for beauties you'd pass,
  Take a lick of the glass,
'Twill mend your complexions, and when they are gone,
The best red we have is the red of the grape.
  Then, sisters, lay't on,
  And damn a good shape.

Dain. Dear brimmer! Well, in token of our openness and plain-dealing, let
us throw our masks over our heads.   40

Horn. So, 'twill come to the glasses anon.

Squeam. Lovely brimmer! Let me enjoy him first.

Lady Fidg. No, I never part with a gallant till I've tried him. Dear brimmer,
that mak'st our husbands short-sighted.

Dain. And our bashful gallants bold.

Squeam. And for want of a gallant, the butler lovely in our eyes. Drink,
eunuch.

Lady Fidg. Drink, thou representative of a husband. Damn a husband!

Dain. And, as it were a husband, an old keeper.

Squeam. And an old grandmother.   50

Horn. And an English bawd, and a French chirurgion.

Lady Fidg. Ay, we have all reason to curse 'em.

Horn. For my sake, ladies?

Lady Fidg. No, for our own, for the first spoils all young gallants' industry.

Dain. And the other's art makes 'em bold only with common women.

Squeam. And rather run the hazard of the vile distemper amongst them
than of a denial amongst us.

Dain. The filthy toads choose mistresses now as they do stuffs, for having
been fancied and worn by others.

Squeam. For being common and cheap.   60

Lady Fidg. Whilst women of quality, like the richest stuffs, lie untumbled
and unasked for.

Horn. Ay, neat, and cheap, and new, often they think best.

Dain. No, sir, the beasts will be known by a mistress longer than by a suit.

Squeam. And 'tis not for cheapness neither.

Lady Fidg. No, for the vain fops will take up druggets and embroider 'em.
But I wonder at the depraved appetites of witty men; they use to be out of
the common road, and hate imitation. Pray tell me, beast, when you were a

66 druggets] cheap wool fabrics

man, why you rather chose to club with a multitude in a common house for an
entertainment than to be the only guest at a good table.   70

Horn. Why, faith, ceremony and expectation are unsufferable to those
that are sharp bent. People always eat with the best stomach at an ordinary,
where every man is snatching for the best bit.

Lady Fidg. Though he get a cut over the fingers. . . . But I have heard
people eat most heartily of another man's meat, that is, what they do not pay
for.

Horn. When they are sure of their welcome and freedom, for ceremony in
love and eating is as ridiculous as in fighting. Falling on briskly is all should
be done in those occasions.

Lady Fidg. Well, then, let me tell you, sir, there is nowhere more freedom
than in our houses, and we take freedom from a young person as a sign of
good breeding, and a person may be as free as he pleases with us, as frolic, as
gamesome, as wild as he will.   83

Horn. Han't I heard you all declaim against wild men?

Lady Fidg. Yes, but for all that, we think wildness in a man as desirable a
quality as in a duck or rabbit. A tame man, foh!

Horn. I know not, but your reputations frightened me, as much as your
faces invited me.

Lady Fidg. Our reputation! Lord, why should you not think that we women
make use of our reputation, as you men of yours, only to deceive the world
with less suspicion? Our virtue is like the statesman's religion, the Quaker's
word, the gamester's oath, and the great man's honour—but to cheat those
that trust us.   93

Squeam. And that demureness, coyness, and modesty that you see in our
faces in the boxes at plays is as much a sign of a kind woman as a vizard-mask
in the pit.

Dain. For, I assure you, women are least masked when they have the velvet
vizard on.

Lady Fidg. You would have found us modest women in our denials only.

Squeam. Our bashfulness is only the reflection of the men's.

Dain. We blush when they are shamefaced.

Horn. I beg your pardon, ladies. I was deceived in you devilishly. But why
that mighty pretence to honour?   103

Lady Fidg. We have told you. But sometimes 'twas for the same reason
you men pretend business often, to avoid ill company, to enjoy the better
and more privately those you love.

Horn. But why would you ne'er give a friend a wink then?

Lady Fidg. Faith, your reputation frightened us as much as ours did you,
you were so notoriously lewd.

72 ordinary] tavern restaurant

Horn. And you so seemingly honest.   110
Lady Fidg. Was that all that deterred you?
Horn. And so expensive . . . you allow freedom, you say?
Lady Fidg. Ay, ay.
Horn. That I was afraid of losing my little money, as well as my little time,
both which my other pleasures required.
Lady Fidg. Money, foh! You talk like a little fellow now. Do such as we
expect money?
Horn. I beg your pardon, madam. I must confess, I have heard that great
ladies, like great merchants, set but the higher prices upon what they have,
because they are not in necessity of taking the first offer.   120
Dain. Such as we make sale of our hearts?
Squeam. We bribed for our love? Foh!
Horn. With your pardon, ladies, I know, like great men in offices, you seem
to exact flattery and attendance only from your followers, but you have re-
ceivers about you, and such fees to pay, a man is afraid to pass your grants.
Besides, we must let you win at cards, or we lose your hearts. And if you make
an assignation, 'tis at a goldsmith's, jeweller's, or china house, where, for
your honour you deposit to him, he must pawn his to the punctual cit, and so
paying for what you take up, pays for what he takes up.
Dain. Would you not have us assured of our gallant's love?   130
Squeam. For love is better known by liberality than by jealousy.
Lady Fidg. For one may be dissembled, the other not. (*Aside.*) But my
jealousy can be no longer dissembled, and they are telling ripe.—Come,
here's to our gallants in waiting, whom we must name, and I'll begin. This is
my false rogue.   [*Claps him on the back.*
Squeam. How!
Horn. (*Aside.*) So, all will out now.
Squeam. (*Aside to* Horner.) Did you not tell me, 'twas for my sake only you
reported yourself no man?
Dain. (*Aside to* Horner.) Oh wretch! Did you not swear to me, 'twas for my
love and honour you passed for that thing you do?   141
Horn. So, so.
Lady Fidg. Come, speak ladies; this is my false villain.
Squeam. And mine too.
Dain. And mine.
Horn. Well, then, you are all three my false rogues too, and there's an end
on't.
Lady Fidg. Well, then, there's no remedy; sister sharers, let us not fall out,
but have a care of our honour. Though we get no presents, no jewels of him,
we are savers of our honour, the jewel of most value and use, which shines yet
to the world unsuspected, though it be counterfeit.   151

Horn. Nay, and is e'en as good as if it were true, provided the world think so; for honour, like beauty now, only depends on the opinion of others.

Lady Fidg. Well, Harry Common, I hope you can be true to three. Swear— but 'tis no purpose to require your oath for you are as often forsworn as you swear to new women.

Horn. Come, faith, madam, let us e'en pardon one another, for all the difference I find betwixt we men and you women, *we* forswear ourselves at the beginning of an amour, *you* as long as it lasts.

Enter Sir Jasper Fidget, *and* Old Lady Squeamish.

Sir Jas. Oh, my lady Fidget, was this your cunning to come to Mr. Horner without me? But you have been nowhere else, I hope.   161

Lady Fidg. No, sir Jasper.

Old L. Squeam. And you came straight hither, biddy?

Squeam. Yes, indeed, lady grandmother.

Sir Jas. 'Tis well, 'tis well. I knew when once they were thoroughly acquainted with poor Horner, they'd ne'er be from him. You may let her masquerade it with my wife and Horner, and I warrant her reputation safe.

Enter Boy.

Boy. Oh, sir, here's the gentleman come whom you bid me not suffer to come up without giving you notice, with a lady too, and other gentlemen.

Horn. Do you all go in there, whilst I send 'em away, and boy, do you desire 'em to stay below 'till I come, which shall be immediately.   171

[*Exeunt* Sir Jasper, Lady Squeamish, Lady Fidget,
Mistress Dainty, Mistress Squeamish.

Boy. Yes, sir.   [*Exit.*

[*Exit* Horner *at t'other door, and returns with* Mistress Pinchwife.

Horn. You would not take my advice to be gone home before your husband came back; he'll now discover all. Yet pray, my dearest, be persuaded to go home, and leave the rest to my management. I'll let you down the back way.

Mrs. Pinch. I don't know the way home, so I don't.

Horn. My man shall wait upon you.

Mrs. Pinch. No, don't you believe that I'll go at all. What, are you weary of me already?

Horn. No, my life, 'tis that I may love you long, 'tis to secure my love, and your reputation with your husband. He'll never receive you again else.

Mrs. Pinch. What care I? D'ye think to frighten me with that? I don't intend to go to him again. You shall be my husband now.   183

Horn. I cannot be your husband, dearest, since you are married to him.

Mrs. Pinch. Oh, would you make me believe that? Don't I see every day at London here, women leave their first husbands, and go and live with other

men as their wives? Pish, pshaw! you'd make me angry, but that I love you so
mainly.

Horn. So, they are coming up.—In again, in, I hear 'em.

[*Exit* Mistress Pinchwife.

Well, a silly mistress is like a weak place, soon got, soon lost, a man has scarce
time for plunder. She betrays her husband first to her gallant, and then her
gallant to her husband. 192

Enter Pinchwife, Alithea, Harcourt, Sparkish, Lucy, *and a* Parson.

Pinch. Come, madam, 'tis not the sudden change of your dress, the confidence of your asseverations, and your false witness there, shall persuade me
I did not bring you hither just now. Here's my witness, who cannot deny it,
since you must be confronted.—Mr. Horner, did not I bring this lady to you
just now?

Horn. (*Aside.*) Now must I wrong one woman for another's sake. But that's
no new thing with me; for in these cases I am still on the criminal's side,
against the innocent. 200

Alith. Pray speak, sir.

Horn. (*Aside.*) It must be so—I must be impudent and try my luck;
impudence uses to be too hard for truth.

Pinch. What, you are studying an evasion, or excuse for her? Speak,
sir.

Horn No, faith, I am something backward only to speak in women's
affairs or disputes.

Pinch. She bids you speak.

Alith. Ay, pray sir do, pray satisfy him.

Horn. Then truly, you did bring that lady to me just now. 210

Pinch. O ho!

Alith. How, sir!

Harc. How, Horner!

Alith. What mean you, sir? I always took you for a man of honour.

Horn. (*Aside.*) Ay, so much a man of honour that I must save my mistress,
I thank you, come what will on't.

Spark. So if I had had her, she'd have made me believe the moon had been
made of a Christmas pie.

Lucy. (*Aside.*) Now could I speak, if I durst, and solve the riddle, who am
the author of it. 220

Alith. O unfortunate woman! A combination against my honour, which
most concerns me now, because you share in my disgrace, sir, and it is your
censure which I must now suffer, that troubles me, not theirs.

Harc. Madam, then have no trouble, you shall now see 'tis possible for me
to love too, without being jealous. I will not only believe your innocence

myself, but make all the world believe it. (*Apart to* Horner.) Horner, I must
now be concerned for this lady's honour.

Horn. And I must be concerned for a lady's honour too.

Harc. This lady has her honour, and I will protect it.

Horn. My lady has not her honour, but has given it me to keep, and I will
preserve it.   231

Harc. I understand you not.

Horn. I would not have you.

Mrs. Pinch. (*Peeping in behind.*) What's the matter with 'em all?

Pinch. Come, come, Mr. Horner, no more disputing. Here's the parson; I
brought him not in vain.

Horn. No, sir, I'll employ him, if this lady please.

Pinch. How! what d'ye mean?

Spark. Ay, what does he mean?

Horn. Why, I have resigned your sister to him; he has my consent.   240

Pinch. But he has not mine, sir. A woman's injured honour, no more than a
man's, can be repaired or satisfied by any but him that first wronged it. And
you shall marry her presently, or . . .   [*Lays his hand on his sword.*

Enter to them Mistress Pinchwife.

Mrs. Pinch. O lord, they'll kill poor Mr. Horner! Besides he shan't marry
her whilst I stand by and look on. I'll not lose my second husband so.

Pinch. What do I see?

Alith. My sister in my clothes!

Spark. Ha!

Mrs. Pinch. (*To* Pinchwife.) Nay, pray now don't quarrel about finding
work for the parson. He shall marry me to Mr. Horner, for now I believe you
have enough of me.   251

Horn. Damned, damned loving changeling!

Mrs. Pinch. Pray, sister, pardon me for telling so many lies of you.

Harc. I suppose the riddle is plain now.

Lucy. No, that must be my work. Good sir, hear me.

   [*Kneels to* Mr. Pinchwife, *who stands doggedly with his hat over his eyes.*

Pinch. I will never hear woman again, but make 'em all silent, thus—

                                   [*Offers to draw upon his wife.*

Horn. No, that must not be.

Pinch. You then shall go first, 'tis all one to me.

                   [*Offers to draw on* Horner; *stopped by* Harcourt.

Harc. Hold!

Enter Sir Jasper Fidget, Lady Fidget, Lady Squeamish,
Mrs. Dainty Fidget, Mrs. Squeamish.

Sir Jas. What's the matter? what's the matter? pray, what's the matter, sir? I beseech you communicate, sir. 261

Pinch. Why, my wife has communicated, sir, as your wife may have done too, sir, if she knows him, sir.

Sir Jas. Pshaw! with him! ha, ha, he!

Pinch. D'ye mock me, sir? A cuckold is a kind of a wild beast, have a care, sir!

Sir Jas. No, sure, you mock me, sir—he cuckold you! It can't be, ha, ha, he! Why, I'll tell you, sir. . . . [*Offers to whisper.*

Pinch. I tell you again, he has whored my wife, and yours too, if he knows her, and all the women he comes near. 'Tis not his dissembling, his hypocrisy, can wheedle me. 271

Sir Jas. How! does he dissemble? Is he an hypocrite? Nay then . . . how . . . wife . . . sister, is he an hypocrite?

Old L. Squeam. An hypocrite, a dissembler! Speak, young harlotry, speak, how?

Sir Jas. Nay, then . . . oh, my head too! . . . Oh thou libidinous lady!

Old L. Squeam. Oh thou harloting harlotry! Hast thou done't then?

Sir Jas. Speak, good Horner, art thou a dissembler, a rogue? Hast thou. . . ?

Horn. So. . . . 280

Lucy. (*Apart to* Horner.) I'll fetch you off, and her too, if she will but hold her tongue.

Horn. (*Apart to* Lucy.) Canst thou? I'll give thee. . . .

Lucy. (*To* Mr. Pinchwife.) Pray, have but patience to hear me, sir, who am the unfortunate cause of all this confusion. Your wife is innocent, I only culpable—for I put her upon telling you all these lies concerning my mistress in order to the breaking off the match between Mr. Sparkish and her, to make way for Mr. Harcourt.

Spark. Did you so, eternal rotten-tooth? Then it seems, my mistress was not false to me, I was only deceived by you. Brother, that should have been, now, man of conduct, who is a frank person now?—to bring your wife to her lover—ha! 292

Lucy. I assure you, sir, she came not to Mr. Horner out of love, for she loves him no more. . . .

Mrs. Pinch. Hold, I told lies for you, but you shall tell none for me, for I do love Mr. Horner with all my soul, and nobody shall say me nay. Pray don't you go to make poor Mr. Horner believe to the contrary, 'tis spitefully done of you, I'm sure.

Horn. (*Aside to* Mrs. Pinchwife.) Peace, dear idiot!

Mrs. Pinch. Nay, I will not peace. 300

Pinch. Not till I make you.

Enter Dorilant, Quack.

Dor. Horner, your servant; I am the doctor's guest, he must excuse our intrusion.

Quack. But what's the matter, gentlemen? For heaven's sake, what's the matter?

Horn. Oh, 'tis well you are come. 'Tis a censorious world we live in; you may have brought me a reprieve, or else I had died for a crime I never committed, and these innocent ladies had suffered with me. Therefore, pray satisfy these worthy, honourable, jealous gentlemen . . . that . . .

[*Whispers.*

Quack. Oh, I understand you; is that all?—Sir Jasper, by heavens and upon the word of a physician, sir . . .   311

[*Whispers to* Sir Jasper.

Sir Jas. Nay, I do believe you truly.—Pardon me, my virtuous lady, and dear of honour.

Old L. Squeam. What, then all's right again?

Sir Jas. Ay, ay, and now let us satisfy him too.

[*They whisper with* Mr. Pinchwife.

Pinch. An eunuch! Pray, no fooling with me.

Quack. I'll bring half the chirurgions in town to swear it.

Pinch. They! . . . They'll swear a man that bled to death through his wounds died of apoplexy.

Quack. Pray hear me, sir. Why, all the town has heard the report of him.

Pinch. But does all the town believe it?   321

Quack. Pray enquire a little, and first of all these.

Pinch. I'm sure when I left the town he was the lewdest fellow in't.

Quack. I tell you, sir, he has been in France since; pray ask but these ladies and gentlemen, your friend Mr. Dorilant. . . . Gentlemen and ladies; han't you all heard the late sad report of poor Mr. Horner?

All Ladies. Ay, ay, ay.

Dor. Why, thou jealous fool, do'st thou doubt it? He's an arrant French capon.

Mrs. Pinch. 'Tis false, sir, you shall not disparage poor Mr. Horner, for to my certain knowledge. . . .   331

Lucy. Oh, hold!

Squeam. (*Aside to* Lucy.) Stop her mouth!

Lady Fidg. (*To* Pinchwife.) Upon my honour, sir, 'tis as true. . . .

Dain. D'ye think we would have been seen in his company?

Squeam. Trust our unspotted reputations with him!

Lady Fidg. (*Aside to* Horner.) This you get, and we too, by trusting your secret to a fool.

Horn. Peace, madam. (*Aside to* Quack.) Well, doctor, is not this a good
design, that carries a man on unsuspected, and brings him off safe?   340
Pinch. (*Aside.*) Well, if this were true, but my wife . . .

> [Dorilant *whispers with* Mrs. Pinchwife.

Alith. Come, brother, your wife is yet innocent you see. But have a care of
too strong an imagination, lest like an over-concerned, timorous gamester, by
fancying an unlucky cast, it should come. Women and fortune are truest
still to those that trust 'em.

Lucy. And any wild thing grows but the more fierce and hungry for being
kept up, and more dangerous to the keeper.

Alith. There's doctrine for all husbands, Mr. Harcourt.

Harc. I edify, madam, so much that I am impatient till I am one.

Dor. And I edify so much by example I will never be one.   350

Spark. And because I will not disparage my parts I'll ne'er be one.

Horn. And I, alas, can't be one.

Pinch. But I must be one—against my will, to a country wife, with a country
murrain to me.

Mrs. Pinch. (*Aside.*) And I must be a country wife still too, I find, for I
can't, like a city one, be rid of my musty husband and do what I list.

Horn. Now, sir, I must pronounce your wife innocent, though I blush
whilst I do it, and I am the only man by her now exposed to shame, which I
will straight drown in wine, as you shall your suspicion, and the ladies'
troubles we'll divert with a ballet. Doctor, where are your maskers?   360

Lucy. Indeed, she's innocent, sir, I am her witness. And her end of coming
out was but to see her sister's wedding, and what she has said to your face of
her love to Mr. Horner was but the usual innocent revenge on a husband's
jealousy—was it not, madam? Speak.

Mrs. Pinch. (*Aside to* Lucy *and* Horner.) Since you'll have me tell more
lies.—Yes, indeed, bud.

Pinch.	For my own sake fain I would all believe;
	Cuckolds, like lovers, should themselves deceive.
	But . . . (*Sighs.*)
	His honour is least safe, too late I find, 370
	Who trusts it with a foolish wife or friend.

A dance of cuckolds.

Horn.	Vain fops, but court, and dress, and keep a pother,
	To pass for women's men with one another;
	But he who aims by women to be prized,
	First by the men, you see, must be despised!

354 murrain] plague

EPILOGUE

spoken by Mrs. Knep.

Now, you the vigorous, who daily here
O'er vizard mask in public domineer,
And what you'd do to her if in place where;
Nay, have the confidence to cry, 'Come out!'
Yet when she says, 'Lead on', you are not stout;
But to your well-dressed brother straight turn round
And cry, 'Pox on her, Ned, she can't be found!'
Then slink away, a fresh one to engage,
With so much seeming heat and loving rage,
You'd frighten listening actress on the stage: 10
Till she at last has seen you huffing come,
And talk of keeping in the tiring-room,
Yet cannot be provoked to lead her home.
Next, you Falstaffs of fifty, who beset
Your buckram maidenheads, which your friends get;
And whilst to them you of achievement boast,
They share the booty, and laugh at your cost.
In fine, you essenced boys, both old and young,
Who would be thought so eager, brisk, and strong,
Yet do the ladies, not their husbands, wrong: 20
Whose purses for your manhood make excuse,
And keep your Flanders mares for show, not use;
Encouraged by our woman's man today,
A Horner's part may vainly think to play;
And may intrigues so bashfully disown
That they may doubted be by few or none;
May kiss the cards at picquet, ombre, loo,
And so be thought to kiss the lady too;
But, gallants, have a care, faith, what you do.
The world, which to no man his due will give,   30
You by experience know you can deceive,
And men may still believe you vigorous,
But then we women—there's no coz'ning us!

FINIS

15 *buckram*] stiff   18 *essenced*] perfumed   22 *Flanders mares*] mistresses   33 *coz'ning*]
cheating

THE RELAPSE

or

Virtue in Danger

BY

SIR JOHN VANBRUGH

SIR JOHN VANBRUGH (1664–1726)

The Relapse, first performed at Drury Lane, 21 November 1696; first published 1697.

[*The Complete Works of Sir John Vanbrugh*, ed. B. Dobrée and G. Webb, 4 vols., 1927.]

THE
RELAPSE;
O R,
Virtue in Danger

Being the Sequel of

The Fool in Fashion,

A
COMEDY.

ACTED AT

The *Theatre-Royal* in *Drury-lane* ;

Printed for *Samuel Briscoe* at the corner of *Charles-street* in *Ruſſel-ſtreet Covent-Garden.* 1697.

Next week will be Publiſh'd Familiar Letters, the Second Volumn written by the Right Honourable John late Earl of *Rocheſter*, the Duke of *Buckingham*, Sir *George Etheridge*, the Honourble *Henry Saville*, Eſq; with other Letters, by a Perſon of Honour.

THE PREFACE

To go about to excuse half the defects this abortive brat is come into the world with, would be to provoke the town with a long useless preface, when 'tis, I doubt, sufficiently soured already by a tedious play.

I do therefore (with all the humility of a repenting sinner) confess it wants everything—but length; and in that I hope the severest critic will be pleased to acknowledge I have not been wanting. But my modesty will sure atone for everything, when the world shall know it is so great, I am even to this day insensible of those two shining graces in the play (which some part of the town is pleased to compliment me with) blasphemy and bawdy. 9

For my part I cannot find 'em out. If there was any obscene expressions upon the stage, here they are in the print; for I have dealt fairly, I have not sunk a syllable that could (though by racking of mysteries) be ranged under that head. And yet I believe with a steady faith, there is not one woman of a real reputation in town, but when she has read it impartially over in her closet, will find it so innocent, she'll think it no affront to her prayer book, to lay it upon the same shelf. So to them, (with all manner of deference,) I entirely refer my cause, and I'm confident they'll justify me against those pretenders to good manners, who at the same time have so little respect for the ladies, they would extract a bawdy jest from an ejaculation, to put 'em out of countenance. But I expect to have these well-bred persons always my enemies, since I'm sure I shall never write anything lewd enough to make 'em my friends. 22

As for the saints (your thorough-paced ones, I mean, with screwed faces and wry mouths) I despair of them, for they are friends to nobody. They love nothing but their altars and themselves. They have too much zeal to have any charity: they make debauches in piety, as sinners do in wine; and are as quarrelsome in their religion as other people are in their drink. So I hope nobody will mind what they say. But if any man (with flat plod shoes, a little band, greasy hair, and a dirty face, who is wiser than I, at the expense of being forty years older) happens to be offended at a story of a cock and a bull, and a priest and a bull-dog: I beg his pardon with all my heart, which I hope I shall obtain by eating my words and making this public recantation. I do therefore for his satisfaction, acknowledge I lied when I said, they never quit their hold; for in that little time I have lived in the world, I thank God I have seen 'em forced to't, more than once; but next time I'll speak with more caution and truth and only say, they have very good teeth. 36

If I have offended any honest gentlemen of the town, whose friendship or good word is worth the having, I am very sorry for it; I hope they'll

28 plod] thudding   29 band] clerical neckband

correct me as gently as they can, when they consider I have had no other design, in running a very great risk, than to divert (if possible) some part of their spleen, in spite of their wives and their taxes.

One word more about the bawdy, and I have done. I own the first night this thing was acted, some indecencies had like to have happened, but 'twas not my fault.   44

The fine gentleman of the play, drinking his mistress's health in Nantes Brandy, from six in the morning to the time he waddled on upon the stage in the evening, had toasted himself up to such a pitch of vigour, I confess I once gave Amanda for gone, and I am since (with all due respect to Mrs. Rogers) very sorry she 'scaped; for I am confident a certain lady, (let no one take it to herself that's handsome) who highly blames the play for the barrenness of the conclusion, would then have allowed it, a very natural close.

45 Nantes] from Nantes, France

FIRST PROLOGUE

Spoken by Miss Cross.

Ladies, this play in too much haste was writ,
To be o'er-charged with either plot or wit;
'Twas got, conceived, and born in six weeks' space,
And wit, you know, 's as slow in growth—as grace.
Sure it can ne'er be ripened to your taste,
I doubt 'twill prove our author bred too fast.
For mark 'em well, who with the muses marry,
They rarely do conceive, but they miscarry.
'Tis the hard fate of those wh' are big with rhyme,
Still to be brought to bed before their time.   10
Of our late poets, nature few has made,
The greatest part—are only so by trade.
Still want of something brings the scribbling fit,
For want of money some of 'em have writ,
And others do't you see—for want of wit.
Honour, they fancy, summons 'em to write,
So out they lug in resty nature's spite,
As some of you spruce beaux do—when you fight.
Yet let the ebb of wit be ne'er so low,
Some glimpse of it a man may hope to show   20
Upon a theme so ample—as a beau.
So, howsoe'er true courage may decay,
Perhaps there's not one smock-face here today,
But's bold as Caesar—to attack a play.
Nay, what's yet more, with an undaunted face
To do the thing with more heroic grace,
'Tis six to four, y'attack the strongest place.
You are such Hotspurs, in this kind of venture,
Where there's no breach, just there you needs must enter.
But be advised.   30
E'en give the hero, and the critic o'er,
For nature sent you on another score,
She formed her beau for nothing but her whore.

17 *resty*] sluggish   23 *smock-face*] effeminate man   28 *Hotspurs*] the impetuous Sir
Henry Percy who figures in Shakespeare's *Henry IV* as Hotspur

PROLOGUE ON THE THIRD DAY

Spoken by Mrs. Verbruggen.

Apologies for plays, experience shows,
Are things almost as useless—as the beaux.
Whate'er we say (like them) we neither move
Your friendship, pity, anger, nor your love.
'Tis interest turns the globe: let us but find
The way to please you, and you'll soon be kind:
But to expect, you'd for our sakes approve,
Is just as though you for their sakes should love,
And that, we do confess, we think a task,
Which (though they may impose) we never ought to ask.   10
This is an age where all things we improve,
But most of all the art of making love.
In former days women were only won
By merit, truth, and constant service done,
But lovers now are much more expert grown.
They seldom wait t'approach by tedious form,
They're for despatch, for taking you by storm,
Quick are their sieges, furious are their fires,
Fierce their attacks, and boundless their desires.
Before the play's half ended, I'll engage   20
To show you beaux come crowding on the stage,
Who with so little pains have always sped,
They'll undertake to look a lady dead.
How I have shook, and trembling stood with awe,
When here, behind the scenes, I've seen 'em draw—
A comb (that dead-doing weapon to the heart,)
And turn each powdered hair into a dart.
When I have seen 'em sally on the stage,
Dressed to the war, and ready to engage,
I've mourned your destiny—yet more their fate,   30
To think, that after victories so great,
It should so often prove their hard mishap
To sneak into a lane and get a clap.

33 *clap*] venereal disease

But hush; they're here already; I'll retire,
And leave 'em to you ladies to admire.
They'll show you twenty thousand airs and graces,
They'll entertain you with their soft grimaces,
Their snuff-box, awkward bows, and ugly faces.
In short, they're after all so much your friends
That, lest the play should fail the author's ends,   40
They have resolved to make you some amends.
Between each act, (performed by nicest rules,)
They'll treat you—with an interlude of fools;
Of which, that you may have the deeper sense,
The entertainment's at their own expense.

DRAMATIS PERSONAE

Men

SIR NOVELTY FASHION, newly created Lord Foppington	*Mr. Cibber*
YOUNG FASHION, his brother	*Mr. Kent*
LOVELESS, husband to Amanda	*Mr. Verbruggen*
WORTHY, a gentleman of the town	*Mr. Powell*
SIR TUNBELLY CLUMSY, a country gentleman	*Mr. Bullock*
SIR JOHN FRIENDLY, his neighbour	*Mr. Mills*
COUPLER, a match-maker	*Mr. Johnson*
BULL, chaplain to Sir Tunbelly	*Mr. Simson*
SYRINGE, a surgeon	*Mr. Haynes*
LORY, servant to Young Fashion	*Mr. Dogget*
Shoemaker, Taylor, Periwig-maker etc.	

Women

AMANDA, wife to Loveless	*Mrs. Rogers*
BERINTHIA, her cousin, a young widow	*Mrs. Verbruggen*
MISS HOYDEN, a great fortune, daughter to Sir Tunbelly	*Mrs. Cross*
NURSE, her gouvernant	*Mrs. Powell*

The

Relapse:

Or,

Virtue In Danger:

Being the sequel of

The Fool In Fashion.

ACT I SCENE I

Enter Loveless *reading.*

Love. How true is that philosophy which says
  Our heaven is seated in our minds?
  Through all the roving pleasures of my youth,
  (Where nights and days seemed all consumed in joy,
  Where the false face of luxury
  Displayed such charms
  As might have shaken the most holy hermit
  And made him totter at his altar;)
  I never knew one moment's peace like this.
  Here—in this little soft retreat,   10
  My thoughts unbent from all the cares of life
  Content with fortune,
  Eased from the grating duties of dependence,
  From envy free, ambition under foot,
  The raging flame of wild destructive lust
  Reduced to a warm pleasing fire of lawful love,
  My life glides on, and all is well within.
                  Enter Amanda.

Love. (*Meeting her kindly.*) How does the happy cause of my content,
  My dear Amanda?
  You find me musing on my happy state,   20
  And full of grateful thoughts to heaven and you.
Aman. Those grateful offerings heaven can't receive
  With more delight than I do:
  Would I could share with it as well
  The dispensations of its bliss,
  That I might search its choicest favours out
  And shower 'em on your head for ever.
Love. The largest boons that heaven thinks fit to grant
  To things it has decreed shall crawl on earth,
  Are in the gift of women formed like you.   30
  Perhaps, when time shall be no more,
  When the aspiring soul shall take its flight
  And drop this pondrous lump of clay behind it,
  It may have appetites we know not of,
  And pleasures as refined as its desires—
  But till that day of knowledge shall instruct me,
  The utmost blessing that my thought can reach
  Is folded in my arms and rooted in my heart.   [*Taking her in his arms.*
Aman. There let it grow for ever.
Love. Well said, Amanda. . . . Let it be for ever. . . .   40
  Would heaven grant that . . .
Aman. 'Twere all the heaven I'd ask.
  But we are clad in black mortality, and the dark curtain
  Of eternal night at last must drop between us.
Love. It must—that mournful separation we must see.
  A bitter pill it is to all; but doubles its ungrateful taste
  When lovers are to swallow it.
Aman. Perhaps that pain may only be my lot:
  You possibly may be exempted from it. Men find out softer
  Ways to quench their fires.   50
Love. Can you then doubt my constancy, Amanda?
  You'll find 'tis built upon a steady basis—
  The rock of reason now supports my love,
  On which it stands so fixed
  The rudest hurricane of wild desire
  Would, like the breath of a soft slumb'ring babe,
  Pass by and never shake it.
Aman. Yet still 'tis safer to avoid the storm;
  The strongest vessels, if they put to sea,

May possibly be lost.   60
Would I could keep you here, in this calm port, for ever!
Forgive the weakness of a woman,
I am uneasy at your going to stay so long in town,
I know its false insinuating pleasures;
I know the force of its delusions;
I know the strength of its attacks;
I know the weak defence of nature;
I know you are a man—and I—a wife.
Love. You know then all that needs to give you rest,
  For wife's the strongest claim that you can urge.   70
  When you would plead your title to my heart,
  On this you may depend; therefore be calm,
  Banish your fears, for they are traitors to your peace;
  Beware of 'em, they are insinuating busy things
  That gossip to and fro, and do a world of mischief
  Where they come. But you shall soon be mistress of 'em all,
  I'll aid you with such arms for their destruction,
  They never shall erect their heads again.
  You know the business is indispensable, that obliges
  Me to go to London; and you have no reason, that I   80
  Know of, to believe I'm glad of the occasion;
  For my honest conscience is my witness.
  I have found a due succession of such charms
  In my retirement here with you;
  I have never thrown one roving thought that way;
  But since, against my will, I'm dragged once more
  To that uneasy theatre of noise,
  I am resolved to make such use on't,
  As shall convince you 'tis an old-cast mistress,
  Who has been so lavish of her favours   90
  She's now grown bankrupt of her charms
  And has not one allurement left to move me.
Aman. Her bow, I do believe, is grown so weak,
  Her arrows (at this distance) cannot hurt you,
  But in approaching 'em, you give 'em strength;
  The dart that has not far to fly
  Will put the best of armour to a dangerous trial.
Love. That trial past, and y'are at ease for ever;
  When you have seen the helmet proved,
  You'll apprehend no more for him that wears it.   100
  Therefore to put a lasting period to your fears,

I am resolved, this once, to launch into temptation.
I'll give you an essay of all my virtues,
My former boon companions of the bottle
Shall fairly try what charms are left in wine:
I'll take my place amongst 'em;
They shall hem me in,
Sing praises to their god, and drink his glory,
Turn wild enthusiasts for his sake,
And beasts to do him honour,   110
Whilst I, a stubborn atheist,
Sullenly look on,
Without one reverend glass to his divinity.
That for my temperance!
Then for my constancy—

Aman. Ay, there take heed.
Love. Indeed the danger's small.
Aman. And yet my fears are great.
Love. Why are you so timorous?
Aman. Because you are so bold.   120
Love. My courage should disperse your apprehensions.
Aman. My apprehensions should alarm your courage.
Love. Fie, fie, Amanda, it is not kind thus to distrust me.
Aman. And yet my fears are founded on my love.
Love. Your love then is not founded as it ought,
    For if you can believe 'tis possible
    I should again relapse to my past follies,
    I must appear to you a thing
    Of such an undigested composition
    That but to think of me with inclination   130
    Would be a weakness in your taste,
    Your virtue scarce could answer.
Aman. 'Twould be a weakness in my tongue,
    My prudence could not answer,
    If I should press you farther with my fears;
    I'll therefore trouble you no longer with 'em.
Love. Nor shall they trouble you much longer;
    A little time shall show you they were groundless.
    This winter shall be the fiery trial of my virtue,
    Which when it once has past,   140
    You'll be convinced 'twas of no false allay.
    There all your cares will end.
Aman. Pray heaven they may.   [*Exeunt hand in hand.*

SCENE [II] *Whitehall.*

Enter Young Fashion, Lory *and* Waterman.

Young Fash. Come, pay the waterman, and take the portmantle.

Lory. Faith, sir, I think the waterman had as good take the portmantle and pay himself.

Young Fash. Why, sure there's something left in't!

Lory. But a solitary old waistcoat, upon honour, sir.

Young Fash. Why, what's become of the blue coat, sirrah?

Lory. Sir, 'twas eaten at Gravesend. The reckoning came to thirty shillings, and your privy purse was worth but two half crowns.

Young Fash. 'Tis very well.

Water. Pray master, will you please to dispatch me?   10

Young Fash. Ay, here, a—Canst thou change me a guinea?

Lory. (*Aside.*) Good.

Water. Change a guinea, master! Ha! ha! Your honour's pleased to compliment.

Young Fash. Egad I don't know how I shall pay thee then, for I have nothing but gold about me.

Lory. (*Aside.*) Hum, hum.

Young Fash. What dost thou expect, friend?

Water. Why master, so far against wind and tide is richly worth half a piece.   20

Young Fash. Why, faith, I think thou art a good conscionable fellow. I'gad I begin to have so good an opinion of thy honesty, I care not if I leave my portmantle with thee, till I send thee thy money.

Water. Ha! God bless your honour! I should be as willing to trust you, master, but that you are, as a man may say, a stranger to me, and these are nimble times. There are a great many sharpers stirring. (*Taking up the portmantle.*) Well master, when your worship sends the money your portmantle shall be forthcoming. My name's Tugg. My wife keeps a brandy-shop in Drab Alley at Wapping.

Young Fash. Very well; I'll send for't tomorrow.   [*Exit* Waterman.

Lory. So.—Now sir, I hope you'll own yourself a happy man. You have out-lived all your cares.   32

Young Fash. How so, sir?

Lory. Why, you have nothing left to take care of.

Young Fash. Yes sirrah, I have myself and you to take care of still.

Lory. Sir, if you could but prevail with somebody else to do that for you, I fancy we might both fare the better for't.

s.d. *waterman*] licensed wherry-man   1 portmantle] portmanteau   20 piece] coin

Young Fash. Why if thou canst tell me where to apply myself—I have at present so little money and so much humility about me, I don't know but I may follow a fool's advice.   40

Lory. Why then, sir, your fool advises you to lay aside all animosity, and apply to Sir Novelty, your elder brother.

Young Fash. Damn my elder brother.

Lory. With all my heart, but get him to redeem your annuity however.

Young Fash. My annuity? 'Sdeath he's such a dog, he would not give his powder puff to redeem my soul.

Lory. Look you, sir, you must wheedle him, or you must starve.

Young Fash. Look you, sir, I will neither wheedle him, nor starve.

Lory. Why? What will you do then?

Young Fash. I'll go into the army.   50

Lory. You can't take the oaths; you are a Jacobite.

Young Fash. Thou may'st as well say I can't take orders because I'm an atheist.

Lory. Sir, I ask your pardon. I find I did not know the strength of your conscience so well as I did the weakness of your purse.

Young Fash. Methinks, sir, a person of your experience should have known that the strength of the conscience proceeds from the weakness of the purse.

Lory. Sir, I am very glad to find you have a conscience, able to take care of us, let it proceed from what it will. But I desire you'll please to consider that the army alone will be but a scanty maintenance for a person of your generosity, (at least as rents now are paid). I shall see you stand in damnable need of some auxiliary guineas, for your *menus plaisirs*. I will therefore turn fool once more for your service and advise you to go directly to your brother.

Young Fash. Art thou then so impregnable a blockhead to believe he'll help me with a farthing?   64

Lory. Not if you treat him *de haut en bas* as you used to do.

Young Fash. Why, how wouldst have me treat him?

Lory. Like a trout—tickle him!

Young Fash. I can't flatter.

Lory. Can you starve?

Young Fash. Yes.

Lory. I can't! Goodbye t'ye sir . . .   [*Going.*

Young Fash. Stay, thou wilt distract me. What wouldst thou have me say to him?

Lory. Say nothing to *him*—apply yourself to his favourites, speak to his periwig, his cravat, his feather, his snuffbox. And when you are well with them—desire him to lend you a thousand pounds. I'll engage you prosper.

Young Fash. 'Sdeath and furies, why was that coxcomb thrust into the world before me? O Fortune! . . . Fortune! . . . Thou art a bitch by Gad! . . . [*Exeunt.*

---

51 Jacobite] supporter of James II's cause   61 *menus plaisirs*] minor entertainments
65 *de haut en bas*] in a high and mighty way

SCENE [III] *A Dressing-Room.*

Enter Lord Foppington *in his night-gown.*

Lord Fop. Page!

Enter Page.

Page. Sir.

Lord Fop. Sir, pray sir, do me the favour to teach your tongue the title the king has thought fit to honour me with.

Page. I ask your lordship's pardon, my lord.

Lord Fop. O, you can pronounce the word then! I thought it would have choked you. D'ye hear?

Page. My lord.

Lord Fop. Call La Vérole, I would dress. ...   [*Exit* Page.
(*Solus.*) Well, 'tis an unspeakable pleasure to be a man of quality! ... Strike me dumb! ... My lord! ... Your lordship! ... My lord Foppington! ... *Ah c'est quelque chose de beau, que le diable m'emporte.* ... Why, the ladies were ready to puke at me, whilst I had nothing but sir Navelty to recommend me to 'em. ... Sure whilst I was but a knight, I was a very nauseous fellow. ... Well, 'tis ten thousand pawnd well given—stap my vitals!   15

Enter La Vérole.

La Vér. Me lord, de shoemaker, de taylor, de hosier, de semstress, de barber, be all ready, if your lordship please to be dress.

Lord Fop. 'Tis well, admit 'em.

La Vér. Hey, *messieurs, entrez!*

Enter Taylor, *etc.*

Lord Fop. So gentlemen, I hope you have all taken pains to show yourselves masters in your professions.

Taylor. I think I may presume to say, sir. ...

La Vér. My *lord*—you clawn you!   23

Taylor. Why, is he made a lord?—My lord, I ask your lordship's pardon, my lord; I hope, my lord, your lordship will please to own, I have brought your lordship as accomplished a suit of clothes as ever peer of England trod the stage in. My lord, will your lordship please to try 'em now?

Lord Fop. Ay, but let my people dispose the glasses so, that I may see myself before and behind, for I love to see myself all raund.

Whilst he puts on his clothes, enter Young Fashion *and* Lory.

12 *Ah ... m'emporte*] What a splendid thing it is—may the devil take me!   15 pawnd] pound (he uses an affected pronunciation throughout the play)

Young Fash. Hey-day, what the devil have we here? Sure my gentleman's grown a favourite at court, he has got so many people at his levee.   31

Lory. Sir, these people come in order to make him a favourite at court. They are to establish him with the ladies.

Young Fash. Good God, to what an ebb of taste are women fallen, that it should be in the power of a laced coat to recommend a gallant to 'em.

Lory. Sir, taylors and periwig-makers are now become the bawds of the nation. 'Tis they debauch all the women.

Young Fash. Thou say'st true, for there's that fop now, has not by nature wherewithal to move a cook-maid, and by that time these fellows have done with him, egad he shall melt down a countess.—But now for my reception. I'll engage it shall be as cold a one as a courtier's to his friend who comes to put him in mind of his promise.   42

Lord Fop. (*To his* Taylor.) Death and eternal tartures, sir, I say the packet's too high by a foot.

Taylor. My lord, if it had been an inch lower, it would not have held your lordship's pocket-handkerchief.

Lord Fop. Rat my packet-handkerchief! Have not I a page to carry it? You may make him a packet up to his chin a purpose for it. But I will not have mine come so near my face.

Taylor. 'Tis not for me to dispute your lordship's fancy.   50

Young Fash. (*To* Lory.) His lordship! Lory, did you observe that?

Lory. Yes sir, I always thought 'twould end there. Now I hope you'll have a little more respect for him.

Young Fash. Respect! Damn him for a coxcomb! Now has he ruined his estate to buy a title, that he may be a fool of the first rate. But let's accost him. (*To* Lord Foppington.) Brother, I'm your humble servant.

Lord Fop. O lard, Tam, I did not expect you in England! Brother, I am glad to see you. (*Turning to his* Taylor.) Look you, sir, I shall never be reconciled to this nauseous packet, therefore pray get me another suit with all manner of expedition for this is my eternal aversion. [*To the* Sempstress.] Mrs. Calico, are not you of my mind?   61

Semp. O, directly, my lord, it can never be too low.

Lord Fop. You are positively in the right on't, for the packet becomes no part of the body but the knee.

Semp. I hope your lordship is pleased with your steenkirk.

Lord Fop. In love with it, stap my vitals! Bring your bill, you shall be paid tomarrow.

Semp. I humbly thank your honour.   [*Exit* Sempstress.

Lord Fop. Hark thee, shoemaker, these shoes an't ugly but they don't fit me.

Shoe. My lord, methinks they fit you very well.   70

31 levee] ceremonial rising from bed   62 directly] frankly   65 steenkirk] neckcloth

Lord Fop. They hurt me just below the instep.

Shoe. (*Feeling his foot.*) My lord, they don't hurt you there.

Lord Fop. I tell thee they pinch me execrably.

Shoe. My lord, if they pinch you, I'll be bound to be hanged, that's all.

Lord Fop. Why, wilt thou undertake to persuade me I cannot feel?

Shoe. Your lordship may please to feel what you think fit, but that shoe does not hurt you. I think I understand my trade!

Lord Fop. Now by all that's Great and Powerful, thou art an incomprehensible coxcomb! But thou makest good shoes, and so I'll bear with thee.

Shoe. My lord, I have worked for half the people of quality in town, these twenty years, and 'twere very hard I should not know when a shoe hurts and when it don't.   82

Lord Fop. Well, prithee begone about thy business.   [*Exit* Shoemaker. (*To the* Hosier.) Mr. Mend-legs, a word with you; the calves of these stockings are thickened a little too much. They make my legs look like a chairman's.

Mend. My lord, methinks they look mighty well.

Lord Fop. Ay, but you are not so good a judge of these things as I am—I have studied 'em all my life. Therefore pray let the next be the thickness of a crawn-piece less.—(*Aside.*) If the town takes notice my legs are fallen away 'twill be attributed to the violence of some new intrigue.—(*To the* Periwigmaker.) Come, Mr. Foretop, let me see what you have done, and then the fatigue of the marning will be over.   92

Fore. My lord, I have done what I defy any prince in Europe t'outdo; I have made you a periwig so long and so full of hair it will serve you for hat and cloak in all weathers.

Lord Fop. Then thou hast made me thy friend to eternity. Come, comb it out.

Young Fash. Well, Lory, what dost think on't? A very friendly reception from a brother after three years' absence.

Lory. Why, sir, it's your own fault. We seldom care for those that don't love what we love. If you would creep into his heart, you must enter into his pleasures. Here have you stood ever since you came in, and have not commended any one thing that belongs to him.   102

Young Fash. Nor never shall, whilst they belong to a coxcomb.

Lory. Then, sir, you must be content to pick a hungry bone.

Young Fash. No, sir, I'll crack it, and get to the marrow before I have done.

Lord Fop. Gad's curse! Mr. Foretop, you don't intend to put this upon me for a full periwig?

Fore. Not a full one, my lord? I don't know what your lordship may please to call a full one, but I have crammed twenty ounces of hair into it.

Lord Fop. What it may be by weight, sir, I shall not dispute, but by tale, there are not nine hairs of a side.   111

85 chairman's] sedan chair carrier's   110 tale] number

Fore. O lord! O lord! O Lord! Why, as God shall judge me, your honour's side-face is reduced to the tip of your nose.

Lord Fop. My side-face may be in eclipse for aught I know, but I'm sure my full-face is like the full-moon.

Fore. Heavens bless my eye-sight! (*Rubbing his eyes.*) Sure I look through the wrong end of the perspective, for by my faith, an't please your honour, the broadest place I see in your face does not seem to me to be two inches [in] diameter.

Lord Fop. If it did, it would be just two inches too broad. Far a periwig to a man should be like a mask to a woman—nothing should be seen but his eyes.   122

Fore. My lord, I have done; if you please to have more hair in your wig, I'll put it in.

Lord Fop. Pasitively, yes.

Fore. Shall I take it back now, my lord?

Lord Fop. No! I'll wear it today, though it show such a manstrous pair of cheeks. Stap my vitals, I shall be taken for a trumpeter.   [*Exit* Foretop.

Young Fash. Now your people of business are gone, brother, I hope I may obtain a quarter of an hour's audience of you.   130

Lord Fop. Faith, Tam, I must beg you'll excuse me at this time, for I must away to the House of Lards immediately. My lady Teaser's case is to come on today, and I would not be absent for the salvation of mankind. Hey page, is the coach at the door?

Page. Yes, my lord.

Lord Fop. You'll excuse me, brother.   [*Going.*

Young Fash. Shall you be back at dinner?

Lord Fop. As Gad shall jidge me, I can't tell; for 'tis passible I may dine with some of aur House at Lacket's.

Young Fash. Shall I meet you there? For I must needs talk with you.

Lord Fop. That I'm afraid mayn't be so praper, far the lards I commonly eat with are people of a nice conversation, and you know, Tam, your education has been a little at large. But if you'll stay here, you'll find a family-dinner. Hey fellow! What is there for dinner? There's beef; I suppose, my brother will eat beef. Dear Tam, I'm glad to see thee in England, stap my vitals.   [*Exit with his equipage.*

Young Fash. Hell and furies, is this to be borne?   147

Lory. Faith, sir, I could almost have given him a knock o'th' pate myself.

Young Fash. 'Tis enough; I will now show thee the excess of my passion by being very calm. Come, Lory, lay your loggerhead to mine, and in cool blood let us contrive his destruction.

114 side-face] profile   117 perspective] telescope   139 Lacket's] Locket's, a fashionable eating-house near Charing Cross   143 at large] haphazard   150 loggerhead] blockhead

Lory. Here comes a head, sir, would contrive it better than us both, if he would but join in the confederacy.

Enter Coupler.

Young Fash. By this light, old Coupler alive still! Why, how now, match-maker, art thou here still to plague the world with matrimony? You old bawd, how have you the impudence to be hobbling out of your grave twenty years after you are rotten!

Coup. When you begin to rot, sirrah, you'll go off like a pippin—one winter will send you to the devil. What mischief brings you home again? Ha! You young lascivious rogue, you. Let me put my hand in your bosom, sirrah.

Young Fash. Stand off, old Sodom.   161

Coup. Nay, prithee now, don't be so coy.

Young Fash. Keep your hands to yourself, you old dog you, or I'll wring your nose off.

Coup. Hast thou then been a year in Italy, and brought home a fool at last? By my conscience, the young fellows of this age profit no more by their going abroad than they do by their going to church. Sirrah, sirrah, if you are not hanged before you come to my years, you'll know a cock from a hen. But come, I'm still a friend to thy person, though I have a contempt of thy under-standing; and therefore I would willingly know thy condition, that I may see whether thou standest in need of my assistance, for widows swarm, my boy, the town's infected with 'em.   172

Young Fash. I stand in need of anybody's assistance, that will help me to cut my elder brother's throat, without the risk of being hanged for him.

Coup. Egad, sirrah, I could help thee to do him almost as good a turn, without the danger of being burnt in the hand for't.

Young Fash. Sayest thou so, old Satan? Show me but that and my soul is thine.

Coup. Pox o'thy soul, give me thy warm body, sirrah. I shall have a sub-stantial title to't when I tell thee my project.   180

Young Fash. Out with it then, dear dad, and take possession as soon as thou wilt.

Coup. Say'st thou so my Hephaestion? Why then, thus lies the scene—but hold! Who's that? If we are heard we are undone.

Young Fash. What, have you forgot Lory?

Coup. Who, trusty Lory, is it thee?

Lory. At your service, sir.

Coup. Give me thy hand, old boy. Egad I did not know thee again, but I

<hr>

158 sirrah] sir (imperious or contemptuous use)   158 pippin] a kind of apple
161 Sodom] implying he is a sodomite   176 burnt in the hand] branded for felony
183 Hephaestion] famous for intimacy with Alexander the Great

remember thy honesty, though I did not thy face. I think thou had'st like
to have been hanged once or twice for thy master?   190

Lory. Sir, I was very near once having that honour.

Coup. Well, live and hope, don't be discouraged! Eat with him, and drink
with him, and do what he bids thee, and it may be thy reward at last, as well
as another's. (*To* Young Fashion.) Well, sir, you must know I have done you
the kindness to make up a match for your brother.

Young Fash. Sir, I am very much beholding to you, truly.

Coup. You may be, sirrah, before the wedding-day yet. The lady is a great
heiress—fifteen hundred pound a year, and a great bag of money. The match
is concluded, the writings are drawn, and the pipkin's to be cracked in a fortnight.—Now you must know, stripling,—with respect to your mother,—
your brother's the son of a whore!   201

Young Fash. Good.

Coup. He has given me a bond of a thousand pounds for helping him to this
fortune, and has promised me as much more in ready money upon the day of
marriage, which I understand by a friend, he ne'er designs to pay me! If
therefore you will be a generous young dog, and secure me five thousand
pounds, I'll be a covetous old rogue and help you to the lady.

Young Fash. Egad, if thou canst bring this about, I'll have thy statue cast
in brass. But don't you dote, you old pander you, when you talk at this rate?

Coup. That your youthful parts shall judge of. This plump partridge that
I tell you of lives in the country, fifty miles off, with her honoured parents, in
a lonely old house which nobody comes near. She never goes abroad, nor sees
company at home. To prevent all misfortunes she has her breeding within
doors, the parson of the parish teaches her to play upon the bass-viol, the
clerk to sing, her nurse to dress, and her father to dance. In short, nobody can
give you admittance there but I, nor can I do it any other way than by making
you pass for your brother.   217

Young Fash. And how the devil wilt thou do that?

Coup. Without the devil's aid, I warrant thee! Thy brother's face, not one of
the family ever saw; the whole business has been managed by me, and all the
letters go through my hands. The last that was writ to sir Tunbelly Clumsy
(for that's the old gentleman's name,) was to tell him his lordship would be
down in a fortnight to consummate. Now you shall go away immediately,
pretend you writ that letter only to have the romantic pleasure of surprising
your mistress; fall desperately in love, as soon as you see her; make that your
plea, for marrying her immediately, and when the fatigue of the wedding-
night's over, you shall send me a swinging purse of gold, you dog you.

---

199 pipkin] small earthenware pot (bawdy innuendo)   209 pander] go-between, pro-
curer   214 bass-viol] a six-stringed musical instrument, precursor of the violoncello
215 clerk] lay officer of parish church

Young Fash. Egad, old dad, I'll put my hand in thy bosom now.

Coup. Ah, you young hot lusty thief, let me muzzle you! (*Kissing.*) Sirrah, let me muzzle you!   230

Young Fash. (*Aside.*) Pshaw, the old lecher. . . .

Coup. Well, I'll warrant thou hast not a farthing of money in thy pocket now, no; one may see it in thy face. . . .

Young Fash. Not a souse, by Jupiter.

Coup. Must I advance then? Well sirrah, be at my lodgings in half an hour, and I'll see what may be done. We'll sign and seal, and eat a pullet, and when I have given thee some farther instructions, thou sha't hoist sail and begone. (*Kissing.*) T'other buss and so adieu.

Young Fash. Hum . . . pshaw. . . .

Coup. Ah, you young warm dog you, what a delicious night will the bride have on't.   [*Exit* Coupler.

Young Fash. So, Lory! Providence, thou see'st at last, takes care of men of merit. We are in a fair way to be great people.   243

Lory. Ay sir, if the devil don't step between the cup and the lip, as he uses to do.

Young Fash. Why, faith, he has played me many a damned trick to spoil my fortune, and egad I'm almost afraid he's at work about it again now. But if I should tell thee how, thou'dst wonder at me.

Lory. Indeed, sir, I should not.

Young Fash. How dost know?

Lory. Because, sir, I have wondered at you so often, I can wonder at you no more.   252

Young Fash. No—what wouldst thou say, if a qualm of conscience should spoil my design?

Lory. I would eat my words, and wonder more than ever.

Young Fash. Why, faith, Lory, though I am a young rakehell, and have played many a roguish trick, this is so full-grown a cheat, I find I must take pains to come up to't. I have scruples.

Lory. They are strong symptoms of death. If you find they increase, pray, sir, make your will.   260

Young Fash. No, my conscience shan't starve me neither. But thus far I will hearken to it, before I execute this project. I'll try my brother to the bottom. I'll speak to him with the temper of a philosopher. My reasons (though they press him home,) shall yet be clothed with so much modesty, not one of all the truths they urge shall be so naked to offend his sight. If he has yet so much humanity about him as to assist me, (though with a moderate aid,) I'll drop my project at his feet, and show him I can do for him much

229 muzzle] to fondle with the mouth   234 souse] pickle, food in pickle   238 buss] kiss   256 rakehell] profligate, rake

more than what I ask he'd do for me. This one conclusive trial of him I resolve to make.

> Succeed or no, still victory's my lot;
> If I subdue his heart, 'tis well; if not,
> I shall subdue my conscience to my plot.   [*Exeunt.*

The End of the First Act.

ACT II   SCENE I

Enter Loveless *and* Amanda.

Love. How do you like these lodgings, my dear? For my part I am so well pleased with 'em, I shall hardly remove whilst we stay in town, if you are satisfied.

Aman. I am satisfied with everything that pleases you; else I had not come to town at all.

Love. O, a little of the noise and bustle of the world sweetens the pleasures of retreat. We shall find the charms of our retirement doubled when we return to it.

Aman. That pleasing prospect will be my chiefest entertainment whilst (much against my will) I am obliged to stand surrounded with these empty pleasures, which 'tis so much the fashion to be fond of.   10

Love. I own most of 'em are indeed but empty—nay, so empty that one would wonder by what magic power they act, when they induce us to be vicious for their sakes. Yet some there are we may speak kindlier of. There are delights, (of which a private life is destitute) which may divert an honest man and be a harmless entertainment to a virtuous woman. The conversation of the town is one; and truly, (with some small allowances) the plays, I think, may be esteemed another.

Aman. The plays I must confess have some small charms, and would have more would they restrain that loose obscene encouragement to vice, which shocks, if not the virtue of some women, at least the modesty of all.   20

Love. But till that reformation can be made I would not leave the wholesome corn for some intruding tares that grow amongst it. Doubtless, the moral of a well-wrought scene is of prevailing force.—Last night there happened one that moved me strangely.

Aman. Pray, what was that?

Love. Why 'twas about—but 'tis not worth repeating.

Aman. Yes, pray let me know it.

Love. No, I think 'tis as well let alone.

Aman. Nay, now you make me have a mind to know.

Love. 'Twas a foolish thing. You'd perhaps grow jealous should I tell it you, though without cause, heaven knows. 31

Aman. I shall begin to think I have cause, if you persist in making it a secret.

Love. I'll then convince you, you have none, by making it no longer so. Know then, I happened in the play to find my very character, only with the addition of a relapse; which struck me so, I put a sudden stop to a most harmless entertainment, which till then diverted me between acts. 'Twas to admire the workmanship of nature in the face of a young lady that sat some distance from me, she was so exquisitely handsome.

Aman. So exquisitely handsome?

Love. Why do you repeat my words, my dear? 40

Aman. Because you seemed to speak 'em with such pleasure, I thought I might oblige you with their echo.

Love. Then you are alarmed, Amanda?

Aman. It is my duty to be so when you are in danger.

Love. You are too quick in apprehending for me. All will be well when you have heard me out. I do confess I gazed upon her,—nay, eagerly I gazed upon her.

Aman. Eagerly? That's with desire.

Love. No, I desired her not. I viewed her with a world of admiration, but not one glance of love. 50

Aman. Take heed of trusting to such nice distinctions.

Love. I did take heed. For, observing in the play that he who seemed to represent me there was by an accident like this unwarily surprised into a net, in which he lay a poor entangled slave, and brought a train of mischiefs on his head, I snatched my eyes away. They pleaded hard for leave to look again, but I grew absolute and they obeyed.

Aman. Were they the only things that were inquisitive? Had I been in your place my tongue, I fancy, had been curious too. I should have asked her name, and where she lived, (yet still without design).—Who was she, pray?

Love. Indeed I cannot tell. 60

Aman. You will not tell.

Love. By all that's sacred then, I did not ask.

Aman. Nor do you know what company was with her?

Love. I do not.

Aman. Then I am calm again.

Love. Why, were you disturbed?

Aman. Had I then no cause?

Love. None certainly.

Aman. I thought I had.

Love. But you thought wrong, Amanda. For turn the case and let it be

your story. Should you come home and tell me you had seen a handsome
man, should I grow jealous because you had eyes?   72

Aman. But should I tell you, he were exquisitely so: that I had gazed
upon him with admiration: that I had looked with eager eyes upon him—
should you not think 'twere possible I might go one step farther and enquire
his name?

Love. (*Aside.*) She has reason on her side: I have talked too much. But I
must turn it off another way. (*To* Amanda.) Will you then make no difference, Amanda, between the language of our sex and yours? There is a
modesty restrains your tongues, which makes you speak by halves when you
commend. But roving flattery gives a loose to ours, which makes us still
speak double what we think. You should not therefore in so strict a sense
take what I said to her advantage.   83

Aman. Those flights of flattery, sir, are to our faces only. When women
once are out of hearing, you are as modest in your commendations as we are.
But I shan't put you to the trouble of farther excuses; if you please this
business shall rest here. Only give me leave to wish both for your peace and
mine, that you may never meet this miracle of beauty more.

Love. I am content.

Enter Servant.

Serv. Madam, there's a young lady at the door in a chair, desires to know
whether your ladyship sees company. I think her name is Berinthia.   91

Aman. O dear! 'tis a relation I have not seen these five years. Pray her to
walk in.   [*Exit* Servant.
(*To* Loveless.) Here's another beauty for you. She was young when I saw her
last; but I hear she's grown extremely handsome.

Love. Don't you be jealous now; for I shall gaze upon her too.

Enter Berinthia.

Love. (*Aside.*) Ha! By heavens the very woman.

Ber. (*Saluting* Amanda.) Dear Amanda, I did not expect to meet with you
in town.

Aman. Sweet cousin, I'm overjoyed to see you. (*To* Loveless.) Mr. Loveless,
here's a relation and a friend of mine I desire you'll be better acquainted with.

Love. (*Saluting* Berinthia.) If my wife never desires a harder thing, madam,
her request will be easily granted.   103

Ber. (*To* Amanda.) I think, madam, I ought to wish you joy.

Aman. Joy! Upon what?

Ber. Upon your marriage. You were a widow when I saw you last.

Love. You ought rather, madam, to wish me joy upon that, since I am the
only gainer.

    s.d. *Saluting*] kissing

Ber. If she has got so good a husband as the world reports, she has gained enough to expect the compliments of her friends upon it.   110

Love. If the world is so favourable to me to allow I deserve that title, I hope 'tis so just to my wife to own I derive it from her.

Ber. Sir, it is so just to you both to own you are (and deserve to be) the happiest pair that live in it.

Love. I'm afraid we shall lose that character, madam, whenever you happen to change your condition.

Enter Servant.

Serv. Sir, my lord Foppington presents his humble service to you, and desires to know how you do. He but just now heard you were in town. He's at the next door, and if it be not inconvenient he'll come and wait upon you.

Love. Lord Foppington! I know him not.   120

Ber. Not his dignity, perhaps, but you do his person. 'Tis Sir Novelty; he has bought a barony in order to marry a great fortune. His patent has not been past eight and forty hours, and he has already sent how do ye's to all the town to make 'em acquainted with his title.

Love. Give my service to his lordship, and let him know I am proud of the honour he intends me. (*Exit* Servant.) Sure this addition of quality must have so improved his coxcomb he can't but be very good company for a quarter of an hour.

Aman. Now it moves my pity more than my mirth to see a man whom nature has made no fool, be so very industrious to pass for an ass.   130

Love. No, there you are wrong, Amanda. You should never bestow your pity upon those who take pains for your contempt. Pity those whom nature abuses, but never those who abuse nature.

Ber. Besides, the town would be robbed of one of its chief diversions, if it should become a crime to laugh at a fool.

Aman. I could never yet perceive the town inclined to part with any of its diversions for the sake of their being crimes, but I have seen it very fond of some I think had little else to recommend 'em.

Ber. I doubt, Amanda, you are grown its enemy, you speak with so much warmth against it.   140

Aman. I must confess I am not much its friend.

Ber. Then give me leave to make you mine, by not engaging in its quarrel.

Aman. You have many stronger claims than that, Berinthia, whenever you think fit to plead your title.

Love. You have done well to engage a second, my dear, for here comes one will be apt to call you to an account for your country principles.

Enter Lord Foppington.

116 change your condition] marry   121 dignity] title   127 coxcomb] conceit

Lord Fop. (*To* Loveless.) Sir, I am your most humble servant.

Love. I wish you joy, my lord.

Lord Fop. O lard, sir. . . . Madam, your ladyship's welcome to tawn.

Aman. I wish your lordship joy.   150

Lord Fop. O heavens, madam. . . .

Love. My lord, this young lady is a relation of my wife's.

Lord Fop. (*Saluting her.*) The beautifull'st race of people upon earth—rat me! Dear Loveless, I'm overjoyed to see you have brought your family to tawn again; I am, stap my vitals. . . . (*Aside.*) Far I design to lie with your wife. (*To* Amanda.) Far Gad's sake, madam, haw has your ladyship been able to subsist thus long under the fatigue of a country life?

Aman. My life has been very far from that, my lord; it has been a very quiet one.

Lord Fop. Why, that's the fatigue I speak of, madam! For 'tis impossible to be quiet, without thinking. Now thinking is to me the greatest fatigue in the world.   162

Aman. Does not your lordship love reading then?

Lord Fop. Oh, passionately, madam—but I never think of what I read.

Ber. Why, can your lordship read without thinking?

Lord Fop. O lard. . . . Can your ladyship pray without devotion . . . madam?

Aman. Well, I must own I think books the best entertainment in the world.

Lord Fop. I am so much of your ladyship's mind, madam, that I have a private gallery (where I walk sometimes) is furnished with nothing but books and looking-glasses. Madam, I have gilded 'em, and ranged 'em so prettily, before Gad, it is the most entertaining thing in the world to walk and look upon 'em.   172

Aman. Nay, I love a neat library too; but 'tis I think the inside of the book should recommend it most to us.

Lord Fop. That I must confess I am nat altogether so fand of. Far to mind the inside of a book, is to entertain oneself with the forced product of another man's brain. Naw I think a man of quality and breeding may be much better diverted with the natural sprauts of his own. But to say the truth, madam, let a man love reading never so well, when once he comes to know this tawn, he finds so many better ways of passing the four and twenty hours, that 'twere ten thousand pities he should consume his time in that. Far example, madam—my life. My life, madam, is a perpetual stream of pleasure, that glides through such a variety of entertainments, I believe the wisest of our ancestors never had the least conception of any of 'em. I rise, madam, about ten a-clock. I don't rise sooner because 'tis the worst thing in the world for the complexion. Nat that I pretend to be a beau! But a man must endeavour to look wholesome, lest he make so nauseous a figure in the side-bax the ladies should be compelled to turn their eyes upon the play. So at ten a-clack

I say, I rise. Naw if I find 'tis a good day, I resalve to take a turn in the park, and see the fine women. So huddle on my clothes and get dressed by one. If it be nasty weather, I take a turn in the chocolate hause, where, as you walk madam, you have the prettiest prospect in the world—you have looking-glasses all round you. But I'm afraid I tire the company?   193

Ber. Not at all. Pray go on.

Lord Fop. Why then, ladies, from thence I go to dinner at Lacket's, where you are so nicely and delicately served, that, stap my vitals, they shall compose you a dish no bigger than a saucer shall come to fifty shillings. Between eating my dinner, (and washing my mauth, ladies) I spend my time, till I go to the play, where till nine a-clack I entertain myself with looking upon the company, and usually dispose of one hour more in leading 'em aut. So there's twelve of the four and twenty pretty well over. The other twelve, madam, are disposed of in two articles. In the first four, I toast myself drunk, and in t'other eight, I sleep myself sober again. Thus, ladies, you see my life is an eternal raund O of delights.   204

Love. 'Tis a heavenly one, indeed.

Aman. But I thought, my lord, you beaux spent a great deal of your time in intrigues. You have given us no account of them yet.

Lord Fop. (*Aside.*) So; she would enquire into my amours—that's jealousy —she begins to be in love with me. (*To* Amanda.) Why, madam, as to time for my intrigues, I usually make detachments of it from my other pleasures, according to the exigency. Far your ladyship may please to take notice, that those who intrigue with women of quality have rarely occasion far above half an hour at a time. People of that rank being under those decorums, they can seldom give you a langer view than will just serve to shoot 'em flying. So that the course of my other pleasures is not very much interrupted by my amours.

Love. But your lordship is now become a pillar of the state. You must attend the weighty affairs of the nation.

Lord Fop. Sir . . . as to weighty affairs . . . I leave them to weighty heads. I never intend mine shall be a burthen to my body.

Love. O but you'll find the House will expect your attendance.   220

Lord Fop. Sir, you'll find the House will compound for my appearance.

Love. But your friends will take it ill if you don't attend their particular causes.

Lord Fop. Not, sir, if I come time enough to give 'em my particular vote.

Ber. But pray, my lord, how do you dispose of yourself on Sundays, for that, methinks, is a day should hang wretchedly upon your hands?

Lord Fop. Why faith, madam . . . Sunday . . . is a vile day I must confess. I intend to move for leave to bring in a bill, that the players may work upon it as well as the hackney-coaches. Though this I must say for the government,

191 chocolate hause] café selling chocolate drinks and coffee   213 decorums] rules of etiquette   220 House] House of Lords   221 compound for] excuse

it leaves us the churches to entertain us. . . . But then again, they begin so
abominable early, a man must rise by candle-light to get dressed by the psalm.

Ber. Pray which church does your lordship most oblige with your presence?

Lord Fop. Oh, Saint James's, madam. . . . There's much the best company.

Aman. Is there good preaching too?   233

Lord Fop. Why faith, madam . . . I can't tell. A man must have very little
to do there, that can give an account of the sermon.

Ber. You can give us an account of the ladies at least?

Lord Fop. Or I deserve to be excommunicated! There is my lady Tattle,
my lady Prate, my lady Titter, my lady Leer, my lady Giggle, and my lady
Grin. These sit in the front of the boxes, and all church time are the prettiest
company in the world, stap my vitals. (*To* Amanda.) Mayn't we hope for the
honour to see your ladyship added to our society, madam?

Aman. Alas, my lord, I am the worst company in the world at church. I'm
apt to mind the prayers or the sermon, or. . . .   243

Lord Fop. One is indeed strangely apt at church to mind what one should
not do. But I hope, madam, at one time or other, I shall have the honour to
lead your ladyship to your coach there. (*Aside.*) Methinks she seems strangely
pleased with everything I say to her! 'Tis a vast pleasure to receive encouragement from a woman before her husband's face! I have a good mind to pursue
my conquest and speak the thing plainly to her at once. Egad I'll do it, and
that in so cavalier a manner, she shall be surprised at it.—Ladies, I'll take my
leave. I'm afraid I begin to grow troublesome with the length of my visit.

Aman. Your lordship's too entertaining to grow troublesome anywhere.

Lord Fop. (*Aside.*) That now was as much as if she had said: 'Pray lie
with me.' I'll let her see I'm quick of apprehension. (*To* Amanda.) O lard,
madam, I had like to have forgot a secret, I must needs tell your ladyship.
(*To* Loveless.) Ned, you must not be so jealous now as to listen.   256

Love. Not I, my lord! I am too fashionable a husband to pry into the secrets
of my wife.

Lord Fop. (*To* Amanda, *squeezing her hand.*) I am in love with you to
desperation, strike me speechless.

Aman. (*Giving him a box o'th' ear.*) Then thus I return your passion! An
impudent fool!

Lord Fop. Gad's curse, madam, I'm a peer of the realm!

Love. Hey! What the devil! Do you affront my wife, sir? Nay then. . . .

They draw and fight. The women run shrieking for help.

Aman. Ah! What has my folly done? Help, murder, help! Part 'em for
heaven's sake.   266

Lord Fop. (*Falling back, and leaning upon his sword.*) Ah . . . quite through
the body . . . stap my vitals.

Enter Servants.

Love. (*Running to him.*) I hope I han't killed the fool however—Bear him
up! Where's your wound?   270

Lord Fop. Just through the guts.

Love. Call a surgeon there. Unbutton him quickly.

Lord Fop. Ay, pray make haste.

Love. This mischief you may thank yourself for.

Lord Fop. I may so. . . . Love's the devil indeed, Ned.

Enter Syringe *and* Servant.

Serv. Here's Mr. Syringe, sir, was just going by the door.

Lord Fop. He's the welcom'st man alive.

Syr. Stand by, stand by, stand by. Pray gentlemen, stand by. Lord have
mercy upon us, did you never see a man run through the body before? Pray
stand by.   280

Lord Fop. Ah Mr. Syringe—I'm a dead man.

Syr. A dead man and I by—I should laugh to see that, egad.

Love. Prithee don't stand prating, but look upon his wound.

Syr. Why, what if I won't look upon his wound this hour, sir?

Love. Why then he'll bleed to death, sir.

Syr. Why, then I'll fetch him to life again, sir.

Love. 'Slife he's run through the guts I tell thee.

Syr. Would he were run through the heart, I should get the more credit
by his cure. Now I hope you're satisfied—Come, now let me come at him—
now let me come at him. (*Viewing his wound.*) Oons, what a gash is here!
Why, sir, a man may drive a coach and six horses into your body.   291

Lord Fop. Oh!

Syr. Why, what the devil, have you run the gentleman through with a
scythe! (*Aside.*) A little prick, between the skin and the ribs, that's all.

Love. Let me see his wound.

Syr. Then you shall dress it, sir, for if anybody looks upon it, I won't.

Love. Why, thou art the veriest coxcomb I ever saw.

Syr. Sir, I am not master of my trade for nothing.

Lord Fop. Surgeon.

Syr. Well, sir.   300

Lord Fop. Is there any hopes?

Syr. Hopes? . . . I can't tell. . . . What are you willlng to give for your
cure?

Lord Fop. Five hundred paunds with pleasure.

Syr. Why then, perhaps there may be hopes. But we must avoid farther
delay. Here—help the gentleman into a chair, and carry him to my house

306 chair] sedan chair

presently, that's the properest place—(*Aside.*) to bubble him out of his money.—Come, a chair, a chair quickly! There, in with him!

[*They put him into a chair.*

Lord Fop. Dear Loveless . . . adieu! If I die . . . I forgive thee, and if I live . . . I hope thou'lt do as much by me. I'm very sorry you and I should quarrel, but I hope here's an end on't, for if you are satisfied—I am.   311

Love. I shall hardly think it worth my prosecuting any farther, so you may be at rest, sir.

Lord Fop. Thou art a generous fellow, strike me dumb. (*Aside.*) But thou hast an impertinent wife, stap my vitals.

Syr. So, carry him off, carry him off, we shall have him prate himself into a fever by and by, carry him off!   [*Exit* Syringe *with* Lord Foppington.

Aman. Now on my knees, my dear, let me ask your pardon for my indiscretion. My own I never shall obtain.

Love. Oh, there's no harm done. You served him well.   320

Aman. He did indeed deserve it. But I tremble to think how dear my indiscreet resentment might have cost you.

Love. Oh, no matter—never trouble yourself about that.

Ber. For heaven's sake, what was't he did to you?

Aman. Oh, nothing—he only squeezed me kindly by the hand, and frankly offered me a coxcomb's heart. I know I was to blame to resent it as I did, since nothing but a quarrel could ensue. But the fool so surprised me with his insolence I was not mistress of my fingers.

Ber. Now I dare swear he thinks you had 'em at great command—they obeyed you so readily.   330

Enter Worthy.

Worthy. Save you, save you, good people! I'm glad to find you all alive. I met a wounded peer carrying off. For heaven's sake, what was the matter?

Love. Oh, a trifle. He would have lain with my wife before my face, so she obliged him with a box o'th'ear, and I run him through the body. That was all.

Worthy. Bagatelle on all sides! But pray madam, how long has this noble lord been an humble servant of yours?

Aman. This is the first I have heard on't. So I suppose 'tis his quality more than his love has brought him into this adventure. He thinks his title an authentic passport to every woman's heart, below the degree of a peeress.

Worthy. He's coxcomb enough to think anything. But I would not have you brought into trouble for him. I hope there's no danger of his life?

Love. None at all. He's fallen into the hands of a roguish surgeon I perceive

307 presently] at once   307 bubble] hoodwink   337 servant] suitor

designs to frighten a little money out of him. But I saw his wound—'tis
nothing. He may go to the play tonight if he pleases.   345

Worthy. I am glad you have corrected him without farther mischief. And
now, sir, if these ladies have no farther service for you, you'll oblige me if
you can go to the place I spoke to you of t'other day.

Love. With all my heart. (*Aside.*) Though I could wish, methinks, to stay
and gaze a little longer on that creature. Good gods! how beautiful she is!—
But what have I to do with beauty? I have already had my portion, and must
not covet more. (*To* Worthy.) Come, sir, when you please.

Worthy. Ladies, your servant.

Aman. Mr. Loveless, pray one word with you before you go.

Love. (*To* Worthy.) I'll overtake you, sir—What would my dear?   355
                                                          [*Exit* Worthy.

Aman. Only a woman's foolish question. How do you like my cousin here?

Love. Jealous already, Amanda?

Aman. Not at all. I ask you for another reason.

Love. (*Aside.*) Whate'er her reason be, I must not tell her true. (*To*
Amanda.) Why, I confess she's handsome. But you must not think I slight
your kinswoman if I own to you, of all the women who may claim that
character, she is the last would triumph in my heart.

Aman. I'm satisfied.

Love. Now tell me why you asked?

Aman. At night I will. Adieu.   365

Love. (*Kissing her.*) I'm yours.   [*Exit* Loveless.

Aman. (*Aside.*) I'm glad to find he does not like her, for I have a great
mind to persuade her to come and live with me. (*To* Berinthia.) Now dear
Berinthia, let me enquire a little into your affairs. For I do assure you I am
enough your friend to interest myself in everything that concerns you.

Ber. You formerly have given me such proofs on't I should be very much
to blame to doubt it. I am sorry I have no secrets to trust you with, that I
might convince you how entire a confidence I durst repose in you.

Aman. Why, is it possible that one so young and beautiful as you should
live and have no secrets?   375

Ber. What secrets do you mean?

Aman. Lovers.

Ber. Oh, twenty—but not one secret one amongst 'em. Lovers in this age
have too much honour to do anything underhand—they do all above board.

Aman. That now methinks would make me hate a man.

Ber. But the women of the town are of another mind—for by this means a
lady may (with the expense of a few coquet glances) lead twenty fools about in
a string, for two or three years together. Whereas, if she should allow 'em

382 coquet] flirting

greater favours, and oblige 'em to secrecy, she would not keep one of 'em a fortnight.

Aman. There's something indeed in that to satisfy the vanity of a woman, but I can't comprehend how the men find their account in it.

Ber. Their entertainment I must confess is a riddle to me. For there's very few of 'em ever get farther than a bow and an ogle. I have half a score for my share, who follow me all over the town; and at the play, the park, and the church, do (with their eyes) say the violent'st things to me—but I never heard any more of 'em.   392

Aman. What can be the reason of that?

Ber. One reason is, they don't know how to go farther. They have had so little practice they don't understand the trade. But besides their ignorance, you must know there is not one of my half-score lovers but what follows half a score mistresses. Now their affections being divided amongst so many, are not strong enough for any one to make 'em pursue her to the purpose. Like a young puppy in a warren they have a flirt at all, and catch none.

Aman. Yet they seem to have a torrent of love to dispose of.   400

Ber. They have so. But 'tis like the rivers of a modern philosopher (whose works, though a woman, I have read); it sets out with a violent stream, splits in a thousand branches, and is all lost in the sands.

Aman. But do you think this river of love runs all its course without doing any mischief? Do you think it overflows nothing?

Ber. O yes, 'tis true it never breaks into anybody's ground that has the least fence about it, but it overflows all the commons that lie in its way. And this is the utmost achievement of those dreadful champions in the field of love—the beaux.

Aman. But prithee, Berinthia, instruct me a little farther, for I'm so great a novice I am almost ashamed on't. My husband's leaving me whilst I was young and fond threw me into that depth of discontent, that ever since I have led so private and recluse a life, my ignorance is scarce conceivable. I therefore fain would be instructed. Not (heaven knows) that what you call intrigues have any charms for me—my love and principles are too well fixed. The practical part of all unlawful love is. . . .   416

Ber. Oh, 'tis abominable! But for the speculative—that we must confess is entertaining! The conversation of all the virtuous women in the town turns upon that and new clothes.

Aman. Pray be so just then to me to believe 'tis with a world of innocency I would enquire, whether you think those women we call women of reputation do really 'scape all other men, as they do those shadows of 'em, the beaux.

Ber. Oh, no Amanda. There are a sort of men make dreadful work amongst

387 account] profit   399 flirt] go   421 women of reputation] respectable women

'em—men that may be called the beaux' antipathy, for they agree in nothing
but walking upon two legs.

These have brains—
The beau has none.
These are in love with their mistress—
The beau with himself.
They take care of her reputation—   430
He's industrious to destroy it.
They are decent—
He's a fop.
They are sound—
He's rotten.
They are men—
He's an ass.

Aman. If this be their character I fancy we had here e'en now a pattern of
'em both.

Ber. His lordship and Mr. Worthy?   440

Aman. The same.

Ber. As for the lord, he's eminently so! And for the other I can assure you,
there's not a man in town who has a better interest with the women that are
worth having an interest with. But 'tis all private. He's like a back-stair
minister at court, who, whilst the reputed favourites are sauntering in the
bed-chamber, is ruling the roost in the closet.

Aman. He answers then the opinion I had ever of him. Heavens! What a
difference there is between a man like him and that vain nauseous fop, sir
Novelty. (*Taking her hand.*) I must acquaint you with a secret, cousin. 'Tis
not that fool alone has talked to me of love. Worthy has been tampering too.
'Tis true, he has done't in vain. Not all his charms or art have power to shake
me. My love, my duty, and my virtue are such faithful guards, I need not
fear my heart should e'er betray me. But what I wonder at is this. I find I did
not start at his proposal as when it came from one whom I contemned. I
therefore mention his attempt, that I may learn from you whence it proceeds.
That vice (which cannot change its nature) should so far change at least its
shape, as that the self-same crime proposed from one shall seem a monster
gaping at your ruin, when from another it shall look so kind as though it
were your friend and never meant to harm you. Whence think you can this
difference proceed, for 'tis not love, heaven knows?   460

Ber. Oh no, I would not for the world believe it were. But possibly, should
there a dreadful sentence pass upon you, to undergo the rage of both their
passions; the pain you'd apprehend from one might seem so trivial to the
other; the danger would not quite so much alarm you.

446 closet] private room   454 contemned] despised

Aman. Fie, fie, Berinthia, you would indeed alarm me, could you incline me to a thought that all the merit of mankind combined could shake that tender love I bear my husband. No, he sits triumphant in my heart and nothing can dethrone him.

Ber. But should he abdicate again, do you think you should preserve the vacant throne ten tedious winters more in hopes of his return?   470

Aman. Indeed I think I should. Though I confess, after those obligations he has to me, should he abandon me once more my heart would grow extremely urgent with me to root him thence and cast him out for ever.

Ber. Were I that thing they call a slighted wife, somebody should run the risk of being that thing they call—a husband!

Aman. Oh fie, Berinthia, no revenge should ever be taken against a husband. But to wrong his bed is a vengeance which of all vengeance. . . .

Ber. Is the sweetest, ha, ha, ha! Don't I talk madly?

Aman. Madly indeed.

Ber. Yet I'm very innocent.   480

Aman. That I dare swear you are. I know how to make allowances for your humour. You were always very entertaining company, but I find since marriage and widowhood have shown you the world a little, you are very much improved.

Ber. (*Aside.*) Alack a day, there has gone more than that to improve me, if she knew all!

Aman. For heaven's sake, Berinthia, tell me what way I shall take to persuade you to come and live with me?

Ber. Why, one way in the world there is—and but one.

Aman. Pray which is that?   490

Ber. It is, to assure me—I shall be very welcome.

Aman. If that be all, you shall e'en lie here tonight.

Ber. Tonight?

Aman. Yes, tonight.

Ber. Why, the people where I lodge will think me mad.

Aman. Let 'em think what they please.

Ber. Say you so, Amanda? Why then, they shall think what they please. For I'm a young widow, and I care not what anybody thinks. Ah, Amanda, it's a delicious thing to be a young widow.

Aman. You'll hardly make me think so.   500

Ber. Pooh—because you are in love with your husband! But that is not every woman's case.

Aman. I hope 'twas yours, at least.

Ber. Mine, say ye? Now have I a great mind to tell you a lie, but I should do it so awkwardly, you'd find me out.

Aman. Then e'en speak the truth.

Ber. Shall I? Then after all I did love him, Amanda—as a nun does penance.

Aman. Why did not you refuse to marry him then?

Ber. Because my mother would have whipped me.

Aman. How did you live together?   510

Ber. Like man and wife—asunder.

   He loved the country—I the town.

   He hawks and hounds—I coaches and equipage.

   He eating and drinking—I carding and playing.

   He the sound of a horn—I the squeak of a fiddle.

   We were dull company at table—worse abed.

   Whenever we met, we gave one another the spleen,

   And never agreed but once, which was about lying alone.

Aman. But tell me one thing, truly and sincerely,

Ber. What's that?   520

Aman. Notwithstanding all these jars, did not his death at last . . . extremely trouble you?

Ber. Oh yes. Not that my present pangs were so very violent, but the after-pains were intolerable—I was forced to wear a beastly widow's band a twelve-month for't!

Aman. Women I find have different inclinations.

Ber. Women I find keep different company. When your husband ran away from you, if you had fallen into some of my acquaintance, 'twould have saved you many a tear. But you go and live with a grandmother, a bishop, and an old nurse—which was enough to make any woman break her heart for her husband. Pray, Amanda, if ever you are a widow again, keep yourself so as I do.

Aman. Why, do you then resolve you'll never marry?   532

Ber. Oh no! I resolve I will.

Aman. How so?

Ber. That I never may.

Aman. You banter me.

Ber. Indeed I don't. But I consider I'm a woman, and form my resolutions accordingly.

Aman. Well, my opinion is, form what resolutions you will, matrimony will be the end on't.   540

Ber. Faith, it won't.

Aman. How do you know?

Ber. I'm sure on't.

Aman. Why, do you think 'tis impossible for you to fall in love?

Ber. No.

Aman. Nay, but to grow so passionately fond that nothing but the man you love can give you rest?

517 spleen] ill temper   524 widow's band] collar or ruff

Ber. Well, what then?

Aman. Why, then you'll marry him.

Ber. How do you know that?   550

Aman. Why, what can you do else?

Ber. Nothing,—but sit and cry.

Aman. Pshaw!

Ber. Ah, poor Amanda. You have led a country life, but if you'll consult the widows of this town, they'll tell you—you should never take a lease of a house you can hire for a quarter's warning.   [*Exeunt.*

The End of the Second Act.

ACT III [SCENE I]

Enter Lord Foppington *and* Servant.

Lord Fop. Hey, fellow, let the coach come to the door.

Serv. Will your lordship venture so soon to expose yourself to the weather?

Lord Fop. Sir, I will venture as soon as I can, to expose myself to the ladies. Though give me my cloak however, for in that side-box, what between the air that comes in at the door on one side, and the intolerable warmth of the masks on t'other, a man gets so many heats and colds 'twould destroy the canstitution of a harse.

Serv. (*Putting on his cloak.*) I wish your lordship would please to keep house a little longer. I'm afraid your honour does not well consider your wound.

Lord Fop. My wound? I would not be in eclipse another day, though I had as many wounds in my guts as I have had in my heart.   11

Enter Young Fashion.

Young Fash. Brother, your servant. How do you find yourself today?

Lord Fop. So well, that I have ardered my coach to the door. So there's no great danger of death this baut, Tam.

Young Fash. I'm very glad of it.

Lord Fop. (*Aside.*) That I believe's a lie.—Prithee, Tam, tell me one thing. Did nat your heart cut a caper up to your mauth when you heard I was run through the bady?

Young Fash. Why do you think it should?

Lord Fop. Because I remember mine did so, when I heard my father was shat through the head.   21

Young Fash. It then did very ill.

556 warning] notice to quit   6 masks] masked women

Lord Fop. Prithee, why so?

Young Fash. Because he used you very well.

Lord Fop. Well! Naw strike me dumb, he starved me! He has let me want a thausand women for want of a thausand paund.

Young Fash. Then he hindered you from making a great many ill bargains, for I think no woman is worth money, that will take money.

Lord Fop. If I were a younger brother I should think so too.

Young Fash. Why, is it possible you can value a woman that's to be bought.

Lord Fop. Prithee, why not as well as a pad-nag?   31

Young Fash. Because a woman has a heart to dispose of—a horse has none.

Lord Fop. Look you, Tam, of all things that belang to a woman, I have an aversion to her heart. Far when once a woman has given you her heart— you can never get rid of the rest of her body.

Young Fash. This is strange doctrine! But pray, in your amours how is it with your own heart?

Lord Fop. Why, my heart in my amours . . . is like my heart aut of my amours—*à la glace*. My bady, Tam, is a watch, and my heart is the pendulum to it; whilst the finger runs raund to every hour in the circle, that still beats the same time.   41

Young Fash. Then you are seldom much in love?

Lord Fop. Never, stap my vitals.

Young Fash. Why then did you make all this bustle about Amanda?

Lord Fop. Because she was a woman of an insolent virtue, and I thought myself picked in honour to debauch her.

Young Fash. Very well. (*Aside.*) Here's a rare fellow for you, to have the spending of five thousand pounds a year. But now for my business with him. (*To* Lord Foppington.) Brother, though I know to talk to you of business (especially of money) is a theme not quite so entertaining to you as that of the ladies, my necessities are such I hope you'll have patience to hear me.

Lord Fop. The greatness of your necessities, Tam, is the worst argument in the world for your being patiently heard. I do believe you are going to make me a very good speech, but, strike me dumb, it has the worst beginning of any speech I have heard this twelve-month.

Young Fash. I'm very sorry you think so.

Lord Fop. I do believe thau art. But come, let's know thy affair quickly, far 'tis a new play and I shall be so rumpled and squeezed with pressing through the crawd, to get to my servant, the women will think I have lain all night in my clothes.   60

Young Fash. Why then (that I may not be the author of so great a mis-fortune) my case in a word is this. The necessary expenses of my travels have so much exceeded the wretched income of my annuity, that I have been

31 pad-nag] easy-paced horse   39 *à la glace*] frozen   46 picked] provoked

forced to mortgage it for five hundred pounds, which is spent. So that unless you are so kind to assist me in redeeming it, I know no remedy but to go take a purse.

Lord Fop. Why, faith Tam . . . to give you my sense of the thing, I do think taking a purse the best remedy in the world! For if you succeed, you are relieved that way. If you are taken—you are relieved t'other.

Young Fash. I'm glad to see you are in so pleasant a humour. I hope I shall find the effects on't.   71

Lord Fop. Why, do you then really think it a reasonable thing I should give you five hundred paunds?

Young Fash. I do not ask it as a due, brother. I am willing to receive it as a favour.

Lord Fop. Thau art willing to receive it anyhaw, strike me speechless! But these are damned times to give money in. Taxes are so great, repairs so exorbitant, tenants such rogues, and periwigs so dear, that the devil take me I am reduced to that extremity in my cash, I have been forced to retrench in that one article of sweet pawder, till I have braught it dawn to five guineas a manth. Naw judge, Tam, whether I can spare you five hundred paunds.

Young Fash. If you can't, I must starve, that's all. (*Aside.*) Damn him!

Lord Fop. All I can say is, you should have been a better husband.

Young Fash. Oons, if you can't live upon five thousand a year, how do you think I should do't upon two hundred?   85

Lord Fop. Don't be in a passion, Tam, far passion is the most unbecoming thing in the world—to the face. Look you, I don't love to say anything to you to make you melancholy, but upon this occasion I must take leave to put you in mind that a running horse does require more attendance than a coach-horse. Nature has made some difference 'twixt you and I.

Young Fash. Yes, she has made you older. (*Aside.*) Pox take her.

Lord Fop. That is nat all, Tam.

Young Fash. Why, what is there else?   93

Lord Fop. (*Looking first upon himself, then upon his brother.*) Ask the ladies.

Young Fash. Why, thou essence-bottle, thou musk-cat, dost thou think thou hast any advantage over me but what fortune has given thee?

Lord Fop. I do—stap my vitals.

Young Fash. Now, by all that's great and powerful, thou art the prince of coxcombs.

Lord Fop. Sir, I am praud of being at the head of so prevailing a party.

Young Fash. Will nothing then provoke thee? Draw coward!   101

Lord Fop. Look you, Tam, you know I have always taken you for a mighty

83 husband] economist   84 Oons] corruption of By God's wounds   89 running horse] race horse   95 essence-bottle] perfume bottle   95 musk-cat] animal providing perfume base; fop

dull fellow, and here is one of the foolishest plats broke out that I have seen a long time. Your paverty makes your life so burthensome to you, you would provoke me to a quarrel in hopes either to flip through my lungs into my estate, or to get yourself run through the guts to put an end to your pain. But I will disappoint you in both your designs, far with the temper of a philasapher and the discretion of a statesman,—I will go to the play with my sword in my scabbard.   [*Exit* Lord Foppington.

Young Fash. So farewell, snuff-box!—And now, conscience, I defie thee.

Enter Lory.

Lory. Sir.   III

Young Fash. Here's rare news, Lory. His lordship has given me a pill has purged off all my scruples.

Lory. Then my heart's at ease again. For I have been in a lamentable fright, sir, ever since your conscience had the impudence to intrude into your company.

Young Fash. Be at peace—it will come there no more! My brother has given it a wring by the nose, and I have kicked it downstairs. So run away to the inn, get the horses ready quickly, and bring 'em to old Coupler's without a moment's delay.

Lory. Then, sir, you are going straight about the fortune?

Young Fash. I am. Away! Fly, Lory!

Lory. The happiest day I ever saw. I'm upon the wing already.

[*Exeunt several ways.*

SCENE [II] *A Garden.*

Enter Loveless *and* Servant.

Love. Is my wife within?

Serv. No, sir, she has been gone out this half hour.

Love. 'Tis well—leave me.

Solus.

Sure fate has yet some business to be done,
Before Amanda's heart and mine must rest:
Else, why amongst those legions of her sex,
Which throng the world,
Should she pick out for her companion

103 plats] plots

The only one on earth,
Whom nature has endowed for her undoing?   10
Undoing was't, I said?—Who shall undo her?
Is not her empire fixed? Am I not hers?
Did she not rescue me, a grovelling slave?
When chained and bound by that black tyrant vice,
I laboured in his vilest drudgery,
Did she not ransom me, and set me free?
Nay more:
When by my follies sunk
To a poor tattered despicable beggar,
Did she not lift me up to envied fortune,   20
Give me herself, and all that she possest,
Without a thought of more return,
Than what a poor repenting heart might make her?
Han't she done this? And if she has,
Am I not strongly bound to love her for it?
To love her! . . . Why, do I not love her then?
By earth and heaven I do.
Nay, I have demonstration that I do:
For I would sacrifice my life to serve her.
Yet hold. . . . If laying down my life
Be demonstration of my love,   30
What is't I feel in favour of Berinthia?
For should she be in danger, methinks I could incline
To risk it for her service too; and yet I do not love her.
How then subsists my proof? . . .
Oh, I have found it out.
What I would do for one, is demonstration of my love;
And if I'd do as much for t'other:
It there is demonstration of my friendship. . . .
Ay, it must be so. I find I'm very much her friend.
Yet let me ask myself one puzzling question more.   40
Whence springs this mighty friendship all at once,
For our acquaintance is of later date?
Now friendship's said to be a plant of tedious growth, its root composed of
tender fibres, nice in their taste, cautious in spreading, checked with the least
corruption in the soil—long e'er it take, and longer still e'er it appear to do so.
Whilst mine is in a moment shot so high, and fixed so fast, it seems beyond
the power of storms to shake it. I doubt it thrives too fast. (*Musing.*)

Enter Berinthia.

Ha, she here! ... Nay, then take heed my heart, for there are dangers towards.

Ber. What makes you look so thoughtful, sir? I hope you are not ill?

Love. I was debating, madam, whether I was so or not; and that was it which made me look so thoughtful. 51

Ber. Is it then so hard a matter to decide? I thought all people had been acquainted with their own bodies, though few people know their own minds.

Love. What if the distemper I suspect be in the mind?

Ber. Why, then I'll undertake to prescribe you a cure.

Love. Alas, you undertake you know not what.

Ber. So far at least then allow me to be a physician.

Love. Nay, I'll allow you so yet farther. For I have reason to believe, should I put myself into your hands, you would increase my distemper.

Ber. Perhaps I might have reasons from the College not to be too quick in your cure; but 'tis possible I might find ways to give you often ease, sir.

Love. Were I but sure of that I'd quickly lay my case before you. 62

Ber. Whether you are sure of it or no, what risk do you run in trying?

Love. Oh, a very great one.

Ber. How?

Love. You might betray my distemper to my wife.

Ber. And so lose all my practice.

Love. Will you then keep my secret?

Ber. I will, if it don't burst me.

Love. Swear. 70

Ber. I do.

Love. By what?

Ber. By woman.

Love. That's swearing by my deity. Do it by your own, or I shan't believe you.

Ber. By man, then.

Love. I'm satisfied. Now hear my symptoms and give me your advice. The first were these:

When 'twas my chance to see you at the play,
A random glance you threw at first alarmed me; 80
I could not turn my eyes from whence the danger came:
I gazed upon you, till you shot again,
And then my fears came on me.
My heart began to pant, my limbs to tremble,
My blood grew thin, my pulse beat quick,
My eyes grew hot and dim, and all the frame of nature
Shook with apprehension.
'Tis true, some small recruits of resolution

My manhood brought to my assistance,
And by their help I made a stand a while,   90
But found at last your arrows flew so thick
They could not fail to pierce me;
So left the field,
And fled for shelter to Amanda's arms.
What think you of these symptoms, pray?

Ber. Feverish, every one of 'em. But what relief pray did your wife afford you?

Love. Why, instantly she let me blood, which for the present much assuaged my flame. But when I saw you, out it burst again, and raged with greater fury than before. Nay, since you now appear, 'tis so increased that in a moment if you do not help me, I shall, whilst you look on, consume to ashes.   [*Taking hold of her hand.*

Ber. (*Breaking from him.*) O lard, let me go. 'Tis the plague, and we shall all be infected.   104

Love. (*Catching her in his arms and kissing her.*) Then we'll die together, my charming angel.

Ber. Oh Ged—the devil's in you! Lord, let me go, here's somebody coming.

Enter Servant.

Serv. Sir, my lady's come home, and desires to speak with you. She's in her chamber.

Love. Tell her I'm coming.   [*Exit* Servant.
(*To* Berinthia.) But before I go, one glass of nectar more to drink her health.

Ber. Stand off, or I shall hate you, by heavens.   112

Love. (*Kissing her.*) In matters of love, a woman's oath is no more to be minded than a man's.

Ber. Um . . .

Enter Worthy.

Worthy. Ha! What's here? My old mistress, and so close, i'faith? I would not spoil her sport for the universe.   [*He retires.*

Ber. Oh Ged!   [*Exit* Loveless *running.*
Now do I pray to heaven, with all my heart and soul, that the devil in hell may take me, if ever . . . I was better pleased in my life. . . . This man has bewitched me, that's certain. (*Sighing.*) Well, I am condemned; but thanks to heaven I feel myself each moment more and more prepared for my execution. Nay, to that degree, I don't perceive I have the least fear of dying. No, I find, let the executioner be but a man, and there's nothing will suffer with more resolution than a woman. Well, I never had but one intrigue yet, but I confess I long to have another! Pray heaven it end as the first did though,

that we may both grow weary at a time—for 'tis a melancholy thing for lovers
to out-live one another.

Enter Worthy.

Worthy. (*Aside.*) This discovery's a lucky one. I hope to make a happy use
on't. That gentlewoman there is no fool, so I shall be able to make her
understand her interest. (*To* Berinthia.) Your servant, madam. I need not
ask how you do, you have got so good a colour.   132

Ber. No better than I used to have, I suppose?

Worthy. A little more blood in your cheeks.

Ber. The weather's hot.

Worthy. If it were not, a woman may have a colour.

Ber. What do you mean by that?

Worthy. Nothing.

Ber. Why do you smile then?

Worthy. Because the weather's hot.

Ber. You'll never leave roguing, I see that.   141

Worthy. (*Putting his finger to his nose.*) You'll never leave . . . I see that!

Ber. Well, I can't imagine what you drive at. Pray tell me what you mean?

Worthy. Do *you* tell me; it's the same thing.

Ber. I can't.

Worthy. Guess!

Ber. I shall guess wrong.

Worthy. Indeed you won't.

Ber. Pshaw! Either tell, or let it alone.

Worthy. Nay, rather than let it alone, I will tell. But first I must put you
in mind that after what has past 'twixt you and I, very few things ought to be
secrets between us.   152

Ber. Why, what secrets do we hide? I know of none.

Worthy. Yes, there are two; one I have hid from you, and t'other you
would hide from me. You are fond of Loveless, which I have discovered. And
I am fond of his wife. . . .

Ber. Which I have discovered.

Worthy. Very well, now I confess your discovery to be true. What do you
say to mine?

Ber. Why, I confess . . . I would swear 'twere false—if I thought you were
fool enough to believe me.   161

Worthy. Now am I almost in love with you again. Nay, I don't know but I
might be quite so, had I made one short campaign with Amanda. Therefore
if you find 'twould tickle your vanity to bring me down once more to your
lure, e'en help me quickly to dispatch her business, that I may have nothing
else to do but to apply myself to yours.

165 lure] enticement (falconry term)

Ber. Do you then think, sir, I am old enough to be a bawd?

Worthy. No, but I think you are wise enough to. . . .

Ber. To do what?

Worthy. To hoodwink Amanda with a gallant, that she mayn't see who is her husband's mistress. 171

Ber. (*Aside.*) He has reason. The hint's a good one.

Worthy. Well, madam, what think you on't.

Ber. I think you are so much a deeper politician in these affairs than I am, that I ought to have a very great regard to your advice.

Worthy. Then give me leave to put you in mind that the most easy, safe, and pleasant situation for your own amour is the house in which you now are —provided you keep Amanda from any sort of suspicion. That the way to do that is to engage her in an intrigue of her own, making yourself her confidant. And the way to bring her to intrigue is to make her jealous of her husband in a wrong place; which the more you foment, the less you'll be suspected. This is my scheme, in short; which if you follow as you should do, my dear Berinthia, we may all four pass the winter very pleasantly. 183

Ber. Well, I could be glad to have nobody's sins to answer for but my own. But where there is a necessity. . . .

Worthy. Right as you say, where there is a necessity, a Christian is bound to help his neighbour. So good Berinthia, lose no time, but let us begin the dance as fast as we can.

Ber. Not till the fiddles are in tune, pray sir. Your lady's strings will be very apt to fly, I can tell you that, if they are wound up too hastily. But if you'll have patience to screw 'em to their pitch by degrees, I don't doubt but she may endure to be played upon. 192

Worthy. Ay, and will make admirable music too, or I'm mistaken. But have you had no private closet discourse with her yet about males and females, and so forth, which may give you hopes in her constitution? For I know her morals are the devil against us.

Ber. I have had so much discourse with her that I believe were she once cured of her fondness to her husband, the fortress of her virtue would not be so impregnable as she fancies.

Worthy. What? She runs I'll warrant you into that common mistake of fond wives, who conclude themselves virtuous because they can refuse a man they don't like, when they have got one they do. 202

Ber. True, and therefore I think 'tis a presumptuous thing in a woman to assume the name of virtuous till she has heartily hated her husband, and been soundly in love with somebody else. Whom, if she has withstood . . . then . . . much good may it do her!

167 bawd] procuress   174 politician] schemer   195 constitution] disposition

Worthy. Well, so much for her virtue. Now, one word of her inclinations, and everyone to their post. What opinion do you find she has of me?

Ber. What you could wish—she thinks you handsome and discreet.

Worthy. Good, that's thinking half seas over. One tide more brings us into port.   211

Ber. Perhaps it may, though still remember there's a difficult bar to pass.

Worthy. I know there is, but I don't question I shall get well over it by the help of such a pilot.

Ber. You may depend upon your pilot, she'll do the best she can. So weigh anchor and be gone as soon as you please.

Worthy. I'm under sail already. Adieu.   [*Exit* Worthy.

Ber. *Bon voyage*.

Sola.

So, here's fine work. What a business have I undertaken. I'm a pretty gentlewoman truly, but there was no avoiding it. He'd have ruined me if I had refused him. Besides, faith, I begin to fancy there may be as much pleasure in carrying on another body's intrigue, as one's own. This at least is certain—it exercises almost all the entertaining faculties of a woman, for there's employment for hypocrisy, invention, deceit, flattery, mischief, and lying.

Enter Amanda, *her* Woman *following her*.

Woman. If you please, madam, only to say whether you'll have me buy 'em or not?

Aman. Yes, no, go fiddle—I care not what you do! Prithee leave me.

Woman. I have done.   [*Exit* Woman.

Ber. What in the name of Jove's the matter with you?   230

Aman. The matter Berinthia! I'm almost mad, I'm plagued to death!

Ber. Who is it that plagues you?

Aman. Who do you think should plague a wife, but her husband?

Ber. O ho, is it come to that? We shall have you wish yourself a widow by and by.

Aman. Would I were anything but what I am. A base ungrateful man, after what I have done for him, to use me thus!

Ber. What, he has been ogling now I'll warrant you?

Aman. Yes, he has been ogling.

Ber. And so you are jealous? Is that all?   240

Aman. That all! Is jealousy then nothing?

Ber. It should be nothing, if I were in your case.

Aman. Why, what would you do?

Ber. I'd cure myself.

Aman. How?

Ber. Let blood in the fond vein! Care as little for my husband as he did for me.

Aman. That would not stop his course.

Ber. Nor nothing else, when the wind's in the warm corner. Look you, Amanda, you may build castles in the air, and fume, and fret, and grow thin and lean, and pale and ugly, if you please. But I tell you, no man worth having is true to his wife, or can be true to his wife, or ever was, or ever will be so.

Aman. Do you then really think he's false to me? For I did but suspect him.   254

Ber. Think so? I know he's so!

Aman. Is it possible? Pray tell me what you know?

Ber. Don't press me then to name names, for that I have sworn I won't do.

Aman. Well I won't—but let me know all you can without perjury.

Ber. I'll let you know enough to prevent any wise woman's dying of the pip. And I hope you'll pluck up your spirits and show upon occasion you can be as good a wife as the best of 'em.

Aman. Well, what a woman can do I'll endeavour.   262

Ber. Oh, a woman can do a great deal if once she sets her mind to it. Therefore pray don't stand trifling any longer, and teasing yourself with this and that, and your love and your virtue, and I know not what—but resolve to hold up your head, get a-tiptoe, and look over 'em all. For to my certain knowledge your husband is a-pickering elsewhere.

Aman. You are sure on't?

Ber. Positively! He fell in love at the play.

Aman. Right, the very same. Do you know the ugly thing?   270

Ber. Yes, I know her well enough, but she's no such an ugly thing neither.

Aman. Is she very handsome?

Ber. Truly I think so.

Aman. Hey ho.

Ber. What do you sigh for now?

Aman. Oh my heart.

Ber. (*Aside.*) Only the pangs of nature. She's in labour of her love. Heaven send her a quick delivery—I'm sure she has a good midwife.

Aman. I'm very ill. . . . I must go to my chamber. Dear Berinthia, don't leave me a moment.   280

Ber. No, don't fear. (*Aside.*) I'll see you safe brought to bed, I'll warrant you.   [*Exeunt* Amanda, *leaning upon* Berinthia.

---

246 fond] loving   249 corner] quarter   260 pip] depression   267 a-pickering] marauding

SCENE [III] *A Country House.*

Enter Young Fashion *and* Lory.

Young Fash. So, here's our inheritance, Lory, if we can but get into possession. But methinks the seat of our family looks like Noah's ark, as if the chief part on't were designed for the fowls of the air and the beasts of the field.

Lory. Pray, sir, don't let your head run upon the orders of building here. Get but the heiress, let the devil take the house.

Young Fash. Get but the house, let the devil take the heiress, I say, at least if she be as old Coupler describes her. But come, we have no time to squander. Knock at the door. [*Lory knocks two or three times.* What the devil, have they got no ears in this house? Knock harder!   10

Lory. Egad, sir, this will prove some enchanted castle. We shall have the giant come out by and by with his club, and beat our brains out.

[*Knocks again.*

Young Fash. Hush—they come.
From within. Who is there?
Lory. Open the door and see. Is that your country breeding?
Within. Ay, but two words to a bargain. Tummas, is the blunderbuss primed?
Young Fash. Oons, give 'em good words, Lory. We shall be shot here a fortune catching.
Lory. Egad, sir, I think y'are in the right on't.—Ho, Mr. What d'ye call 'um!
Serv. (*Appears at the window with a blunderbuss.*) Weall, naw what's yare business?   22
Young Fash. Nothing, sir, but to wait upon sir Tunbelly, with your leave.
Serv. To weat upon sir Tunbelly? Why, you'll find that's just as sir Tunbelly pleases.
Young Fash. But will you do me the favour, sir, to know whether sir Tunbelly pleases or not?
Serv. Why, look you, do you see, with good words much may be done. Ralph, go thy weas, and ask sir Tunbelly if he pleases to be waited upon. And dost hear—call to nurse, that she may lock up Miss Hoyden before the geats open.   31
Young Fash. D'ye hear that Lory?
Lory. Ay, sir, I'm afraid we shall find a difficult job on't. Pray heaven that old rogue Coupler han't sent us to fetch milk out of the gunroom.
Young Fash. I'll warrant thee all will go well. See, the door opens.

34 gunroom] mess-room on ships of war, i.e., an impossible task

Enter Sir Tunbelly, *with his* Servants *armed with guns, clubs,*
pitchforks, scythes, etc.

Lory. (*Running behind his master.*) O lord, O lord, O lord—we are both
dead men!

Young Fash. Take heed, fool, thy fear will ruin us.

Lory. My fear, sir? 'Sdeath, sir, I fear nothing. (*Aside.*) Would I were
well up to the chin in a horse-pond.   40

Sir Tun. Who is it here has any business with me?

Young Fash. Sir, 'tis I, if your name be sir Tunbelly Clumsy.

Sir Tun. Sir, my name is sir Tunbelly Clumsy, whether you have any
business with me or not. So you see I am not ashamed of my name—nor my
face neither.

Young Fash. Sir, you have no cause, that I know of.

Sir Tun. Sir, if you have no cause neither, I desire to know who you are;
for till I know your name I shall not ask you to come into my house; and
when I know your name—'tis six to four I don't ask you neither.

Young Fash. (*Giving him a letter.*) Sir, I hope you'll find this letter an
authentic passport.   51

Sir Tun. God's my life, I ask your lordship's pardon ten thousand times.
(*To his* Servants.) Here, run in a-doors quickly. Get a Scotch coal fire in the
great parlour. Set all the turkey-work chairs in their places. Get the great
brass candlesticks out, and be sure stick the sockets full of laurel. Run!
(*Turning to* Young Fashion.) My lord, I ask your lordship's pardon. (*To other*
Servants.) And do you hear, run away to nurse, bid her let Miss Hoyden
loose again, and if it was not shifting-day, let her put on a clean tucker quick.
                                                    [*Exeunt* Servants *confusedly.*
(*To* Young Fashion.) I hope your honour will excuse the disorder of my
family. We are not used to receive men of your lordship's great quality every
day. Pray, where are your coaches and servants, my lord?   61

Young Fashion. Sir, that I might give you and your fair daughter a proof of
how impatient I am to be nearer akin to you, I left my equipage to follow
me and came away post, with only one servant.

Sir Tun. Your lordship does me too much honour. It was exposing your
person to too much fatigue and danger, I protest it was, but my daughter
shall endeavour to make you what amends she can. And though I say it, that
should not say it—Hoyden has charms.

Young Fashion. Sir, I am not a stranger to them, though I am to her.
Common fame has done her justice.   70

Sir Tun. My lord, I am common fame's very grateful humble servant. My

53 Scotch coal] mined in Scotland   54 turkey-work] Turkish tapestry   58 shifting-
day] clothes changing day   58 tucker] cloth covering neck and shoulders   64 post] on
horseback

lord—my girl's young, Hoyden is young, my lord; but this I must say for her, what she wants in art, she has by nature; what she wants in experience, she has in breeding; and what's wanting in her age, is made good in her constitution. So pray, my lord, walk in; pray my lord, walk in.

Young Fash. Sir, I wait upon you.   [*Exeunt.*

[*Enter*] Miss Hoyden, *sola.*

[*Hoy.*] Sure never nobody was used as I am. I know well enough what other girls do, for all they think to make a fool of me. It's well I have a husband a-coming, or i'cod I'd marry the baker, I would so. Nobody can knock at the gate, but presently I must be locked up, and here's the young greyhound bitch can run loose about the house all day long, she can, 'tis very well.

Nurse. (*Without, opening the door.*) Miss Hoyden! Miss! Miss! Miss! Miss Hoyden!   83

Enter Nurse.

Hoy. Well, what do you make such a noise for, ha? What do you din a body's ears for? Can't one be at quiet for you?

Nurse. What do I din your ears for? Here's one come will din your ears for you!

Hoy. What care I who's come? I care not a fig who comes, nor who goes, as long as I must be locked up like the ale-cellar.

Nurse. That, Miss, is for fear you should be drank before you are ripe.

Hoy. Oh, don't you trouble your head about that! I'm as ripe as you, though not so mellow.   92

Nurse. Very well! Now have I a good mind to lock you up again, and not let you see my lord tonight.

Hoy. My lord? Why, is my husband come?

Nurse. Yes, marry is he, and a goodly person too.

Hoy. (*Hugging* Nurse.) Oh, my dear nurse, forgive me this once, and I'll never misuse you again. No, if I do, you shall give me three thumps on the back, and a great pinch by the cheek.

Nurse. Ah the poor thing, see how it melts! It's as full of good nature as an egg's full of meat.   101

Hoy. But, my dear nurse, don't lie now. Is he come, by your troth?

Nurse. Yes, by my truly, is he.

Hoy. O lord! I'll go put on my laced smock, though I'm whipped till the blood run down my heels for't.   [*Exit running.*

Nurse. Eh—the lord succour thee, how thou art delighted!

[*Exit after her.*

Enter Sir Tunbelly, *and* Young Fashion.
A Servant *with wine.*

Sir Tun. My lord, I am proud of the honour to see your lordship within my doors, and I humbly crave leave to bid you welcome in a cup of sack wine.

Young Fash. Sir, to your daughter's health.   [*Drinks.*

Sir Tun. Ah poor girl, she'll be scared out of her wits on her wedding night. For, honestly speaking, she does not know a man from a woman, but by his beard and his britches.   112

Young Fash. Sir, I don't doubt but she has a virtuous education, which with the rest of her merit makes me long to see her mine. I wish you would dispense with the canonical hour, and let it be this very night.

Sir Tun. Oh, not so soon neither—that's shooting my girl before you bid her stand. No, give her fair warning. We'll sign and seal tonight, if you please, and this day seven-night—let the jade look to her quarters.

Young Fash. This day sennight? Why, what do you take me for—a ghost, sir? 'Slife, sir, I'm made of flesh and blood, and bones and sinnews, and can no more live without your daughter—(*Aside.*) than I can live a month with her!

Sir Tun. Oh, I'll warrant you, my hero, young men are hot I know, but they don't boil over at that rate, neither. Besides, my wench's wedding gown is not come home yet.   124

Young Fash. Oh, no matter sir, I'll take her in her shift. (*Aside.*) A pox of this old fellow, he'll delay the business till my damned star finds me out and discovers me. (*To* Sir Tunbelly.) Pray, sir, let it be done without ceremony— 'twill save money.

Sir Tun. Money! Save money when Hoyden's to be married? Udswoons I'll give my wench a wedding dinner, though I go to grass with the king of Assyria for't. And such a dinner it shall be as is not to be cooked in the poaching of an egg. Therefore, my noble lord, have a little patience, we'll go and look over our deeds and settlements immediately. And as for your bride, though you may be sharp set before she's quite ready, I'll engage for my girl, she stays your stomach at last.   [*Exeunt.*

The End of the Third Act.

ACT IV   SCENE I

Enter Miss Hoyden *and* Nurse.

Nurse. Well, miss, how do you like your husband that is to be?

Hoy. Oh lord, nurse, I'm so overjoyed I can scarce contain myself.

Nurse. Oh but you must have a care of being too fond, for men now-a-days hate a woman that loves 'em.

108 sack] sherry   118 quarters] haunches   129 Udswoons] God's wounds   130–31 grass with the king of Assyria] Nebuchadnezzar ate grass as punishment   135 stays] appeases

Hoy. Love him? Why do you think I love him, nurse? I'cod I would not care if he were hanged, so I were but once married to him! No, that which pleases me is to think what work I'll make when I get to London! For when I am a wife and a lady both, nurse, i'cod I'll flant it with the best of 'em.

Nurse. Look, look, if his honour be not coming again to you! Now if I were sure you would behave yourself handsomely, and not disgrace me that have brought you up, I'd leave you alone together.   11

Hoy. That's my best nurse. Do as you would be done by, trust us together this once, and if I don't show my breeding from the head to the foot of me, may I be twice married and die a maid.

Nurse. Well, this once I'll venture you, but if you disparage me. . . .

Hoy. Never fear, I'll show him my parts, I'll warrant him. [*Exit* Nurse.

Sola.

These old women are so wise when they get a poor girl in their clutches, but e'er it be long I shall know what's what as well as the best of 'em!

Enter Young Fashion.

Young Fash. Your servant, madam. I'm glad to find you alone for I have something of importance to speak to you about.   20

Hoy. Sir, (my lord, I meant,) you may speak to me about what you please, I shall give you a civil answer.

Young Fash. You give me so obliging a one, it encourages me to tell you in few words what I think both for your interest and mine. Your father, I suppose you know, has resolved to make me happy in being your husband, and I hope I may depend upon your consent to perform what he desires.

Hoy. Sir, I never disobey my father in anything, but eating of green gooseberries.

Young Fash. So good a daughter must needs make an admirable wife. I am therefore impatient till you are mine—and hope you will so far consider the violence of my love, that you won't have the cruelty to defer my happiness so long as your father designs it.   32

Hoy. Pray, my lord, how long is that?

Young Fash. Madam, a thousand year—a whole week.

Hoy. A week—why I shall be an old woman by that time.

Young Fash. And I an old man, which you'll find a greater misfortune than t'other.

Hoy. Why, I thought 'twas to be tomorrow morning, as soon as I was up. I'm sure nurse told me so.

Young Fash. And it shall be tomorrow morning still, if you'll consent?

Hoy. If I'll consent? Why, I thought I was to obey you as my husband?

8 flant] flaunt   15 disparage] bring discredit on

Young Fash. That's when we are married—'till then I am to obey you.

Hoy. Why then, if we are to take it by turns it's the same thing—I'll obey you now, and when we are married you shall obey me.   44

Young Fash. With all my heart. But I doubt we must get nurse on our side or we shall hardly prevail with the chaplain.

Hoy. No more we shan't indeed, for he loves her better than he does his pulpit, and would always be a-preaching to her by his good will.

Young Fash. Why then, my dear little bedfellow, if you'll call her hither we'll try to persuade her presently.

Hoy. Oh lord, I can tell you a way how to persuade her to anything.

Young Fash. How's that?   52

Hoy. Why, tell her she's a wholesome, comely woman—and give her half a crown.

Young Fash. Nay, if that will do, she shall have half a score of 'em.

Hoy. Oh Gemini, for half that she'd marry you herself. I'll run and call her.
                                                            [*Exit* Miss Hoyden.

Young Fash. (*Solus.*) So, matters go swimmingly! This is a rare girl, i'faith. I shall have a fine time on't with her at London. I'm much mistaken if she don't prove a March hare all the year round. What a scampering chase will she make on't when she finds the whole kennel of beaux at her tail. Hey to the park and the play and the church and the devil; she'll show 'em sport I'll warrant 'em! But no matter—she brings an estate will afford me a separate maintenance.   63

Enter Miss Hoyden *and* Nurse.

Young Fash. How do you do, good mistress nurse? I desired your young lady would give me leave to see you, that I might thank you for your extra-ordinary care and conduct in her education. Pray accept of this small acknow-ledgment for it at present, and depend upon my farther kindness when I shall be that happy thing, her husband.

Nurse. (*Aside.*) Gold, by makings, your honour's goodness is too great.—Alas, all I can boast of is I gave her pure good milk, and so your honour would have said, an you had seen how the poor thing sucked it. . . . Eh, God's blessing on the sweet face on't, how it used to hang at this poor tett, and suck and squeeze, and kick and sprawl it would, till the belly on't was so full it would drop off like a leech.   74

Hoy. (*To* Nurse, *taking her angrily aside.*) Pray one word with you! Prithee nurse, don't stand ripping up old stories, to make one ashamed before one's

56 Oh Gemini] the Twins of the Zodiac, used as interjection of surprise   59 March
hare] sexually eager (as in breeding season)   69 by makings] by mackins (an oath)
72 tett] teat   76 ripping up] opening up again

love. Do you think such a fine proper gentleman as he cares for a fiddlesome
tale of a draggle-tailed girl? If you have a mind to make him have a good
opinion of a woman, don't tell him what one did then, tell him what one can
do now! (*To* Young Fashion.) I hope your honour will excuse my mismanners
to whisper before you—it was only to give some orders about the family.

Young Fash. Oh everything, madam, is to give way to business. Besides,
good housewifry is a very commendable quality in a young lady.   83

Hoy. Pray sir, are the young ladies good housewives at London town? Do
they darn their own linen?

Young Fash. Oh no, they study how to spend money, not to save it.

Hoy. I'cod, I don't know but that may be better sport than t'other, ha,
nurse?

Young Fash. Well, you shall have your choice when you come there.

Hoy. Shall I? Then by my troth I'll get there as fast as I can. (*To* Nurse.)
His honour desires you'll be so kind as to let us be married tomorrow.

Nurse. Tomorrow, my dear madam?   92

Young Fash. Yes, tomorrow, sweet nurse . . . privately. Young folks, you
know, are impatient, and sir Tunbelly would make us stay a week for a
wedding dinner. Now all things being signed and sealed and agreed, I fancy
there could be no great harm in practising a scene or two of matrimony in
private, if it were only to give us the better assurance when we come to play
it in public.

Nurse. Nay, I must confess stolen pleasures are sweet, but if you should
be married now, what will you do when sir Tunbelly calls for you to be wed?

Hoy. Why then we'll be married again.   101

Nurse. What, twice my child?

Hoy. I'cod I don't care how often I'm married, not I.

Young Fash. Pray nurse, don't you be against your young lady's good, for
by this means she'll have the pleasure of two wedding days.

Hoy. (*To* Nurse *softly*.) And of two wedding nights too, nurse.

Nurse. Well, I'm such a tender-hearted fool, I find I can refuse nothing.
So you shall e'en follow your own inventions.

Hoy. Shall I? (*Aside.*) Oh lord, I could leap over the moon.

Young Fash. Dear nurse, this goodness of yours shan't go unrewarded.
But now you must employ your power with Mr. Bull the chaplain, that he
may do us his friendly office too, and then we shall all be happy. Do you think
you can prevail with him?   113

Nurse. Prevail with him?—or he shall never prevail with me, I can tell him
that!

Hoy. My lord, she has had him upon the hip this seven year.

77 fiddlesome] trivial   78 draggle-tailed] with untidily trailing skirts   80 mismanners]
bad manners   116 upon the hip] in her power

Young Fash. I'm glad to hear it. However, to strengthen your interest
with him, you may let him know I have several fat livings in my gift, and that
the first that falls shall be in your disposal.

Nurse. Nay, then I'll make him marry more folks than one, I'll promise
him.   121

Hoy. Faith, do nurse, make him marry you too! I'm sure he'll do't for a fat
living, for he loves eating more than he loves his bible—and I have often
heard him say, a fat living was the best meat in the world.

Nurse. Ay, and I'll make him commend the sauce too, or I'll bring his
gown to a cassock, I will so.

Young Fash. Well, nurse, whilst you go and settle matters with him, then
your lady and I will go take a walk in the garden.

Nurse. I'll do your honour's business in the catching up of a garter.

[*Exit* Nurse.

Young Fash. (*Giving her his hand.*) Come, madam, dare you venture yourself alone with me?

Hoy. Oh dear yes, sir, I don't think you'll do anything to me I need be
afraid on.   [*Exeunt.*

[SCENE II. Loveless's *Lodgings.*]

Enter Amanda *and* Berinthia.

A SONG.

I.

'*I smile at love, and all its arts,*'
   The charming Cynthia cried;
'*Take heed, for love has piercing darts,*'
   A wounded swain replied.
'*Once free and blessed as you are now,*
   I trifled with his charms,
   I pointed at his little bow,
   And sported with his arms:
'*Till urged too far, "Revenge!" he cries,*
   A fatal shaft he drew,   10
   It took its passage through your eyes,
   And to my heart it flew.'

118 livings] benefices   118 gift] i.e., his to bestow   125–6 bring his gown to a cassock]
tear his clothes off him

II.

'To tear it thence, I tried in vain,
To strive, I quickly found,
Was only to increase the pain,
And to enlarge the wound.
Ah! much too well I fear you know
What pain I'm to endure,
Since what your eyes alone could do,
Your heart alone can cure.   20
And that (grant heaven I may mistake)
I doubt is doomed to bear
A burthen for another's sake,
Who ill rewards its care.'

Aman. Well now, Berinthia, I'm at leisure to hear what 'twas you had to say to me.

Ber. What I had to say was only to echo the sighs and groans of a dying lover.

Aman. Pooh, will you never learn to talk in earnest of anything?

Ber. Why this shall be in earnest, if you please. For my part I only tell you matter of fact, you may take it which way you like best, but if you'll follow the women of the town, you'll take it both ways—for when a man offers himself to one of them, first she takes him in jest, and then she takes him in earnest.   34

Aman. I'm sure there's so much jest and earnest in what you say to me, I scarce know how to take it. But I think you have bewitched me, for I don't find it possible to be angry with you, say what you will.

Ber. I'm very glad to hear it, for I have no mind to quarrel with you, for more reasons than I'll brag of. But quarrel or not, smile or frown, I must tell you what I have suffered upon your account.

Aman. Upon my account?

Ber. Yes, upon yours. I have been forced to sit still and hear you commended for two hours together, without one compliment to myself! Now don't you think a woman had a blessed time of that?   44

Aman. Alas! I should have been unconcerned at it. I never knew where the pleasure lay of being praised by the men. But pray who was this that commended me so?

Ber. One you have a mortal aversion to—Mr. Worthy. He used you like a text. He took you all to pieces, but spoke so learnedly upon every point, one might see the spirit of the church was in him. If you are a woman, you'd have been in an ecstasy to have heard how feelingly he handled your hair, your

49 text] a biblical text expounded in detail

eyes, your nose, your mouth, your teeth, your tongue, your chin, your neck, and so forth. Thus he preached for an hour, but when he came to use an application, he observed that all these without a gallant were nothing.—Now consider of what has been said, and heaven give you grace to put it in practice.

Aman. Alas! Berinthia, did I incline to a gallant, (which you know I do not) do you think a man so nice as he could have the least concern for such a plain unpolished thing as I am? It is impossible!

Ber. Now have you a great mind to put me upon commending you.

Aman. Indeed that was not my design.   61

Ber. Nay, if it were, it's all one, for I won't do't. I'll leave that to your looking-glass. But to show you I have some good nature left, I'll commend him, and may be that may do as well.

Aman. You have a great mind to persuade me I am in love with him.

Ber. I have a great mind to persuade you, you don't know what you are in love with.

Aman. I am sure I am not in love with him, nor never shall be, so let that pass. But you were saying something you would commend him for.

Ber. Oh you'd be glad to hear a good character of him however!   70

Aman. Pshaw!

Ber. Pshaw!—Well 'tis a foolish undertaking for women in these kind of matters, to pretend to deceive one another—have not I been bred a woman as well as you?

Aman. What then?

Ber. Why then I understand my trade so well, that whenever I am told of a man I like, I cry *pshaw*! But that I may spare you the pains of putting me a second time in mind to commend him, I'll proceed and give you this account of him—that though 'tis possible he may have had women with as good faces as your ladyship's (no discredit to it neither) yet you must know your cautious behaviour, with that reserve in your humour, has given him his death's wound. He mortally hates a coquette, he says 'tis impossible to love where we cannot esteem, and that no woman can be esteemed by a man who has sense, if she makes herself cheap in the eye of a fool. That pride to a woman is as necessary as humility to a divine; and that far-fetched, and dear bought, is meat for gentlemen, as well as for ladies—in short, that every woman who has beauty may set a price upon herself, and that by under-selling the market they ruin the trade. This is his doctrine—how do you like it?

Aman. So well, that since I never intend to have a gallant for myself, if I were to recommend one to a friend, he should be the man.   90

Enter Worthy.

53-4 use an application] draw a moral

Aman. Bless me! He's here! Pray heaven he did not hear me.

Ber. If he did, it won't hurt your reputation. Your thoughts are as safe in his heart as in your own.

Worthy. I venture in at an unreasonable time of night, ladies. I hope if I'm troublesome you'll use the same freedom in turning me out again.

Aman. I believe it can't be late, for Mr. Loveless is not come home yet, and he usually keeps good hours.

Worthy. Madam, I'm afraid he'll transgress a little tonight, for he told me about half an hour ago, he was going to sup with some company he doubted would keep him out till three or four o'clock in the morning, and desired I would let my servant acquaint you with it, that you might not expect him. But my fellow's a blunder-head, so lest he should make some mistake, I thought it my duty to deliver the message myself.   103

Aman. I'm very sorry he should give you that trouble, sir, but. . . .

Ber. But since he has, will you give me leave, madam, to keep him to play at ombre with us?

Aman. Cousin, you know you command my house.

Worthy. (*To* Berinthia.) And, madam, you know you command me, though I'm a very wretched gamester.

Ber. Oh you play well enough to lose your money, and that's all the ladies require. So without any more ceremony let us go into the next room and call for the cards.   112

Aman. With all my heart.   [*Exit* Worthy, *leading* Amanda.

Ber. (*Sola.*) Well, how this business will end, heaven knows, but she seems to me to be in as fair a way—as a boy is to be a rogue, when he's put clerk to an attorney.   [*Exit* Berinthia.

SCENE [III] Berinthia's *Chamber.*

Enter Loveless *cautiously in the dark.*

Love. So, thus far all's well. I'm got into her bed-chamber, and I think nobody has perceived me steal into the house. My wife don't expect me home till four o'clock, so if Berinthia comes to bed by eleven, I shall have a chase of five hours. Let me see, where shall I hide myself? Under her bed? No—we shall have her maid searching there for something or other. . . . Her closet's a better place, and I have a master key will open it. I'll e'en in there and attack her just when she comes to her prayers—that's the most likely to prove her critical minute, for then the devil will be there to assist me.

106 ombre] card game

He opens the closet, goes in, and shuts the door after him.
Enter Berinthia *with a candle in her hand.*

Ber. Well, sure I am the best natured woman in the world. I that love cards
so well (there is but one thing upon earth I love better,) have pretended letters
to write, to give my friends a tête-à-tête. However, I'm innocent, for piquet
is the game I set 'em to—at her own peril be it if she ventures to play with
him at any other. But now what shall I do with myself? I don't know how in
the world to pass my time—would Loveless were here to *badiner* a little.
Well, he's a charming fellow . . . I don't wonder his wife's so fond of him.
What if I should sit down and think of him till I fall asleep . . . and dream of
the lord knows what? Oh but then if I should dream we were married, I
should be frightened out of my wits. (*Seeing a book.*) What's this book? I
think I had best go read. O *splenatique*! it's a sermon. Well, I'll go into my
closet, and read the *Plotting Sisters*.   20
                    [*She opens the closet, sees* Loveless, *and shrieks out.*
O lord, a ghost, a ghost, a ghost, a ghost!

Enter Loveless, *running to her.*

Love. Peace, my dear, it's no ghost! Take it in your arms, you'll find 'tis
worth a hundred of 'em.
Ber. Run in again, here's somebody coming.

Enter her Maid.

Maid. Lord, madam, what's the matter?
Ber. O heavens! I'm almost frighted out of my wits. I thought verily I
had seen a ghost, and 'twas nothing but the white curtain, with a black hood
pinned up against it. You may be gone again, I am the fearful'st fool.

Exit Maid, *re-enter* Loveless.

Love. Is the coast clear?
Ber. The coast clear! I suppose you are clear—you'd never play such a
trick as this else.   31
Love. I'm very well pleased with my trick thus far, and shall be so till I
have played it out, if it ben't your fault. Where's my wife?
Ber. At cards.
Love. With whom?
Ber. With Worthy.
Love. Then we are safe enough.
Ber. Are you so? Some husbands would be of another mind, if he were at
cards with their wives.

14 *badiner*] jest   19 O *splenatique*!] an oath   20 *Plotting Sisters*] D'Urfey's saucy
comedy, performed in 1677

Love. And they'd be in the right on't too. But I dare trust mine . . .
besides, I know he's in love in another place, and he's not one of those who
court half a dozen at a time.   42

Ber. Nay, the truth on't is, you'd pity him if you saw how uneasy he is at
being engaged with us, but 'twas my malice—I fancied he was to meet his
mistress somewhere else, so did it to have the pleasure of seeing him fret.

Love. What says Amanda to my staying abroad so late?

Ber. Why she's as much out of humour as he. I believe they wish one
another at the devil.

Love. Then I'm afraid they'll quarrel at play, and soon throw up the cards.
(*Offering to pull her into the closet.*) Therefore my dear charming angel, let
us make a good use of our time.   51

Ber. Heavens, what do you mean?

Love. Pray, what do you think I mean?

Ber. I don't know.

Love. I'll show you.

Ber. You may as well tell me.

Love. No, that would make you blush worse than t'other.

Ber. Why, do you intend to make me blush?

Love. Faith, I can't tell that, but if I do, it shall be in the dark.
                                                                   [*Pulling her.*

Ber. Oh heavens! I would not be in the dark with you for all the world.

Love. (*Puts out the candles.*) I'll try that.   61

Ber. Oh lord, are you mad! What shall I do for light?

Love. You'll do as well without it.

Ber. Why, one can't find a chair to sit down.

Love. Come into the closet, madam, there's moon-shine upon the couch.

Ber. Nay, never pull, for I will not go.

Love. Then you must be carried.   [*Carrying her.*

Ber. (*Very softly.*) Help, help, I'm ravished, ruined, undone! Oh lord, I
shall never be able to bear it.

SCENE [IV] Sir Tunbelly's *House.*

Enter Miss Hoyden, Nurse, Young Fashion *and* Bull.

Young Fash. This quick dispatch of yours, Mr. Bull, I take so kindly, it
shall give you a claim to my favour as long as I live, I do assure you.

Hoy. And to mine too, I promise you.

Bull. I most humbly thank your honours, and I hope, since it has been my
lot to join you in the holy bands of wedlock, you will so well cultivate the soil,

which I have craved a blessing on, that your children may swarm about you like bees about a honeycomb.

Hoy. I'cod with all my heart, the more the merrier I say—ha, nurse?

Enter Lory *taking his master hastily aside.*

Lory. One word with you for heaven's sake.

Young Fash. What the devil's the matter?   10

Lory. Sir, your fortune's ruined, and I don't think your life's worth a quarter of an hour's purchase! Yonder's your brother arrived with two coaches and six horses, twenty footmen and pages, a coat worth fourscore pound, and a periwig down to his knees, so judge what will become of your lady's heart.

Young Fash. Death and furies, 'tis impossible.

Lory. Fiends and spectres, sir, 'tis true.

Young Fash. Is he in the house yet?

Lory. No, they are capitulating with him at the gate. The porter tells him, he's come to run away with Miss Hoyden, and has cocked the blunderbuss at him. Your brother swears 'Gad damme, they are a parcel of clawns', and he has a good mind to break off the match. But they have given the word for sir Tunbelly, so I doubt all will come out presently. Pray sir resolve what you'll do this moment, for egad they'll maul you.   24

Young Fash. Stay a little. (*To* Miss [Hoyden].) My dear, here's a troublesome business my man tells me of, but don't be frightened, we shall be too hard for the rogue. Here's an impudent fellow at the gate (not knowing I was come hither *incognito*) has taken my name upon him in hopes to run away with you.

Hoy. Oh the brazen-faced varlet! It's well we are married, or may be we might never 'a been so.

Young Fash. (*Aside.*) Egad, like enough!—Prithee, dear doctor, run to sir Tunbelly, and stop him from going to the gate before I speak with him.

Bull. I fly, my good lord. . . .   [*Exit* Bull.

Nurse. An't please your honour, my lady and I had best lock ourselves up till the danger be over.   36

Young Fash. Ay, by all means.

Hoy. Not so fast! I won't be locked up any more. I'm married.

Young Fash. Yes, pray my dear do, till we have seized this rascal.

Hoy. Nay, if you pray me, I'll do anything.

                    [*Exeunt* Miss [Hoyden] *and* Nurse,

Young Fash. Oh, here's sir Tunbelly coming! (*To* Lory.) Hark you, sirrah, things are better than you imagine. The wedding's over.

Lory. The devil it is, sir.

19 capitulating] parleying

Young Fash. Not a word, all's safe. But sir Tunbelly don't know it, nor must not yet. So I am resolved to brazen the business out and have the pleasure of turning the impostor upon his lordship, which I believe may easily be done.

Enter Sir Tunbelly, Chaplain, *and* Servants *armed.*

Young Fash. Did you ever hear, sir, of so impudent an undertaking?
Sir Tun. Never, by the mass, but we'll tickle him I'll warrant him.
Young Fash. They tell me, sir, he has a great many people with him disguised like servants.　51
Sir Tun. Ay, ay, rogues, enough; but I'll soon raise the posse upon 'em.
Young Fash. Sir, if you'll take my advice, we'll go a shorter way to work. I find whoever this spark is, he knows nothing of my being privately here. So if you pretend to receive him civilly he'll enter without suspicion, and as soon as he is within the gate, we'll whip up the drawbridge upon his back, let fly the blunderbuss to disperse his crew, and so commit him to gaol.
Sir Tun. Egad, your lordship is an ingenious person, and a very great general. But shall we kill any of 'em or not?
Young Fash. No, no, fire over their heads only to fright 'em. I'll warrant the regiment scours when the colonel's a prisoner.　61
Sir Tun. Then come along my boys, and let your courage be great—for your danger is but small.　[*Exeunt.*

SCENE [V] *The Gate.*

Enter Lord Foppington *and* Followers.

Lord Fop. A pax of these bumkinly people, will they open the gate, or do they desire I should grow at their moat-side like a willow? (*To the* Porter.) Hey, fellow . . . prithee do me the favour, in as few words as thou canst find to express thyself, to tell me whether thy master will admit me or not, that I may turn about my coach and be gone.
Porter. Here's my master himself now at hand. He's of age—he'll give you his answer.

Enter Sir Tunbelly, *and* Servants.

Sir Tun. My most noble lord, I crave your pardon, for making your honour wait so long, but my orders to my servants have been to admit nobody, without my knowledge, for fear of some attempt upon my daughter, the times being full of plots and roguery.　11

49 tickle] beat　61 scours] runs away

Lord Fop. Much caution, I must confess, is a sign of great wisdom. But stap my vitals, I have got a cold enough to destroy a porter . . . he, hem. . . .

Sir Tun. I am very sorry for't, indeed, my lord. But if your lordship please to walk in, we'll help you to some brown sugar-candy. My lord, I'll show you the way.

Lord Fop. Sir, I follow you with pleasure.   [*Exeunt.*

As Lord Foppington's Servants *go to follow him in,
they clap the door against* La Vérole.

Servants. (*Within.*) Nay, hold you me there, sir.
La Vér. Jernie, qu'est-ce que veut dire ça?
Sir Tun. (*Within.*) Fire, porter!   20
Porter. (*Fires.*) Have among ye, my masters!
La Vér. Ah, je suis mort. . . .   [*The* Servants *all run off.*
Porter. Not one soldier left, by the mass.

SCENE [VI] *changes to the Hall.*

Enter Sir Tunbelly, *the* Chaplain *and* Servants, *with*
Lord Foppington *disarmed.*

Sir Tun. Come, bring him along, bring him along.

Lord Fop. What the pax do you mean, gentlemen! Is it fair time, that you are all drunk before dinner?

Sir Tun. Drunk, sirrah? Here's an impudent rogue for you. Drunk or sober, bully, I'm a justice of the peace, and know how to deal with strollers.

Lord Fop. Strollers!

Sir Tun. Ay, strollers. Come give an account of yourself. What's your name? Where do you live? Do you pay scot and lot? Are you a Williamite, or a Jacobite? Come.

Lord Fop. And why dost thou ask me so many impertinent questions?

Sir Tun. Because I'll make you answer 'em before I have done with you, you rascal you.   12

Lord Fop. Before Gad, all the answer I can make thee to 'em, is, that thou art a very extraordinary old fellow, stap my vitals. . . .

Sir Tun. Nay, if you are for joking with deputy lieutenants, we'st know how to deal with you. Here, draw a warrant for him immediately.

Lord Fop. A warrant! What the devil is't thou would'st be at, old gentleman?

19 *Jernie* . . . *ça?*] Gad, what does this mean?   5 strollers] vagrants   8 scot and lot] borough taxes   8 Williamite] supporter of William III   15 we'st] we shall

Sir Tun. I would be at you, sirrah, (if my hands were not tied as a magistrate) and with these two double fists beat your teeth down your throat, you dog you.

20

Lord Fop. And why would'st thou spoil my face at that rate?

Sir Tun. For your design to rob me of my daughter, villain.

Lord Fop. Rab thee of thy daughter!—Now do I begin to believe I am a-bed and asleep, and that all this is but a dream. If it be, 'twill be an agreeable surprise enough to waken by and by, and instead of the impertinent company of a nasty country justice, find myself, perhaps, in the arms of a woman of quality. (*To* Sir Tunbelly.) Prithee, old father, wilt thou give me leave to ask thee one question?

Sir Tun. I can't tell whether I will or not, till I know what it is.

Lord Fop. Why, then it is—whether thou didst not write to my lord Foppington to come down and marry thy daughter?

31

Sir Tun. Yes, marry did I. And my lord Foppington is come down, and shall marry my daughter before she's a day older.

Lord Fop. Now give me thy hand, dear dad, I thought we should understand one another at last.

Sir Tun. This fellow's mad! Here, bind him hand and foot.

[*They bind him down.*

Lord Fop. Nay, prithee, knight, leave fooling, thy jest begins to grow dull.

Sir Tun. Bind him, I say, he's mad! Bread and water, a dark room and a whip, may bring him to his senses again.

Lord Fop. (*Aside.*) Egad, if I don't waken quickly, by all I can see this is like to prove one of the most impertinent dreams that ever I dreamed in my life.

Enter Miss [Hoyden] *and* Nurse. (Miss [Hoyden] *going up to him.*)

Hoy. Is this he that would have run away with me? Faugh, how he stinks of sweets! Pray, father, let him be dragged through the horse pond.

Lord Fop. (*Aside.*) This must be my wife by her natural inclination to her husband.

45

Hoy. Pray, father, what do you intend to do with him, hang him?

Sir Tun. That, at least, my child.

Nurse. Ay, and its e'en too good for him too.

Lord Fop. (*Aside.*) *Madame la gouvernante*, I presume. Hitherto this appears to me to be one of the most extraordinary families that ever a man of quality matched into.

Sir Tun. What's become of my lord, daughter?

Hoy. He's just coming, sir.

Lord Fop. (*Aside.*) My lord? What does he mean by that, now?

Enter Young Fashion, *and* Lory.

43 sweets] perfumes   49 *gouvernante*] governess, or, chaperon

(*Seeing him.*) Stap my vitals, Tam, now the dream's out.

Young Fash. Is this the fellow, sir, that designed to trick me of your daughter?

Sir Tun. This is he, my lord; how do you like him? Is not he a pretty fellow to get a fortune?

Young Fash. I find by his dress, he thought your daughter might be taken with a beau.   61

Hoy. O gimmeni! Is this a beau? Let me see him again—ha! I find a beau's no such an ugly thing neither.

Young Fash. Egad, she'll be in love with him presently. I'll e'en have him sent away to gaol. (*To* Lord Foppington.) Sir, though your undertaking shows you are a person of no extraordinary modesty, I suppose you han't confidence enough to expect much favour from me?

Lord Fop. Strike me dumb, Tam, thou art a very impudent fellow.

Nurse. Look if the varlet has not the frontery to call his lordship plain Thomas.   70

Bull. The business is, he would feign himself mad, to avoid going to gaol.

Lord Fop. (*Aside.*) That must be the chaplain, by his unfolding of mysteries.

Sir Tun. Come, is the warrant writ?

Clerk. Yes, sir.

Sir Tun. Give me the pen, I'll sign it. . . . So. Now constable, away with him!

Lord Fop. Hold one moment! . . . Pray, gentlemen; my lord Foppington, shall I beg one word with your lordship?

Nurse. O ho, it's *my lord* with him now. See how afflictions will humble folks.   80

Hoy. Pray, my lord, don't let him whisper too close lest he bite your ear off.

Lord Fop. I am not altogether so hungry as your ladyship is pleased to imagine. (*To* Young Fashion.) Look you, Tam, I am sensible I have not been so kind to you as I ought, but I hope you'll forget what's past, and accept of the five thousand pounds I offer. Thou may'st live in extreme splendour with it, stap my vitals.

Young Fash. It's a much easier matter to prevent a disease than to cure it. A quarter of that sum would have secured your mistress; twice as much won't redeem her. (*Leaving him.*)

Sir Tun. Well, what says he?   90

Young Fash. Only the rascal offered me a bribe to let him go.

Sir Tun. Ay, he shall go, with a pox to him. Lead on, constable.

Lord Fop. One word more, and I have done.

Sir Tun. Before Gad, thou art an impudent fellow to trouble the court at this rate, after thou art condemned! But speak once for all.

62 gimmeni] variant of Gemini

Lord Fop. Why then once for all, I have at last luckily called to mind that there is a gentleman of this country, who I believe cannot live far from this place, if he were here would satisfy you I am Novelty, Baron of Foppington, with five thousand pounds a year, and that fellow there a rascal not worth a groat.   100

Sir Tun. Very well; now who is this honest gentleman you are so well acquainted with? (*To* Young Fashion.) Come, sir, we shall hamper him.

Lord Fop. 'Tis Sir John Friendly.

Sir Tun. So; he lives within half a mile, and came down into the country but last night. This bold-faced fellow thought he had been at London still, and so quoted him. Now we shall display him in his colours. I'll send for Sir John immediately. Here, fellow, away presently, and desire my neighbour he'll do me the favour to step over upon an extraordinary occasion. And in the meanwhile you had best secure this sharper in the gatehouse.

Const. An't please your worship, he may chance to give us the slip thence. If I were worthy to advise, I think the dog-kennel's a surer place.   111

Sir Tun. With all my heart, anywhere!

Lord Fop. Nay, for heaven's sake, sir, do me the favour to put me in a clean room, that I mayn't daub my clothes.

Sir Tun. Oh, when you have married my daughter, her estate will afford you new ones! Away with him.

Lord Fop. A dirty country justice . . . is a barbarous magistrate . . . stap my vitals. . . .   [*Exit* Constable *with* Lord Foppington.

Young Fash. (*Aside.*) Egad, I must prevent this knight's coming, or the house will grow soon too hot to hold me. (*To* Sir Tunbelly.) Sir, I fancy 'tis not worth while to trouble Sir John upon this impertinent fellow's desire. I'll send and call the messenger back. . . .   122

Sir Tun. Nay, with all my heart; for to be sure he thought he was far enough off, or the rogue would never have named him.

Enter Servant.

Serv. Sir, I met sir John just lighting at the gate—he's come to wait upon you.

Sir Tun. Nay, then it happens as one could wish.

Young Fash. (*Aside.*) The devil it does! Lory, you see how things are. Here will be a discovery presently, and we shall have our brains beat out; for my brother will be sure to swear he don't know me. Therefore run into the stable—take the two first horses you can light on—I'll slip out at the back door, and we'll away immediately.   132

Lory. What, and leave your lady, sir?

Young Fash. There's no danger in that, as long as I have taken possession.

109 sharper] swindler

I shall know how to treat with 'em well enough, if once I am out of their reach. Away, I'll steal after thee.

[*Exit* Lory, *his master follows him out at one door,*
as Sir John *enters at t'other.*
Enter Sir John.

Sir Tun. Sir John, you are the welcom'st man alive. I had just sent a messenger to desire you'd step over, upon a very extraordinary occasion. We are all in arms here!

Sir John. How so?   140

Sir Tun. Why, you must know . . . a finical sort of a tawdry fellow here (I don't know who the devil he is, not I) hearing, I suppose, that the match was concluded between my lord Foppington and my girl Hoyden, comes impudently to the gate, with a whole pack of rogues in liveries, and would have passed upon me for his lordship. But what does I? I comes up to him boldly at the head of his guards, takes him by the throat, strikes up his heels, binds him hand and foot, dispatches a warrant, and commits him prisoner to the dog-kennel!

Sir John. So—but how do you know but this was my lord? For I was told he set out from London the day before me, with a very fine retinue, and intended to come directly hither.   151

Sir Tun. Why now to show you how many lies people raise in that damned town—he came two nights ago post, with only one servant, and is now in the house with me. But you don't know the cream of the jest yet. This same rogue (that lies yonder neck and heels among the hounds) thinking you were out of the country, quotes you for his acquaintance, and said if you were here, you'd justify him to be lord Foppington, and I know not what.

Sir John. Pray will you let me see him?

Sir Tun. Ay, that you shall presently.—Here, fetch the prisoner.

[*Exit* Servant.

Sir John. I wish there ben't some mistake in this business. Where's my lord? I know him well.   161

Sir Tun. He was here just now. See for him, doctor; tell him sir John is here to wait upon him.   [*Exit* Chaplain.

Sir John. I hope, sir Tunbelly, the young lady is not married yet.

Sir Tun. No, things won't be ready this week. But why do you say you hope she is not married?

Sir John. Some foolish fancies only—perhaps I'm mistaken.

Re-enter Chaplain.

Bull. Sir, his lordship is just rid out to take the air.

Sir Tun. To take the air! Is that his London breeding to go take the air when gentlemen come to visit him?   170

135 treat with] negotiate terms with   141 finical] paltry

Sir John. 'Tis possible he might want it . . . he might not be well—some sudden qualm perhaps.

                Enter Constable, *etc. with* Lord Foppington.

Lord Fop. Stap my vitals, I'll have satisfaction!

Sir John. (*Running to him.*) My dear lord Foppington.

Lord Fop. Dear Friendly, thou art come in the critical minute, strike me dumb.

Sir John. Why, I little thought I should have found you in fetters.

Lord Fop. Why truly, the world must do me the justice to confess I do use to appear a little more *dégagé*. But this old gentleman, not liking the freedom of my air, has been pleased to skewer down my arms like a rabbit.

Sir Tun. Is it then possible that this should be the true lord Foppington at last?

Lord Fop. Why, what do you see in his face to make you doubt of it? Sir, without presuming to have any extraordinary opinion of my figure, give me leave to tell you, if you had seen as many lords as I have done, you would not think it impossible a person of a worse *taille* than mine might be a modern man of quality.   185

Sir Tun. Unbind him, slaves. My lord, I'm struck dumb. . . . I can only beg pardon by signs . . . but if a sacrifice will appease you, you shall have it. Here, pursue this tartar, bring him back! Away, I say, a dog-oons—I'll cut off his ears, and his tail, I'll draw out all his teeth, pull his skin over his head,—and—and what shall I do more?

Sir John. He does indeed deserve to be made an example of.

Lord Fop. He does deserve to be *châtré*, stap my vitals.

Sir Tun. May I then hope I have your honour's pardon?

Lord Fop. Sir, we courtiers do nothing without a bribe. That fair young lady might do miracles.   195

Sir Tun. Hoyden, come hither, Hoyden.

Lord Fop. Hoyden is her name, sir?

Sir Tun. Yes, my lord.

Lord Fop. The prettiest name for a song I ever heard.

Sir Tun. My lord—here's my girl—she's yours. She has a wholesome body, and a virtuous mind. She's a woman complete, both in flesh and in spirit. She has a bag of milled crowns, as scarce as they are, and fifteen hundred a year stitched fast to her tail—so go thy ways Hoyden.   203

Lord Fop. Sir, I do receive her like a gentleman.

Sir Tun. Then I'm a happy man, I bless heaven, and if your lordship will give me leave, I will like a good Christian at Christmas, be very drunk by way of thanksgiving. Come, my noble peer, I believe dinner's ready. If your honour pleases to follow me, I'll lead you on to the attack of a venison pasty.

                                                              [*Exit* Sir Tunbelly.

178 *dégagé*] free and easy   184 *taille*] figure   188 tartar] savage person   188 dog-oons] God's bones   192 *châtré*] castrated   202 milled crowns] coins

Lord Fop. Sir, I wait upon you. Will your ladyship do me the favour of your little finger, madam? 210

Hoy. My lord, I'll follow you presently—I have a little business with my nurse.

Lord Fop. Your ladyship's most humble servant. Come, sir John, the ladies have *des affaires.*   [*Exeunt* Lord Foppington *and* Sir John.

Hoy. So nurse, we are finely brought to bed! What shall we do now?

Nurse. (*Crying.*) Ah dear miss, we are all undone! Mr. Bull, you were used to help a woman to a remedy.

Bull. A-lack a day, but it's past my skill now. I can do nothing.

Nurse. Who would have thought that ever your invention should have been drained so dry. 220

Hoy. Well, I have often thought old folks fools, and now I'm sure they are so. I have found a way myself to secure us all.

Nurse. Dear lady, what's that?

Hoy. Why, if you two will be sure to hold your tongues and not say a word of what's past, I'll e'en marry this lord too.

Nurse. What! two husbands, my dear?

Hoy. Why you have had three, good nurse, you may hold your tongue.

Nurse. Ay, but not all together, sweet child.

Hoy. Pshaw, if you had, you'd ne'er ha' thought much on't.

Nurse. O but 'tis a sin, sweeting. 230

Bull. Nay that's my business to speak to, nurse. I do confess, to take two husbands for the satisfaction of the flesh is to commit the sin of exorbitancy, but to do it for the peace of the spirit is no more than to be drunk by way of physic. Besides, to prevent a parent's wrath is to avoid the sin of disobedience, for when the parent's angry the child is froward. So that upon the whole matter, I do think, though miss should marry again, she may be saved.

Hoy. I'cod and I will marry again then, and so there's an end of the story.

The End of the Fourth Act.

ACT V   SCENE [I] *London.*

Enter Coupler, Young Fashion *and* Lory.

Coup. Well, and so sir John coming in—

Young Fash. And so sir John coming in, I thought it might be manners in me to get out, which I did, and getting on horseback as fast as I could, rid

214 *des affaires*] business   235 froward] refractory

away as if the devil had been at the rear of me. What has happened since, heaven knows.

Coup. Egad sirrah, I know as well as heaven.

Young Fash. What do you know?

Coup. That you are a cuckold.

Young Fash. The devil I am! By who?

Coup. By your brother.   10

Young Fash. My brother! Which way?

Coup. The old way—he has lain with your wife.

Young Fash. Hell and furies, what dost thou mean?

Coup. I mean plainly—I speak no parable.

Young Fash. Plainly! Thou dost not speak common-sense. I cannot understand one word thou say'st.

Coup. You will do soon, youngster. In short, you left your wife a widow, and she married again.

Young Fash. It's a lie.

Coup. I'cod if I were a young fellow, I'd break your head, sirrah.

Young Fash. Dear dad, don't be angry, for I'm as mad as Tom of Bedlam.

Coup. Then I had fitted you with a wife, you should have kept her.

Young Fash. But is it possible the young strumpet could play me such a trick?   24

Coup. A young strumpet, sir . . . can play twenty tricks.

Young Fash. But prithee instruct me a little farther—whence comes thy intelligence?

Coup. From your brother in this letter. There you may read it.

Young Fash. (*Reads, pulling of his hat.*) *Dear Coupler, I have only time to tell thee in three lines, or thereabouts, that here has been the devil, that rascal Tam having stole the letter thou hadst formerly writ for me to bring to sir Tunbelly, formed a damnable design upon my mistress, and was in a fair way of success when I arrived. But after having suffered some indignities, (in which I have all daubed my embroidered coat) I put him to flight. I sent out a party of horse after him, in hopes to have made him my prisoner, which if I had done, I would have qualified him for the* seraglio, *stap my vitals. The danger I have thus narrowly 'scapt, has made me fortify myself against further attempts, by entering immediately into an association with the young lady, by which we engage to stand by one another, as long as we both shall live. In short, the papers are sealed, and the contract is signed, so the business of the lawyer is* achevé, *but I defer the divine part of the thing till I arrive at London; not being willing to consummate in any other bed but my own.—Postscript—'Tis passible I may be in tawn as soon as this letter, far I find the lady is so violently in love with me, I have determined*

21 Bedlam] hospital of St. Mary of Bethlehem, used as a lunatic asylum   36 seraglio] harem   40 achevé] completed

to make her happy with all the dispatch that is practicable, without disardering my coach-harses. So, here's rare work, i'faith.

Lory. Egad, Miss Hoyden has laid about her bravely.

Coup. I think my country girl has played her part as well as if she had been born and bred in St. James's parish.

Young Fash. That rogue the chaplain!

Lory. And then that jade the nurse, sir.   50

Young Fash. And then that drunken sot Lory, sir, that could not keep himself sober to be a witness to the marriage.

Lory. Sir—with respect—I know very few drunken sots that do keep themselves sober.

Young Fash. Hold your prating, sirrah, or I'll break your head. Dear Coupler, what's to be done?

Coup. Nothing's to be *done*—till the bride and bridegroom come to town!

Young Fash. Bride and bridegroom! Death and furies, I can't bear that thou should'st call 'em so.

Coup. Why what shall I call 'em—dog and cat?   60

Young Fash. Not for the world—that sounds more like man and wife than t'other.

Coup. Well, if you'll hear of 'em in no language, we'll leave 'em for the nurse and the chaplain.

Young Fash. The devil and the witch.

Coup. When they come to town. . . .

Lory. We shall have stormy weather.

Coup. Will you hold your tongues gentlemen, or not?

Lory. Mum.

Coup. I say when they come, we must find what stuff they are made of . . . whether the church-man be chiefly composed of the flesh, or the spirit—I presume the former. For as chaplains now go, 'tis probable he eats three pound of beef to the reading of one chapter. . . . This gives him carnal desires . . . he wants money, preferment, wine, a whore. Therefore we must invite him to supper, give him fat capons, sack and sugar, a purse of gold, and a plump sister. Let this be done and I'll warrant thee, my boy, he speaks truth like an oracle.

Young Fash. Thou art a profound statesman, I allow it, but how shall we gain the nurse?

Coup. Oh, never fear the nurse. If once you have got the priest, for the devil always rides the hag. Well, there's nothing more to be said of the matter at this time, that I know of. So let us go and enquire if there's any news of our people yet. Perhaps they may be come. But let me tell you one thing by the way, sirrah. I doubt you have been an idle fellow—if thou had'st behaved thyself as thou should'st have done, the girl would never have left thee.   [*Exeunt.*

SCENE [II] Berinthia's *Apartment*.

Enter her Maid *passing the stage, followed by* Worthy.

Worthy. Hem, Mrs. Abigail . . . is your mistress to be spoken with?
Abi. By you, sir, I believe she may.
Worthy. Why 'tis by me I would have her spoken with.
Abi. I'll acquaint her, sir.   [*Exit* Abigail.
Worthy. (*Solus.*) One lift more I must persuade her to give me, and then
I'm mounted. Well, a young bawd and a handsome one for my money—'tis
they do the execution! I'll never go to an old one but when I have occasion
for a witch. Lewdness looks heavenly to a woman, when an angel appears in
its cause; but when a hag is advocate, she thinks it comes from the devil. An
old woman has something so terrible in her looks, that whilst she is persuad-
ing your mistress to forget she has a soul, she stares hell and damnation full in
her face.   12

Enter Berinthia.

Ber. Well sir, what news bring you?
Worthy. No news, madam—there's a woman going to cuckold her hus-
band.
Ber. Amanda?
Worthy. I hope so.
Ber. Speed her well.
Worthy. Ay, but there must be more than a *God speed*, or your charity
won't be worth a farthing.   20
Ber. Why han't I done enough already?
Worthy. Not quite.
Ber. What's the matter?
Worthy. The lady has a scruple still, which you must remove.
Ber. What's that?
Worthy. Her virtue—she says.
Ber. And do you believe her?
Worthy. No, but I believe it's what she takes for her virtue—it's some relics
of lawful love. She is not yet fully satisfied her husband has got another
mistress, which unless I can convince her of, I have opened the trenches in
vain—for the breach must be wider before I dare storm the town.   31
Ber. And so I'm to be your engineer?
Worthy. I'm sure you know best how to manage the battery.
Ber. What think you of springing a mine? I have a thought just now come
into my head, how to blow her up at once.
Worthy. That would be a thought indeed.

Ber. Faith, I'll do't, and thus the execution of it shall be—we are all invited to my lord Foppington's tonight to supper. He's come to town with his bride and makes a ball with an entertainment of music. Now you must know, my undoer here, Loveless, says he must needs meet me about some private business (I don't know what 'tis) before we go to the company. To which end he has told his wife one lie, and I have told her another. But to make her amends, I'll go immediately and tell her a solemn truth.   43

Worthy. What's that?

Ber. Why, I'll tell her that to my certain knowledge her husband has a rendez-vous with his mistress this afternoon, and that if she'll give me her word she'll be satisfied with the discovery without making any violent enquiry after the woman, I'll direct her to a place where she shall see 'em meet. Now, friend, this I fancy may help you to a critical minute. For home she must go again to dress. You (with your good breeding) come to wait upon us to the ball. Find her all alone,—her spirit enflamed against her husband for his treason—and her flesh in a heat from some contemplations upon the treachery—her blood on a fire—her conscience in ice—a lover to draw, and the devil to drive—Ah poor Amanda!   54

Worthy. (*Kneeling.*) Thou angel of light, let me fall down and adore thee?

Ber. Thou minister of darkness, get up again, for I hate to see the devil at his devotions.

Worthy. Well, my incomparable Berinthia—how shall I requite you?

Ber. Oh, ne'er trouble yourself about that. Virtue is its own reward. There's a pleasure in doing good which sufficiently pays itself. Adieu.

Worthy. Farewell, thou best of women.   [*Exeunt several ways.*

Enter Amanda, *meeting* Berinthia.

Aman. Who was that went from you?

Ber. A friend of yours.

Aman. What does he want?

Ber. Something you might spare him, and be ne'er the poorer.

Aman. I can spare him nothing but my friendship. My love already's all disposed of,—though I confess to one ungrateful to my bounty.

Ber. Why there's the mystery. You have been so bountiful, you have cloyed him. Fond wives do by their husbands as barren wives do by their lap-dogs—cram 'em with sweet-meats till they spoil their stomachs.   70

Aman. Alas! Had you but seen how passionately fond he has been since our last reconciliation! You would have thought it were impossible he ever should have breathed an hour without me.

Ber. Ay, but there you thought wrong again Amanda. You should consider that in matters of love men's eyes are always bigger than their bellies. They have violent appetites, 'tis true—but they have soon dined.

Aman. Well, there's nothing upon earth astonishes me more, than men's inconstancy.

Ber. Now there's nothing upon earth that astonishes me less when I consider what they and we are composed of. For nature has made them children and us babies. Now, Amanda, how we used our babies you may remember. We were mad to have 'em as soon as we saw 'em—kissed 'em to pieces as soon as we got 'em. Then pulled off their clothes, saw 'em naked, and so threw 'em away. 84

Aman. But do you think all men are of this temper?

Ber. All but one.

Aman. Who is that?

Ber. Worthy.

Aman. Why, he's weary of his wife too, you see.

Ber. Ay, that's no proof.

Aman. What can be a greater?

Ber. Being weary of his mistress.

Aman. Don't you think 'twere possible he might give you that too?

Ber. Perhaps he might, if he were my gallant; not if he were yours.

Aman. Why do you think he should be more constant to me than he would to you? I'm sure I'm not so handsome. 96

Ber. Kissing goes by favour; he likes you best.

Aman. Suppose he does? That's no demonstration he would be constant to me.

Ber. No, that I'll grant you. But there are other reasons to expect it. For you must know after all, Amanda, the inconstancy we commonly see in men of brains, does not so much proceed from the uncertainty of their temper, as from the misfortunes of their love. A man sees perhaps a hundred women he likes well enough for an intrigue, and away. But possibly, through the whole course of his life, he does not find above one who is exactly what he could wish her. Now her, 'tis a thousand to one, he never gets. Either she is not to be had at all, (though that seldom happens you'll say) or he wants those opportunities that are necessary to gain her. Either she likes somebody else much better than him, or uses him like a dog because he likes nobody so well as her. Still something or other fate claps in the way between them and the woman they are capable of being fond of. And this makes them wander about, from mistress to mistress, like a pilgrim from town to town, who every night must have a fresh lodging, and's in haste to be gone in the morning.

Aman. 'Tis possible there may be something in what you say, but what do you infer from it as to the man we were talking of? 115

Ber. Why, I infer, that you being the woman in the world the most to his humour, 'tis not likely he would quit you for one that is less.

Aman. That is not to be depended upon, for you see Mr. Loveless does so.

Ber. What does Mr. Loveless do?

Aman. Why, he runs after something for variety, I'm sure he does not like
so well as he does me.   121

Ber. That's more than you know, madam.

Aman. No, I'm sure on't. I'm not very vain, Berinthia, and yet I'd lay my
life, if I could look into his heart, he thinks I deserve to be preferred to a
thousand of her.

Ber. Don't be too positive in that neither. A million to one but she has the
same opinion of you. What would you give to see her?

Aman. Hang her, dirty trull! Though I really believe she's so ugly she'd
cure me of my jealousy.

Ber. All the men of sense about town say she's handsome.   130

Aman. They are as often out in those things as any people.

Ber. Then I'll give you farther proof—all the women about town say she's a
fool. Now I hope you're convinced?

Aman. Whate'er she be, I'm satisfied he does not like her well enough to
bestow anything more than a little outward gallantry upon her.

Ber. Outward gallantry? (*Aside.*) I can't bear this. (*To* Amanda.) Don't
you think she's a woman to be fobbed off so. Come, I'm too much your
friend to suffer you should be thus grossly imposed upon by a man who does
not deserve the least part about you, unless he knew how to set a greater
value upon it. Therefore in one word, to my certain knowledge, he is to meet
her—now, within a quarter of an hour, somewhere about that Babylon of
wickedness, Whitehall. And if you'll give me your word that you'll be content
with seeing her masked in his hand, without pulling her headclothes off, I'll
step immediately to the person, from whom I have my intelligence, and send
you word whereabouts you may stand to see 'em meet. My friend and I'll
watch 'em from another place, and dodge 'em to their private lodging. But
don't you offer to follow 'em, lest you do it awkwardly, and spoil all. I'll
come home to you again, as soon as I have earth'd 'em, and give you an account
in what corner of the house the scene of their lewdness lies.

Aman. If you can do this, Berinthia, he's a villain.   150

Ber. I can't help that, men will be so.

Aman. Well! I'll follow your directions, for I shall never rest till I know the
worst of this matter.

Ber. Pray, go immediately, and get yourself ready then. Put on some of
your woman's clothes, a great scarf and a mask, and you shall presently
receive orders. (*Calls within.*) Here, who's there? Get me a chair quickly.

Serv. There are chairs at the door, madam.

Ber. 'Tis well; I'm coming.

Aman. But pray, Berinthia, before you go—tell me how I may know this

128 trull] whore   148 earth] run to earth

filthy thing if she should be so forward (as I suppose she will) to come to the rendezvous first, for methinks I would fain view her a little. 161

Ber. Why she's about my height, and very well shaped.

Aman. I thought she had been a little crooked. . . .

Ber. Oh no, she's as straight as I am. But we lose time, come away.

[*Exeunt.*

[SCENE III Fashion's *Lodgings*.]

Enter Young Fashion, *meeting* Lory.

Young Fash. Well, will the doctor come?

Lory. Sir, I sent a porter to him as you ordered me. He found him with a pipe of tobacco and a great tankard of ale, which he said he would dispatch while I could tell three and be here.

Young Fash. He does not suspect 'twas I that sent for him?

Lory. Not a jot sir. He divines as little for himself as he does for other folks.

Young Fash. Will he bring nurse with him?

Lory. Yes.

Young Fash. That's well. Where's Coupler?

Lory. He's half-way up the stairs taking breath. He must play his bellows a little before he can get to the top. 11

Enter Coupler.

Young Fash. Oh, here he is. Well, old Phthisic? The doctor's coming.

Coup. Would the pox had the doctor—I'm quite out of wind. (*To Lory.*) Set me a chair, sirrah. Ah—(*Sits down. To* Young Fashion.) Why the plague can'st not thou lodge upon the ground floor.

Young Fash. Because I love to lie as near heaven as I can.

Coup. Prithee let heaven alone; ne'er affect tending that way. Thy centre's downwards.

Young Fash. That's impossible. I have too much ill luck in this world, to be damned in the next. 20

Coup. Thou art out in thy logic. Thy major is true, but thy minor is false, for thou art the luckiest fellow in the universe.

Young Fash. Make out that.

Coup. I'll do't. Last night the devil ran away with the parson of fat-goose living.

Young Fash. If he had run away with the parish too, what's that to me?

12 Phthisic] consumptive   21 major; minor] terms of a syllogism   24–25 fat-goose living] a rich benefice

Coup. I'll tell thee what it's to thee. This living is worth five hundred pound a year, and the presentation of it is thine, if thou can'st prove thyself a lawful husband to Miss Hoyden.

Young Fash. Say'st thou so, my protector? Then egad I shall have a brace of evidence here presently.   31

Coup. The nurse and the doctor?

Young Fash. The same. The devil himself won't have interest enough to make 'em withstand it.

Coup. That we shall see presently. Here they come.

Enter Nurse *and* Chaplain: *they start back, seeing* Young Fashion.

Nurse. Ah goodness, Roger, we are betrayed!

Young Fash. (*Laying hold on 'em.*) Nay, nay, ne'er flinch for the matter, for I have you safe. Come, to your trials immediately. I have no time to give you copies of your indictment. There sits your judge.

Both. (*Kneeling.*) Pray, sir, have compassion on us.   40

Nurse. I hope, sir, my years will move your pity. I am an aged woman.

Coup. That is a moving argument indeed.

Bull. I hope, sir, my character will be considered. I am heaven's ambassador.

Coup. (*To* Bull.) Are not you a rogue of sanctity?

Bull. Sir, with respect to my function, I do wear a gown.

Coup. Did you not marry this vigorous young fellow to a plump young buxom wench?

Nurse. (*To* Bull.) Don't confess, Roger, unless you are hard put to it indeed.

Coup. Come, out with't! Now is he chewing the cud of his roguery, and grinding a lie between his teeth.   50

Bull. Sir ... I cannot positively say ... I say, sir ... positively I cannot say. ...

Coup. Come, no equivocations—no Roman turns upon us. Consider thou standest upon Protestant ground, which will slip from under thee, like a Tyburn cart, for in this country we have always ten hangmen for one jesuit.

Bull. (*To* Young Fashion.) Pray, sir, then will you but permit me to speak one word in private with nurse.

Young Fash. Thou art always for doing something in private with nurse.

Coup. But pray let his betters be served before him for once. I would do something in private with her myself. Lory, take care of this reverend gown-man in the next room a little. Retire priest.   [*Exit* Lory *with* Bull.

Now, virgin, I must put the matter home to you a little. Do you think it might not be possible to make you speak truth?

Nurse. Alas! sir, I don't know what you mean by truth.

53 Roman turns] Roman Catholic casuistry   55 Tyburn cart] from which a condemned man was hanged at Tyburn

Coup. Nay, 'tis possible thou may'st be a stranger to it.

Young Fash. Come, nurse, you and I were better friends when we saw one another last, and I still believe you are a very good woman in the bottom. I did deceive you and your young lady, 'tis true, but I always designed to make a very good husband to her, and to be a very good friend to you. And 'tis possible in the end she might have found herself happier, and you richer, than ever my brother will make you.   71

Nurse. Brother! Why, is your worship then his lordship's brother?

Young Fash. I am—which you should have known, if I durst have stayed to have told you; but I was forced to take horse a little in haste you know.

Nurse. You were indeed, sir—poor young man, how he was bound to scour for't. Now won't your worship be angry, if I confess the truth to you? When I found you were a cheat (with respect be it spoken) I verily believed miss had got some pitiful skip-jack varlet or other to her husband, or I had ne'er let her think of marrying again.

Coup. But where was your conscience all this while, woman? Did not that stare in your face, with huge saucer eyes and a great horn upon the forehead? Did not you think you should be damned for such a sin? Ha?   82

Young Fash. Well said, divinity, pass that home upon her.

Nurse. Why, in good truly sir, I had some fearful thoughts on't, and could never be brought to consent, till Mr. Bull said it was a peccadilla, and he'd secure my soul, for a tithe pig.

Young Fash. There was a rogue for you.

Coup. And he shall thrive accordingly—he shall have a good living! Come, honest nurse, I see you have butter in your compound—you can melt. Some compassion you can have of this handsome young fellow.   90

Nurse. I have indeed, sir.

Young Fash. Why then, I'll tell you what you shall do for me. You know what a warm living here is fallen, and that it must be in the disposal of him who has the disposal of miss. Now if you and the doctor will agree to prove my marriage, I'll present him to it, upon condition he makes you his bride.

Nurse. Naw the blessing of the lord follow your good worship both by night and by day. Let him be fetched in by the ears! I'll soon bring his nose to the grindstone.

Coup. (*Aside.*) Well said, old whiteleather. Hey! Bring in the prisoner there.

Enter Lory *with* Bull.

Coup. Come, advance holy man. Here's your duck—does not think fit to retire with you into the chancel at this time, but she has a proposal to make to

---

78 skip-jack] a jumping toy   81 with huge saucer eyes ... forehead] a hobgoblin
83 pass that home upon her] drive it home to her   85 peccadilla] peccadillo, trifling
offence   99 whiteleather] tough, white-coloured leather

you in the face of the congregation. Come, nurse, speak for yourself—you are
of age.   103

Nurse. Roger, are not you a wicked man, Roger, to set your strength against
a weak woman, and persuade her it was no sin to conceal miss's nuptials?
My conscience flies in my face for it, thou priest of Baal, and I find by woeful
experience thy absolution is not worth an old cassock. Therefore I am resolved
to confess the truth to the whole world, though I die a beggar for it. But his
worship overflows with his mercy and his bounty. He is not only pleased to
forgive us our sins, but designs thou sha't squat thee down in fat-goose
living, and which is more than all, has prevailed with me to become the wife of
thy bosom.   112

Young Fash. All this I intend for you, doctor. What you are to do for me,
I need not tell you.

Bull. Your worship's goodness is unspeakable. Yet there is one thing seems
a point of conscience—and conscience is a tender babe. If I should bind
myself, for the sake of this living, to marry nurse and maintain her afterwards,
I doubt it might be looked on as a kind of simony.

Coup. (*Rising up.*) If it were sacrilege, the living's worth it! Therefore no
more words, good doctor. But with the parish—here—take the parsonage
house. (*Giving* Nurse *to him.*) 'Tis true, 'tis a little out of repair; some
dilapidations there are to be made good; the windows are broke, the wainscot
is warped; the ceilings are peeled, and the walls are cracked; but a little
glazing, painting, whitewash, and plaster will make it last thy time.   124

Bull. Well, sir, if it must be so, I shan't contend. What providence orders,
I submit to.

Nurse. And so do I, with all humility.

Coup. Why, that now was spoke like good people. Come my turtle doves,
let us go help this poor pigeon to his wandering mate again, and after institu-
tion and induction you shall all go a-cooing together.   [*Exeunt.*

[SCENE IV. Loveless's *Lodgings*.]

Enter Amanda *in a scarf, etc. as just returned,* her Woman *following her.*

Aman. Prithee, what care I who has been here.

Woman. Madam, 'twas my lady Bridle and my lady Tiptoe.

Aman. My lady Fiddle and my lady Faddle! What, dost stand troubling

---

106 Baal] a false god   118 simony] buying or selling of ecclesiastical preferment
129–30 institution] establishment in cure of souls   130 induction] formal introduction
into possession (of a benefice etc.)

me with the visits of a parcel of impertinent women? When they are well
seamed with the small-pox, they won't be so fond of showing their faces—
there are more coquettes about this town.

Woman. Madam, I suppose they only came to return your ladyship's
visit, according to the custom of the world.

Aman. Would the world were on fire, and you in the middle on't. Be gone;
leave me.   [*Exit* Woman.

Amanda, sola.

At last I am convinced. My eyes are testimonies of his falsehood.
The base, ungrateful, perjured villain. . . .
Good gods . . . what slippery stuff are men composed of?
Sure, the account of their creation's false,
And 'twas the woman's rib that they were formed of!
But why am I thus angry?
This poor relapse should only move my scorn. . . .
'Tis true. . . . The roving flights of his unfinished youth
Had strong excuse from the plea of nature;
Reason had thrown the reins loose on his neck,   20
And slipped him to unlimited desire.
If therefore he went wrong,
He had a claim to my forgiveness, and I did him right.
But since the years of manhood rein him in,
And reason well digested into thought,
Has pointed out the course he ought to run—
If now he strays? . . .
'Twould be as weak and mean in me to pardon,
As it has been in him t'offend.
But hold—   30
'Tis an ill cause indeed, where nothing's to be said for't.
My beauty possibly is in the wane;
Perhaps sixteen has greater charms for him:
Yes, there's the secret.
But let him know,
My quiver's not entirely emptied yet—
I still have darts, and I can shoot 'em too;
They're not so blunt, but they can enter still;
The want's not in my power, but in my will.
Virtue's his friend, or through another's heart   40
I could find the way to make his smart.

Going off she meets Worthy.

Ha! he here? Protect me heaven, for this looks ominous.

Worthy. You seem disordered, madam. I hope there's no misfortune happened to you?

Aman. None that will long disorder me, I hope.

Worthy. Whate'er it be disturbs you, I would to heaven 'twere in my power to bear the pain, till I were able to remove the cause.

Aman. I hope e're long it will remove itself. At least, I have given it warning to be gone.

Worthy. Would I durst ask, where 'tis the thorn torments you? Forgive me, if I grow inquisitive—'tis only with desire to give you ease.   51

Aman. Alas! 'tis in a tender part. It can't be drawn, without a world of pain. Yet out it must, for it begins to fester in my heart.

Worthy. If 'tis the sting of unrequited love, remove it instantly. I have a balm will quickly heal the wound.

Aman. You'll find the undertaking difficult. The surgeon who already has attempted it, has much tormented me.

Worthy. I'll aid him with a gentler hand—if you will give me leave.

Aman. How soft soe'er the hand may be, there still is terror in the operation.   60

Worthy. Some few preparatives would make it easy, could I persuade you to apply 'em. Make home reflections, madam, on your slighted love. Weigh well the strength and beauty of your charms. Rouse up that spirit women ought to bear, and slight your god, if he neglects his angel. With arms of ice receive his cold embraces, and keep your fire for those who come in flames! Behold a burning lover at your feet, his fever raging in his veins. See how he trembles, how he pants! See how he glows, how he consumes! Extend the arms of mercy to his aid—his zeal may give him title to your pity, although his merit cannot claim your love.

Aman. Of all my feeble sex, sure I must be the weakest should I again presume to think on love. (*Sighing.*) Alas! my heart has been too roughly treated.

Worthy. 'Twill find the greater bliss in softer usage.   72

Aman. But where's that usage to be found?

Worthy. 'Tis here, within this faithful breast, which if you doubt I'll rip it up before your eyes, lay all its secrets open to your view, and then you'll see 'twas sound.

Aman. With just such honest words as these the worst of men deceived me.

Worthy. He therefore merits all revenge can do. His fault is such the extent and stretch of vengeance cannot reach it. Oh make me but your instrument of justice—you'll find me execute it with such zeal, as shall convince you I abhor the crime.   82

Aman. The rigour of an executioner has more the face of cruelty than

62 home] about yourself

justice. And he who puts the cord about the wretch's neck is seldom known
to exceed him in his morals.

Worthy. What proof then can I give you of my truth?

Aman. There is on earth but one.

Worthy. And is that in my power?

Aman. It is—and one that would so thoroughly convince me, I should be
apt to rate your heart so high I possibly might purchase't with a part of mine.

Worthy. Then heaven thou art my friend, and I am blessed . . . for if 'tis
in my power, my will I'm sure will reach it. No matter what the terms may be,
when such a recompense is offered! Oh tell me quickly what this proof must
be. What is it will convince you of my love?   94

Aman. I shall believe you love me as you ought, if from this moment you
forbear to ask whatever is unfit for me to grant. You pause upon it, sir. I
doubt, on such hard terms, a woman's heart is scarcely worth the having.

Worthy. A heart like yours on any terms is worth it—'twas not on that I
paused. (*Drawing nearer to her.*) But I was thinking whether some things
there may not be, which women cannot grant without a blush and yet which
men may take without offence. (*Taking her hand.*) Your hand, I fancy, may be
of the number. Oh pardon me, if I commit a rape upon it, and thus devour
it with my kisses. (*Kissing it eagerly.*)   103

Aman. Oh heavens! let me go.

Worthy. Never whilst I have strength to hold you here! (*Forcing her to sit
down on a couch.*) My life, my soul, my goddess—Oh forgive me!

Aman. Oh whither am I going? Help, heaven, or I am lost!

Worthy. Stand neuter, gods, this once I do invoke you.

Aman. Then save me, virtue, and the glory's thine.

Worthy. Nay, never strive.

Aman. I will—and conquer too. My forces rally bravely to my aid, and thus
I gain the day.   [*Breaking from him.*

Worthy. Then mine as bravely double their attack! (*Seizing her again.*)
And thus I wrest it from you! Nay struggle not, for all's in vain. Or death or
victory—I am determined.   115

Aman. And so am I. (*Rushing from him.*) Now keep your distance, or we part
for ever.

Worthy. (*Offering again.*) For heaven's sake—

Aman. (*Going.*) Nay, then farewell.

Worthy. (*Kneeling and holding by her clothes.*) Oh stay, and see the magic
force of love. Behold this raging lion at your feet, struck dead with fear and
tame as charms can make him. What must I do to be forgiven by you?

Aman. Repent, and never more offend.   123

Worthy. Repentance for past crimes is just and easy. But *sin no more*'s a
task too hard for mortals.

Aman. Yet those who hope for heaven must use their best endeavours to perform it.

Worthy. Endeavours we may use, but flesh and blood are got in t'other scale, and they are ponderous things.

Aman. Whate'er they are, there is a weight in resolution sufficient for their balance. The soul, I do confess, is usually so careless of its charge, so soft, and so indulgent to desire, it leaves the reins in the wild hand of nature, who like a Phaeton drives the fiery chariot and sets the world on flame. Yet still the sovereignty is in the mind, whene'er it pleases to exert its force. Perhaps you may not think it worth your while to take such mighty pains for my esteem, but that I leave to you.   136

> You see the price I set upon my heart;
> Perhaps 'tis dear: but spite of all your art,
> You'll find on cheaper terms we ne'er shall part.

[*Exit* Amanda.

Worthy. (*Solus.*) Sure there's divinity about her, and sh'has dispensed some portion on't to me. For what but now was the wild flame of love, or (to dissect that specious term) the vile, the gross desires of flesh and blood, is in a moment turned to adoration. The coarser appetite of nature's gone, and 'tis methinks the food of angels I require. How long this influence may last, heaven knows. But in this moment of my purity, I could on her own terms accept her heart. Yes, lovely woman, I can accept it. For now 'tis doubly worth my care. Your charms are much increased, since thus adorned. When truth's extorted from us then we own the robe of virtue is a graceful habit.

> Could women but our secret counsels scan,
> Could they but reach the deep reserves of man,   150
> They'd wear it on, that that of love might last,
> For when they throw off one, we soon the other cast.
> Their sympathy is such—
> The fate of one, the other scarce can fly—
> They live together, and together die.

[*Exit.*

[SCENE V. *A room in* Lord Foppington's *house.*]

Enter Miss [Hoyden] *and* Nurse.

Hoy. But is it sure and certain, say you, he's my lord's own brother?

Nurse. As sure as he's your lawful husband.

Hoy. I'cod if I had known that in time, I don't know but I might have kept

133 Phaeton] son of Phoebus (the sun), nearly set the earth on fire by driving his father's sun-chariot too near to it, and was struck down by Zeus.

him—for between you and I nurse, he'd have made a husband worth two of this I have. But which do you think you should fancy most, nurse?

Nurse. Why truly, in my poor fancy, madam, your first husband is the prettier gentleman.

Hoy. I don't like my lord's shapes, nurse.

Nurse. Why in good truly, as a body may say, he is but a slam.

Hoy. What do you think now he puts me in mind of? Don't you remember, a long, loose, shambling sort of a horse my father called Washy?   11

Nurse. As like as two twin brothers!

Hoy. I'cod, I have thought so a hundred times. Faith, I'm tired of him.

Nurse. Indeed, madam, I think you had e'en as good stand to your first bargain.

Hoy. Oh but nurse, we han't considered the main thing yet. If I leave *my lord*, I must leave *my lady* too; and when I rattle about the streets in my coach, they'll only say, *there goes mistress ... mistress ...* mistress what? What's this man's name, I have married, nurse?

Nurse. Squire Fashion.   20

Hoy. Squire Fashion is it? Well, squire, that's better than nothing. Do you think one could not get him made a knight, nurse?

Nurse. I don't know but one might, madam, when the king's in a good humour.

Hoy. I'cod, that would do rarely. For then he'd be as good a man as my father, you know?

Nurse. Birlady, and that's as good as the best of 'em.

Hoy. So 'tis, faith, for then I shall be *my lady*, and *your ladyship* at every word, and that's all I have to care for. Ha, nurse, but hark you me; one thing more, and then I have done. I'm afraid, if I change my husband again, I shan't have so much money to throw about, nurse?   31

Nurse. Oh, enough's as good as a feast! Besides, madam, one don't know, but as much may fall to your share with the younger brother as with the elder. For though these lords have a power of wealth indeed, yet, as I have heard say, they give it all to their sluts and their trulls, who joggle it about in their coaches, with a murrain to 'em, whilst poor madam sits sighing and wishing, and knotting and crying, and has not a spare half crown to buy her a *Practice of Piety*.

Hoy. Oh, but for that, don't deceive yourself, nurse. For this I must say for my lord, and a—for him. (*Snapping her fingers.*) He's as free as an open house at Christmas. For this very morning he told me I should have two hundred a

---

9 slam] ill-shaped person   27 Birlady] By our Lady   35 joggle] shake   36 murrain] plague   37 knotting] knitting the brows   38 *Practice of Piety*] a popular religious manual   40 open house] hospitality to all

year to buy pins. Now, nurse, if he gives me two hundred a year to buy pins,
what do you think he'll give me to buy fine petticoats?   43

Nurse. Ah, my dearest, he deceives thee foully, and he's no better than a
rogue for his pains. These Londoners have got a gibberidge with 'em, would
confound a gipsy. That which they call pin-money is to buy their wives
everything in the varsal world, dawn to their very shoe-ties. Nay, I have
heard folks say, that some ladies, if they will have gallants, as they call 'um,
are forced to find them out of their pin-money too.

Hoy. Has he served me so, say ye?—Then I'll be his wife no longer, so
that's fixed. Look, here he comes, with all the fine folk at's heels. I'cod,
nurse, these London ladies will laugh till they crack again, to see me slip my
collar and run away from my husband. But d'ye hear? Pray take care of one
thing. When the business comes to break out, be sure you get between me
and my father, for you know his tricks—he'll knock me down.   55

Nurse. I'll mind him, ne'er fear, madam.

Enter Lord Foppington, Loveless, Worthy, Amanda *and* Berinthia.

Lord Fop. Ladies and gentlemen, you are all welcome. (*To* Loveless.)
Loveless . . . that's my wife. Prithee do me the favour to salute her. (*Aside to
him.*) And dost hear, if thau hast a mind to try thy fartune, to be revenged of
me—I won't take it ill, stap my vitals.

Love. You need not fear, sir, I'm too fond of my own wife to have the least
inclination to yours.   [*All salute* Miss [Hoyden].

Lord Fop. (*Aside.*) I'd give you a thausand paund he would make love to
her, that he may see she has sense enough to prefer me to him, though his own
wife has not. (*Viewing him.*) He's a very beastly fellow in my opinion.   65

Hoy. (*Aside.*) What a power of fine men there are in this London! He that
kissed me first is a goodly gentleman, I promise you. Sure those wives have a
rare time on't that live here always!

Enter Sir Tunbelly *with* Musicians, Dancers, *etc.*

Sir Tun. Come; come in, good people, come in, come tune your fiddles,
tune your fiddles. (*To the* Hautboys.) Bag-pipes, make ready there. Come
strike up. (*Sings.*)

> For this is Hoyden's wedding-day,
> And therefore we keep holy-day,
> And come to be merry.

Ha! There's my wench i'faith. Touch and take, I'll warrant her—she'll
breed like a tame rabbit.

---

45 gibberidge] gibberish   47 varsal] corruption of universal   47 dawn] down
52 crack again] split their sides   s.d. Hautboys] oboe players   75 Touch and take]
copulate and become pregnant

Hoy. (*Aside.*) I'cod, I think my father's gotten drunk before supper.

Sir Tun. (*To* Loveless *and* Worthy.) Gentlemen, you are welcome. (*Saluting* Amanda *and* Berinthia.) Ladies by your leave. Ha!—they bill like turtles. Udsookers, they set my old blood a-fire; I shall cuckold somebody before morning. 81

Lord Fop. (*To* Sir Tunbelly.) Sir, you being master of the entertainment, will you desire the company to sit?

Sir Tun. Oons, sir, I'm the happiest man on this side the Ganges.

Lord Fop. (*Aside.*) This is a mighty unaccountable old fellow. (*To* Sir Tunbelly.) I said, sir, it would be convenient to ask the company to sit.

Sir Tun. Sit? With all my heart! Come, take your places, ladies, take your places, gentlemen; come sit down, sit down; a pox of ceremony, take your places. [*They sit, and the masque begins.*

Dialogue between Cupid *and* Hymen.

1.

Cupid.
Thou bane to my empire, thou spring of contest, 90
Thou source of all discord, thou period to rest;
Instruct me what wretches in bondage can see,
That the aim of their life is still pointed to thee.

2.

Hymen.
Instruct me, thou little impertinent god,
From whence all thy subjects have taken the mode;
To grow fond of a change, to whatever it be,
And I'll tell thee why those would be bound, who are free.

Chorus.

For change, w'are for change, to whatever it be,
We are neither contented with freedom nor thee.
   Constancy's an empty sound, 100
   Heaven, and earth, and all go round,
   All the works of nature move,
   And the joys of life and love
     Are in variety.

80 Udsookers] God save us   s.d. Hymen] god of marriage

3.
Cupid.
Were love the reward of a painstaking life,
Had a husband the art to be fond of his wife,
Were virtue so plenty, a wife could afford,
These very hard times to be true to her lord,
Some specious account might be given of those,
Who are tied by the tail, to be led by the nose.   110

4.
But since 'tis the fate of a man and his wife
To consume all their days in contention and strife:
Since whatever the bounty of heaven may create her,
He's morally sure, he shall heartily hate her,
I think 'twere much wiser to ramble at large,
And the volleys of love on the herd to discharge.

5.
Hymen.
Some colour of reason thy counsel might bear,
Could a man have no more than his wife to his share:
Or were I a monarch, so cruelly just,
To oblige a poor wife to be true to her trust.   120
But I have not pretended for many years past,
By marrying of people to make 'em grow chaste.

6.
I therefore advise thee to let me go on,
Thou'll find I'm the strength and support of thy throne;
For hadst thou but eyes, thou would'st quickly perceive it,
How smoothly thy dart
Slips into the heart
Of a woman that's wed,
Whilst the shivering maid,
Stands trembling and wishing, but dare not receive it.   130

Chorus.
For change, etc.

The Masque ended, enter Young Fashion, Coupler, *and* Bull.

Sir Tun. So, very fine, very fine i'faith, this is something like a wedding.
Now if supper were but ready, I'd say a short grace, and if I had such a
bedfellow as Hoyden tonight—I'd say as short prayers. (*Seeing* Young

Fashion.) How now? What have we got here—a ghost? . . . Nay it must be
so, for his flesh and his blood could never have dared to appear before me.
(*To him.*) Ah rogue!

Lord Fop. Stap my vitals, Tam again.

Sir Tun. My lord, will you cut his throat—or shall I?

Lord Fop. Leave him to me, sir, if you please. Prithee Tam, be so ingenuous
now, as to tell me what thy business is here?   141

Young Fash. 'Tis with your bride.

Lord Fop. Thau art the impudent'st fellow that nature has yet spawned into
the warld, strike me speechless.

Young Fash. Why, you know my modesty would have starved me. I sent
it a-begging to you, and you would not give it a groat.

Lord Fop. And dost thau expect by an excess of assurance to extart a
maintenance fram me?

Young Fash. (*Taking* Miss [Hoyden] *by the hand.*) I do intend to extort
your mistress from you, and that I hope will prove one.   150

Lord Fop. I ever thaught Newgate or Bedlam would be his fartune, and
naw his fate's decided. Prithee Loveless dost know of ever a mad-doctor
hard by?

Young Fash. There's one at your elbow will cure you presently. (*To* Bull.)
Prithee doctor, take him in hand quickly.

Lord Fop. Shall I beg the favour of you, sir, to pull your fingers out of my
wife's hand.

Young Fash. His wife! Look you there, now I hope you are all satisfied he's
mad!

Lord Fop. Naw is it nat possible far me to penetrate what species of fally it
is thau art driving at.   161

Sir Tun. Here, here, here, let me beat out his brains, and that will decide
all.

Lord Fop. No, pray sir, hold, we'll destray him presently, accarding to
law.

Young Fash. (*To* Bull.) Nay, then advance doctor. Come, you are a man of
conscience, answer boldly to the questions I shall ask. Did not you marry me
to this young lady before ever that gentleman there saw her face?

Bull. Since the truth must out, I did.

Young Fash. Nurse, sweet nurse, were not you a witness to it?   170

Nurse. Since my conscience bids me speak—I was.

Young Fash. (*To* Miss [Hoyden].) Madam, am not I your lawful husband?

Hoy. Truly I can't tell, but you married me first.

Young Fash. Now I hope you are all satisfied?

---

140 ingenuous] frank   151 Newgate] prison   152 mad-doctor] specialist in mental
disorders

Sir Tun. (*Offering to strike him, is held by* Loveless *and* Worthy.) Oons and thunder, you lie!

Lord Fop. Pray sir be calm, the battle is in disarder, but requires more canduct than courage to rally our forces. Pray dactar, one word with you. (*To* Bull *aside.*) Look you, sir, though I will not presume to calculate your notions of damnation fram the description you give us of hell, yet since there is at least a passibility you may have a pitchfark thrust in your backside, methinks it should not be worth your while to risk your saul in the next warld, far the sake of a beggarly yaunger brather who is nat able to make your bady happy in this.   184

Bull. Alas! my lord, I have no worldly ends, I speak the truth, heaven knows.

Lord Fop. Nay prithee never engage heaven in the matter, for by all I can see, 'tis like to prove a business for the devil.

Young Fash. Come, pray sir, all above-board, no corrupting of evidences, if you please. This young lady is my lawful wife, and I'll justify it in all the courts of England. So your lordship (who always had a passion for variety) may go seek a new mistress if you think fit.

Lord Fop. I am struck dumb with his impudence, and cannot passitively tell whether ever I shall speak again or nat.   194

Sir Tun. Then let me come and examine the business a little. I'll jerk the truth out of 'em presently. Here, give me my dog-whip!

Young Fash. Look you, old gentleman, 'tis in vain to make a noise. If you grow mutinous I have some friends within call have swords by their sides, above four foot long. Therefore be calm, hear the evidence patiently, and when the jury have given their verdict, pass sentence according to law. Here's honest Coupler shall be foreman and ask as many questions as he pleases.

Coup. All I have to ask is, whether nurse persists in her evidence. The parson I dare swear will never flinch from his.   204

Nurse. (*To* Sir Tunbelly, *kneeling.*) I hope in heaven your worship will pardon me. I have served you long and faithfully, but in this thing I was over-reached. Your worship however was deceived as well as I, and if the wedding dinner had been ready you had put madam to bed to him with your own hands.

Sir Tun. But how durst you do this without acquainting of me?

Nurse. Alas! if your worship had seen how the poor thing begged, and prayed, and clung and twined about me, like ivy to an old wall, you would say, I who had suckled it, and swaddled it, and nursed it both wet and dry, must have had a heart of adamant to refuse it.   214

Sir Tun. Very well.

207 over-reached] deceived   214 adamant] hard as loadstone, or, diamond

Young Fash. Foreman, I expect your verdict.

Coup. Ladies, and gentlemen, what's your opinions?

All. A clear case, a clear case!

Coup. Then my young folks, I wish you joy.

Sir Tun. (*To* Young Fashion.) Come hither stripling. If it be true then that thou hast married my daughter, prithee tell me who thou art?   221

Young Fash. Sir, the best of my condition is, I am your son-in-law; and the worst of it is, I am brother to that noble peer there.

Sir Tun. Art thou brother to that noble peer? Why then, that noble peer and thee, and thy wife, and the nurse, and the priest—may all go and be damned together!   [*Exit* Sir Tunbelly.

Lord Fop. (*Aside.*) Now for my part, I think the wisest thing a man can do with an aching heart is to put on a serene countenance, for a philosophical air is the most becoming thing in the world to the face of a person of quality. I will therefore bear my disgrace like a great man, and let the people see I am above an affront. (*To* Young Fashion.) Dear Tam, since things are thus fallen aut, prithee give me leave to wish thee jay. I do it *de bon cœur*, strike me dumb. You have married a woman beautiful in her person, charming in her airs, prudent in her canduct, canstant in her inclinations, and of a nice marality, split my wind-pipe.   235

Young Fash. Your lordship may keep up your spirits with your grimace if you please, I shall support mine with this lady, and two thousand pound a year. (*Taking* Miss [Hoyden].) Come, madam.

> We once again you see are man and wife,
> And now perhaps the bargain's struck for life;
> If I mistake, and we should part again,
> At least you see you may have choice of men:
> Nay, should the war at length such havoc make,
> That lovers should grow scarce, yet for your sake,
> Kind heaven always will preserve a beau,   245

[*Pointing to* Lord Foppington.

> You'll find his lordship ready to come to.

Lord Fop. Her ladyship shall stap my vitals if I do.

---

232 *de bon cœur*] sincerely

EPILOGUE
Spoken by Lord Foppington.

Gentlemen, and Ladies,
These people have regaled you here today
(In my opinion) with a saucy play;
In which the author does presume to show,
That coxcomb, ab origine—*was beau.*
Truly I think the thing of so much weight,
That if some smart chastisement ben't his fate,
Gad's curse it may in time destroy the state.
I hold no-one its friend, I must confess,
Who would discauntenance your men of dress.   10
Far give me leave t'abserve good clothes are things,
Have ever been of great support to kings;
All treasons come fram slovens, it is not
Within the reach of gentle beaux to plart.
They have no gaul, no spleen, no teeth, no stings,
Of all Gad's creatures the most harmless things.
Through all recard, no prince was ever slain,
By one who had a feather in his brain.
They're men of too refin'd an education,
To squabble with a court—for a vile dirty nation.   20
I'm very pasitive, you never saw
A thorough republican a finished beau.
Nor truly shall you very often see
A Jacobite much better dressed than he;
In shart, through all the courts that I have been in,
Your men of mischief—still are in faul linen.
Did ever one yet dance the Tyburn jig,
With a free air, ar a well pawdered wig?
Did ever highway-man yet bid you stand,
With a sweet bawdy snuff-box in his hand;   30
Ar do you ever find they ask your purse
As men of breeding do? Ladies, Gad's curse,
This auther is a dag, and 'tis not fit
You should allow him ev'n one grain of wit.
To which, that his pretence may ne'er be named,
My humble motion is—he may be damed.

FINIS

---

5 *ab origine*] originally   14 plart] plot   27 dance the Tyburn jig] suffer hanging
36 *damed*] pun: 'damned' or 'emasculated'